SYLLOGE OF COINS
OF THE BRITISH ISLES
71

SYLLOGE OF COINS
OF THE BRITISH ISLES

A British Academy Research Project

The British Sylloge project was first promoted in the early 1950s by Christopher Blunt and other members of the British and Royal Numismatic Societies. An informal committee was formed under the chairmanship of Sir Frank Stenton, who in 1956 secured its admission as a Committee of the British Academy. The first volume, on Anglo-Saxon coins in the Fitzwilliam Museum, Cambridge, was published by the British Academy in 1958.

The aim of the series is to publish detailed and fully illustrated catalogues of coins of the British Isles in British and foreign collections. The volumes range in scope from Ancient British coins to seventeenth-century tokens, with most detailed coverage of the Anglo-Saxon coinage. The collections recorded include those in more than two hundred national, university and provincial museums in Britain and Ireland and of museums in Scandinavia, Germany, Poland, Latvia, Estonia, Russia and the United States of America.

A full listing of the series is printed at the end of this volume. The SCBI Database can be consulted on https://www.thebritishacademy.ac.uk/publishing/scbi or https://emc.fitzmuseum.cam.ac.uk/

SYLLOGE OF COINS OF THE BRITISH ISLES

71

THE LORD STEWARTBY COLLECTION
of Scottish Coins
at the Hunterian,
University of Glasgow

Part I
JAMES IV TO JAMES VI
1488–1625

BY

WILLIAM A. MACKAY

Published for THE BRITISH ACADEMY
by OXFORD UNIVERSITY PRESS
2021

Oxford University Press, Great Clarendon Street, Oxford OX2 6DP

First edition published in 2021

British Library Cataloguing in Publication Data
Data available

Library of Congress Cataloging in Publication Data
Data available

Typeset by New Leaf Design, Malton, North Yorkshire
Printed in Great Britain by TJ Books Ltd, Padstow, Cornwall

ISBN 978–0–19–726687–8

In Memoriam
Carol, wife of William MacKay
1963-2019

CONTENTS

PREFACE

What makes the Lord Stewartby collection so important is its depth and the scale of its coverage of the Scottish coinage. His intention was to build a complete collection of the Scottish coinage from its beginnings under David I in 1136, to its end in 1707 with the Act of Union. This goal, a lifetime's work, was effectively completed in that only the rarest coins eluded him, such as the David II noble or Mary and Francis ducat. The end result, with just over 6000 coins, had very few gaps and provided a comprehensive picture of the Scottish coinage across all metals, coinages, denominations and varieties. Sadly the burglaries in June 2007 and November 2008 removed the earlier and later coins, the former covering the period from the start of the Scottish coinage to the single-cross coinage of Alexander III, 1136–1280, the only exception to this being nearly 143 crescent and pellet pence of William the Lion, which were on loan at the time, and so avoided the fate of the other early coins. The size of this parcel, covering just one coinage, hints at the scale of the loss to the record of the Scottish mints of the twelfth- and the thirteenth-centuries. The later coins included the silver and copper of William II and Anne.

It continues to be the hope of Lady Stewartby, her family and the numismatic community that one day the missing coins will be returned to join the rest of the collection.

In addition to his Scottish Collection, Lord Stewartby built up a substantial collection of English hammered coins from *c.* 620–1660, with a small number of later milled pieces. In 2016 increasing illness made it necessary for him to consider the future of both collections. It was decided that the English coins, numbering just under 3700, were to be sold. A series of auctions duly took place in 2016–17 at Spink, the London auction house, in which they were offered as *The Academic Collection of Lord Stewartby*. An alternative approach was chosen for the Scottish collection. This was not to be dispersed and in early 2017 Lord Stewartby gifted it to the Hunterian at the University of Glasgow. Despite the loss of the earliest and latest coins, it still amounted to 5000 coins.

Shortly before Lord Stewartby died in March 2018, it was agreed that the collection should be published in the Sylloge of Coins of the British Isles series (SCBI). This was a welcome decision, given Lord Stewartby's long association with the project, on the committee of which he had served from 1967, and presided over as Chairman during the period 1993–2007. The decision to begin with the period from James IV to James VI (1488–1625) sought to complement and build on the SCBI publication of the Edinburgh National Museums collections covering 1526–1603, the second coinage of James V to the English accession of James VI (vol. 58). For Part I of the Stewartby collection it was decided to include James IV and the first coinage of James V, to allow for the unicorn and plack coinages of each to be considered, and to include the post-1603 coinage of James VI, so the whole of his Scottish coinage is covered in one place. The result is a Sylloge with 1458 coins, along with 9 non-contemporary copies or forgeries.

The commentary that accompanies the catalogue seeks to bring together an overview of the coinage within the context of its production and the politics of each reign. With three of the four monarchs included in this Sylloge ascending the throne as minors with lengthy, often fractious, periods of regency and the ascendency of the Protestants under James VI, this is a period of Scottish history that is politically complex, turbulent and economically challenging, but also at times vibrant with change and ideas. The Scottish coinage of this period was produced against this background, which is reflected in its issues, designs, production and management. Commentary on numismatic interpretation is limited, so as to avoid the risks inherent in drawing conclusions from one collection without assessing the evidence of coins held elsewhere. Nevertheless with such substantial holdings for some areas of the coinage in the Stewartby collection, it is appropriate to make observations on some aspects of the coinage, notably the sequencing of that of James IV. This is intended to provide a foundation on which future researchers can build.

In preparing this volume, the author is grateful to those individuals and institutions without whose support and resources it could not have been completed. Foremost among these are Lady Stewartby and her family, without whose generous and kind support this book could not have been undertaken or completed at what proved a most difficult time for the author. Their understanding and patience while my wife was ill and then after her death, which all occurred while this Sylloge was being written, was second to none. Throughout this time Scottish coinage gave me a lifeline to keep going. For this I will always be most grateful.

For access to the coins in the Kelvin Hall study centre at The Hunterian I must thank Jesper Ericsson who was always accommodating in fitting me in for my visits and providing me with the necessary flow of coins for recording as well as guid-ing me through the Lord Stewartby Scottish Numismatic Archive, comprising his correspondence on the collection and his research notes, *c.* 1950–2010, also held at The Hunterian. Jesper has also been a tower of support in taking on coordination of the photography of the coins, working with the University of Glasgow photo-graphic unit, to whom I am also grateful. Donal Bateson not only provided me with feedback but also pointed me in the direction of key publications and offered gentle encouragement in the earlier days when the billon coinage of James IV proved challenging. Elsewhere, the staff at the Fitzwilliam Museum in Cambridge have been a great help in allowing me access to their library of sale catalogues. In the absence of access to this resource, due to the 2020–1 pandemic, the on-line library of numismatic catalogues at The George Washington University in St Louis, USA, and Tim Webb-Ware helped close some outstanding gaps. Lord Stewartby noted provenances for some coins which proved challenging to verify and I am grateful to Peter Mitchell, Peter Preston-Morley, Hugh Pagan and Arent Pol for helping resolve some of these. In creating this volume I would like to also thank Erin McGowan of Oxford University for patiently editing the images of the coins and creating the plates.

Finally I would like to thank Rory Naismith for his feedback on the draft of this volume. It is possible that there are others who I have overlooked and their omission from this record is unintended. All responsibility for any errors that remain lies solely with the author.

AUTUMN 2020

WILLIAM A. MACKAY
BARKWAY,
NORTH HERTFORDSHIRE

THE LORD STEWARTBY COLLECTION OF SCOTTISH COINS

The Lord Stewartby collection is the most important assemblage of Scottish coins ever formed by a private individual. The first coins were acquired in the 1940s; the last *c.* 2010. These were purchased in the main from the London dealers A. H. Baldwin, Spink and Seaby and supplemented by some significant private acquisitions of portions of other collections, as well as at auctions. Many of the coins had passed through other important collections of Scottish coins formed in the nineteenth- and twentieth-centuries. Some coins were acquired from the finders of hoards following disclaimer decisions under the Scottish treasure-trove process.

Apart from a holding of crescent and pellet pence of William the Lion, the loss of the early coins of the Stewartby collection in the 2007 burglary (a second burglary in 2008 did not result in the loss of coins from the Scottish collection) mean that its contents start with the single-cross coinage of Alexander III (1249–86), which was continued under his successors, John Baliol (1292–6) and Robert I (1306–29). The collection contains 389 pence and fractions of Alexander III, 127 of John Baliol and 18 of Robert I. The introduction of the groat in 1357 increased the denominations in use, and the collection comprises 621 coins of David II (1329–71), 266 of Robert II (1371–90) and 341 (including 13 gold) of Robert III (1390–1406). The fifteenth-century coinage was marked by increasing debasement and remains a difficult series to interpret. Lord Stewartby's holding includes 228 coins (8 gold) of James I (1406–37), 188 (7 gold) of James II (1437–60), and 327 (9 gold) of James III (1460–88). In 1484 James III introduced the first coins to be struck in the British Isles with a renaissance style life-like bust of the king, and the collection is especially rich in this issue. He also introduced the first copper coins, and these are also well represented, as is the Crux-Pellit coinage, of which there are 46 specimens.

Table 1: The Lord Stewartby collection of Scottish coins at the Hunterian

Monarch	*Number of gold coins*	*HSAN sequence, gold*	*Number of silver, billon and copper coins*	*HSAN sequence, silver, billon and copper*	*Number of coins in the collection*
William I	None issued		143	4865–5007	143
Alexander III	None issued		389	1–389	389
John Baliol	None issued		127	390–516	127
Robert I	None issued		18	517–534	18
David II	0		621	535–1155	621

Table 1: *Continued*

Monarch	*Number of gold coins*	*HSAN sequence, gold*	*Number of silver, billon and copper coins*	*HSAN sequence, silver, billon and copper*	*Number of coins in the collection*
Robert II	None issued		266	1156–1421	266
Robert III	13	4744–4756	328	1422–1749	341
James I	8	4757–4764	220	1750–1942, 1995–2019, 2020, 2023	228
James II	7	4765–4771	181	1943–1994, 2024–2150	188
James III	9	4772–4779	318	2151–2423, 4698–4743	327
James IV	17	4780–4797	313	2424–2735	330
James V	17	4798–4814	196	2736–2931	213
Mary	8	4815–4825	495	2932–3433	503
James VI	27	4827–4852	385	3434–3824	412
Charles I	9	4854–4861	415	3824–4238	424
Charles II	None issued		413	4239–4651	413
James VII	None issued		20	4652–4671	20
William and Mary	None issued		26	4672–4697	26
William II	2	4862–4863	0	–	2
Forgeries and copies	4		5		9
Total coins	121		4879		5000

Notes.
1. The HSAN sequence includes modern copies and forgeries, as well as jettons and medals.
2. The William I group excludes one English coin of Henry II of England which is included in the HSAN numbering.
3. The Crux Pellet issue coins are included within the silver, billon and copper of James III.
4. A group of 442 coins, of which 425 are Scottish, were added to the collections at the Hunterian in May 2021. By origin these can also be associated with the collection formed by Lord Stewartby.

There follow 330 coins of James IV (1488–1513) (17 gold), with an especially good holding of his rare silver groats and halves; 213 coins (17 gold) of James V (1513–42); and 503 coins (8 gold) of Mary (1542–67). The billon coinages are especially well represented for James IV, James V and Mary. The collection includes 412 (27 gold) coins of James VI (1567–1625), among them rare silver pieces of the second and third coinages, as well as examples of all the gold denominations from both before and after his accession to the English throne in 1603. The later coinages include 424 coins of Charles I (1625–49) (9 gold); 413 of Charles II (1649–85); 20 of James VII (1685–8); and 26 of William and Mary (1688–94). The burglary means that the Stewartby collection ends at this point with the silver and copper of William II and Anne lost to the 2007 burglary. The gold having been stored separately means a pistole and half-pistole of William II (1694–1702) were retained, meaning that with the exceptions, notably, of the 1357 noble of David II and the Mary and Francis ducat, the Stewartby collection's gold covers the entirety of its issue in Scotland. In total there are 117 gold coins including 28 lions and demi-lions from the reigns of Robert III and James I and II. The unicorn issues of James III to V are well represented and include rarities such as the roman-lettering half of James IV/V (**15**). The ducat issue of James V, 1539–40, is present for both dates and all denominations, as are all denominations of the lion noble of the fourth coinage of James VI.

Within the coinage of James IV to James VI (1488–1625), there is much that is exceptional and of importance to researchers. The gold of James IV is well covered with 9 unicorns, 7 halves and one lion. The entire silver coinage of James IV is rare, and the holding of 32 groats and halves is among the best. It includes an example of the 1512 'Maundy' groat (**45**) showing the bearded facing 'older-style' bust of James IV. The billon coinage of placks and pence of James IV, with 281 coins, along with 57 placks and 53 bawbees of James V and 219 bawbees of Mary, is also well represented. When combined with placks, twelve-penny groats and hardheads of Mary, the 1583 and 1588 billon and 1597, 1614 and 1623 copper issues of James VI, the collection provides a comprehensive cross-section of the small-change in use in Scotland in the sixteenth- and early-seventeenth centuries. The first coinage gold of James V is well covered, with 5 unicorns and one half (**335**, a very rare coin). From the second coinage, types II to IV are represented for the gold crown; the silver by 70 groats and 16 thirds, along with a single example of the 1533 issue of the plack (**489**). From the 1538–42 third coinage, examples of both the 1539 (**343**) and 1540 (**344**) ducat are present, along with an example each of the two-thirds (**345**) and third fractions (**346**).

Holdings of the gold coinages of Mary are strong, with examples of the 1543 Abbey crown (**543–4**) and twenty shillings (**545**), along with the 1553 forty-four (**546–7**) and twenty-two shilling (**548**) pieces. There is an example each of the gold ryal (**549**) and its half (**550**). For the sake of completeness, Lord Stewartby acquired an electrotype of the 1558 Francis and Mary ducat, and this is included with the copies and forgeries (**1462**). The silver of Mary is substantial, with all types and halves of the testoon covered, including an example of the type I of 1553 (**551**) and 8 examples (**1014–21**) of the 1561–2 first widowhood portrait issues. Although lacking the Mary and Darnley 1565 type I ryal, the 1565–7 ryals and fractions include all denominations and most dates as well as some rare varieties.

Lord Stewartby had a high regard for the coinage of James VI before his accession to the English throne, appreciating its originality and freshness of design. This coinage is well represented in the collection. All issues of the gold are present including a 1575 twenty-pound piece (**1046**), the 1580 ducat (**1047**), one each of the lion noble (**1048**) and its fractions (**1049–50**), two examples of the thistle noble (**1051–2**) and an example of the hat piece. The gold from after his accession to the English throne covers all denominations, including an example of the rare ninth coinage double-crown (**1364**). All the silver coinage and denominations are present, with a few extremely rare exceptions. The very rare second and third coinage 'thistle-dollar' issues are especially well represented. In addition, there is a forty-shilling piece (**1163**) from the fourth coinage. The billon issues include an exceedingly rare type I two-penny plack (**1330**) of the 1583–90 issue. The coinage from after the accession to the English throne is less imaginative than that from before, but nevertheless is fully covered in the collection. All the silver denominations, including a good selection of six-shilling pieces with most dates, are in the Stewartby collection.

With publication of this Sylloge it is hoped the gift of his collection, and his Scottish numismatic archive, to the Hunterian at the University of Glasgow, will not only enable it to be an exceptional resource for research but also provide a further body of reference material which can assist collectors. Lord Stewartby would have approved of both these aims.

OVERVIEW OF THE COINAGE

JAMES IV (1488–1513)

The coinage of this reign of 25 years consisted, in gold, of unicorns (18 shillings), and halves; lions or crowns (13 shillings and 4 pence) and halves. In silver, there were heavier and lighter coinages. The heavier continued the standard of James III, comprising fourteen pence groats and halves; the lighter, commenced *c.* 1496, introduced a new standard with twelve pence groats, halves and a penny (3 pence). All gold and silver is rare. Base metal coinage, on the other hand, was more plentiful and comprised the billon plack (4 pence), its half, and the penny. The reign saw innovation with the introduction of roman-lettering on unicorns, on a rare (possibly special issue) groat and on placks, as well as the use of a number within the royal title, this either an abbreviation of quartus, **QRA**, **QTR**, **QR**, a roman **IIII**, or an Arabic numeral **4** in either old or new style. The only mint to be named is Edinburgh.

Interpretation of the coinage of James IV is challenging as the documentary evidence is limited. This offers fragments of information, and little that can assist in providing clear evidence to establish sequencing of the coinage with confidence. Scholars of this period, notably Joan Murray, have attempted to overcome this by looking at the coins themselves to seek linkages between letter styles and other features which may provide a plausible structure for particular denominations (J. E. L. Murray 1971). While this was helpful, it still remains hard to build a clear picture of the ordering of the whole coinage. The coinage does however have some clear divisions. The two silver coinages are distinguished by weight and style. The first was struck at a heavier weight, with the groat (value 14 pence) at 47 grains. The second was lighter with the groat, valued now at 12 pence, at 39 grains. There are no apparent weight or fineness changes which assist in dividing the gold and billon issues. For these, stylistic variations in legends, punctuation and lettering have been used to define types and varieties (Stewart 1967, p. 71–3; J. E. L. Murray, 1971). These are used in the ordering of the coins here.

The initial heavy coinage period of James IV, 1488–c. 1490

To make some sense of the patterns in this coinage the limited documentary evidence has to be considered, as this can provide some chronological anchors to assist with ordering the coinage. James IV succeeded to the throne as a consequence of a successful rebellion against his father that resulted in the latter's death at the battle of Sauchieburn on 11 June 1488. An initial Act of 17 October 1488 ordered a new coinage, to include a gold coin equivalent to the English rose noble, a groat of fourteen pence and half-groats (C-P I, p. 46, I; Stewart 1967, p. 68). With the exception of the gold, which was never struck, this order maintained silver denominations of the same weight and fineness as the previous reign. This would appear to have been its intention.

Some four months later a further Act of 14 January 1489 ordered a new coinage. This specified the issue of a gold crown, value fourteen shillings, to be the same size as the French écu, with the king shown seated enthroned. This seems to have been more an aspiration, as such a coin was never issued. It also set out a revised design for the fourteen pence groat and seven pence half which 'was to have prent sic as the xiiiid grote has that now Is except that the visage sall stand eywyn in the new groit.' This retained the reverse design of the profile type VI groat of James III, with crowns and pellets in alternate angles and annulet stops, while replacing the obverse realistic portrait of James III with a facing bust more appropriate for the younger new king (Stewart 1967, p. 68). The **DOMINVS PROTECTOR MEVS ET LIBERATOR MEVS** (God is my defender and redeemer) legend was retained. Groats and matching half-groats were struck (type I). A cross fleury initial mark occurs on the groat and a cross pattée on the halves, as with the preceding James III issue. There is a variety (Ic) on which James was for the first time named as the fourth of that name with an old Arabic 4 appearing with king's name on the obverse. Similar minor change and continuity seems to have applied for the unicorn and half, which retained the design of James III, notably the three-lis crown on the neck of the unicorn (Stewart 1967, type I; J. E. L. Murray 1971, type Y). These can confidently be regarded as the earliest coinage of James IV. The rare second issue billon pence, with pellets in all angles on the reverse and the plain-cross initial mark, also belongs to this period; the same initial mark is found on the type I half-groat, with a crown and pellets in the angles (Stewart 1967, p. 68).

The later heavy coinage period of James IV, 1490–c. 1496

The duration of the initial heavy coinage was short, as a further new silver coinage was ordered in an Act of 3 February 1490. Groats were to be of the same weight, value and fineness but were to bear a mark that would distinguish them from earlier issues: 'this said cunye sall haf a signe and takin made in the prenting hafand difference fra the first cunye' (C-P I, p. 48, IV). The resulting coins are recognised as the type II groat of James IV, where a lis replaced the second of the crowns in the angles of the cross on the reverse, providing the token mark that distinguishes this coin from earlier issues (J. E. L. Murray 1971, p. 79). Only groats are known of this issue. As with the type I silver, all have the cross fleury initial mark and use the **DOMINVS** legend on the reverse, with various renditions in an abbreviated form (J. E. L. Murray 1971, pp. 79–80). New styles of bust appear and the annulet stops of type I are replaced with stars. There are several varieties: IIa, with a five-fleur crown and annulet on the breast; IIb, crown with three fleurs; IIc, crown with tall spikes between fleurs in the crown. There are extensive stylistic variations on the obverse, notably as regards the tressure, where the number of arcs and devices on the cusps vary, and it may be broken or unbroken by the bust. With scope for so much variation, it is accepted that this was an issue of some duration and it is thought to have continued until *c.* 1496 (J. E. L. Murray 1971, p. 63 and p. 72–3), as opposed the earlier interpretation of it ceasing as early as 1492 (Stewart 1967, p. 69).

Gold unicorns were struck in this period. Murray thought all unicorns with the five-lis crown and lombardic-lettering (class II) corresponded with the light coinage groats, where the Arabic 4 also appears, which she dated to after *c.* 1496. This suggests the type I unicorn, with the three-lis crown and lombardic letter N, continued to be struck until the mid–1490s. These have in common the lis initial mark or, in some cases, a cross potent (described as a cross pommée by Stewart and Murray), and there are a number of varieties, designated by Murray as Ib to Id, based on the punctuation (J. E. L. Murray 1971, p. 70). Type I half-unicorns also date from before *c.* 1496 and were designated by Murray as type Ic to Ie (J. E. L. Murray 1971, p. 70).

Billon coinage attributable to before 1496 is more uncertain, but there is good reason to believe it was struck. The first reference to placks is in a Treasurer's Account from 1505–6 (C-P I, p. 53, XIV). Murray thought this indicated there was a gap of about twenty years in the production of placks after 1486 (J. E. L. Murray 1971, p. 64). There are problems with this proposition that affect all the light coinage silver denominations of groats, half-groats and pennies bearing the crown initial mark. This mark is significant as it occurs across several denominations. It represents a common feature, perhaps signifying the coins were produced under the authority of the same official or were all part of the same issue of coinage commencing *c.* 1496, even if struck at different times thereafter. In the gold, the crown initial mark is also found on the type III roman-lettering unicorns and half-unicorns, and on the lion and half-lion. In the silver, as noted, it occurs with the groat, half-groat and penny. On the billon it occurs with some lombardic-lettered placks, all roman-lettered and on some half-placks and on second-issue type II and III billon pence with lis and crowns in the reverse angles. It therefore seems plausible that all these coins should be associated with the light coinage silver and date to after *c.* 1496.

That though leaves a problem with the billon placks carrying the cross fleury and cross potent (cross pommée) initial marks. The Stewartby collection has a large holding of billon placks and pence of James IV, which allows for greater assessment of the series than Joan Murray was able to provide. In many ways they are key to helping explain the wider coinage of James IV. The cross fleury initial mark, a distinctive feature of the heavy silver, is found on placks with forked and star stops (types IId-f), both of which are also found on type I unicorns. Similarly, the cross potent initial mark on Stewart type IIa unicorns (noted as cross pattée by Stewart and Murray) is found on placks (types IIa to IIc), half-placks (types I and II) and unicorns (Murray type Id), where it is found with pellet, lis, forked and star stops, and one plack variety without stops, as also found on a half-unicorn (Murray Ib).

It seems plausible that placks with the cross fleury and cross potent (pommée) initial marks date from before *c.* 1496, and that the plack was a part of the coinage produced in the early to mid–1490s. So while the written evidence for the issue of placks between 1486 and 1505–6 is lacking, the numismatic evidence provides a compelling argument that they were issued from early in the reign of James IV and a twenty-year pause in production, as proposed by J. E. L. Murray, did not occur.

Types III and IV billon pence, attributed to the second issue by Stewart (1967, p. 146), might be added to this period of the coinage. These have in common the lis and crowns reverse and Edinburgh is named as the mint. The type III coins have the cross potent initial mark, suggesting they should be associated with others bearing the same initial mark. This points to these all being issues from before *c.* 1496. The type IV billon pence are more problematic. These base coins all have small flans, crude production, and a distinctive moonlike-face. The reverse legend reads **VILLA DE EDINBVRG**. They all seem to have in common a small plain-cross initial mark on both sides and pellet, saltire, trefoil, or star stops, or none (Stewart 1967, p. 146, varieties IVa to IVe), some of which occur on the placks and unicorns with the cross potent (pommée) mark. It may be that this different and distinctive initial mark indicates these were the work of a specific moneyer or workshop. Alternatively, it is possible they were a separate coinage that ran parallel with the changes in the silver coinage *c.* 1496, but with a lack of evidence to draw on, it is not possible to be more specific. These groupings are too marked to ignore and the most plausible explanation is that these all began before the adoption of the homogenous crown initial mark. The deduction to be made is that type IId to IIf placks, with the cross fleury mark, date from the earlier years of the reign, while those with the cross potent follow on from them before *c.* 1496. With some placks having obverse and reverse dies with the cross potent and crown marks, these would appear to mule different types and point to coins with the cross potent initial mark preceding the crown. The conclusion that can be inferred, in the absence of documentary evidence, is that the heavy coinage silver of 1490 to *c.* 1496 was issued in parallel with pence, placks and unicorns and that the plack was issued from the start of the reign. This assessment vindicates other scholars who have suggested this was so (Stewart 1967, p. 72).

The light coinage period of James IV, c. 1496–c. 1512

The great omission from the record of the coinage under James IV is a lack of any Act that sets out the introduction of the new light coinage. In the absence of this, deductions can be made from other documents that have been shown to provide sound suggestions that the revised light coinage began around 1496 (J. E. L. Murray 1971, p. 72–3). The central part of this argument is an Act of 13 June 1496 in which it was ordered that 'ane famous and wise man that is expert and vnderstandis the maner and fassoun of cunye to be maister of the money and anent the strikeing the form thairof the fynace and the course and anent the inbringing of bulyeoun' (C-P I, p. 50, VIII). There is supplementary evidence for the gathering of bullion, as indicated was to be done in the Act, as gold and silver from the Treasury was given over to be coined at this time (J. E. L. Murray 1971, p. 73), along with an Act of 18 June 1496 forbidding clerks (*kirkman*) from taking money out of the kingdom. A further comment in the Treasurer's Account for 1496–7 notes the use of links in the great gold chain being used to strike unicorns. All this provides evidence that something was happening at this time with regard to the coinage.

Evidence for coinage production between *c.* 1496 and 1513 is scanty. There are some suggestions in surviving fragments of the Treasurer's Accounts for the striking of pence and unicorns noted for 1496–7 (C-P I, p. 51, XII, XIII), placks in 1505–6 (C-P I, p. 53, XIV), a sizeable coinage of silver and gold in 1506–7, with some of the gold sourced from French écus (C-P I, p. 52, XV), and a further striking of silver and gold for the year to August 1508 (C-P I, p. 52, XVI).

The focus of the reforms carried out at this time appears to have been the silver coinage. Given the previous coinage Acts in 1489 and 1490 had both specified the introduction of a gold coin, it is possible the same might have occurred in the 'lost Act' which would have enacted the new coinage, and this may explain the introduction of the gold lion and its half. The old groat of 14 pence was replaced by one of 12 pence with the weight reduced from 47 to 39 grains. The design changed, introducing a neat facing crowned bust with bushy hair within a tressure on the obverse. On the reverse, the plain long-cross was changed to be more decorative with a long-cross fourchée, in the manner of the type III English groat of Henry VII. A mullet and trefoil of pellets appear alternately in the angles of the long-cross. The **SALVVM FAC POPVLVM TVVM DOMINE** (O Lord, save thy people), legend previously used on the gold of James I, II and III, appears on the reverse. On the obverse a crown initial mark appears. These features were applied across the groat, half-groat (6 pence) and penny (3 pence), indicating this reform was intended to provide a new silver coinage across three denominations.

The light coinage groats are classified as group III. All have lombardic-lettering. There are varieties defined by how James is described as the fourth king of that name in the obverse legend, with types IIIa, using an old Arabic 4; IIIc, **QRA** (for Quartus); IIId, **QT**; and IIIe, with a roman **IIII**. Type IIIb has no numeral. Various forms of punctuation, stars and Vs, have been associated with these types and used in interpreting the coinage (Stewart 1967, p. 70–2 and p. 145; J. E. L. Murray 1971, p. 73). On types IIIc and IIIe, a star sometimes appears each side of the neck on the obverse. The number of arcs in the tressure is commonly between seven and nine. The half-groat occurs for two types; IIIa, without a numeral on the obverse, and IIIb, with the numeral **IIII** at the end of the obverse legend. The extremely rare penny is of one type only, which has no numeral in the obverse legend.

Gold coinage of this period comprises two denominations: the new lion (13 shillings and 4 pence) and the unicorn. The lion restores the type last issued under James II with the crowned arms of Scotland on the obverse and St Andrew on the reverse. There are two types; I, a unique coin, where St Andrew holds a saltire cross; and II, in the style used before, where he is crucified upon a saltire cross. The numeral IIII appears in the type II obverse legend. Half-lions were also struck with two types; I, as the lion type II, without IIII on the obverse, and II, with IIII in the obverse legend. All have the SALVVM legend, lombardic-lettering and the crown initial mark, linking them to the light coinage silver. Unicorns with the crown initial mark and lombardic-lettering do not exist, but they seem to have been in production at this time, probably periodically, and it has been shown that the type II unicorn, with a crown of five lis, has punctuation and lettering which aligns with the groats (J. E. L. Murray 1971, p. 74). There are four types: IIa, lis/pellets stops obverse/reverse; IIb, pellets/lis stops obverse/reverse and IId, without stops. A type II half-unicorn is known with a slightly different obverse design and QR in the obverse legend.

In the absence of any evidence to suggest otherwise, billon coinage with the crown initial mark can be given to this period by association. This comprises placks and pence. A few placks, type IIa (without QRA in the obverse legend), with design unchanged, have the crown initial mark appearing with lombardic-lettering. In a few cases the initial mark is a cross potent on one side and crown on the other, suggesting muling of dies. All these coins are rare, which may suggest production of the plack after 1496 was much reduced until the roman-lettered type was issued. Types I and II of the second issue pence can be associated with the silver of the light coinage period. The rare type I billon penny, with lis and crowns in alternate angles of the long-cross, has in common with the light coinage silver the SALVVM legend on the reverse, and the crown initial mark. It would seem to belong to this period. Type II, with the same reverse design as type I, also has the crown initial mark on most coins but replaces the SALVVM legend to name the mint, VILLA EDINBVRGH. The issue can be associated with this period through its use of the crown initial mark.

The coinage of James IV with roman-lettering, c. 1512–13

Coins with roman-lettering are later than those with lombardic and must date from towards the end of the reign of James IV. The type III unicorn has roman-lettering on one (IIIa) or both sides (IIIb). James IV roman-lettering unicorn dies are found muled with those of James V, as also occurs for James V placks, both suggesting continuity in production across the change in ruler. Similarly the only silver known with roman-lettering is the type IV groat with the bearded bust of James and the EXVRGAT legend, which can be dated with confidence to 1512, and is thought to have been struck for ceremonial purposes connected with royal maundy (Stewart 1966, pp. 261–6). This has similarities to a pattern angel also with roman-lettering and a new legend format. It is accepted that the angel is a pattern that belongs to the preparatory phase of a new coinage at the very end of the reign which was cut short by the death of James IV at Flodden in September 1513 (Stewart 1967, p. 74). The specific date for the introduction of the roman-lettering into the coinage is unclear, but it would certainly seem to be in the last year or two of the reign for the gold and silver. Roman-lettered placks, types IV and V, may have been introduced a little earlier, for not only was this a large-volume production, unlike the silver and gold, but they are found muled with lombardic-lettered dies (Stewart, type III). It is possible that plack production was reduced after *c.* 1496, when the lombardic die would have been old when used with a type IV roman-lettered die. All type IV and V placks have the crown initial mark and the obverse legend **IACOBVS 4**. Varieties are defined by the punctuation, with the four varieties of type IV (IVa to IVd) designated by differing formats of pellets and trefoils, while the three varieties of type V (Va to Vc) are distinguished by the varying forms of the stars (Stewart 1967, p. 146). There is evidence in the Treasurer's Accounts for production of placks in 1505–6, but it is not clear if these were type IV and V, both with roman-lettering both sides, or type III, with lombardic-lettering.

Coins of James IV in the Stewartby collection

The Stewartby collection contains 330 coins (**1–13, 13A–329**) of James IV of which 17 are gold (**1–13, 13A–16**), 32 silver (**17–48**) and 281 billon (**49–329**). The holdings of gold and silver are especially strong, and include coins from the specialist collection of this series built up by Joan Murray, a portion of which was acquired by Lord Stewartby in 1998. This included one of the three known examples of the 1512 'Maundy groat' on which the roman-lettering and the **EXVRGAT** legend first appear on silver (**45**). The gold includes examples of both the unicorn and the half with roman-lettering.

The gold has examples of all three types of the unicorn. Type I, with a three-lis crown on the unicorn's neck (all with initial mark lis), is represented by 4 coins (**1–4**), the first being a James III/IV obverse/reverse mule (**1**), while the others belong to varieties Ic (star stops, **2–3**) and Id (v stops, **4**). Type II, with the five-lis crown (**5–8**), has examples with pellet stops (IIa, **5**) and with v-shaped stops (IId, **6–8**). All type II unicorns carry the cross potent initial mark, distinctive for its bar at the end of limb. The rare roman-lettering type III unicorn, reading **IACOBVS 4**, with the crown initial mark and star stops, is represented by one coin (**9**). Half-unicorns (**12–13, 13A–14**), all type I (with stops denoting varieties Ia to Ic), are represented, as also is an example of type III (**15**) with roman-letters, including an F for E. Some uncertainty exists as to the position of this in the sequence of the Scottish coinage, and it was assigned by Lord Stewartby to James IV or V, perhaps as a transitional issue between 1513 and 1518. It is also possible it may belong to a planned new coinage that was stalled by James's death at Flodden and to which a pattern angel in the name for James IV is attributed (Stewart 1967, p. 74).

The Stewartby collection's holdings of the notably rare heavy coinage silver (**17–26**), with the DOMINVS PROTECTOR legend, are also considerable. With 9 groats (**17–25**) and a very rare half (**26**), the Stewartby collection provides an exceptional group of these coins which suggests that there was much variety in them. Following Joan Murray's revised division of the heavy coinage silver (J. E. L. Murray 1971), the earliest issues (from 1489–90: type I (**17–18**)) have a facing bust within an unbroken tressure of twelve arcs with annulet colon stops, in the manner of the last groat issue of James III, and include an old style Arabic 4 after the king's name. The type II heavy groats (**19–25**), dated 1490 to *c.* 1496, have star stops, with the bust appearing on some (type IIa) in an unbroken tressure (**19–20**), and on others (type IIb) in a broken tressure (**21–5**), of either twelve or ten arcs. All examples are without the numeral. Heavy coinage silver in the Stewartby collection usually has a cross fleury as the initial mark on the obverse and reverse, the exceptions to this being one groat (**17**) of type I that has a cross pattée with what looks to be a cross patonce on the obverse and the single half-groat (**26**) with a cross pattée on both sides.

The Stewartby collection light coinage silver (**27–48**), while lacking a penny, is as significant as the element of heavy coinage. This coinage, with a neater facing bust, pellets and mullets in the angles and the reintroduced SALVVM legend, is thought to have commenced *c.* 1496, (J. E. L. Murray 1971, pp. 72–3). The light coinage groats in the Stewartby collection follow the core sub-division (Stewart 1967, pp. 45 and 145) of those without the numeral and those with: types IIIa (with old Arabic 4, **27–30**); IIIb (without numeral, **31–2**); IIIc (with QRA, **33–8**) and IIIe (with roman IIII at the end of the legend, **39–44**). Varieties are noted with different forms of stops, stars by the neck (or not), as well as the number of arcs in the unbroken tressure, with nine, eight or seven all noted in the Stewartby collection. The light coinage half-groat is represented by three coins (**46–8**), one similar to the IIIb groat, without numeral, and two, as the IIIe groat with the roman IIII at the end of the obverse legend.

The billon coinage of James IV is well-represented in the Stewartby collection, with 140 placks, 5 halves, 14 first issue and 122 second issue pence. The placks continued on from those issued under James III, the only significant difference being a crown each side of the shield on the obverse. They were divided into types I to IV by Lord Stewartby based on the obverse inscription (Stewart 1967, pp. 73 and 145–6). Type I have the inscription SCOTORVM QRA. This is not represented in the Stewartby collection, suggesting it may be rare. Type II (**49–161**), with lombardic-lettering, omits a numeral or abbreviation at the end of the obverse legend; its five varieties (IIa to IIf) are defined by the stops and the initial marks. Holdings of IIa to IIc include coins with the cross potent initial mark, some muled with a crown (**49–60, 65–108**), as well as with the crown initial mark alone (**61–4**). IId to IIf (**109–61**) all have the cross fleury initial mark, with varieties defined by the stops. Type III combines a type II die with a type IV die (**162**), so one side has roman-lettering. This is not categorised as a type in the Stewartby collection, being regarded by him as a muling of dies (according to a note by Lord Stewartby on the packet in which this coin (HSAN 2703, Sylloge 162) is stored). Type IV, reading **IACOBVS 4** with roman-lettering on both the obverse and reverse, has four varieties, IVa to IVd (**163–85**), each defined by the stops. The final type V (**186–8**), is as type IV, but with star stops. All type IV and V placks have the crown initial mark. 5 examples of the rare half-placks (**189–93**) are in the Stewartby collection with a single example of type I, with **QR**, three examples of type II, without **QR**, and a single example (**193**) of type IV, reading **SCOTORVM . 4**. This last coin is noted by Lord Stewartby as the only known example of a half-plack with the Arabic 4.

The first issue billon penny, with the pellets reverse (**194–207**), divides into type 1, with annulets by the neck and annulet stops (**194–5**), and type 2, without annulets by the neck or annulet stops (**196–207**) (Stewart 1967, pp. 73 and 146). Both types name the mint, Edinburgh, on the reverse, and have an initial mark which is a plain-cross with indented arms on both sides. These are believed to be the earliest of the billon pence (Bateson 1997, p. 46). A second issue, with crown and lis reverse, followed on from this and consisted of four types (Stewart 1967, pp. 73 and 146). Type I, with the **SALVVM FAC** legend on the reverse and crown initial mark (**208–9**), is represented by two examples in the collection; type II, naming the mint on the reverse but also with the crown initial mark, is represented by 14 coins (**210–23**). Better represented in the Stewartby collection are types III and IV. Type III (**224–58**) is similar to type II but with a different style bust, and is usually found with the cross potent initial mark or, sometimes, cross potent on the obverse and crown on the reverse. Type IV (**259–329**) consists of rather crude coins, often struck on a dumpy flan and generally very base and badly made. They were also readily counterfeited (**323–9**). Type IV retains the crown and lis obverse but has a round moon-like face on the obverse. The initial mark is often small and appears to be a small cross pattée. Varieties are noted in the Stewartby collection based on the stops: IVa has pellets; IVb, saltires; IVc, trefoils; IVd, no stops; IVe, stars. Many of these coins are unclear, so the type is not subdivided into its varieties but these have been noted where it is possible to see the stops clearly.

JAMES V (1513–42)

The numismatic history of the reign follows the broad periodisation of the life of James V. The first part aligns with the regency up to 1524, initially under his mother, Queen Margaret and, from 1514, the Duke of Albany and the Earl of Arran; the second part from then until his marriage in 1538, with James V ruling in his own right from 1528; and the third part until his death in December 1542. These periods are reflected in the designation of his reign into three coinages, the first belonging to the period 1513–26; the second to 1526–38; and the third to 1538–42.

The coinage of James V

In the first coinage no silver was struck. Otherwise, continuity was maintained with the coinage of James IV. Adam Boyd was appointed Warden of the Mint, 'wardane principale and Keper of the Kingis Cunyie Irnis', in 1514 (C-P I, p. cxxxii). In the years to 1517–8, mint output was predominantly billon placks, with muling of James IV and James V dies indicative of the smooth transition from James IV to James V. It is unclear if any gold was struck before 1517–8, but in March 1517 Robert Bertoune, the Controller of the Mint, was given permission to coin 80 oz. of gold into unicorns and the Earl of Arran, likewise for 30 oz. (C-P I, p. 62, XXVIII). In March 1518, an instruction was given for the 'irnis of the Unicorne' to be delivered to the Treasurer to coin 50 oz. of gold into unicorns for the Earl of Arran (C-P I, p. 62, XXIX). Authority was again given to the Earl of Arran in March 1519 for coining 50 oz. of gold (C-P I, p. 62, XXXI).

The second coinage began in 1526 and marked a significant change, with the introduction of the gold crown, in the manner of the French écu, and a new silver coinage of groats and third-groats. Billon coinage would appear to have ceased save for an issue in 1533 (Stewartby and Holmes 2008). This coinage was initiated in March 1525 when the Lords in secret council authorised a new coinage in silver and gold, 'ane crown of gold and ane grote of silver.' Gold was to be struck at 21.5 carats, with the crown valued at twenty shillings, and the silver at ten deniers (0.833) fine, with the groat valued at 18 pence (C-P I, p. 62, XXXII). At this time James Achesoun, an Edinburgh goldsmith, was appointed as Mint Master, commencing the Achesoun family's long association with the mint (C-P I, p. 55, IV; p. 80, XXIII). Following the Earl of Angus taking custody of the king in 1525, a contract was let to Joachim Hochstetter, a mining entrepreneur, and his brother to produce the coinage for ten years (C-P I, p. 64, XXXIV). It is now accepted that this agreement did not survive the downfall of Angus in 1528 and that no coinage was ever produced under it (Stevenson 1991, pp. 39 and 49). Production of crowns and groats continued into the 1530s.

The third coinage comprises gold and billon, but no silver. It witnessed the minting of gold ducats (forty shillings) and billon bawbees (6 pence). No authorisation initiating this coinage survives, but the introduction of two new denominations indicates it was intended to be a significant change. It is thought instructions would have been given in the first half of 1538 (Holmes 1996, p. 2). The resignation of James Achesoun, when he refused to strike billon bawbees in 1538 (Hopetoun MSS, C-P I, p. 96), and the appointment of Alexander Orrok of Sillebawby in his place, suggests this was the time the new coinage began (Stewart 1967, p. 78). A Treasurer's Account for 1539 indicates it was underway by then as it records the striking of 'braidbonnets', referring to the bonneted bust of James V on the ducats, using gold supplied from Scottish goldfields at Craufurd Moor and Corehead (C-P I, p. 59, XXII). For the first time the date appeared on the 1539 ducats. Further ducats and fractions were struck in 1540, and the striking of 159 oz. of Scottish gold into ducats is noted in accounts for 1541–2. No coins survive bearing these dates, suggesting that the dies dated 1540 continued to be used to strike the ducat and its fractions in 1541–2. James Achesoun made his peace with Alexander Orrok and was reappointed to the mint in 1540, working there until 1554 (Stewart 1967, p. 78). Orrok on the other hand is last heard of in 1541 (Stewart 1967, p. 78).

Coins of James V in the Stewartby collection

The Stewartby collection contains 213 coins (**330–542**) of James V of which 17 are gold (**330–46**), 86 silver (**347–432**) and 110 billon (**433–542**). The first coinage is represented by 63 coins; the second- by 93; and the third- by 57. The gold includes examples of all the denominations of the reign. The first coinage unicorns divide into two types (Stewart 1967, pp. 75 and 146): type Ia, with a cinquefoil countermark, the symbol of the Regent Arran, on the reverse (**330–1**); and type II, without the countermark (**333–4**). In addition there is a half-unicorn, a rare coin (**335**), and a base metal contemporary counterfeit of a type Ia unicorn (**332**). The second coinage gold crowns are known for four types (Stewart 1967, p. 77 and 147). Type I differs from types II to IV in having the legend PER LIGNVM CRVCIS SALVI SVMVS ('by the wood of the cross we are saved') on the reverse, as opposed to CRVCIS ARMA SEQVAMVR ('let us follow the arms of the cross') found on types II to IV. Types I and II, the earliest of the crowns, both have a pointed shield on the obverse, in the same way that the type I and II groats have this feature. These features are represented by a type II/I mule (**336**) and a type II/III mule (**337**), with the Stewartby collection not having a true example of either type. The collection contains three examples of the type III crown, with the rounded base shield (**338–41**), and one example of type IV, this as type III but with pellet colon stops (**342**). The third coinage gold is fully covered with examples of both dates for the ducat (**343–4**), and of each of the fractional denominations, the two-thirds (**345**) and the one-third (**346**).

The silver holdings, all of the second coinage (1526–38), comprise 70 groats (**347–416**) and 16 one-third groats (**417–32**). The groat divides into four types, I to IV (Stevenson 1991), with a good selection of varieties for each. There are 11 examples of the type I groat, with the VILLA EDINBRVGH reverse and pointed shield (**347–57**); these coins include several die-links, indicating few dies were used for these, the earliest coins of the issue. Type II, inscribed with OPPIDVM EDINBVRGI and a pointed shield on the reverse, is represented by two examples (**358–9**). 4 examples of type II/III mules (**360–3**) show that type II preceded type III. The most numerous of the groats, representing an issue that continued for some years, are type III (**364–414**), on which the reverse legend is amended to read OPPIDV EDINBVRGI, with a shield with a rounded base. The last of the groats is type IV (**415–6**), which is similar to type III, but with distinctive lis-tipped points on the central fleur of the crown. One type IV example (**416**) has initial marks, a plain-cross on the obverse and a lis on the reverse, which varies from the usual plain-cross on the obverse alone found on the rest of the groats. The one-third groat (**417–32**) all use the type III groat reverse style. There are a number of variations as set out by Stevenson (1989) and these are well represented.

The billon coinage of James V is formed of placks (**433–88**), from the first coinage (1513–26), along with bawbees and halves (**490–542**) from the third coinage (1538–42). There is one plack (**489**), which is dated to 1533, during the time of the second coinage. James IV obverse dies muled with a James V reverse demonstrate continuity of output of the plack coinage after 1513, with two coins in the Stewartby collection combining a James IV type II obverse (**433–4**) with dies of James V, while two other coins (**435–6**) mule a James IV type IV obverse with a James V reverse die. The James V placks all have roman-lettering and divide into two types, I and II (Stewart 1967, pp. 75 and 148). Type I (**437–41**) has star stops on one of or both of the obverse and reverse, with variety Ia on both sides and Ib with stars on the obverse and trefoils on the reverse or the other way round. Type II (**442–88**) placks have pellet (IIa) or trefoil stops (IIb) on both sides, or the pellets on the obverse and the trefoils on the reverse (IIb). Type I are thought to be the earliest. Placks were not known to have been part of the second coinage of James V but Joan Murray discovered that James V had ordered a coinage of billon in 1533, struck as placks or otherwise (Stewartby and Holmes 2008). An example (**489**) of the second coinage plack, similar to type II but with more elegant lettering, is in the Stewartby collection. The third coinage saw the introduction of the billon bawbee (**490–535**), which was also struck in fractions; halves (**536–42**) and quarters are also known. The last is not represented. The bawbee divides into two broad types; those with no annulet on the obverse (**490–509**) and those with (**510–35**). A number of varieties based on the stops and form of the crown have been identified by Stevenson (1989) and these are well represented in the Stewartby collection. The rare half-bawbee is divided in the same manner as the bawbee into those without an annulet on the obverse (**536–7**), and those with (**538–42**).

MARY (1542–67)

The coinage of Mary's reign is traditionally divided into five periods defined by her marriages. The first period runs from her accession in 1542 to her marriage to the Dauphin Francis in 1558; the second period coincides with her first marriage, April 1558 to December 1560, including the brief reign (10 July 1559 to 5 December 1560) of her husband as Francis II; the third period is her first widowhood, including her return to Scotland, 1561–5; the fourth period represents the marriage to Lord Darnley (1565–7); and the fifth period covers her second widowhood, embracing the final months of her reign in 1567 (February-July). This approach fits neatly with the coinage, on which her titles change according to her marital status, and this has provided an easy means to divide and classify it into five periods.

The political context of Mary's reign and its impact on the coinage

The story of the Scottish coinage at this time was not defined so much by the events of Mary's private life but by the external and internal politics of Scotland. Her position as a woman, a catholic, for much of her reign, a minor, and as a legitimate great-granddaughter of Henry VII of England, placed her and Scotland in a position where the interests of the greater powers of England and France would dictate events for much of her life. Seen from this angle Mary's reign can be divided differently, into three distinct phases, defined by the dominant forces influencing events and politics in Scotland.

The first phase (1542–50) was dominated by English military intervention, the so called 'Rough Wooing' in pursuit of a dynastic marriage between Mary and Prince Edward. This led to the Scots appealing for French military support, which was provided, leading to the 1550 Treaty of Boulogne and English withdrawal from Scotland. The second phase, 1550–60, was dominated by a deepening alliance with France, culminating with the attempted union of the two kingdoms through the marriage of Mary to the Dauphin Francis. French forces continued to be present in Scotland after 1550, with the government under a Regent, the Earl of Arran until 1554, and then Mary of Guise, until her death in June 1560, after which French domination of Scottish affairs began to unravel. Following the 5 July 1560 Treaty of Edinburgh, both French and English troops – the latter having intervened again to support Scottish protestants – withdrew, and Scotland entered a period of being in control of its own destiny, with the Protestant Lords of the Congregation in the ascendancy. The third and final phase (1560–7), which might be described as 'Scotland alone,' included Mary's return in 1561 following the unexpected death of Francis II in December 1560, and her sole rule. This was a politically toxic period during which the catholic queen was unable to reach an accommodation with the newly politically dominant Protestant Lords and the changed religious beliefs they represented.

Numismatically, the coinage of Mary is a reflection of these three politically defined phases. The first, 'Rough Wooing' phase to 1550, continued the coinage begun under James V, with billon bawbees from 1543–9, the reissue of the penny and a small output of gold, but no silver. In the second, French dominated phase, 1550–60, Arran's rule continued until 1554, with a further issue of bawbees (group IV) in 1553/4. Near the end of Arran's rule in 1553, a new gold issue, along with the introduction of the silver testoon, took place. From 1554 to 1560, under the regency of Mary of Guise, a period of significant coinage output took place with gold, predominantly ryals and fractions, silver testoons and halves, along with billon placks, hardheads, pence and the twelve-penny groat. The third, 'Scotland alone' phase, 1560–7, saw a cessation of the billon coinage but the silver testoon coinage continued, initially as before. A gold coinage may have been planned at this time but none was produced (Stewart 1967, p. 89). No coinage seems to have been produced in 1563–4. In 1565 a new silver coinage of ryals and fractions was begun.

The coinage of Mary in the first phase, 1542–50

Coinage production in the first years of Mary's reign was a continuation of her father's. James Achesoun continued as Master of the Mint until 1554. Gold crowns in the same style as those of James V, with the CRVCIS ARMA SEQVAMVR legend, were produced in 1543 with the value raised from 20 shillings under James V to 22 shillings and 10 pence, and a new twenty-shilling piece was introduced in 1543, dated and with the reverse legend reading ECCE ANCILLA DOMINE ('behold the handmaid of the Lord'). All gold production was small and between 1543 and 1553 no further gold was struck. The main mint output of the years 1543–9 was billon bawbees (6d) and halves, which again continued a strand of the coinage of James V. These were produced in Edinburgh, except in the summer and autumn of 1544, when production was based under Mary of Guise at Stirling Castle, a move made necessary by the exposure of Edinburgh to English military operations at that time. The bawbee is classified into four groups by Stevenson (1989), with groups 1 to 3 dated to this period and group 4 (authorised in January 1553) (C-P I, p. 76, XV), to 1553–4.

It is noticeable from the Stewartby collection holding of just under 200 bawbees that some variation exists in initial marks, which may reflect production at different times, with both a plain-cross and a slipped-cross (a cross where the lower arm is tapered) appearing on the obverse of group 2 coins and a thinner plain-cross, as well as the usual form, on group 3. Metal for the bawbee issues was acquired from the French in the form of clipped *sous*, and it was noted at the time that 'the maist pairt of the saidis bawbeis were conyeit of clippit soussis quhilkis than were proclamit for bullion and send heir to be conuertit in bawbeis for payment of their men of weir lying heir aganis Ingland' (Hopetoun MSS, C-P I, p. 97; Holmes 1998, p. 34). The presence of many clipped French coins coming into circulation as small-change ultimately required them to be prohibited in July 1550 (C-P I, p. 71, VIII). The authorities had to manage this influx of foreign coins from as early as 1545, when it was necessary to pass an Act of the Privy Council to allow French testerns to circulate and to set the value of French small-change in circulation, with the *sou* at 6d, the half-*sou* at 3d, the *carolus* at 5d and the *liard* at three-halfpence (C-P I, p.69, III). In addition to the bawbee, an issue of billon pence and halves was authorised by the Privy Council on 3 May 1547 (C-P I, p. 71, VII), and this reintroduced a denomination not issued since before 1513. The pence were struck in two issues, initially in 1547 (type I), and a second issue (type II) a little later, the date of which is uncertain, but likely before 1554. No halves were struck.

The coinage of Mary in the second phase, 1550–60

The first significant developments in the coinage in the years after 1550 were the introduction of a new denomination, the testoon, and a small issue of gold in 1553. It is recorded that James Achesoun went to Paris in 1553 with permission to engrave portraits of Mary for her coins (*PSAS* IX, p. 506). The resulting new coin, the testoon, with a crowned bust of Mary on the obverse, and the legend **DA PACEM DOMINE** ('give peace O Lord') on the reverse, was struck on French mill presses at eleven deniers fine (91.67 per cent), with a value of 4 shillings. As Mint Master in 1553 (C-P I, pp. 75 and 76, XIV, XV), Achesoun would also seem to have also been responsible for the issue of two new gold coins, the forty-four and twenty-two shilling pieces, both dated, with a monogram of *Maria Regina* and the legend **DILIGITE IVSTICIAM** ('observe justice') on the reverse. Like the new testoon, these are associated with Arran, then still regent. Both have his heraldic mark of the cinquefoil, and on the gold the letters I G divided by the arms of Scotland on the obverse, standing for *Iacobus Gubernator* ('James [Hamilton], the Regent').

The tenure of James Achesoun as Mint Master ended in 1554. His place was taken by November by John Missaruy (also given as Missarwy or Misserwy), apparently an Englishman (C-P I, p. 82, XXXI). His tenure was short, for by October 1555 he was detained in the Edinburgh Tolbooth (C-P I, p. 83, XXXIII), after which he disappears from the record. His place was taken by David Stevinson from 1555–8 (Hopetoun MSS, C-P I, p. 99). Between 1555 and 1558 gold in the form of ryals (60 shillings) and halves (30 shillings) was being struck. With production of the bulk of the issue commencing in 1555, it seems Missaruy was responsible for this coin, one of just five issues on which a realistic portrait of Mary appears (the others being the 1553 and 1561–2 testoons, the 1558 Mary and Francis ducat and the Mary and Darnley 1565 type I silver ryal). Stevinson took over this issue in 1555 and was responsible for the rare 1557–8 ryals and halves. The reverse legend on these coins reads **IVSTVS FIDE VIVIT** ('the just man lives by faith').

A new silver coinage of testoons and halves was begun in 1555. This was associated with the regency of Mary of Guise. The first of these (type II), dated 1555, was valued at 5 shillings instead of 4 shillings, as with the 1553 issues, and issued at a lower silver fineness at 0.725, which was compensated for with a higher weight (7.63g as opposed to 5.08g). The reverse of the type II testoon and halves has the arms of Scotland set over a large cross potent and the legend **DILICIE DNI COR HVMILE** ('a humble heart is the delight of the Lord'). A further issue of testoons and halves (type III) followed in 1556–8. The reverse changed to a large cross potent with a small cross in each angle and the legend to **IN VIRTVTE TVA LIBERA ME** ('in thy strength deliver me'). These were also valued at 5 shillings, but with improved fineness at 0.916 and a lower weight, 6.12 g. This was to be the standard for the testoon through to 1562. At the end of 1558 John Achesoun became Mint Master.

Some testoons and halves with a letter A in the field on the obverse are thought to be his work at this time (C-P I, p. 83, XXXII and XXXIII).

John Achesoun was responsible for the production of the gold ducat (Hopetoun MSS, C-P I, p. 100), the only gold coin of the second period. This may have been produced to mark Mary's marriage to Francis. This was authorised by the Privy Council on 23 January 1559 (C-P I, p. 76, XVI), to be 22 carats fine, and to weigh a quarter of an ounce with a value of 60 shillings. The design of the coin was specified in some detail, and the Council also authorised halves to be produced, which did not happen. The obverse has facing busts of Mary and Francis vis à vis, and the reverse carries cruciform interlinked dolphins with the legend **HORVM TVTA FIDES** ('the faith of these is whole'). All are dated 1558, the year in which the issue was authorised according to the old style (counting the year's end as 25 March).

Testoons and halves were issued during the period of the French marriage. The first, type I, dated 1558 and 1559, was from before Francis became king of France. It has a reverse with a distinctive cross of Lorraine each side of the FM (Francis and Mary) monogram, with the legend **FECIT VTRAQVE VNVM** ('he has made both one'). The obverse has the halved shield of the arms of Scotland with those of the Dauphiné and of Scotland over a cross potent and the titles, with Francis as Dauphin.

The second type, dated 1560–1, was from after Francis became king and after the death of Mary of Guise. With some dated 1561, it continued to be struck after his death. On this the obverse inscription proclaimed Francis and Mary as king and queen of France and Scotland, with the arms of Scotland no longer set over a cross potent. The absence of this symbol recognised the death of Mary of Guise in June 1560. Similarly, the Lorraine crosses on the reverse are replaced by a crowned thistle and lis each side of the monogram. On the reverse the legend **VICIT LEO DE TRIBV IVDA** ('the Lion of the tribe of Judah has prevailed') was used.

The **VICIT LEO** legend, along with removal of the Guise symbols, is symbolic of the decisive change taking place in Scottish politics as the Protestant Lords seized control. Its source is Revelation 5:5, where the opening of the sealed scrolls is described: 'then one of the Elders said to me 'weep not; lo the Lion of the tribe of Judah, the root of David, has conquered so that he can open the scroll and its seven seals.' This is a marked departure from preceding legends where the message addressed matters such as the French alliance, faith, the image of the Virgin and the power of the cross. Instead this inscription is about the bible and getting access to scripture for salvation. It could not be better chosen for making a political point, in this case the regime change arising from the takeover of the Protestant Lords of the Congregation and the rise of the new religion, with its emphasis on finding salvation in the word of God as set out in scripture. As such, this historically resonant issue should be attributed to the third, and final political phase of Mary's reign, but before her presence and sole rule in Scotland required some toning down of the strident protestant message on the coinage.

The **VICIT** testoon and halves are known for two obverse defined varieties. One reads **SCOTOR *B*** with a small high Scottish crown; the other **SCOTOR Q**, with a flat wide crown. The significance of the ***B*** and **Q** suffix has been much debated (Stewart 1967, p. 87; J. K. R. Murray 1967; J. K. R. Murray and J. E. L. Murray 1980) and it is now accepted that those with ***B*** were struck earlier than those with **Q**, as **Q** coins are known dated 1561 (struck after the death of Francis and before Mary returned to Scotland). A possible explanation for the variation in the ***B*** and **Q** obverse dies is that they are the work of different die-cutters or different die batches. This is plausible, as the Mint Master changed in 1560. Prior to that date the coins were made under the tenure of John Achesoun, who on being displaced from his position went to France, and was briefly replaced by John Hairt, before Achesoun returned in 1561 (Hopetoun MSS, C-P I, p. 101).

Billon coinage was a major part of mint output in the 1550s. The bawbee ceased production for a period after 1549, until a new issue in 1553–4 (C-P I, p. 75, XIV and p. 76, XV) which is notable for bearing the cross potent initial mark, a device associated with Mary of Guise. The plack (4d) was issued in 1557, when 606 stones of metal were coined between 1 July 1557 and 19 January 1558 (Hopetoun MSS, C-P I, p. 99). The penny was issued again, firstly, type III, under a licence granted to Monsieur D'Oysel, the French ambassador and authorised shortly after Mary of Guise assumed the regency. This was struck in December to January 1554–5 (C-P I, p. 98, L). A further issue, with a new design, was authorised in February 1554 (C-P I, p. 76, XVI), but not struck until 1555–6 (Holmes 1998, pp. 40–1). A new denomination, the lion (three-halfpence), commonly known as the hardhead, a derivation from the French *hardi*, was authorised on 23 February 1554 (C-P I, p. 98, L; Holmes 1998, p. 40) and first produced in 1555. Hardheads were struck until 1560, with fineness reduced to 0.5 from 1 denier fine in 1558 (Hopetoun MSS, C-P I, p. 99). The design was altered at the end of 1558 to reflect Mary's marriage. The lion/hardhead was supplemented with another new denomination the twelve-penny groat 'the kingis and quenis twelff penny groate,' authorised on 4 March 1558, and issued during the period of Mary's marriage to Francis in 1558–9 (C-P I, p. 77, XVIII; Holmes 1998, pp. 42–3). This was commonly called a 'nonsunt' on the basis of the reverse inscription **IAM NONSVNT DVO SED VNA CARO** ('now they are not two but one flesh').

The coinage of Mary in the third phase, 1560–7

The **VICIT LEO** legend on the type-II second period testoons and halves marked a significant departure from what had gone before, with a decisive shift towards the protestant cause and belief in the politics of Scotland. Perhaps reflecting this changed political environment with the return of Mary, John Achesoun was reinstalled as Mint Master in 1561 (Hopetoun MSS, C-P I, p. 101) and remained in post until 1580. He had responsibility for the mint output during the final phase of Mary's reign, covering the periods of her first widowhood, marriage to Darnley and second widowhood. No gold (a crown of 1560 is known but is thought to be a pattern) or billon coinage was struck during this period (Stewart 1967, p. 89). A silver coinage of testoons and halves, with an elegant realistic bust of Mary on the obverse, was struck in 1561–2. The VICIT legend was dropped in favour of the less radical and more traditional SALVM FAC POPVLVM TVVM DOMINE ('o Lord save thy people') legend on the reverse, where the halved Scottish and French arms were retained. No coinage appears to have been struck in 1563–4, which may have been due to the fall in the price of silver noted at the time because, 'all men abstractit thair handis throw the downe crying of the pryces of silver from 24s to 22s.' (Hopetoun MSS, C-P I, p. 101).

A new silver denomination, a ryal of 30 shillings, was introduced in this phase in 1565. The earliest issue of this commemorated the marriage of Mary and Darnley (type I). The obverse, with facing busts of Mary and Darnley and the legend, HENRICVS & MARIA DEI GRA R & R SCOTORVM proved controversial for, by putting Darnley's name first, it implied his being both superior and king. It was withdrawn. On 22 December 1565 an Act of the Privy Council authorised the striking of a second-issue of ryals with the design revised (type II), with fractions at 20 (two-thirds) and 10 shillings (one-third). Fineness was set at 11 deniers and weight of 1 oz. (C-P I, p. 78, XX). The obverse replaced the facing busts with the crowned arms of Scotland and Mary's name was placed first in the legend. The reverse, on which the date appears, reintroduced EXVRGAT DEVS ET DISSIPENTVR INIMICI EIVS ('let God arise and let his enemies be scattered'), a legend last seen on unicorns of James V. A curious design was used of a crowned palm tree with a tortoise ascending its trunk over which there is a banner proclaiming DAT GLORIA VIRES ('glory gives strength'). Various explanations have been proposed for the significance of this iconography, one of which led to these coins being popularly referred to by contemporaries as 'Crookston dollars', with the palm representing a yew tree at Crookston under which, it was said, Mary and Darnley had sat during their courtship (Stewartby and Stewartby, p. 225). This is now proven as erroneous (Stewart 1967, p. 90; Archibald and Cook, p. 169). The design was dropped after Mary's abdication. This would suggest that the type's significance was associated directly with Mary herself and its relevance no longer applied after her removal. Explanations put forward for this intriguing design have included that it was a personal expression of her religious faith, or that it celebrated the defence of Malta against the Turks in 1565 (Stewartby and Stewartby 2007, p. 226). A recently published suggestion is that it is a personal and dynastic message setting out Mary's self-image as resilient, fecund and wise along with the hopes for the survival of the Stewart dynasty through the anticipated birth of an heir who would unite the thrones of England and Scotland (Archibald and Cook 2020, pp. 172–9). The new ryal was authorised by an Act of the Privy Council on 22 December 1565 (C-P I, p. 78, XX) and James VI was born in June 1566 (ryals dated 1565 would have been struck before 25 March 1566). Ryals and two-thirds ryals are dated 1565–7 and the one-third ryal 1565–6. A final issue of the ryal and its fractions (but not the one third), was made in 1567, with the obverse naming Mary alone and the reverse unchanged. These probably include the eight stones of silver struck on 15–16 July 1567 when 'the Lords causit streik the Quenis wark in xx shilling xxx shilling and x shilling pieces' (C-P I, p. cxlii, noted 'Diurnal of Occurents', Maitland Club, Edinburgh).

Some denominations of the coinage of Mary were subject to later countermarking. Testoons and halves, along with the ryal and its fractions, were subject to revaluation in 1578 (C-P I, p.110, VIII). On recall to the mint these coins were marked with a crowned thistle before reissue. Forgery of billon placks and hardheads was also a problem. In 1575 these were recalled for examination, with coins deemed not to be forgeries reissued with a star in heart countermark, which was the device of James Douglas, the Earl of Morton, regent to James VI.

Coins of Mary in the Stewartby collection

The Stewartby collection contains 503 coins (**543–1045**) of Mary of which 8 are gold (**543–50**), 151 silver (**551–626, 922–64, 1014–21, 1022–45**) and 344 billon (**627–821, 965–1013**). Counterfeiting was a particular problem under Mary, and the collection includes examples of counterfeit bawbees (**821**), placks (**920–1**), hardheads (**1006–13, 989**) and a twelve-penny groat (**979**). The Stewartby collection is arranged in the traditional numismatic ordering of five-periods with 393 coins from the first period, before the French marriage (1542–58) (**543–921**); 92 coins from the second-, French marriage, period (1558–60) (**922–1013**); 8 coins from the third period, Mary's first widowhood (1560–5) (**1014–21**); 14 coins from the fourth period, her second-marriage (1565–7) (**1022–38**); and 8 from the fifth period of her second widowhood (1567) (**1039–45**). If considered according to the politically defined phases of Mary's reign, the first phase (1542–50) is represented by 211 coins including bawbee groups 1 to 3, and halves; the second- (1550–60) by 230 (including group 4 bawbees); and the third (1560–7), by 62 coins including the VICIT testoons and halves.

From the earliest years of the reign, the gold element of the collection contains examples of the Abbey crown (**543–4**), and the 1543 twenty-shilling piece (**545**). There is an example each of the first issue 1553 forty-four-shilling piece (**546–7**), the 1553 twenty-two-shilling piece (**548**), the portrait ryal (**549**) and the half-ryal (**550**), the last two both dated 1555. The second issue 1557 forty-four-shilling piece and the second period Francis and Mary ducat are not in the Stewartby collection, although the latter is represented by a nineteenth-century electrotype (copies and later forgeries, **1462**).

The silver coinage commences with an example of the 1553 group I testoon (**551**). The testoon issues that followed in the first period 1555–8, under the regency of

Mary of Guise but before Mary's marriage to Francis, are well represented with 75 coins (**552–626**), comprising 56 testoons (**552–6, 562–612**) and 19 halves (**557–61, 613–26**). There are 10 examples of the group II issue (**552–61**), dated 1555 with reverse legend **DILICIE DNI COR HVMILE** ('a humble heart is the delight of the Lord'), with 5 testoons (**552–6**) and 5 halves (**557–61**). One group II testoon is a variety with an annulet over the left small crown on the obverse (**556**). There are 65 examples of the group III issue (**562–626**), dated 1556–8, with the **IN VIRTVTE TVA LIBERA** ('in Thy strength deliver me') legend, with 51 testoons (**562–612**) and 14 halves (**613–26**). The group III testoon varieties are all represented, with 20 (**562–81**) examples of the first-variety (dated 1556–7, with small high crown), of which 17 are with an annulet below the M and R (**562–78**) and three without (**579–81**). There are 31 examples in the Stewartby collection (**582–612**) of the second-variety of group III testoons (dated 1557–8, with the low crown) of which 19 are of the variety without annulets on the obverse (**582–600**); three are similar but with a letter A (Achesoun) in the obverse field (**601–3**); and 9 are the variety with annulets on the obverse (**604–12**). The group III half-testoons (**613–26**), 14 coins, all of the first-variety, are divided into those with an annulet on the obverse (**613–4**); those without (**615–23**); those without but dated 1558 on the reverse only (**624–5**); and one example of the rare 1558 half with the letter A (Achesoun) in the obverse field (**626**).

The silver coinage of the second period (marriage to Francis) comprises two issues. There are 13 examples of the first, type I (**922–34**), dated 1558–9 with the **FECIT VTRAQVE VNVM** ('he has made both one') reverse legend and the Lorraine crosses on the obverse, with 10 testoons (**922–31**) and three halves (**932–4**). The second issue, type II, dated 1560–1, with the revised obverse and the **VICIT LEO DE TRIBV IVDA** reverse legend, is represented by 30 coins (**935–64**), with 24 testoons (**935–58**) and 6 halves (**959–64**). Of these 13 are variety A, **SCOTOR *B*** (11 testoons, **935–45**, and two halves, **959–60**) and 17 are variety B, **SCOTOR Q** (14 testoons, **946–58**, and 4 halves, **961–4**). The sole coinage struck in the third period 1560–5 (first widowhood), are testoons and halves dated 1561, or less commonly, 1562, with a bust of Mary on the obverse and the **SALVVM** legend on the reverse. There are 6 examples of the third period testoon (**1014–9**) in the Stewartby collection, with 5 dated 1561 (**1014–18**), one 1562 (**1019**); and two examples of the half (**1020–1**), with one dated 1561 and one 1562.

The final silver coinage, covering the fourth (marriage to Darnley) and fifth periods (second widowhood), comprises the silver ryal coinage of 1565–7. The Stewartby collection does not have an example of the 1565 type I 'marriage' ryal, but the coinage of Mary and Darnley is represented by 17 coins, comprising 6 ryals (**1022–7**), 6 two-thirds ryals (**1028–33**) and 5 one-third ryals (**1034–8**). The 1567 two-thirds ryal is not in the collection (the one-third was not struck in 1567 naming Darnley). There is an example of the rare undated two-thirds ryal (**1028**). The fifth period ryal coinage, dated 1567 in the name of Mary only, is represented by 7 coins (**1039–45**), with three ryals (**1039–41**), two two-thirds ryals (**1042–3**) and two one-third ryals (**1044–5**).

Two-thirds of all the coins of Mary in the Stewartby collection are billon. The majority of these are bawbees (**627–821**) and halves (**822–46**) from the first period (1542–58). The bawbees are listed according to Stevenson's classification groups 1 to 4, where 1 and 2 have a solid saltire, and 3 and 4 a fluted saltire (Stevenson 1989). There are 28 group 1 Edinburgh bawbees (**627–41** and **656–68**) and 14 (dating to the summer-autumn 1544) from Stirling Castle (**642–55**), struck while the mint relocated there away from English military activity. Group 2 is represented by 49 coins (**669–717**). There are 79 examples of Group 3, with the voided saltire on the reverse (**718–96**). The issue of 1553–4, with the cross potent initial mark (group 4 in Stevenson's classification), is represented by 24 coins (**797–820**). One example in the collection is a counterfeit bawbee (**821**). The halves are listed by Stevenson's classification, A to D, with types A and B, represented by six and two coins respectively (**822–7** and **828–9**). Types C and D, with a fluted rather than solid saltire, account for 9 (**830–8**) and 8 coins (**839–46**) respectively. Both the first and second issue pence are represented in the Stewartby collection. The first issue, *c.* 1547, type Ia, with the 'baby face' bust and reading OPIDVM, is represented by 6 examples (**847–52**). Type Ib, similar to Ia but with an open crown, is not represented in the collection. There are two examples of the slightly later type II penny, which carries a child's bust with an open crown and reads OPIDV (**853–4**), and 4 of type III (**855–8**), similar to type II but with a double-arched crown and, on the reverse, a lis replacing Arran's cinquefoil in the angles of the long-cross and the reading OPPIDVM.

There are 6 of the second issue pence in the Stewartby collection (**859–64**). These are all dated 1556 (but struck in 1557), and have a cross potent on the obverse and the legend VICIT VERITAS on the reverse. The hardhead, first issued in the first period and dated 1555 and 1556, is represented by 10 coins (**865–74**) of two varieties: type I with annulets on the obverse (**865–7**), and type II without (**868–74**). There are 14 examples of the second issue hardheads, all dated 1558 (**875–88**), which are similar to type II of the first issue, dated 1555. The plack of 1557 is represented by 33 coins (**889–921**). Two are counterfeits (**920–1**). The placks are classified based on an unpublished typology by Stevenson (Holmes 2006, plates 32–3) with four types, A to D, where A has crowns on the reverse with a beaded arch (**889–904**); B, a plain arch (**905–11**); C, a plain arch disconnected from the outer fleurs of the crown (**912–13**); and D, similar to C, but with a re-cut arch connected to the fleurs (**914–19**).

The last of Mary's billon coinage dates from the second period, the time of her marriage to Francis. The twelve-penny groat, or 'nonsunt,' is dated 1558 or 1559. It is represented in the Stewartby collection by 15 coins (**965–79**) and one counterfeit (**979**). The twelve-penny groat is divided into two types; type I with the dolphin on the obverse looking right and dated 1558 or 1559 (**965–72**), and type II with the dolphin looking left and dated 1559 (**973–8**). The hardhead continued to be struck in the second period, with 34 examples in the collection (**980–1013**), including counterfeits (**989** and **1006–13**). Thes latter provide evidence for the problem that would be addressed in 1575 with the recall and re-issue of good coins, now bearing the star in heart countermark that is found on many surviving examples. The second period hardhead divides into two types: type 1, dated 1559, with the dolphins on the obverse looking right (**980–8**); and type 2, dated 1559 or 1560, with dolphins looking left (**990–1005**) (Stewart 1967, pp. 88 and 150).

JAMES VI (1567–1625)

The coinage of James VI is divided by his accession to the English throne in 1603. Before this there were eight coinages, each involving new issues as authorised by the Privy Council or the Scottish Parliament. No billon coinage was issued before 1583 and copper replaced billon for small-change denominations after 1597. In 1604 the English and Scottish coinages were aligned in terms of denominations, types and fineness to form a single currency across the two kingdoms, one part produced in Edinburgh under Scottish authority, the other in London under English, distinguishable from each other only by minor differences in design. In the 37 years between 1567 and 1604 there were eight coinages; in the 21 years after 1604, there were two. Before 1604 there is great variety, but little thereafter. From 1567 to 1581 Scotland was governed by a series of regents, who ensured that James VI was brought up as a protestant, the most enduring of which was James Douglas, Earl of Morton, between 1572 and 1581.

The coinage of James VI, 1567–1605; gold and silver issues

The first coinage of James, authorised on 31 August 1567 (C-P I, p. 138, XXXIX), was a continuation of the ryal (30 shillings) and fractions (20 shillings and 10 shillings) issued by Mary. The obverse named James and had a crowned I and R each side the crowned arms of Scotland. The reverse replaced the tortoise and palm design of Mary with an upright sword, with a crown on its tip and a hand, left, pointing to the value, right. A new legend, PRO ME SI MEREOR IN ME ('for me; against me if I deserve it'), appeared on the reverse. The ryal is commonly called a sword dollar, and each denomination was dated and issued for the years 1567–71. No gold coinage was issued in these years.

The second coinage (1572–80), initially authorised in 1571, was to comprise merks and halves. The design was specified to show a crowned thistle and the legend NEMO ME LEDET ('no one will harm me'), but this intended new coinage did not happen (C-P I, p. 139, XL). Instead an alternative issue of half- (6 shillings and 8 pence) and quarter-merks (3 shillings and 4 pence) was authorised by an Act of the Privy Council at Leith on 15 May 1572 (C-P I, p. 140, XLI). This Act stated the coins were to be struck at 8 deniers fine (0.667), with a debasement due to the need 'for payment and sustentatioun of the chargeis of the present ciuile and intestine weare rasit aganis his hienes and his authoritie.' The reverse, defined in detail in the Act, was to be a cross with thistle heads and crowns in alternate angles, with the traditional **SALVVM FAC POPVLVM TVVM DOMINE** ('o Lord save thy people') legend last seen on Mary's 1561–2 testoons and halves. Initial production was undertaken at Dalkeith as a consequence of political unrest, with Edinburgh Castle in the hands of supporters of Mary, known as the 'Marians.' They had access of coining skills and equipment and struck their own 1572 half-merks as well as, it is thought, ryals in the form of Mary's last issue dated 1567 (J. E. L. Murray 1987; Rampling and Murray 1989). The second coinage half-merks are dated 1572–7 and 1580; quarters are dated 1572–4, 1576–7 and 1580. The final issue of half- and quarter-merks in 1580, authorised on 4 May 1580 (C-P I, p. 152, XV), was an extension as a new issue of the two- and one-merk coins with improved fineness at 11 deniers fine had commenced in 1578. These 'thistle dollars' had been previously authorised on 18 September 1578 (CP I, p. 146, XLIV), and were struck 1578–80. The **NEMO ME IMPVNE LACESSET** ('no one shall hurt me with impunity') legend appears on these for the first time. They are assigned to James's second coinage, as also is the earliest gold issue, the 22 carat 1 oz. twenty-pound piece, struck in 1575 and 1576 with a half-length bust of the young king and reverse legend **PARCERE SVBIECTIS & DEBELLARE SVPERBOS** ('to spare the humbled and subdue the proud') taken from Virgil's *Aeneid* (VI, 853). This was a small issue struck from 12 pounds and one ounce of gold (Holmes 2006, p. 11). A gold crown of 22 carats and value 2 pounds was authorised on 20 October 1579 (C-P I, p. 147, XLIX) but this was not produced.

In the late 1570s and early 1580s the Scottish authorities were struggling to cope with a monetary crisis. Gold and silver were being lost from the Scottish economy, requiring bans on their export (C-P I, p. 145, XLVII). In addition to this, rising silver and gold prices were affecting the intrinsic value of the coinage, as well as undermining any profit to be had at the mint. Gold rose in price from £20 per oz. in September 1578 (C-P I, p. 148, XLIX) to £21 by November 1579 (C-P I, p. 252, CXLVI) and silver from 34s to 36s in the same period. This had two consequences: a revaluation of silver coinage in circulation in 1578; and the introduction of a new coinage in 1580. By order of the Privy Council on 29 July 1578 all silver coins (testoons and ryal issues of Mary and ryal issues of James VI) were recalled to the mint by 1 March 1579 to be reissued with a crowned thistle countermark with the testoon revalued at 7 shillings 4 pence and the ryal at 36 shillings and 9 pence (C-P I, p. 146, XLVIII). This seems to have had a slow uptake, with deadline extensions necessary to 1 May (C-P I, p. 149, LI) and 1 October 1579 (C-P I, pp. 150–1, LII).

The new, third coinage, was authorised on 28 April 1580 for gold (C-P I, p. 152, LIV) and on 4 May 1580 for silver (C-P I, p. 152, LV). The gold was to be a new coin, the ducat, at 21 carats and valued at 4 pounds, with a bareheaded bust of the young king wearing a ruff on the obverse and, on the reverse, the crowned arms of Scotland dividing the date, 1580, with the legend **EXVRGAT DEVS ET DISSIPENTVR**

INIMICI EIVS ('let God arise and let his enemies be scattered'). The silver, at 11 deniers (0.916) fine, was in four denominations (sixteen-, eight-, four- and two-shilling pieces), with the design similar to the previous two- and one-merk coins, the main difference being that the thistle on the reverse was to be surmounted with a crown. These are dated 1581 only.

The silver of this coinage was to be of short duration, being recalled in October 1581 (C-P I, p. 113–4, XI), since continued volatility of silver prices made it unprofitable to produce (Stewart 1967, p. 94). A new silver coinage of ten-shilling pieces, as before, at 11 deniers fine and 0.25 oz., was authorised to take its place (C-P I, p. 156, LXI). This got underway in 1582 and forty-, thirty- and twenty-shilling pieces were struck, as well as the ten-shilling pieces stated in the authorisation. The forty-shilling coin was to be 1 oz. silver. These denominations form the silver of the fourth coinage. The new coins all feature a half-length armoured figure of the king on the obverse, crowned and holding a sword. The dies for this coinage were prepared by Thomas Foulis based on a drawing of the king by Lord Seytoun's painter (C-P I, p. 248, CXXXIX), and with the reverse legend, HONOR REGIS IVDICIVM DILIGIT ('the kings power loveth judgement'), last seen on the ducats of James V. The forty-shilling pieces are dated 1582 only; the thirty-shilling coins are dated 1581–6, although the examples dated 1581 were not actually struck in that year, and the date is thought to be a die-error (Stewartby 1997a); the twenty-shilling coins to 1582–5; and the ten-shilling coins to 1582–4.

This silver issue was joined by a new gold coinage in 1584. Authorised on 19 May 1584, the lion noble or crown was to be struck at 21.5 carats in two denominations valued at 3 pounds and 15 shillings (75 shillings) and £2 pounds 10 shillings (50 shillings) (C-P I, p. 116, XIV). Although not specified in the authorisation, a one-third lion noble (25 shillings) was also struck, as examples survive. The lion noble neither names the king nor carries his portrait, and his authority is marked only through the cypher on the reverse. Instead, on the obverse it has a facing lion sejant, crowned and holding a sword, left, and sceptre right, with the legend POST 5 & 100 PROAVOS INVICTA MANENT HAEC ('after one hundred and five ancestors these remain unconquered'). The reverse has four crowned IR cyphers, arranged cruciform around a central S, and the legend DEVS IVDICIVM TVVM REGI DA ('give the king thy judgements, O God'). The lion noble and its fractions are mostly found dated 1584, but coins dated 1585–8 are known for the full denomination, and 1585–6 for the two-thirds. The one-third is only known for 1584. Lion nobles circulated until 1590, and their value was raised in August 1588 to 4 pounds (C-P I, pp. 171–2, LXXVII), a reflection of the rising price of gold at this time.

The fifth coinage is only known for the gold thistle noble, authorised in September 1588 (C-P I, pp. 172–3, LXXIX) to be struck at 23.5 carats, 0.25 oz. and with value 11 merks or 7 pounds 6 shillings and 8 pence (146s 8d). The dies for this were prepared by Thomas Foulis and the coin was to be exchangeable at a ratio of just under

10:1 to its English equivalent, the rose noble or ship ryal (15 shillings English). This ratio marked a deterioration in the exchange rate of 8:1 Scots to English which the English had set in 1579 (Holmes 2006, p. 12). The design of the thistle noble uses that of the English and continental rose ryal, but without the standing figure in the ship; this was replaced with the arms of Scotland. The reverse has cruciform sceptres with lions in the angles over a central thistle plant in a tressure, with thistle heads in the arcs, and the legend **FLORENT SCEPTRA PIIS REGNA HIS IOVA DAT NVMERATQVE** ('sceptres flourish with the pious. God gives them kingdoms and numbers them'). A half-noble was authorised as well but is not known to have been produced. Thistle nobles are thought to have been struck from 1588 to 1590 (Stewart 1967, p. 95).

An Act of Parliament, dated 6 August 1590, authorised the sixth coinage to be struck in gold and silver, with a new gold coin, at 22 carats with value 4 pounds, and silver half- (6 shilling and 8 pence) and quarter-merks at 10.5 deniers (0.875) fine (C-P I, pp. 117–19, XVII). The gold coin, known as a hat piece, on account of the bust of James VI right wearing a fashionable-looking tall hat, has a reverse with a crowned lion standing facing left holding a sceptre aloft, connecting with the Hebrew word Jehovah in a cloud above, and the legend **TE SOLVM VEREOR** ('thee alone do I fear'). These were struck in the years 1591–3. This new gold coin was to replace all previous gold except the thistle nobles. The silver has the scales of justice set over a sword, which has led to these being called balance half- and quarter-merks, and uses the legend **HIS DIFFERT REGE TYRANNVS** ('in these a tyrant differs from a king'). The half-merk is dated 1591–3, while the quarter- is only known for 1591 (Stewart 1967, p. 95).

The seventh coinage, authorised on 17 January 1594 (1593 according to the the old calendar ending 25 March), marked a break with the past in that all circulating gold and silver was recalled (C-P I, pp. 122–4, XXI). It was to be replaced with a new coinage consisting, in gold, of riders (and halves), at 22 carats valued at 5 pounds and, in silver, coins denominated at ten shillings, five shillings, thirty pence and twelve pence, all 11 deniers fine. In response to profiteering from the export of coin, values were aligned at an exchange rate of 10:1 with the English coinage in December 1598 (C-P I, pp. 192–5, XCVII), with the rider equivalent to ten shillings English and the Scottish ten-shillings piece equivalent to the English one shilling, five-shillings piece to the sixpence and thirty-pence piece to the threepence. The alignment of the coinage with that of England foreshadowed that which followed after the union of the crowns in 1603. The 1598 Act also revalued the rider to 5 pounds 6 shillings 8 pence and the ten-shilling piece to 10 shillings and 6 pence. The seventh coinage gold reintroduced the king on horseback charging right, a design last seen on the denomination of the same name under James III. The reverse legend changed again to read **SPERO MELIORA** ('I hope for better things'). On the silver a bust of the king, half-length with head bare, appears on the obverse. The reverse has a thistle of three heads with a crown above the central head and the **NEMO ME IMPVNE LACESSET** legend. Riders and halves were struck with the dates 1593–5 and 1598–9 and 1600; the silver 1593–5, 1598–1601. A disagreement over the contract let for production of the coinage meant no coins were produced in 1596–7 although coins with an 8 over a 6 in the date suggest dies were prepared for use in 1596 and later reused in 1598 (Stewart 1967, p. 97).

The actions of December 1598 did not solve the underlying instability of the Scottish coinage and it was necessary to authorise a new coinage on 11 September 1601 (C-P I, pp. 136–8, XXXVII), when a new exchange rate of 12:1 Scots-English was implied. The eighth coinage comprised gold sword and sceptre pieces (and halves), at 22 carats and value 6 pounds (English 10 shillings), and silver, merks, halves, quarters and eighths, with the merk at value 13 shillings and 4 pence. The move to the merk-based unit meant that the easy-to-use 10:1 alignment with the English silver was broken with the Scots merk worth 13½ pence English. The design of the new gold coin has a crossed sword and sceptre on the reverse with the legend **SALVS REIPVBLICAE SVPREMA LEX** ('the safety of the people is the supreme law'), a slight variation on words from Cicero in his work *De legibus* (Stewart 1967). The silver reverse design returns to the crowned thistle seen in the second coinage merk and third coinage issues, with the legend **REGEM IOVA PROTEGIT** ('God protects the king'). All coins are dated 1601–4. No eighth-merks were struck dated 1604.

The coinage of James VI, 1567–1605; base-metal issues

A key strand of the coinage of James's predecessors had been base-metal, and by 1567 a substantial quantity of twelve-penny groats, bawbees, placks and hardheads was in circulation. Perhaps for this reason no further billon issues were made until 1583. Yet these coins already demanded attention in 1567 when they were subject to counterfeiting, and considerable effort was expended in the first decade of the reign in dealing with this problem. An early action of the new regime was an order in December 1567 that specified twelve-penny groats would be worth 6 pence, bawbees 3 pence, placks 2 pence and hardheads a halfpenny. There is some doubt as to whether this revaluation was carried out (Lord Stewartby noted, in an annotation to his copy of C-P I, p. cxliii, that J. E. L. Murray thought this was a proposal only). The aim was to cut the margin between the value of the metal and the face value of the coin, thereby curtailing the profit to be had in counterfeiting. If not carried out in 1567, it would reflect some wisdom on the part of the authorities as these small-change coins were used for daily transactions by the general public, and devaluation would have been an unpopular move at the start of the new reign. At the same time, it was agreed that no new 'llayit' money would be issued without the agreement of all three estates of parliament and punishments for false coining were set out again (C-P I, p. 107, I). These had to be reiterated in 1570 when batches of false hardheads had been arriving from Flanders (Records of the Convention of the Boroughs, p. 22). In August 1572, placks of Mary were banned from circulation as so many were counterfeit (C-P I, p. 140, XLII). Finally, in March 1575 hardheads and placks were recalled to the mint to enable checking of 'the trew fra the fals' (C-P I, p. 142, XLV). Those deemed official issues were returned to circulation with a star in heart countermark, the device of Morton, the Regent, and those deemed false were sent to the melting pot. Placks deemed true were returned to circulation with value set at 2 pence as specified in 1567. Hardheads were to exchange for 1 penny, an improvement on the halfpenny value proposed in 1567. This, and further restatement of punishments for importing false coin (C-P I, p. 141, XLIII), may have eased the problem. Thereafter the issue of dealing with counterfeiting appears less in the records suggesting the action taken had gone some way to bringing matters under control.

Low-value base-metal coinage formed a key part of the Scottish currency, being the majority of that in daily use, so maintaining an adequate supply was a key consideration for the authorities. Consequently, at various times it was necessary for new issues to be made of base-metal coins. The first issue of billon coins by James VI was authorised on 24 December 1583 when all twelve-penny groats, bawbees and placks, as well as fractions, were recalled to be melted for a new billon coinage of eight-penny groats and two-penny placks at 3 denier fine (C-P I, p. 158, LXIII). The new coins, with some varieties, are of the same common design each having a crowned thistle on the reverse with the mint, Edinburgh, named, and the arms of Scotland on the obverse. They are undated but were struck until 1590. A further issue of billon was authorised in August 1588 with penny and two-penny placks, 'ane penny and twa penny plakkis' to be struck to remedy a shortage of small-change (C-P I, p. 170, LXXVII). The two pence is known as a hardhead and the penny as the half-hardhead. An initial issue of hardheads had the arms of Scotland on the reverse and, as it was found that this made the coins hard to distinguish from the eight-penny placks, it was changed to show a lion rampant with two pellets behind denoting the value. The design of the half-hardhead or penny is similar to the revised second-type hardhead.

A small issue of four-penny placks at 1 denier fine was authorised to be struck on 27 December 1593 (C-P I, p. 120, XIX), with the coins actually struck in 1594. With all billon coins remaining in circulation, except the recently issued hardheads and half-hardheads that were recalled in August 1591, there was a shortage of mid-range base-metal denominations. The 1594 issue set out to address this. The new coin is known as the saltire plack on account if its design of crossed sceptres over a thistle on the obverse. This is the last billon issue. Small-denomination coinage thereafter would be copper.

In April 1597 Thomas Achesoun proposed that a pure copper coinage of two-pence and penny coins could be minted using new production methods to provide better struck and more accurate weight coins that would be harder to forge (C-P I, p. 268,

CLX). As a result, on 13 May 1597 the production of the proposed copper coinage was authorised (C-P I, p. 129, XXIX). The two-pence has a bust of James VI on the obverse, and three thistle heads and the mint name on the reverse. The penny is the same but for a single pellet denoting the denomination behind the king's bust. The obverse and reverse of these issues were thought to look like the *doubles tournois* of Henri II of France (1547–59). This led to their being named 'turners' which stuck for future issues of copper two-pence coins in Scotland after 1603 and under Charles I and II (Holmes 1998, p. 53).

Symbolism, belief and power – projecting the regime of James VI on the coinage 1567–1605

There is a freshness and originality about the pre–1603 Scottish coinage that merits consideration. Lord Stewartby himself believed the designs of this reign combined a mix of the imposing and majestic English designs with the lighter and prettier French, the result being a perfect harmony of simplicity and elegant beauty (Stewart 1967, p. 91). There is little conservatism about how the coinage should appear in Scotland, which contrasts with the conventions and traditions guiding matters south of the border. Unlike in England, in Scotland it was not customary that the monarch's bust should appear on most denominations of the coinage. Under James IV and V the king's image is absent on all the gold and on the billon placks, and its appearance on the ducat and groat issues of James V is one of the distinctions of his coinage. Mary is only portrayed on the early billon pence (a stylised facing bust), gold ryals, the 1553 and 1561–2 testoons, and jointly with Francis on the 1558 ducat and with Darnley on the type I 1565 silver ryal. On the vast majority of the coinage in general use, most testoons, ryals, bawbees, 'nonsunts', placks and hard-heads, her image is absent. Given this legacy, it is unsurprising that the coinage of James VI followed suit. His portrait appears on the gold as a half-length figure on the twenty-pound piece of 1575–6, as the bust of a child on the 1580 ducat, as an adult bust on the 1591–3 hat piece and as a horseman on the 1593–1601 rider, but is not used on the 1580s lion noble and the 1601–4 sword and sceptre piece. On the silver his portrait is used more sparingly, appearing only on the fourth (1582–6) and seventh coinage (1593–1601) issues. It is absent on all the billon coinage, while the copper adopts the bust used on the seventh coinage silver being struck at the same time.

In the Scottish coinage of this period it is the inscriptions and symbolism of the overall design, rather than the presence of the monarch's image, that take centre stage. This contrasts markedly with the English coinage where the monarch's bust almost always appeared on every denomination, except for those with impractically small flans. In Scotland numerous legends appeared on Mary's coinage, These range from those reused such as the SALVVM FAC (Psalm 28, v. 10) and EXVRGAT (Psalm 68, v. 1) forms, to the novel, some of which also draw on the biblical sources as with **ECCE ANCILLA DOMINI** (Luke 1, v.38), and **VICIT LEO TRIBV IVDA** (Revelation 5, v.5), while others make statements about the political priority of the moment; appealing for peace, **DA PACEM DOMINE** (1553); an appeal for Divine support, **IN VIRTVTE TVA LIBERA ME** (1556–8) and extolling the benefits of the French marriage, **FECIT VTRAQUE VNVM** (1558–9). The frequency of variation suggests each was quite deliberately chosen to make a point about the regime at a particular point in time.

The overthrow of Mary in 1567 placed the Protestant faction firmly in control of Scotland, whose new king lay at the centre of their ambitions. They advocated a new vision of the kingdom, in which the conventions of medieval Christendom were confronted by humanism in both thought and art (Stewart 1983). In this world individuals harnessed God into their lives, overcoming sin through piety, justice and virtue as set out in the word of God contained in the bible. By extension, a ruler who exercised power through personal piety, justice and virtue, drawn from personal revelation through the bible, would bring good fortune to the people. This changed outlook made its first appearance in Scotland with the **VICIT LEO** legend on the testoons of 1560–1, which coincided with rise of the Protestant Lords after the death of Mary of Guise. At the same time the revival of classical learning offered new sources to draw on in expressing ideas and beliefs, whether in word or art, and ambitious princes throughout Europe were aware of how this could benefit them (Stewart 1983). Under James VI, protestant belief and classicism come together in the coinage design, in a kingdom where juxtaposition of symbolic images and inscriptions was already an established tradition by 1567.

It is widely accepted that the key figure in shaping this was George Buchanan, the king's tutor in the early years of the reign, Moderator of the General Assembly in 1567 and the leading intellectual apologist for the Protestant faction. Buchanan (d. 1584) was a Sorbonne-educated Latinist and leading scholar of the period who, in the 1550s converted to Calvinism and returned to Scotland in 1561 (Stewart 1983, pp. 453–4). He became an anti-Marian only after the murder of Darnley, and his political writing sought to justify the overthrow of Mary as lawful and constitutional, drawing on precedents from the past. James undoubtedly absorbed Buchanan's ideas as he developed his own political philosophy and theology, which came to be expressed in the 1590s in his works *Basilikon Doron* and *The Trew Law of Free Monarchies.* These explored the constitutional relationship between God, the King and the People (Stewart 1983, p. 459). Given this interest, there can be little doubt that James himself would have been involved in selecting inscriptions and designs to project the beliefs he and his regime held through the medium of the coinage. That this was so is evident in the detailed descriptions of designs and legends found in Acts relating to the coinage (C-P I, p. 251, CXLVI and p. 253, CXLVII). Not all the coinage was given this careful treatment, and the bulk continued to use established legends and design conventions such as the crowned arms of

Scotland and the thistle, although the latter emerged larger and bolder under James VI (Stewart, 1983, p. 453).

From the start of the reign new messaging and symbolism appear. The legend **PRO ME SI MEREOR IN ME** ('for me; or against me if I deserve it') was used on the first coinage ryals first struck in 1567, very soon after the accession of James. This set out a political and legal principle that the regime was accountable to the law for its actions. It was accompanied by carefully arranged symbolism with the sword of Justice, a wholly new device on Scottish coinage, being placed centrally on the reverse. This design and inscription can with some confidence be attributed to Buchanan, who, in his work *De Iure Regni,* demonstrated his theme that kings can be overthrown when they act against the people using the example (taken from Cassius Dio) of Trajan, who on his accession presented the symbolic unsheathed sword to the Prefect of the Praetorian Guard and asked him to use it either 'for him or against him according to his deserts' (Stewart 1983, p. 454). The political message implied in this legend is that the king (i.e. the new Protestant regime) will rule justly and, should he fail to do so, the people can justly seek redress. The symbolism of the crowned sword and hand suggests that the sword (of Justice) upholds the crown (of the regal authority), while the hand to the left points to the sword to emphasise the intended message.

The **SALVVM** legend, used for the second coinage half-merk issue, is appropriate for 1571–2, when discord divided the people of Scotland. Its use offered a less strident message more appropriate at this time. It was a considered decision to use this legend, as the design was specified in detail in the Act authorising this coinage (C-P I, p. 140, XLI). The symbolism of the design is a complete contrast to that of 1567, which further adds to the likelihood of deliberate caution here on the part of the authorities, and it uses the formulaic crowned arms on the obverse and floriated cross with thistle heads and crowns in the angles on the reverse. By 1575 the regime felt secure enough to throw caution to the wind with the magnificent gold twenty-pound piece. This foregrounded the young king by using his image, and it projected a political message offering mercy and punishment with the words **PARCERE SVBIECTIS ET DEBELLARE SVPERBOS** ('to spare the humbled and subdue the proud': Virgil, *Aeneid* VI, 84) and **IN VTRVNQVE PARATVS** ('prepare for either': Virgil, *Aeneid* II, 61). The Latin scholarship evident in this, and the use of similar words in lines of his *Epigrams,* again point firmly to Buchanan having a hand in the specification of this magnificent coin (Stewart 1983, p. 455). The symbolism of the obverse shows James VI, looking rather older than his nine years, perhaps more a personification of the Crown than a true portrait. He is armoured and shouldering a sword in one hand, and holding out an olive branch in the other; seeking peace for the people but prepared to wage war to achieve it.

The proposal in 1571 of **NEMO ME LEDET** and of **NEMO ME IMPVNE LACESSET** ('no one shall hurt me with impunity', the motto of the Order of the Thistle) in 1577 are also connected to Buchanan, who is said to have suggested the *Nemo* motto, which he may have borrowed from Francesco Sforza, Duke of Milan (1450–66) (Stewart 1983, p. 452). These legends both project the principle that wrongdoing will always be corrected, with the authorities (represented by the symbol of the thistle) forthright in prosecuting those who might seek to overturn what they stand for. A different angle seems to be pursued in the use of the **EXVRGAT** legend on the ducat of 1580, which presented the young James VI as a child (he was 14 by this time) on one side, and on the other the message that God would be with him in defeating his enemies.

With the execution of Morton in 1581, the regency came to an end and James VI began his personal rule. The fourth coinage silver portrayed James VI as a young armoured king holding the sword of justice and used the legend **HONOR REGIS IVDICIVM DILIGIT** ('the king's power loveth judgement', from Psalm 99:4) on the reverse, previously found on the ducats of James V. It is thought that the meaning of this had been subtly changed, for whereas in 1539–40 the 'king' referred to was God, in 1582 the context was the earthly monarch (Stewart 1983, p. 452). The symbolism of the accompanying design has James crowned and holding the sword of Justice before him, the image of the just ruler he aspires to be. This was a further expression of a political philosophy about the earthly exercise of power by kings.

The remarkable lion nobles of 1584, issued after James VI was fully in control of government, represented his regime as enduring and just, and Scotland as subject to no-one. The strength of the obverse design lies in its integration of the legend and image. The lion sejant, symbol of the proud kingdom of Scotland ruled by James VI, holds out the sword and sceptre in a symbolic gesture that implies a determination to deliver justice and order to the Scottish people. The accompanying legend, **POST 5 & 100 PROAVOS INVICTA MANENT HAC** ('after 100 and five ancestors these remain unconquered'), reinforces that message. This legend is probably derived from Buchanan's *History*, which addressed the long and fabulous ancestry of the Scottish kings and drew on earlier works of Scottish history by Hector Boece, published in 1527, and John Major, in 1521. Boece made James V the 106th Scottish king, so in the reign of his grandson, James VI, it could be said that the symbols of Scottish kingship had passed through 105 generations of forebears (*proavi*), where these were counted as ancestral generations remoter than a grandparent (Stewart 1983, p. 456). The reverse, rather than naming James, presents cyphers symbolising his regime, and the legend, **DEVS IVDICIVM TVVM REGI DA** ('give the king thy judgements O God', from Psalm 57:1), expresses a relationship between the king and the Divine, an expression of the political theology central to James's views on kingship and its direct relationship with God. The king's judgment is therefore shown to draw on the will of God (Stewart 1983, p. 456), the implication being that good earthly government derives from the Divine whose word, in protestant belief, is to be found in the bible.

The 1588 thistle noble took this message a step further with the legend **FLORENT SCEPTRA PIIS REGNA HIS IOVA DAT NVMERATQVE** ('sceptres flourish with the pious. God gives them kingdoms and numbers them'). This further developed the theme of political theology, linking God-fearing and pious kingship with successful kingdoms, the implication being that James VI and his pious and God-fearing rule will make Scotland successful, and numbered among the chosen kingdoms of God. The symbolism of the design, unusally, did not support the legend. It used the ship ryal design, drawn from the English and Burgundian fourteenth- and fifteenth-century nobles and ryals, which had been revived in the low-countries in the 1570s. The design is strictly merchantile, with an eye to participation in an internationally-used coinage (Stewart 1983, p. 457).

In the sixth coinage of 1591, the gold hat piece also elaborated on the theme of political theology with the legend **TE SOLVM VEREOR** ('thee alone do I fear'). This placed James VI's rule as accountable only to God with just government exercised by following His word. The image of the crowned lion holding a sceptre, placed centrally on the flan and connected to a cloud above containing the Hebrew word 'Jehovah', drives home this message. The sceptre, symbol of kingly rule, provides the link between the divine and the Scottish state, symbolised in the lion sejant (Stewart, 1983, p. 458). The presence of the Divine, designated by the Hebrew Jehovah, reflected renewed interest in the Hebrew studies at this time, which James and those around him appear to have recognised. This offered a way to symbolise God, creating a neat expression of James's political theology (Stewart 1983, pp. 458–9).

The silver, with its balance and sword and legend **HIS DIFFERT REGE TYRANNVS** ('in these a tyrant differs from a king'), returned to the theme of James VI as a just ruler (good), who judges based on the law, rather than the tyrant (bad), who imposes his own will outside the law. The reverse symbolism supported the message of the legend, with the scales of justice set over a sword, here perhaps representing oppression. The 1594 seventh coinage legend **SPERO MELIORA** ('I hope for better things', from Ovid, *Metamorphoses* VIII, 20–1) on the rider implied that James VI is driven to build a better Scotland, a message which develops aspects of the theme expressed on the thistle noble of 1588–90. The silver of the same coinage sticks with the **NEMO** legend, perhaps chosen to appear on the coinage accompanying the **SPERO MELIORA** message used on the gold, to emphasise the commitment of the regime to standing up to those who would challenge the law and its authority. The 1601 eighth coinage sword and sceptre piece used the legend **SALVS POPVLI SVPREMA LEX** ('the safety of the people is the supreme law', from Cicero, *De legibus* III, 8). This returned to the established theme with a new angle that implied the focus of James VI's rule was to deliver security to the Scottish nation and people. The silver coinage, issued at the same time, returned to the issue of the relationship between earthly and heavenly kingship with the legend **REGEM IOVA PROTEGIT** ('God protects the king'), expressing that the king draws his authority from God and a pious king is rewarded and protected by God. That this God is Jehovah, the God of the Old Testament, who also appears on the sixth coinage hat piece, shows a continued interest in Hebrew studies.

The precious metal coinage before 1604 went to great lengths to present the regime of James VI as just and drawing its authority from God and scripture. This programme was well thought out, with the chosen themes consistently pursued. It showed that the new Protestant regime James headed, initially in name and from 1583 in person, was committed to projecting its beliefs and virtues through the legends and designs used on the coinage. Only while James VI ruled in Scotland were these messages pursued with intensity. With union of the crowns, the priority moved from just rule in Scotland to promoting the union of England, Ireland and Scotland. This was a regime that saw the coinage as a tool for the projection of its political beliefs targeting the political, religious and professional elite, on whose support the regime depended, with statements on the coinage that could only be understood by them. This elite was a small minority of the Scottish population, but more likely to regularly handle gold and silver coins, and to be better educated and able to understand the Latin, than the majority. It is notable that base-metal coinage, intended as small-change to be used by the majority of the people for daily low-value transactions, lies outside the regime messaging found on the gold and silver. These coins name the king on one side and on the other, the place of minting or, as on the hardhead, use the **VINCIT VERITAS** legend, following the form found on similar coins under Mary. Their design used only the symbolism of Scotland – the arms, thistle and lion rampant – along with the IR cypher, the exception being the portrait on the 1597 copper issues.

The administration of the Scottish coinage, 1567–1605

The Achesoun family maintained their hold on the mint as Master with John Achesoun, in this position from 1561–80, succeeded by Thomas Achesoun in 1581 (C-P I, p. 248, CXL). He then held the position until 1611, when he was succeeded by George Foulis (C-P I, p. 219, CXIII). Thomas Achesoun was an assayer before this and is first noted in the mint records in 1572 (C-P I, p. 103, L). Another Achesoun, James, appears in 1597, when he made proposals to James VI for introducing and producing copper coinage (C-P I, p. 268, CLX). The Foulis family also appears at this time, with Thomas, a die-sinker, between 1583 and 1598 (C-P I, p. 191, XCVI) and George, an assayer, between 1601 and 1610 (C-P I, p. 199, CIII). The General of the Mint for much of the pre-union period (*c.* 1576 to 1608) was Sir Archibald Napier of Edinbillie, Laird of Merchiston (C-P I, p. 216, CXII). These individuals seem to have assured continuity in the running of the mint before the union of the crowns.

James VI himself appears to have taken a direct interest in the mint and its operation. In his proposal to James VI on introducing a copper coinage in 1597,

James Achesoun entreated the king to visit the mint, 'that your Maiestie micht tak occasioun to visite your awin cunyiehous as ye was accustumit to do and be the better sein in the knowledge thairof, Quhilk knowledge appertenis to nane bot your Maiestie and your counsall' (CP I, p. 269, CLX). So even if James was not particularly interested in his mint in 1597, he had been in the past. It is notable the level of detail in which the Privy Council set out the authorisation of new issues, usually specifying the design. Sketches survive of intended designs for a proposed gold issue in 1579 (Hopetoun MSS, C-P I, p. 251, CXLVI), as well as very detailed images for the design of the balance half-merk in 1591, including specification of the reverse legend **HIS DIFFERT** (Hopetoun MSS, C-P, I, p. 253, CXLVIII). The Privy Council also took an interest in the coins produced and it is known from the mint accounts that specimen examples of coins were presented to officials in 1582 (C-P I, p. 248, CXL). These were produced to a higher standard than the usual coinage, using specially cut dies and carefully prepared flans. They are similar to the patterns noted under Elizabeth I and the 'fine work' coins of James I and Charles I.

The coinage seems to have been a regular concern of the government not only in setting out and authorising new issues, usually in response to external factors such as a rising gold or silver price or a change in the exchange rate with the English currency, but also protecting bullion resources held in Scotland. In the 1570s, when disparity developed between the value of silver and the face value of coinage in circulation in Scotland, the authorities responded with orders forbidding the export of gold and silver in 1574 and 1577 (C-P, I, p. 141, XLIV and p. 145, XLVII), and the export of Scottish money was specifically forbidden in 1578 (C-P I, p. 110, VIII), the last part of a wider response to a currency crisis in 1578 which also required revaluation of silver coins (C-P I, p. 146, XLVIII). The need to make best use of the metal available in existing coin in circulation, as well as managing the relationship between its bullion and face value, saw frequent recalls for melting and restriking, notably the recall of third coinage thistle dollars in 1581 (C-P I, p. 153, LVII), of all nonsunts, placks and bawbees in 1583–4 (C-P I, p. 158, LXIII), and of all earlier silver and gold (excluding thistle nobles) in 1593 (C-P I, p. 117, XVII). In some cases there was resistance to the recall and extensions had to be made to the order, notably in 1584, to ensure effective recall of the old billon coinage (C-P I, p. 163, LXIX).

A major concern in the earlier years of James's reign was the eradication of forgery in the billon coinage. This was a response to local fabrication, as well as the importation into Scotland of counterfeit Marian placks and hardheads made in Flanders, which sapped confidence in small-change currency (Holmes 1998, p. 46). The initial response of devaluation in 1567 was a clever move intended to remove the profit from forging. Demonetisation of the 1557 plack for a period in 1572 attempted to address problems with this specific denomination (C-P I, p. 140, XLII; Holmes 1998, p. 46). These do not appear to have been successful as more drastic action of recall, and separation of false coin, with countermarking of good coin, was necessary in

1575. In the meantime, frequent orders for the punishment of false coiners appear throughout this period. The action taken in 1575 seems to have worked, as less is heard of counterfeiting thereafter. It shows, though, the degree of attention the government of James VI was prepared to give to the probity of the coinage and how capable it was of reacting when the need arose. The regime was happy to delay the issue of new billon coinage until 1583, but was prepared to ensure new issues to meet demand, such as in 1588, when it set out to remedy a lack of small-change, or to innovate with a copper coinage in 1597. The overall impression that emerges is of James VI's government taking a vigorous interest in the coinage and actively managing it in terms of the value of metals, design, messaging, availability of small-change and the probity of coins in circulation.

The coinage of James VI after the union of the Crowns, 1605–25

The diversity, distinctiveness and instability of the Scottish coinage ended after the union the crowns in 1603. Both kingdoms had the same currency in gold and silver, but each retained control of their own production. Prior to Elizabeth I's death in March 1603 attempts had been made to set an exchange rate between the Scottish and English currencies, initially in 1598 at an exchange rate of 10 Scots to 1 English, with all Scottish silver denominations neatly matching English at this ratio. The eighth coinage in 1601 had sought to respond to changes in bullion value with a move to 12 Scots to 1 English, but the silver, denominated in merks, was far less easily transferable. Following the English accession, the Scottish eighth coinage continued, while in England the first coinage of James I (1603–4) comprised gold and silver at the established English standards. In November 1604 it was necessary to finally address the coinage of both kingdoms. The first steps, on 15 November 1604, confirmed all the privileges of the Scottish mint, perhaps needed to address a perceived risk of encroachment by the English (C-P I, p. clxiv). On the same day, James I and VI, with the advice of the Privy Council of England and the Estates Council of Scotland, stated that there would be a reduction of gold and silver in the coinage in both countries to perfect equality, which was essential preparation for the union of the two kingdoms (C-P I, p. 210, CIX). A Whitehall warrant for the new coinage the union necessitated was issued on 13 February 1605 (C-P I, p. 217, CXII) and the new, ninth coinage of James VI was authorised in Edinburgh on 4 March 1605 (C-P I, p. clxv).

The ninth coinage gold, at 22 carats fine, comprised five denominations: the unit, often called the sceptre piece, of 12 pounds Scots (1 pound English); the double-crown, 6 pounds (10 shillings); Britain crown, 3 pounds (5 shillings); thistle crown, 48 shillings (4 shillings); and halfcrown, 30 shillings Scots (30 pence (halfcrown) English). Coinage design was brought in line with the English style with a bust of James VI appearing on all denominations except the thistle crown. James's representation was expected to be in the same overall style as in England with only small differences, such as the presence of the small thistle-head initial mark and the use of the Scottish style crown (with a lis at the centre of the band), allowing the English and Scottish coins of this issue to be distinguished from each other. The ninth coinage silver follows the same route with six denominations: sixty-shillings (5 shillings English); thirty-shillings (halfcrown, 30 pence); twelve-shillings (1 shilling); six-shillings (6 pence); two-shillings (2 pence); and one-shilling (1 pence). The six-shilling denomination was issued sparingly and is the only denomination to carry the date (1605, 1606, and the altered date 1609/7). All but the two- and one-shilling coins featured the king's portrait. On the sixty- and thirty-shilling pieces he appears as a horseman riding right, while his crowned bust was used on the twelve- and six-shilling coins. The small size two- and one-shilling coins have the rose and thistle each side denoting each kingdom. As with the gold, only minor design details allow Scottish-issued and English-issued coins to be told apart. On the sixty- and thirty-shilling pieces a thistle appears on the rear caparison of the horse, where the English coinage has a rose.

In 1609 the coinage was revised, with a tenth coinage authorised at Edinburgh on 7 December (C-P I, p. 215, CX). This would be the final coinage of James VI. The gold denominations remained as in the ninth coinage, but without the thistle crown. In the silver, the two-shilling and one-shilling coins were no longer issued. The principal design revision was that the arms on the reverse were amended so the Scottish arms appear in two rather than one quarter as before. The six-shilling denomination continued to carry the date and was issued, again sparingly, dated 1610 to 1619 and 1622. During the tenth coinage two undated copper issues of two pence ('turners') and pence were made, in 1614 (C-P I, p. 233, CXXVI and CXXVII) and again in 1623 (C-P I, p. 241, CXXXIV). On the obverse each features the triple-headed thistle, and the reverse has the lion rampant with minor variations, with the denomination indicated by one or two pellets behind. The legend, with the king's titles, is divided between the two sides of the coin, with a longer version on the 1614 coins.

On both the ninth and tenth coinages the royal title reflected James's change in status, with the numeral left out as he has become IACOBVS REX, James I of Great Britain, MAG BRIT, and the additional titles of FRAN & HIB REX are included. The reverse legends on all the gold changed to emphasise the union and no other theme is pursued: the unit reads FACIAM EOS IN GENTEM VNAM ('I will make them one nation'); the double and Britain crowns HENRICVS ROSAS REGNA IACOBVS ('Henry [VII united] the roses; James the kingdom'); the halfcrown TVEATVR VNITA DEVS ('may God guard these united [kingdoms]'). The silver for both coinages has the same reverse legend on the sixty-, thirty-, twelve- and six-shilling coins: QVAE DEVS CONIVNXIT NEMO SEPARET ('what God has joined together let no man put asunder'), this a variation of the reverse legend used on the controversial 1565 'marriage' ryal of Mary and Darnley. The TVEATVR legend is used on the two- and one-shilling coins of the ninth coinage.

Coins of James VI in the Stewartby collection

The Stewartby collection comprises 412 coins (**1046–1457**) of James VI of which 27 are gold (**1046–59** and **1363–75**), 300 silver (**1060–1299** and **1376–1435**), 58 billon (**1300–57**) and 27 copper (**1358–62** and **1436–57**). There are 317 coins (**1046–1362**) from before the English accession and 95 from after (**1363–1457**).

The gold coinage from before the English accession is comprehensively represented. From the second coinage there is an example of the 1575 twenty-pound piece (**1046**) and from the third coinage of the ducat of 1580 (**1047**). The Stewartby collection has an example of the fourth coinage lion noble, dated 1586 (**1048**), and both its fractions, the two-thirds, 1584 (**1049**), and the rare one-third, only known for 1584 (**1050**). There are two examples of the fifth coinage thistle nobles (**1051–2**), these differing from each other with minor variations in the legends. A single example of the hat piece (**1053**), dated 1592, covers the sixth coinage gold, while from the seventh coinage there are three examples of the rider (**1054–6**), dated 1593, 1599 and 1601, with the 1593 from early style dies (**1054**), and a half-rider (**1057**), dated 1599. From the eighth coinage there is an example of both the sword and sceptre piece (**1058**), dated 1604, and the half (**1059**), dated 1601.

Examples of the silver coinage of James VI from before the English accession exist for all coinages and all denominations with the exception of the very rare 1581 third coinage two-shillings. From the first coinage of 1567–71 there are 12 ryals (**1060–71**) covering all dates; 6 two-thirds ryals (**1072–7**), all dates, including an example erroneously dated 1561 (**1072**); and 6 one-third ryals, also all dates (**1078–83**). A number of these bear the 1578 revaluation countermark (e.g. **1060, 1069, 1072–3, 1079, 1083**). The collection's run of coins from the second coinage of 1571–80 is extensive, with 76 coins (**1084–1159**) comprising 71 examples (**1084–1154**) of the half- and quarter-merk issues of 1572–7 and 1580, as well as 5 examples of the very rare two-merk and merk issues (**1155–9**) of 1578–80. Examples of all dates known for the half-merk (**1084–1131**) are represented, including the 1580 issue (**1128–31**). There are two examples (dated 1572) which were attributed by Joan Murray to the Marians at Edinburgh Castle (**1094, 1097**). The quarter-merk is represented by 23 coins (**1132–54**), with only that of 1576 absent (no examples are known dated 1575). One quarter-merk (**1154**), dated 1573, is a contemporary counterfeit. There are three examples in the Stewartby collection of the two-merks or 'thistle dollar' of 1578–80 (**1155–7**), with each date, 1578–80, represented; and two examples of the merk (**1158–9**), with dates, 1579 and 1580.

All coins of the short-lived third coinage of 1581 are rare. The Stewartby collection has a single example each of the sixteen- (**1160**), eight- (**1161**) and four-shilling (**1162**) pieces but no two-shilling piece, the rarest denomination of this coinage. There are examples of all denominations of the fourth coinage of 1582–8 including the rare 1582 forty-shillings (**1163**). There are 9 examples of the thirty-shilling piece (**1164–72**), with all dates (1582–6); 7 of the twenty-shilling piece (**1173–9**), with dates 1582–4 but no 1585; and 4 of the ten-shilling pieces (**1181–4**), with all dates (1582–4). In addition one coin, of base-metal and coarse style, is a contemporary counterfeit of a 1582 twenty-shilling piece (**1180**). No silver coins were struck for the fifth coinage 1588–90. The sixth coinage is represented by 12 coins with 10 examples of the balance half-merk (**1185–94**), covering all dates, 1591–3. One coin, dated 1591, is a 'fine work' specimen (**1185**), a rare example from the coinage of James VI. There are two examples of the rare balance quarter-merk denomination (**1195–6**), only struck in 1591.

The later silver coinages from before the English accession are well covered. From the seventh coinage there are 49 coins and 54 from the eighth. All denominations of the seventh coinage are covered with 19 examples of the ten-shilling piece (**1197–1215**), covering all dates, except 1601 (with no coins struck dated 1596–7), and two have the erroneous date 1564 (**1201, 1203**); 13 examples of five-shilling pieces (**1216–28**), with all dates, including an example of the 1598/6 altered date coin (**1223**); 8 of the thirty-pence piece (**1229–36**), with all dates except 1601, including an example with the 1598/6 altered date (**1235**) and a 'fine work' specimen (**1229**); and 9 of the twelve-pence piece (**1237–45**), covering all dates. The collection contains examples of all denominations of the final coinage before the accession to the English throne, the eighth. There are 21 examples of the thistle merk (**1246–66**), with all dates (1601–4) represented; 11 of the half-thistle merk (**1267–77**), with all dates (1601–4); 12 of the quarter (**1278–89**), with all dates (1601–4); and 10 of the eighth (**1290–9**), also with all dates (1601–3).

The first billon coinage of James VI commenced in 1583 with an issue of eight-penny groats and two-penny placks. There are 34 examples of this issue in the Stewartby collection (**1300–33**), with 30 specimens of the eight-penny groat (**1300–29**), and 4 examples of the two-penny plack (**1330–3**). All are undated. There are three types of the eight-penny groat: type 1, with reverse legend OPPIDVM EDINBVRGI, represented by 11 examples (**1300–10**) and two contemporary counterfeits (**1311–12**); type 2, reading OPPID EDINB, with 9 examples (**1313–21**), and also one contemporary counterfeit (**1322**); and type 3, as type 2 but with the addition of beaded inner-circles each side, with 7 examples (**1323–8**), and one contemporary counterfeit (**1329**). The two-penny plack, also referred to as the half-plack, undated, is represented by 4 coins (**1330–3**). There are three types, each the same as the types for the eight-penny groat. The collection contains one example of type 1 (**1330**), a very rare type which was unlisted in Burns and which Lord Stewartby thought uncertain to exist prior to his acquiring this example; one example of type 2 (**1331**); and two of type 3 (**1332–3**).

The 1588 issue of the two-penny plack or hardhead and one-penny plack, both undated, is represented by 22 coins in the Stewartby collection. There are 21 examples of the two-penny plack or hardhead (**1334–54**), with two types: 5 of type I, struck in August 1588, with a crowned shield on the reverse (**1334–8**); and 11 of type II, with the type I crowned shield reverse, that led to this coin being confused with the

1583 issue of two-penny placks, replaced with the lion rampant with two pellets in the field denoting the value (**1339–49**). There are also 5 examples of counterfeits of the type II two-penny plack or hardhead (**1350–4**). One-penny placks from the 1588 issues are very rare and appear to have only been struck in small numbers in November 1588. The reverse matched that of the type II two-penny plack or hardhead but with a single pellet denoting the value of one penny. There is one example of this coin (**1355**). A further issue of billon coins followed in 1594, which was to be the last. Comprising four-penny placks only, these are often known as saltire placks on account of the design, with a thistle over crossed sceptres on the obverse, and four thistle heads cruciform on the tips of a lozenge on the reverse. It is a rare coin, and there are two examples (**1356–7**) in the Stewartby collection.

The remaining base-metal coinage from before the accession to the English throne consists of copper, all from the 1597 issue of the twopence ('turners') and penny, both undated. The twopence, with the bust of James VI on the obverse and three thistle heads on the reverse, is represented by 4 coins (**1358–61**). The much rarer penny has the same design but with the addition of a single pellet behind the king's head. There is one example in the Stewartby collection (**1362**).

The gold and silver from after the accession of James VI to the English throne in 1603 comprises the ninth (1604–9) and tenth coinages (1609–25). The ninth is represented in the Stewartby collection by 38 coins, and tenth by 35 coins. From the ninth coinage there are 5 gold (**1363–7**) and 34 silver (**1376–1409**); from the tenth, 8 gold (**1368–75**) and 26 silver coins (**1410–35**). The copper issues of this period are covered as well, with 22 coins (**1436–57**).

There is one example of each denomination of the ninth coinage gold: unit (**1363**); double-crown (**1364**); Britain crown (**1365**); halfcrown (**1366**), and thistle crown (**1367**). From the tenth coinage there are three examples of the unit (**1368–70**); two of the double-crown (**1371–2**); two of the Britain crown (**1373–4**); and one halfcrown (**1375**).

The Stewartby collection holding of the silver from after the English accession has examples of all denominations. From the ninth coinage there are 3 examples of the sixty-shilling piece (**1376–8**); 6 thirty-shillings (**1379–84**); 3 twelve-shillings (**1385–7**); 5 six-shillings (**1388–92**), 3 dated 1605 (**1388–90**) and 2 1606 (**1391–2**), with no example of the altered date 1609/7; 13 two-shillings (**1393–1405**); and 4 one-shilling (**1406–9**). From the tenth coinage there are two examples of the sixty-shillings (**1410–11**); 7 thirty-shillings (**1412–18**); 6 twelve-shillings (**1419–24**) and 11 six-shillings (**1425–35**), with the dates 1610 (**1425**), 1611 (**1426**), 1612 (**1427**), 1615 (**1428–30**), 1617 (**1431**), 1618 (**1432**), 1619 (**1433–4**), 1622 (**1435**), but not 1613, 1614, 1616. The two- and one-shilling coins ceased to be issued after 1609.

The copper issues of 1614 and 1623 are covered for both issues and denominations. From the 1614 issue, there are 6 examples of the twopence or 'turner' (**1436–41**) and two of the penny (**1442–3**). From the 1623 issues, there are 13 examples of the twopence or 'turner' (**1444–56**) and one of the penny (**1457**).

It should be noted that the Stewartby collection also contains 9 coins which are non-contemporary copies and forgeries (**1458–66**). A lion or crown of James IV is likely a nineteenth-century Jons forgery (**1458**). Two base-metal examples of the 1555 Mary ryal are likely also to be non-contemporary fabrications (**1459–60**). Similarly, a first period Mary penny is a forgery from the eighteenth- or nineteenth-century (**1461**). The Mary second period ducat of 1558 is represented in the collection for completeness by a yellow-metal electrotype of the NMAS example (**1462**). Two examples of the second period 1560 **VICIT LEO** testoon are both cast copies (**1463–4**). The holdings of James VI include two curious coins, a fourth coinage 1585 thirty-shilling piece and a seventh coinage 1598 ten-shillings both of light weight with stylistic anomalies (**1465–6**). These are also thought to be non-contemporary forgeries.

SOURCES OF THE COLLECTION

Where known to him, details of the date and place of purchase, along with earlier provenances, were noted by Lord Stewartby on the back of the packet in which he stored each coin. In some cases this has been cross referenced with invoices and other notes within The Lord Stewartby Scottish Numismatic Archive held at the Hunterian. All of the old collection and auction provenances noted by Lord Stewartby have been verified, with occasional errors in his annotation corrected. Biographical profiles of individuals, draws on Manville 2009, Stewartby 1996 and Eaglen, Pagan and Mitchell 2001. Coins acquired from, or which passed through, auctions where the name of the vendor is not stated are not included here: such provenances are noted with the coin.

Addington — Samuel Addington (1806–86), a London cloth merchant. Scottish coins from his collection appear to have been acquired privately by A. B. Richardson (see below). The rest of his collection was acquired en bloc by H. Montagu in 1883.

9.

Asherson — Nehemiah Asherson (1896–1989), an ENT surgeon, who bought extensively at the Lockett Scottish sales and sold his collection to Spink in 1967. 19 coins, all acquired by Lord Stewartby in September 1967, derive from the Asherson collection, retailed by Spink. All are coins of James VI including the ex Lockett half-merk attributed to the Marians at Edinburgh Castle by J. E. L. Murray.

1072, 1082, 1094, 1105, 1158, 1166, 1204, 1210, 1213, 1214, 1215, 1220, 1229, 1234, 1237, 1250, 1293, 1419, 1466.

Two coins, a rare undated two-thirds ryal of Mary and a 1580 merk piece, acquired from 'Dundee' 1976 (see below), were previously in the Asherson collection.

1028, 1159.

Baldwin — A. H. Baldwin and Son, London dealer (Baldwin). Founded as a privately owned dealership by Albert Henry Baldwin (1858–1936), who first traded coins as a schoolboy in 1872. He issued his first list of coins for sale in 1880, and in 1900 opened retail premises at 4A Duncannon Street, Charing Cross, London WC2. The firm was later based at 3 Adelphi House Terrace, 1928-63, The Adelphi 1963-71 and 11 Adelphi Terrace 1971-2014. Auctioneers from 1994 until 2018. Became a limited company in 1920 with all shares held by the family. A. H. Baldwin was succeeded in the business by his second son Albert Henry Frederick Baldwin (1889–1970, known as Fred) who ran the business until 1967, assisted by his nephew, Albert Baldwin (1912–67) and David Dewar Mitchell (another nephew, known as Dougie (1906–2000) until 1986. Peter Mitchell (b. 1933), son of Dougie Mitchell, joined the business in 1949 and served as Managing Director from 1967 until retirement in 1997, when he was succeeded by Edward Baldwin (b. 1949), Albert Baldwin's son. From 1972 to 2002 Michael Baruch Sharp (1940-2012) assisted with the British series. In 2013 Baldwin became part of the Stanley Gibbons group, and relocated to their premises on the Strand in 2014. Lord Stewartby had a long relationship with Baldwin and acquired extensively from their stock, which contained portions of old collection sales, in some cases dating back many decades.

See below - for coins acquired through Baldwin from the collection of Fred Baldwin.

The earliest noted date of an acquisition from Baldwin in this portion of the Stewartby collection is 1953 and the latest 2004. Lord Stewartby acquired a substantial tranche of *c.* 85 coins in 1976. Coins with dated purchases from Baldwin are:

4, 14, 58, 64, 73, 118, 119, 140, 154, 164, 165, 179, 180, 199, 201, 204, 210, 212, 219, 222, 229, 246, 312, 313, 314, 315, 325, 345, 376, 381, 388, 389, 390, 392, 396, 398, 404, 410, 411, 413, 414, 419, 437, 442, 451, 458, 501, 534, 536, 539, 540, 554, 560, 570, 597, 598, 599, 610, 624, 630, 649, 651, 656, 672, 687, 690, 705, 721, 722, 771, 818, 838, 916, 917, 926, 933, 957, 964, 995, 996, 997, 1016, 1023, 1053, 1057, 1058, 1060, 1065, 1069, 1074, 1086, 1087, 1090, 1093, 1103, 1104, 1110, 1115, 1126, 1154, 1156, 1169, 1173, 1175, 1197, 1200, 1206, 1207, 1218, 1221, 1226, 1230, 1233, 1242, 1243, 1249, 1252, 1255, 1257, 1258, 1260, 1261, 1262, 1263, 1264, 1265, 1267, 1269, 1273, 1274, 1277, 1280, 1283, 1292, 1294, 1295, 1296, 1297, 1299, 1305, 1306, 1307, 1310, 1320, 1339, 1342, 1343, 1344, 1345, 1346,

1348, 1349, 1350, 1351, 1352, 1353, 1354, 1360, 1361, 1366, 1369, 1371, 1372, 1378, 1401, 1408, 1413, 1415, 1416, 1418, 1421, 1427, 1443, 1457, 1458, 1461, 1463, 1464.

Lord Stewartby notes a number of coins as having been purchased at Baldwin but does not give a date of acquisition.

370, 662, 684, 688, 689, 695, 699, 716, 740, 742, 759, 796, 816, 1198, 1211, 1219, 1231, 1270, 1271, 1282, 1323, 1324, 1325, 1340, 1341, 1400, 1404, 1420, 1430, 1442.

One coin, **548** (a Mary 1553 twenty-two shilling piece), is remembered by Peter Mitchell as having been acquired by Baldwin from Lady Mitchison, who is named by Lord Stewartby with the coin, and it seems he then acquired this from Baldwin.

A listing in the Lord Stewartby Scottish Numismatic Archive of provenances in Lord Stewartby's handwriting, *c.* 1985, added additional details on the origins on for the coins of James VI. This indicated that much of the post-English accession copper coins of 1614 and 1623 (**1436–57**) in the Stewartby collection, were acquired from Baldwin but a date of acquisition was not given. It has not been possible to align individual coins with this provenance which is noted here for the record.

Three coins gifted by Baldwin staff: **332** (1971, noted by Peter Mitchell), **1180** (1968), **1459** (1970).

F. Baldwin

Members of the Baldwin family at various times built up privately held holdings of stock, as a form of dividend payment from the business to its owners. Among such holdings was that of Albert Henry Frederick Baldwin (1889–1970, known as Fred Baldwin) which contained a large number of Scottish coins. Lord Stewartby acquired 169 coins from this source, noted with the date and 'ex F. Baldwin'. They consisted of two major blocs: one in 1975 (51 coins), and another in 1976 (84 coins). A much smaller group of 3 followed in 1978. 31 other coins are noted by Lord Stewartby as 'ex F Baldwin' but without a date of acquisition. The 1975 tranche added 46 coins of Mary to the collection, including 28 first and second period testoons and halves. From the 1976 tranche is the 1562 Mary third period testoon (**1019**), three James IV groats (**19, 35, 44**), 26 billon pence of James IV and 28 billon coins of the first period of Mary.

Acquired in 1975:

166, 176, 177, 203, 217, 552, 553, 557, 563, 564, 576, 577, 578, 586, 588, 592, 595, 596, 597, 601, 604, 616, 622, 625, 924, 927, 930, 936, 937, 939, 940, 946, 949, 958, 966, 969, 975, 978, 985, 986, 987, 988, 994, 998, 1005, 1009, 1017, 1019, 1034, 1037, 1040, 1045.

Acquired in 1976:

19, 35, 44, 65, 79, 80, 136, 137, 145, 148, 213, 214, 238, 239, 240, 241, 242, 243, 244, 247, 248, 257, 259, 274, 275, 308, 310, 311, 316, 317, 318, 320, 326, 327, 328, 329, 350, 418, 420, 421, 440, 443, 450, 463, 482, 488, 505, 541, 709, 723, 822, 828, 831, 832, 836, 839, 849, 850, 855, 856, 857, 858, 860, 863, 869, 873, 876, 877, 878, 881, 882, 883, 888, 902, 908, 921, 1019, 1061, 1073, 1244, 1245, 1301, 1302, 1313.

Acquired in 1978:

353, 360, 402.

Noted as 'Ex F. Baldwin', without date of acquisition:

349, 372, 373, 374, 378, 380, 382, 387, 400, 408, 423, 428, 429, 729, 797, 810, 811, 813, 1063, 1122, 1165, 1236, 1311, 1315, 1319, 1322, 1326, 1327, 1328, 1329, 1332.

Banes — Arthur Alexander Banes (1856–1922), a solicitor from Upton, Essex. His collection was sold at Sotheby 30–1 October 1922. Three coins, all James V groats, derive from lot 377 (26 coins including 19 Scottish). All three were later part of the collection of Dr A. N. Brushfield (see below).

368, 384, 403.

Basmadjieff — Luben Alexandre Basmadjieff (1911–2000), a French art dealer, who created a choice collection of English, Scottish and other gold, which was sold anonymously at Glendining on 15 July 1953 in 180 lots.

544.

Bearman — Thomas Bearman (1846–1921), a baker and confectioner of Hackney, London. His collection was acquired by Baldwin after his death.

9, 46, 148, 194, 197, 215, 239, 337, 343, 414, 621, 652, 788, 812, 1003, 1072, 1074, 1082, 1117, 1166, 1171, 1209, 1419.

Beaufoy

Henry Benjamin Hanbury Beaufoy (1786–1851), a south Lambeth distiller. The collection of coins, including Scottish, attributed to Beaufoy as 'collected in the early nineteenth-century', was sold at Christie's 18 June 1909, in 226 lots.

432, 1117.

Beresford-Jones

Richard Duncan Beresford-Jones (1903–2000), an accountant, of Sible Hedingham, Essex, formed a collection including English and Scottish hammered gold, with the Scottish gold coins sold in a named portion within Spink, auction 108, 17 March 1995, lots 473 to 517. Lord Stewartby acquired a Mary crown from this sale.

544.

Two other coins later acquired by Lord Stewartby were in the Beresford-Jones collection.

334, 1372.

Blunt

Christopher Evelyn Blunt (1904–87), of Ramsbury, Wiltshire, a merchant banker by profession. He was a collector and eminent private scholar in the second half of the twentieth-century. Lord Stewartby and Blunt were friends from *c.* 1950 until the latter's death, and they corresponded regularly, collaborating on several projects. Blunt was also instrumental in setting up the Sylloge of the Coins of the British Isles series. His collection of Anglo-Saxon coins and medieval jettons was acquired after his death by the Fitzwilliam Museum, Cambridge.

Lord Stewartby was given **231**, a James IV penny, by Blunt, but no date is noted for when this happened, although the coin itself derives from the Shirley Fox collection which was bequeathed to Blunt in 1939. Coins **399**, a James V groat, and **490**, a James V bawbee, are both noted as '1987' and may have been acquired by Lord Stewartby from the Blunt family after his death. Lord Stewartby also acquired a number of books from Blunt's library at this time.

Boyd

Two coins, both acquired by Lord Stewartby on 30 March 1957 from Spink: a Mary third period 1561 testoon: and a James

VI 1578 two-merk piece are cited as 'ex Boyd collection'. The identity of this collection has not been established.

1015, 1155.

Brand

Virgil Michael Brand (1862–1926), an American brewer and collector. His huge collection, including Scottish, was widely dispersed at varying times after his death with a portion acquired by Seaby in 1935. Two important gold coins passed through this collection.

16, 1047.

Bridgewater House

Collection created by the Earls of Bridgewater, for the most part before 1745, with portions likely dating to before 1700. The collection contained a number of the Scottish coins, mostly dating to after 1526. The collection, after being held for many years at the British Museum, was sold by the descendants of the Earls of Bridgewater at Sotheby on 15 June 1972, the Scottish coins lots 477 to 547. Lord Stewartby acquired a 1567 one-third ryal of James VI from this sale, lot 506.

1078.

Coin **1179** also derives from this source, but was acquired from J. K. R. Murray in 1986.

Brunn

Lars Emil Bruun (1852–1923), a butter merchant of Copenhagen. His Scottish coins (lots 898 to 930) were sold with other British and colonial coins at Sotheby 25–7 May 1925.

375, 1049.

Brushfield

Dr. Archibald Nadauld Brushfield (1870–1960), medical practitioner of Halifax, Yorkshire, and later Bognor Regis, Sussex. His Scottish coins were sold Glendining 28 March 1940 as lots 1 to 131.

26, 368, 374, 384, 394, 403, 945, 947, 963.

Bute

A collection of coins, largely formed in the late 1760s by John Stuart, 3rd Earl of Bute (1718–92), Prime Minister and First Lord of the Treasury, 1762–3, a personal favourite of George III. His collection contained contained 58 Scottish gold coins and 144 silver. Further additions mean that when sold at Sotheby on 11 June 1951 the collection contained 81 gold and over 400 silver. Lord Stewartby's James IV/V half-unicorn (**15**) and James VI 1582 forty-shilling piece (**1164**) passed through the Bute collection.

13A, 15, 20, 334, 422, 426, 430, 515, 1163.

Butterfield

Dudley St George Butterfield (1911–2003), of the Bermuda banking family, formed a collection of Scottish gold in the mid–1970s which was later sold as an unnamed property, 'Important Scottish Gold Including Many Rarities' within Spink auction 82, 27 March 1991 (lots 1 to 45). Lord Stewartby acquired four lots from this sale, all rare gold.

9, 336, 545, 1048.

Cairncross

A collection which formed a portion of an unnamed Glendining auction, 14 June 1995, lots 426 to 485, for which Lord Stewartby noted the vendor being a person by name of Cairncross. The identity of this person has not been verified.

255, 282, 283, 1064, 1096, 1100, 1102, 1106, 1107, 1108, 1113, 1114, 1125, 1127, 1128, 1135, 1140, 1141, 1147, 1150, 1151.

Caledon

A group of coins was offered under the name of 'Earl of Caladon' (sic) in a Christie's auction, 4 April 1967, lots 49 to 168, which was the property of Eric Alexander, 5th Earl of Caledon (1885–1968). This had passed to the vendor's family in 1695, on the marriage of Katharine Butler, eldest daughter of James Butler of Amberley Castle, Sussex, to Sir Thomas Pope Blount, at which time a collection of coins and curiosities was noted to be in her possession. These were traditionally said to have been owned by Sir Henry Blount (1602–82) who fought for the king at the battle of Edgehill. Lord Stewartby had one coin from lot 104, a multiple lot, noted in the catalogue at the Fitzwilliam Museum as acquired by 'Parker.' The attribution of this provenance to a single coin suggests it was acquired by Lord Stewartby sometime after the original sale.

361.

Carlyon-Britton, R.C.

Raymond Carlyon Carlyon-Britton (1893–1960), of Chichester, Sussex. The bulk of his collection, including the Scottish coins, was sold for him on commission by Seaby between 1955 and 1961.

26, 153, 187, 191, 196, 200, 209, 391, 409, 455, 470, 484, 499, 512, 517, 527, 533, 535, 542, 572, 620, 827, 868, 872, 915, 1119, 1121, 1153, 1163, 1183, 1196, 1212, 1287, 1288, 1334, 1337, 1390, 1391, 1398, 1403, 1433.

Chown

John Francis Chown (b. 1929), a Cambridge educated monetary economist, resident in north London. He assembled various collections of coins, with Tudor sold at Glendining in April 1979 and Viking at Spink, auction 150 (named 'The Viking Collection') on 14 March 2001, with a further offering within Spink auction 191 on 28 November 2007. His collection of Scottish coins was bought from him by Spink in 1977. Stewartby acquired three coins from this collection by way of J. E. L. Murray, who had bought them from Spink.

27, 59, 188.

Clonterbrook

Clonterbrook Trust holdings of coins, the property of Gerald Derek Lockett (1909–93), acquired from the R. C. Lockett sales, sold at Glendining 7 June 1974. Lord Stewartby acquired a James VI 1585 thirty-shilling piece from this sale.

1171.

Cochran-Patrick

Robert William Cochran-Patrick (1842–97), landowner and member of Parliament for North Ayrshire (1880–5). His collection of Scottish coins sold at Sotheby 30 March 1936, consisted of 945 coins. The gold accounted for lots 1 to 190 and the silver lots 191 to 357. A further sale of the remaining coins took place, Sotheby 9 December 1957, lots 126 to 157. His Scottish medals were largely sold at Sotheby in 1949. Lord Stewartby acquired a half-unicorn of James IV at the 1957 sale.

11.

Forty-one coins derive from the 1936 sale and three others from the 1957 sale.

Coins from the 1936 sale:

18, 22, 192, 356, 362, 379, 417, 561, 562, 594, 609, 623, 928, 942, 944, 959, 1030, 1048, 1085, 1099, 1111, 1123, 1136, 1142, 1143, 1149, 1164, 1188, 1192, 1251, 1254, 1259, 1268, 1272, 1275, 1285, 1290, 1298, 1372, 1377, 1381.

Coins from the 1957 sale:

11, 24, 1201.

Cowley

A single coin is noted to have been the property of the first Lady Cowley, Georgiana Cecil (d. 1860), daughter of the first Marquess of Salisbury. She married Henry Wellesley (d. 1847), created first Baron Cowley in 1828. He was a brother of the Duke of Wellington and had a career as a politician and diplomat. The coin is noted to have subsequently been the property of 'Lord Rockley' (see below). This title is that of a junior arm of the Cecil family: the first Baron Rockley, Evelyn Cecil (d. 1941), was a grandson of the second Marquess of Salisbury and therefore related to Lady Cowley. It is not clear if the Baron Rockley referred to is the first or second. The second Baron Rockley died in 1976, and the coin was acquired by Lord Stewartby in February 1970.

1059.

Dakers

Captain Colin Hugh Dakers (1897–1942), a colonial civil servant in Malaya (1933–42). He formed a collection of Scottish and British hammered coins in conjunction with his father, Hugh John Dakers (1863–1945), a retired schoolmaster in St Albans, Hertfordshire. Scottish coins sold at Glendining 9 October 1946, lots 274 to 543, with a number of large lots.

18, 31, 36, 48, 347, 348, 352, 538, 575, 642, 643, 654, 677, 698, 719,738, 749, 751, 752, 757, 770, 772, 785, 787, 789, 800, 801, 802, 807, 809, 814, 823, 837, 840, 841, 842, 843, 846, 865, 875, 889, 892, 893, 905, 943, 961, 967, 968, 970, 971, 973, 974, 979, 984, 1004, 1007, 1013, 1021, 1029, 1032, 1145, 1062, 1077, 1081, 1186, 1187, 1191, 1194, 1248, 1262, 1336, 1356, 1357, 1410, 1443, 1457.

A number of coins were noted by Stewartby as 'ex Dakers', but the limitations of the 1946 sale catalogue make it impossible to assign these with confidence to specific lots.

199, 201, 204, 216, 229, 276, 303, 309, 1417.

Davidson

Dr James Davidson (1896–1985), forensic scientist of Maxwelltown, Dumfriesshire, usually referred to as the younger to distinguish him from his father, from whom he inherited a coin collection formed in the first half of the twentieth-century.

Lord Stewartby had a cordial relationship with Davidson and his family. He acquired 151 coins at various times between 1985 and 2003, mostly bought from Spink who had acquired a substantial portion of the Davidson collection after his death.

The following is likely a private acquisition from the Davidson family from June 1985:

991

Lord Stewartby purchased three large groups of Davidson's coins from Spink in July 1987, on 25 October 1988 and in June 1989.

July 1987, all silver:

18, 22, 355, 364, 375, 377, 385, 555, 565, 566, 571, 580, 611, 852, 952, 1092, 1138.

25 October 1988, bawbees, half-bawbees and placks:

497, 634, 644, 646, 647, 650, 653, 666, 667, 669, 671, 680, 686, 692, 693, 694, 725, 731, 734, 737, 739, 745, 747, 754, 760, 764, 766, 768, 778, 781, 791, 792, 806, 808, 817, 820, 824, 830, 890, 901, 909, 912, 913, 920.

June 1989, base-metal coins of James IV (38), James V (17), Mary (8) and James VI (1):

61, 62, 69, 71, 74, 76, 77, 83, 84, 86, 87, 88, 90, 93, 96, 97, 104, 110, 112, 113, 115, 116, 120, 121, 134, 138, 139, 141, 144, 146, 147, 149, 150, 151, 152, 174, 186, 190, 434, 444, 448, 449, 453, 456, 457, 466, 467, 468, 469, 472, 477, 478, 479, 481, 486, 853, 861, 862, 983, 993, 999, 1000, 1001, 1289.

A number of individual coins and smaller groups were also acquired from Spink at other times.

1988:

514.

October 1989, all James IV pence:

220, 230, 233, 258, 265, 266, 267, 268, 284, 298, 323.

1990, all Mary placks:

891, 898, 899, 903.

March 1990:

8.

No stated year or date:

524, 531, 874.

Davidson (auctions, part I and II, Dix Noonan Webb 2003)

The residue of the collection of Dr J. Davidson was consigned to auction with the London auction house Dix Noonan Webb (DNW) in 2003 and offered in two parts. Lord Stewartby acquired coins at both sales.

Davidson I, part of DNW auction 59, 7 October 2003:

342, 1056.

Davidson II, part of DNW auction 60, 9 December 2003:

558, 1022.

Dolphin

Dolphin Coins and Medals, dealers, operated by Robert (Bob) Clive Ilsley (b. 1943) from 1967 until *c.* 2000s. Initially based in Hampstead, London, and then at Leighton Buzzard, Bedfordshire, from *c.* 1999. He offered an extensive collection of Scottish coins in his List 2 issued in the Spring of 1992. Lord Stewartby bought several coins from this at different times. A number of these coins appear to derive from the J. K. R. Murray collection sold at auction in April 1987 by Spink.

Acquired 18 December 1991:

1079.

Acquired 4 February 1992:

613, 621, 1152.

Acquired 25–6 May 1992:

567, 569, 619, 1129, 1167, 1288, 1465.

Acquired 10 June 1992:

612.

'Douglas'

A portion of Spink sale 119, 4 March 1997, lots 257 to 385, was named 'The Douglas Collection of Scottish Gold and Silver Coins and other Ancient, English and Foreign Coins and Medals.' The identity of 'Douglas' is not known and the name used for the auction portion is a pseudonym. This contained a number of rarities and Lord Stewartby acquired a James IV crown, James V half-unicorn and a Mary half-ryal from this sale.

16, 335, 550.

Drabble

Gilbert Creswick Drabble (1875–1939), who retired from business interests in Argentina to Los Altos, Sundown, Isle of Wight. His collection included Scottish coins, sold at Glendining in two parts: the Scottish gold coins were lots 220 to 226 in part I, 4–6 July 1939; and the silver lots 1161 to 1204 in part II, 13–14 December 1943. Three coins, all silver, from part II were in this collection:

194, 321, 1209.

Dunbar

A collection of Scottish coins, largely formed in the 1970s, which was sold as that of Dr C. Dunbar', in Spink, auction 64, 23 June 1988, lots 76 to 127. No further details on the identity of this person are known.

46.

Duncan

A collection formed by Mrs. M. Duncan of 312 Goulburn Street, Aberdeen, and sold in Glendining, 5 July 1972, lots 254 to 332.

1080.

'Dundee'

An extensive collection of Scottish coins was formed by Sheldon Paige Fay (1904–81), an American collector based in Los Angeles, and sold as 'The Dundee Collection' (his wife had been born in Dundee) by Bowers and Ruddy Galleries, in conjunction with Spink, in Los Angeles on 19 February 1976, consisting of 347 lots.

1028.

A further 8 coins, previously in the 'Dundee' Collection, came into the Stewartby collection, via the Joan Murray, Jock Murray, Lucien LaRiviere and Dudley Butterfield collections. **1159** was acquired in a Glendining auction on 21 July 1976 when a number of coins from the 'Dundee' Collection were reoffered in London.

6, 46, 338, 339, 545, 1044, 1157, 1159.

Elsen

Jean Elsen et Fils, a Brussels based auctioneer and dealer in coins and medals since 1976, who hold regular auctions and offer coins for retail. One coin, a James V crown, was acquired by Lord Stewartby from a retail list (no. 194) in October 1997.

341.

Finn

Patrick Finn (1942–2000), on the staff of Spink 1978–93 before setting up as an independent dealer from 1994 based in Kendal, Cumbria, issuing lists of British and Irish hammered coins for retail. Lord Stewartby acquired one coin from his winter 1996 list (no. 6) on 17 January 1996.

1088.

One coin, a James VI thistle noble, later acquired by Lord Stewartby in 2007, was in his list 18 (2000).

1051.

Ford

John Kermack Ford (*c.* 1818–83), a solicitor, of Southsea, Hampshire, formed a major collection of Scottish coins which was sold Sotheby 12 June 1884, lots 788 to 974. A light coinage half-groat of James IV acquired by Lord Stewartby once formed part of this collection.

46.

Format

Format Coins, a dealership in coins operated by Peter Ireland, based in Birmingham. Lord Stewartby acquired one coin on 4 April 1997 in a postal auction held by them.

546.

Foster

A collection including Scottish coins was formed by Richard Manley Foster (*c.* 1815–1902), a colliery owner, of Waterloo, Liverpool. The Scottish coins were sold at Sotheby 3–5 November 1903, lots 265 to 301. A 1539 ducat of James V acquired by Lord Stewartby was in this collection.

343.

Gantz

Revd William Lewis Gantz (1873–1940), of Stanstead Abbots, Hertfordshire. The principal collection, including Scottish coins, was sold in two parts at Glendining: part I, 27–30 May

1941; and part II, 23–7 June 1941. His Scottish coins were in part II, lots 1522 to 1587.

335.

Glendining

A London based auctioneer founded in 1900 by Douglas Glendining (1863–1951), incorporated into Bonhams *c.*1995. Lord Stewartby notes a number of coins as having been purchased at Glendining sales. These may have been acquired on commission on his behalf or, in some cases, offered to him by dealers buying with him in mind and then selling to him shortly after the sale with the origin of the coin noted by Lord Stewartby as the auction. This may explain why some coins are part of a multiple lot from which there are no other coins in the collection.

Glendining, 21 July 1976 contained a number of coins from the 'Dundee' collection sale (see above) in February 1976 and reoffered in London, where Lord Stewartby acquired one coin.

1159.

Glendining, 30 March 1983, an unnamed sale within which a portion was named as an 'Old Scottish Collection'. Lord Stewartby acquired one coin.

549.

J. E. L. Murray acquired a James IV half-unicorn at this auction from whom it came to Lord Stewartby.

10.

Note: Coin **394**, ex A. N. Brushfield, has with it a ticket indicating it was lot 32 in Glendining auction on 29 April 1924. No such sale took place.

Gordon

The provenance 'ex Gordon Collection' is given in the R. C. Lockett (part I, 1957) catalogue against lot 373, a 1580 two-merk piece later acquired by Lord Stewartby, in 2006. Lockett acquired this from Baldwin for £52, suggesting it was one of his later acquisitions. It seems likely that the coin came from a collection which was acquired by Baldwin *c.* 1930–40. The identity of the owner of this collection is uncertain.

1157.

Grantley

John Richard Brinsley Norton, 5th Baron Grantley (1855–1943), a landowner, latterly at Weeke Manor, Hampshire. His large collection was sold after his death in a series of sales by Glendining 1943–4; the Scottish coins were in part V, 18 May 1944, lots 1671 to 1824.

1189.

Grover

Brian Henry Grover (1924–2015), a UK dealer active *c.* 1950–2007. He formed a private collection mainly of English coins, from which a small group of Anglo-Saxon coins was sold at DNW in 2011. One coin was acquired from him.

1338.

Harris

Dr Eric James Harris (1915–2003), a biologist residing in south-east London. He was a scholar collector of Plantagenet and early Tudor coins, well known to Lord Stewartby, who privately acquired coins from him at various times, including (in November 2005, after Harris's death), a large number of his fourteenth- and fifteenth-century English coins. One Scottish coin was acquired privately from Harris earlier in 1968.

805.

Higginson

Philip Peter Higginson (b. 1949), a resident of Llandudno, Clwyd, and active collector. He was the owner of a group of coins sold in the *NCirc*, February 2006 (from which Lord Stewartby acquired several other coins).

1170.

Hird

Horace Hird (1899–1973), Bradford Alderman and Lord Mayor, who formed a collection of English and Scottish coins, some of which was dispersed in his lifetime, including the gift of a portion of the Scottish hammered gold to the Ashmolean Museum, Oxford. The remaining Scottish gold was sold at Glendining, catalogued by Spink, 6 March 1974, lots 1 to 166. 10 coins, including a number of the important gold, were acquired by Lord Stewartby from this collection.

9, 16, 330, 335, 336, 337, 545, 583, 1048, 1364.

Hurley

W. Hurley, a collector, active *c.* 1950 to *c.* 1970, who also bought and sold coins when attending coin fairs. Lord Stewartby acquired a number of coins directly from him, with the last group changing hands in October 1967.

232, 301, 302, 305, 306, 556, 603, 618, 932, 960, 1043, 1178, 1190.

Some coins also appear to have passed through Hurley's hands before entering into other collections, and were then later acquired by Lord Stewartby.

207, 425, 1174, 1182.

Huth

Reginald Huth (1853–1926), a member the Huth family of City financiers. His collection, including Scottish, was sold at Sotheby 4–7 April 1927, lots 644 to 696. One coin, owned by Lord Stewartby, a Mary half-ryal was formerly part of this collection.

550.

Kirke

Robert Kirke (1815–94) of Burntisland, Fife, at one time an estate owner in Surinam, and one the last Scots to own slaves, formed a collection including Scottish coins which was sold at Sotheby, 1 February 1897. 'Lot 78 R Kirke' is noted by Bearman as the sale source for one coin. This was described in the Kirke sale as a 1571 two-thirds ryal later acquired by Lord Stewartby in 1967.

1072.

Kirton

Ronald Kirton, a collector active as of 2020 who disposed of coins at various times at auction and through dealers.

1176.

Laing

A coin formerly in the Dakers collection (see above), has an old ticket noting an earlier provenance, 'Laing 1923'.

The precise identity of 'Laing' is uncertain. It may be David Laing (1793–1878), a Scottish antiquary, who formed a collection of coins, including Scottish, sold at Sotheby 19 November 1879 and February 1881.

575.

LaRiviere

Lucien LaRiviere (d. 2012), a Canadian, formed a collection of British and Irish hammered coins in the 1980s and 1990s. The Scottish portion was sold in Spink auction 179, 29 March 2006. Lord Stewartby acquired two coins, both rare James VI third coinage issues, a 1580 two-merks and 1581 four-shilling piece.

1157, 1162.

Lawrence, F. G.

Frederick George Lawrence (*c.* 1851–1927), a dealer in coins and antiquities whose stock, including Scottish coins (lots 195 to 197), was sold at Sotheby, 7–8 June 1910.

652, 727.

Lawrence, L. A.

Laurie Asher Lawrence (1857–1949), a surgeon, of Belsize Park, London. The principal part of the collection was sold in four parts at Glendining, 1950–1, with the Scottish in part IV, 28 November 1951, lots 1312 to 1316.

1130.

Lingford

Herbert Muschamp Lingford (1891–1950) of Cotherstone, Barnard Castle, a manufacturer of baking powder. A portion of his collection was sold in two parts at Glendining, with Scottish crown-size coins in part I, 24–6 October 1950 (lots 615 to 618), and gold, silver and base-metal coins of James VI and I in part II, 20–1 June 1951, lots 830 to 1284. The residue of his collection was acquired by Baldwin. The following coins were in Lingford's collection, offered in part II.

1075, 1091, 1097, 1098, 1132, 1133, 1139, 1184, 1247, 1253, 1256, 1330, 1364, 1372, 1435.

One coin was not in the sales but in the residue acquired by Baldwin.

1156.

Lockett

Richard Cyril Lockett (1873–1950), member of a family of Liverpool ship owners and based from 1922 at 58 Cadogan Place, London. Lockett was responsible for one of the greatest private collections of coins ever formed, which was sold after his death at Glendining in 13 parts from 1955 to 1962. His Scottish coins were sold in two parts: part I, 18–19 June 1956, lots 1 to 485; and part II, lots 679 to 968, 26 October 1960.

Coins that were in Lockett I:

46, 343, 652, 701, 724, 727, 788, 798, 803, 812, 1044, 1049, 1082, 1157, 1166, 1214, 1215, 1288.

Coins that were in Lockett II:

31, 337, 550, 621, 1048, 1072, 1159, 1171, 1210, 1213, 1220, 1250, 1419.

414 was part of either lot 887 or 888 in Lockett II.

Longstaffe

William Hylton Dyer Longstaffe (1826–98), a solicitor of Gateshead, Co. Durham, formed a collection of English coins with some Scottish. A portion of his collection was sold at Sotheby 20–1 January 1903 (as the property of his son, J. E. D. Longstaffe), the Scottish coins being lots 341 to 343.

992.

Lorimer

H. B. Lorimer, a launderer in Stirling, formed a collection of Scottish coins in the first half of the twentieth-century which was acquired by Spink in 1960. Two coins derive from his collection. Lord Stewartby's records do not state they were acquired from Spink in 1961–2, although this seems likely.

340, 1370.

Lornie

John Guthrie Lornie, a J. P., of Kirkcaldy, whose collection was sold after his death with other properties in Sotheby, 26–7 November 1917, lots 63 to 172, with gold forming lots 76 to 80. One coin was in this collection.

342.

Mallinson

Revd. Arnold Mallinson (1896–1985) of Oxford, vicar of St Frideswide's, Oxford, formed a collection of ancient, English, Scottish and European coins. A portion was sold to Paramount Coins, London, 1976, from whom three coins were acquired by Lord Stewartby. The remainder, the principal part, was sold at Spink, auction 39, 6 December 1984, the Scottish coins being lots 124 to 141.

1239, 1241, 1462.

Mann

Alexander Mann (1859–1916) of Kew Gardens, London, put together a collection, including Scottish coins, which was sold after his death at Sotheby 29–31 October 1917, the Scottish coins being lots 418 to 480.

38.

Marr

H. J. Marr, a solicitor in Enfield, Middlesex, who sold his collection, begun in the 1920s, to Spink in 1965. 70 coins derive from this source having been acquired by Lord Stewartby in 1965 or soon after with his notes stating they were purchased from 'Spink ex Marr.' These comprise 21 coins of James IV (including a heavy groat and two light groats); 19 of James V; 17 of Mary; and 13 of James VI.

21, 28, 38, 41, 56, 78, 117, 175, 187, 198, 200, 202, 225, 226, 228, 234, 270, 272, 273, 300, 304, 354, 357, 365, 371, 395, 409, 425, 435, 438, 452, 455, 471, 473, 476, 483, 485, 487, 489, 542, 559, 572, 587, 602, 645, 678, 825, 827, 847, 866, 868, 886, 907, 929, 976, 980, 1041, 1124, 1153, 1172, 1181, 1193, 1195, 1203, 1208, 1227, 1359, 1402, 1406, 1436.

One coin was acquired from this collection by J. K. R. Murray and subsequently bought by Lord Stewartby at the sale of his coins in 1987.

621.

Marshall

Lieut. William Somerville Marshall (1923–44), killed in action at Tienray, near Venlo, Holland on 26 November 1944. Marshall had been actively building a collection including Scottish coins, and acquired lots in the Brushfield and Grantley sales (see above). Four coins were in his collection sold at Glendining 29 April 1946, where the Scottish gold were lots 22 to 23, and the silver lots 160 to 183.

945, 947, 963, 1189.

Marsham

The Hon. Robert William Marsham (1834–1914), formed a large collection of coins including some Scottish, which was sold at Sotheby 19 November 1888, the Scottish coins being lots 861 to 934.

550.

Mackenzie

Thomas Mackenzie (1831–1916), 'Sheriff Mackenzie,' of Dornoch and later Tain, Sheriff of Sutherland, formed a collection with many Scottish coins. A portion of it was dispersed at Chapman's in Edinburgh, 14–15 March 1883, lots 1 to 183; the remainder, including a final group of Scottish, was sold after his death at Sotheby, 21–2 February 1921. Coins from Mackenzie's collection acquired by Lord Stewartby all derive from the 1921 auction.

385, 626, 701, 724, 798, 803, 1162, 1210.

Mcfarlan

David Mcfarlan, a long standing collector and occasional dealer, resident in Glasgow. He is best known for his collection of Scottish countermarked dollars, now in the Hunterian, but he also collected other Scottish coins. Lord Stewartby acquired a number of coins from him privately at various times.

23, 122, 142, 193.

Mitchison

Naomi Margaret Mitchison, Lady Mitchison CBE (1897–1999), Scottish poet and author, lived at Carradale, Argyllshire, and Hammersmith, London, and was wife to Gilbert Mitchison (d. 1970), Labour MP for Kettering (1945–64). She was remembered by Peter Mitchell as having sold a twenty-two shilling piece to Baldwin in the late 1960s or early 1970s, which was acquired from them by Lord Stewartby.

548.

Murdoch

John Gloag Murdoch (1830–1902), a piano manufacturer and publisher, who formed a large coin collection, including Scottish, which was sold in eight sales at Sotheby in 1903–4. The bulk of his Scottish coins were in part II, 406 lots, sold 5 May 1903, the Scottish coins being lots 1 to 373. Some further Scottish coins were offered in part VIII, 14–16 December 1904, lots 1007 to 1080.

Six coins were in Murdoch part II:

9, 46, 337, 550, 621, 953.

Two coins were in Murdoch part VIII:

1229, 1372.

Mure

A James V groat acquired at Baldwin, ex F. Baldwin and Brushfield lot 53, is noted by Lord Stewartby as also 'ex Mure bequest 1 July 1930.' This source has not been identified with certainty. It may relate to the collection of William Mure, at one time British Consul in New Orleans, which was sold at Sotheby, 22–3 May 1865, and included some Scottish coins. It seems likely the coin derives from a batch acquired by a dealer, possibly Baldwin, with this origin noted on subsequent tickets.

374.

J. E. L. Murray

Joan Elizabeth Lowther Murray (1917–96). A mathematician and wartime Bletchley Park cryptographer where she worked closely with Alan Turing. She later worked at GCHQ where she met and married J. K. R Murray (see below) in 1952. They jointly built a collection of Scottish coins between *c.* 1950 and 1986. The coins of James I to IV, her area of academic study, along with some others, were retained by her after the disposal of her husband's collection at Spink 29 April 1987 following his death. Lord Stewartby came to know Joan Murray through his correspondence with her husband on Scottish coinage that commenced in 1964 and which continued with her after her husband's death in 1986. She worked closely with Lord Stewartby on a number of papers and subjects and he had a high regard for her. He privately acquired a portion of her collection after her death in 1998, including 21 coins of James IV (among them five unicorns, four half-unicorns, two light coinage groats, the 'Maundy groat' and a light coinage half-groat) as well as two James V unicorns and her 1572 half-merk attributed to the Marians at Edinburgh Castle.

Acquired directly from her estate in 1998:

1, 2, 5, 6, 7, 10, 12, 13, 13A, 15, 27, 30, 45, 46, 49, 55, 59, 109, 167, 168, 188, 330, 334, 445, 459, 480, 1091, 1097, 1098, 1132, 1133, 1139.

One coin, a James IV light coinage groat, is noted as having been exchanged at an unertain date for another (unidentified) coin.

32.

The residue of her collection was sold by Baldwin, auction 26, 9 May 2001, lots 1863–83.

J. K. R. Murray

Col. John Kenneth Ronald Murray (1910–86, known as Jock), an officer of the Indian Army who later worked at GCHQ, where he met his wife Joan. Along with his wife he formed a collection that spanned the whole Scottish series, while he himself was specifically interested in Scottish coinage from the mid-sixteenth to late seventeenth-centuries. The collection was sold after his death in Spink auction 57, 29 April 1987, save for the fifteenth-century coinage (James I to James IV), which was retained by Joan Murray. Lord Stewartby acquired 24 coins from this sale.

510, 583, 606, 867, 870, 887, 896, 900, 904, 911, 914, 918, 941, 950, 951, 989, 1027, 1037, 1044, 1364, 1387, 1422, 1423, 1424.

In addition five coins, all of James VI, were acquired privately from Jock Murray.

4 April 1984: **1134.**

1968, no date noted: **1144.**

28 May 1986: **1179, 1183, 1391.**

One coin was bought from Spink who had acquired it as stock from the sale of his collection (Spink 57, 29 April 1987).

415.

The following coins are noted as from his collection but were not acquired by Lord Stewartby from Spink auction 57, 29 April 1987, when Murray's collection was sold.

567, 612, 621, 1129, 1288, acquired from Dolphin Coins in 1992 where they were noted as from the 1987 sale of the Scottish coins of J. K. R. Murray.

1131, acquired in October 1967, was a duplicate in Murray's collection sold at that time.

1170, acquired from a group of coins offered in *NCirc* Feb 2006, from the collection of P. Higginson - see above - who acquired it at the 29 April 1987 sale of the coins of J. K. R. Murray.

See also note under 'Rose', below.

Napier — Duncan Scott Napier (1879–1956), an Edinburgh herbalist, whose collection (including Scottish coins) was sold at Glendining, 30 May 1956. The gold accounting for lots 56 to 83 and the silver, lots 203 to 249.

193, 1411.

O'Hagan — Henry Osborne O'Hagan (1853–1930), a financier, whose large collection was sold in four parts at Sotheby, with the Scottish coins, in Part I, 16–20 December 1907, lots 608 to 640.

333.

Paramount — Paramount International Coin Corporation, based at Englewood, Ohio, USA, which had a London office at Trafalgar Square in the mid–1970s headed by Alan Rayner. Paramount published lists of coins for sale at this time, and purchased a portion of the English and Scottish coins in the collection of Revd. A. W. Mallinson (see above) of Oxford in 1975, some of which were offered in a list in January 1976. Lord Stewartby acquired three coins, all ex Mallinson, all presumably offered retail as they cannot be located in printed lists.

1239, 1241, 1462.

Parsons

Harry Alexander Parsons (1876–1952), a post-office employee based in London and the home counties. He formed two collections both including Scottish coins. The first was sold at Sotheby 28 October–1 November 1929, the Scottish coins being lots 750 to 784; the second was sold after his death, Glendining 11–13 May 1954, with Scottish coins accounting for lots 697 to 803. He also traded coins, with many passing through his hands over the years. No coins are noted from the 1929 sale with all 'ex Parsons' coins being from the 1954 sale.

39, 43, 209, 473, 551, 572, 581, 582, 584, 585, 589, 593, 607, 608, 620, 868, 872, 961, 1028, 1067, 1071, 1119, 1153, 1163, 1312, 1316, 1323, 1331, 1341, 1358, 1386, 1420, 1430.

Parsons lot 733, consisting of eight coins (**581, 582, 584, 585, 589, 593, 607, 608**), was acquired at the sale by Baldwin and subsequently acquired en bloc by Lord Stewartby in 1975, presumably after being kept as stock since 1954.

Plumbridge

Robert Ernest Plumbridge (1917–75), of Burnley, Lancashire, was a senior executive in the textile industry who built up a major collection of gold patterns and British Empire coins. He initially bought through Spink but later became a loyal Baldwin client. A portion of these coins were disposed of at Spink after his death, catalogued by Baldwin. A further portion, including some Scottish, would appear to have been acquired as stock by Baldwin *c.* 1993 and offered for retail. Four coins were acquired from Baldwin in 1993 which derive from the collection of R. E. Plumbridge. All four were Mary bawbees purchased 16 July 1993.

672, 676, 682, 744.

Pollexfen

John Hutton Pollexfen (1813–99), initially a doctor qualifying at Edinburgh, but later ordained in 1844. He was vicar at

St Runwald, Colchester, Essex (1851–70), East Witton, Bedale (1870–4) and Middleton Tyas, North Yorkshire (1874–99). His collection, especially strong in Scottish coins, was sold after his death at Sotheby 26–8 June 1900, the Scottish coins being lots 139 to 453.

197, 215, 414, 432, 867.

Pye

Mr C. Pye formed a distinguished collection of Scottish coins between *c.* 1940 and *c.* 1960. These were sold as an unnamed block in Spink auction 20, 31 March 1982, lots 100 to 277. The collection was consigned to the Spink auction by Baldwin with the addition of a few medals and jetons from their stock. All coins acquired by Lord Stewartby from this sale were of James VI, including the 1575 twenty-pound piece, the 1580 ducat and very rare 1583 billon issue half-plack.

1046, 1047, 1075, 1247, 1253, 1256, 1330, 1367, 1435.

In addition five coins from this auction, lots 201 and 206, were bought by J. E. L. Murray and later acquired by Lord Stewartby.

1097, 1098, 1132, 1133, 1139.

No coins derive from the other Scottish offering in this sale, unnamed, but known to have been the property of Mr C. Brady (lots 290 to 320).

Ready

William Talbot Ready (1857–1914), a coin and medal dealer in London and, from 1907–14, manager of the London branch of Rollin and Feuardent. His private collection, including Scottish coins, was sold at Sotheby 15–19 November 1920, the Scottish as lots 814 to 840.

565.

Richardson

Adam Black Richardson (1851–1909), of Edinburgh. He was appointed Curator of Coins at the National Museum of Antiquities in 1888, and also formed a personal collection. The latter's Scottish portion was sold privately, probably to John Gloag Murdoch (see above). His English collection was sold at Sotheby on 22–4 May 1895.

9, 46.

871 (a type II Mary 1555 hardhead) is noted by Lord Stewartby as 'ex Richardson lot 172'. This cannot be A. B. Richardson as his Scottish coins were sold to Murdoch and nor is it from the Glendining, R. Richardson sale of 7 April 1982.

Rockley

A single coin is said to have been the property of a 'Lord Rockley.' The coin is noted to have previously been the property of 'Lady Cowley' (see above), identified as the first Lady Cowley (d. 1860). The Rockley title is that of a junior arm of the Cecil family – the 1st Baron Rockley, Evelyn Cecil (d. 1941), was a grandson of the 2nd Marquess of Salisbury and therefore related to Lady Cowley, a daughter of the 1st Marquess of Salisbury. It is not clear if the Baron Rockley referred to is the first or second. The 2nd Baron Rockley died in 1976, and the coin was acquired by Lord Stewartby in February 1970.

1059.

Rose

The collection of the late William Frederick Rose (1883–1973) of Devizes, Wiltshire, formed largely in the 1940s and 1950s. This formed the principal part of an unnamed joint Glendining-Seaby auction, 13 March 1974 (Scottish coins lots 362 to 389).

196 (part lot).

This lot is annotated in one copy as having been bought by J. K. R. Murray, who may have acquired this specific coin for Lord Stewartby, since other coins in this lot did not in enter his collection.

Roth

Bernard Mathias Simon Roth (1852–1915), a surgeon in London and then Brighton. His collection was sold in two parts, the second of which (Sotheby 14 October 1918), included his Scottish in lots 323 to 393.

566, 1372.

1220, is ticketed as 'ex Roth' but no such coin was in his sales.

'Rotterdam'

A single coin (a James VI post-English accession tenth coinage Britain crown), is noted as having been purchased in Rotterdam in 1960. No more details are recorded.

1373.

Ryan

Valentine John Eustace Ryan (1882–1947), a landowner from Ireland, based successively Switzerland, Channel Islands and London. Ryan was the financial backer of Seaby, a relationship from which he benefited as a collector. His large collection was sold in five parts at Glendining, 1950–2 with the Scottish gold, in part I, 28–30 June 1950, lots 557 to 578, the Scottish silver in part II, 22–4 January 1952, lots 1353 to 1370.

From Part I, **544, 1050.**

From Part II, **401, 573, 1068, 1089, 1276, 1284, 1300.**

Scaife

John Scaife (1940–2004), of Annan, Dumfriesshire, formed a collection of English, Scottish and Irish hammered coins. This was sold as a named portion of Spink auction 175, 28–9 September 2005, lots 1158 to 1287, the Scottish coins being lots 1194 to 1285.

1042, 1431.

Scott-Plummer

A small collection formed in the eighteenth-century and sold at Sotheby 9 December 1929, lots 354 to 382, as the property of Charles Henry Scott-Plummer (1859–1948) of Middlestead and of Sunderland Hall, Selkirkshire, who was a landowner and Lord Lieutenant of Selkirkshire.

544, 1050.

Seaby

B. A. Seaby Ltd, London based coin dealers founded in 1926 by H. A.'Bert' Seaby (1898–1979), with financial backing from V. J. E. Ryan (see above). Peter Seaby (1921–92) took over from his father running the business in 1966. Seaby was sold to Batsford, the publisher, in 1984. In 1991 the publishing activities of Seaby were acquired by Spink and the coin business by Classical Numismatic Associates (CNA), of Pennsylvania, USA, who later became Classical Numismatic Group (CNG) and as of 2020 still trade in London retaining the Seaby Coins name. Seaby published *Seaby's Coin and Medal Bulletin* (*SCMB*) several times each year offering coins for sale; the last issue appeared in February 1991. Seaby sold English and Scottish coins from the large Raymond Carlyon-Britton collection on commission between 1959 and *c*. 1966.

31 coins are noted by Lord Stewartby as having been acquired from Seaby between 1948 and 1984:

c. 1948: **1278.**
c. 1949: **1308.**
1951: **192.**
1953: **386, 821, 1266, 1362.**
1954: **195, 1403.**
1955: **42, 1382.**
1964: **450.**
1965: **1130, 1145.**
1966: **391, 427, 462, 464, 484.**
1971: **363, 1120, 1196, 1389, 1433.**
1972: **211, 322, 1225.**
1975: **1148.**
1980: **162.**
1983: **1176.**
1984: **1055.**

Additionally Lord Stewartby purchased four coins from Seaby between 1967 and 1988 which were listed in the *Seaby's Coin and Medal Bulletin*:

1967: **1052.**
1975: **1287.**
1978: **1224.**
1981: **1363.**
1988: **1038.**

One coin was acquired from a Seaby CNA mail bid auction, CNA XX, held by Classical Numismatic Associates in conjunction with Seaby, on 25 March 1992, some months after their acquisition of the coin business of Seaby.

568.

Senior

Mark Paul Senior (1947–2017), a dealer, active *c*. 1980–*c*. 2010, based in Brighton, Sussex. Two coins were acquired from him.

223, 224.

Shand

The collection formed by Frederick John Shand (1854–1929), general manager, Nobel's Explosives Company, Glasgow, was dispersed following the death of his widow in 1948 at Glendining 8–9 March 1949, with his Scottish coins being lots 213 to 283.

330.

Shirley-Fox

John Shirley Shirley-Fox (1860–1939), portrait painter, based latterly at Marlborough and Bath. He bequeathed his collection of English coins, with a few others, to C. E. Blunt (see above).

231, 681.

Shuttlewood

Roger Alan Shuttlewood (1941–2000), a stockbroker, was from the mid-1960s until his death an active collector, mainly of Tudor and Stuart pre-1660 coins, along with seventeenth-century tokens. His English coins were sold in Spink auction 151, 15 March 2001. Five Scottish coins offered from his collection in *NCirc* in June 2001 were acquired by Lord Stewartby.

1392, 1425, 1426, 1429, 1434.

Sotheby

International auctioneers of coins until 2001, after which its coin sales were operated by Morton and Eden Ltd. Coins with a Sotheby provenance are often single coins from a multiple lot, with the coin likely purchased by Stewartby from a dealer who had acquired the lot. Named portions of Sotheby auctions from which coins derive are:

Sotheby, 24 June 1914, the property of a 'Gentleman'.

1074.

Spink

An old London firm, initially established in the seventeenth-century as gold and silversmiths, and from the 1880s as a leading player in the coin trade. Coin dealers until 2013, publishers of the *Numismatic Circular (NCirc)* from 1892 until January 2014 and auctioneers since 1978. Lord Stewartby purchased many coins from Spink, mostly through their retail offerings, listed here by year of acquisition:

1948: **447.**
c. 1950: **1286.**
1955: **40, 416, 864, 1137, 1232.**
1956: **446, 461, 465, 474, 522, 1321.**
1957: **37, 333, 1015, 1066, 1155, 1217.**
1959: **1146.**
1960: **1409.**
1961: **3.**
1962: **1020.**
1968: **1161.**

1970: **1014.**
c. 1972: **66.**
1972: **1375.**
1973: **1368.**
1975: **351, 615.**
1976: **319.**
1978: **436.**
1980: **503** (given), **1185.**
1986: **1428.**
1988: a group of 7 coins acquired on 25 October 1988 from Spink stock at the same time as a portion of the Davidson collection (see above): **629, 655, 673, 679, 685, 702, 714.**
1988: **715.**
1994: **1025, 1222, 1223.**
2007: **1051.**

In addition to retail purchases Lord Stewartby acquired coins advertised in Spink's *Numismatic Circular* (*NCirc*), the earliest noted being in 1965 and the latest in 2006.

1118, 1160, 1170, 1392, 1425, 1426, 1429, 1434.

The last four of these are James VI post-English accession six-shilling pieces, all acquired in May 2001, from an offering of coins in the *Numismatic Circular* from the collection of Roger Shuttlewood (see above).

Two coins passed through the *NCirc* stock and were acquired later by Lord Stewartby.

22, 680.

Lord Stewartby acquired two coins from unnamed Spink auctions.

344, 1374.

Spufford

Professor Peter Spufford (1934–2017), Professor of European History at the University of Cambridge and a numismatic scholar with a special interest in the economy and coinages of the Netherlands in the later Middle Ages. He was a friend of Lord Stewartby and gifted him a plack of James V in 1958.

433.

Stanley Gibbons — A London based dealer in stamps, who periodically dealt in coins, notably in the late 1970s and early 1980s, and bought the coin dealers A. H. Baldwin. One coin was acquired from them in 1975.

1216.

Stoate — William Stoate of Weston-super-Mare, Somerset, a named portion, of Glendining 21 November 1907.

1171.

Strauss — Ronald Strauss (1907–90), was a senior partner at the stockbroking firm Strauss Turnbull in London. He assembled a collection of British gold coins, including Scottish, between the 1950s and 1970s. This collection was sold at Sotheby, 26 May 1994, with the Scottish gold as lots 103 to 144. Lord Stewartby acquired a two-thirds and a one-third lion noble of James VI from this sale.

1049, 1050.

Thellusson — Augustus Thellusson (1862–1931), of St Peter's, Broadstairs, Kent, formed an impressive collection of coins including Scottish, which was sold at Sotheby 19–23 October 1931; the Scottish gold accounted for lots 155 to 166, and silver, lots 343 to 355.

1051.

Thorburn — Philip Thorburn (1900–64), son of the ornithologist, Archibald Thorburn, formed a collection of Scottish coins which was acquired by Baldwin in 1953. Lord Stewartby received from Thorburn a list of priced coins at the time he was disposing of the collection, and acquired a number of coins, all Mary bawbees, direct from him at that time.

658, 661, 691, 707, 741, 780, 793, 799, 804, 819, 826, 833, 845.

Further coins were acquired from him in 1954.

1070, 1314, 1333, 1355, 1407.

In addition to acquiring some coins directly from Thorburn in 1953 and 1954, Lord Stewartby subsequently acquired other coins from this collection via dealers' stock.

26, 431, 626, 1238.

Trampitsch

Armand Trampitsch (1893–?1970), a member of a French brewing family, was a collector since his adolescence. His coins were sold at auction in Monte Carlo and Paris in 1986 and 1988 respectively. The James IV 'Maundy groat' formerly in his collection appeared on the London Market in early 1989 and was acquired by J. E. L Murray, and later bought by Lord Stewartby from her estate.

45.

In a letter to Lord Stewartby (STE/2/7/21) dated 30 January 1989, Joan Murray commented on this acquisition:

'I was very surprised to be offered the James IV bearded bust groat. This is apparently in a collection in France, of which the gold went to auction – no Scottish among the gold, I understand. I might check whether any French hoard seems likely to have contained this groat.'

Villeneuve

Arthur Stanley Villeneuve (1918–91), noted by Lord Stewartby as the vendor of an unnamed portion of Christie's auction 4 December 1984, described as 'A Collection of Scottish Coins.' Lord Stewartby acquired a very rare James IV light coinage half-groat at this sale.

47.

Walters

Frederick Arthur Walters (1849–1931), an architect, living at Temple Ewell, Dover, Kent. He formed two collections, the first (sold in 1913) had no Scottish; the second, sold after his death at Sotheby 24–7 October 1932, included Scottish coins as lots 601 to 676.

33, 34, 358, 359, 367, 369, 383, 397, 405, 407, 412, 520, 879, 925, 938, 948, 955, 1031, 1033, 1039, 1083, 1084, 1101, 1112, 1168, 1198, 1199, 1205, 1211, 1219, 1231, 1240, 1246, 1271, 1279, 1291, 1303, 1304, 1309, 1317, 1318, 1324, 1325, 1376, 1383, 1385.

Westfälische Auktions

Dortmund, Germany, based auctioneers. One coin, a James V crown, was acquired from their Auction 26, 13–16 April 2004, lot 4256.

337.

Whitton	Cuthbert Alexander Whitton (1890–1950), a schoolmaster at Newcastle under Lyme, Staffordshire, and later at Wellingborough, Northamptonshire. The principal part of his collection was acquired by Seaby in 1950. **192, 452.**
Wigan	John Alfred Wigan (1787–1869), a hop merchant of Malling, Kent, who formed a collection of Anglo-Saxon, English and related coins which was inherited by his nephew, Edward Wright Wigan (1823–71), who also formed a collection of Greek and Roman coins. He donated a portion of his collection to the British Museum in 1864 and the remainder of the amalgamated collection was purchased after his death by Rollin and Feuardent in 1872. Three coins, all ex Cochran-Patrick, derive from Wigan. **623, 1188, 1192.**
Wingate	James Wingate (*c.* 1827–77), a marine insurance broker of Glasgow. He wrote *Illustrations of the Coinage of Scotland* (1868), which drew on coins from his collection for the illustrations. He formed an important collection of Scottish coins, sold at Sotheby 29 November–1 December 1875. **9, 1048.**
Winstanley	Edgar Joseph Winstanley (1892–1977), a dentist of Belsize Park, London, later retiring to Deal, Kent. He was primarily a collector of English hammered coins, and his collection was variously dispersed, with portions purchased over a period of time by Baldwin. It appears to have included some Scottish coins, and Lord Stewartby's coins noted as having a Winstanley provenance were most likely purchased from Baldwin, mostly in the period 1974–6. **95, 439, 605, 931, 1035, 1116, 1197, 1340.**

Lord Stewartby notes a date of acquisition for many coins without noting where they were acquired. It is likely that many of these were acquired from Baldwin.

Without source, but with date of acquisition only	*c.* 1946: **977.** 1947: **748.** *c.* 1950: **406, 591, 626, 1008, 1109, 1202.** 1950: **657.**

c. 1951: **1281.**
1954: **579, 1024, 1414.**
1955: **848, 1095, 1336.**
1956: **631, 956, 961, 962, 972, 1411.**
1957: **422, 426, 430, 515, 641, 758, 965, 1015.**
1959: **834.**
'Before 1960': **910.**
1960: **1071, 1163, 1410, 1417.**
1961: **547, 1370.**
1962: **1248.**
c. 1965: **617.**
1965, with many acquired on 13 February: **537, 551, 635, 659, 670, 674, 683, 706, 708, 712, 718, 720, 726, 730, 736, 743, 746, 750, 753, 755, 756, 779, 784, 786, 795, 829, 1077, 1081, 1238, 1356, 1357.**
1966: **1337.**
1967: **590, 1131.**
1968: **431.**
1969: **574, 614, 1067, 1182.**
1970: **475, 543.**
1971: **1059, 1119, 1121, 1390.**
1972: **943.**
1973: **934.**
1974: **1116.**
1975: **562, 573, 575, 581, 582, 584, 585, 589, 593, 594, 605, 607, 608, 609, 623, 925, 928, 931, 938, 942, 944, 945, 947, 948, 953, 955, 959, 963, 967, 968, 970, 971, 973, 974, 979, 984, 1004, 1007, 1013, 1029, 1030, 1031, 1032, 1033, 1035, 1039.**
1976: **417, 439, 677, 698, 719, 749, 751, 752, 757, 770, 772, 785, 875, 889, 1085, 1089, 1136, 1240, 1303, 1376, 1377.**
1989: **460, 640, 664, 665, 769, 788.**
1990: **954.**
1991: **441.**
2000: **561.**

HOARDS AND SINGLE FINDS

Information on coin hoards is in the main drawn from the Metcalf 1977. This has been supplemented by notes and correspondence on specific finds in The Lord Stewartby Scottish Numismatic Archive as well as details given in more recent publications.

'From Mr. J. S. Cole, Coombe Bisett', Salisbury, Wiltshire

A James VI 1601 five-shilling piece, acquired by Lord Stewartby from the finder, in October 1988, was a single find from near Salisbury, Wiltshire.

1228.

'Found in Kent'

A James VI 1604 'thistle' merk, acquired from Seaby on 10 August 1953, is stated as having been 'found in Kent.'

1266.

Kirkcudbright, 1912

Three coins (two James V bawbees and a Mary bawbee), all from the Davidson Collection, are ticketed by him as from the Kirkcudbright hoard. A date of 24 July 1924 – probably of acquisition rather than discovery – is given with one coin. The three coins may derive from a hoard found at Kirkcudbright in 1912 (Metcalf 1977, hoard 217, p. 51), thought to have contained 108 billon and two silver coins, deposited *c.* 1558.

This would appear to be the same hoard as one supposedly found in 1910 and described in a typescript of an article on 'Medieval Coin finds in Dumfries and Galloway' in the Lord Stewartby Scottish Numismatic Archive (STE/2/3/10, author not known, possibly Davidson), which was found at Kirkcudbright, 'under a clay floor in a long close opening off the High Street in a medieval glazed pirlie jug or savings bank'. Stewartby's typescript notes that the hoard contained 130 coins, with billon of James IV (placks, 11), James V (placks, 15, and bawbees, 4) and Mary (placks, 18, bawbees, 13, hardheads, 64, and a penny), along with two Mary testoons and two small billon coins of Francis I. The latest coins noted were first period issues of Mary, suggesting deposition *c.* 1558–60. It is possible that Davidson senior acquired some coins in 1924 from this hoard, which were later acquired by Lord Stewartby:

524, 531, 671.

Three coins, all James IV placks and acquired from Davidson in June 1989, are noted as 'Kirkcudbrightshire find.' One, **87**, has an old nineteenth-century ticket with the coin; another, **121**, is noted as 'Kirkcudbrightshire find 24 July 1924'. It seems likely these also derive from the Kirkcudbright 1912 hoard.

87, 97, 121.

Two further coins, both acquired from Davidson; the first, a Mary first period testoon, July 1987, noted found Kirkcudbright; the second, a Mary bawbee, on 25 October 1988, noted found at Kirkcudbright' may also derive from the Kirkcudbright 1912 hoard.

571, 778.

'found at Lincluden Abbey, Dumfries' — A Mary first period type II penny, acquired from Davidson on 3 June 1989, and noted as having been found at this location. This would appear to be a single find, with no date of discovery stated, but probably acquired locally by Davidson's father in the first half of the twentieth-century.

853.

Linlithgow, 1963 — Two coins, one a later type of James IV, the second a plack of James V, are stated by Lord Stewartby as 'ex Linlithgow hoard'. Neither has a source of acquisition, but both were acquired on 31 May 1970. Two hoards are known from Linlithgow, one found in the 1930s and another in 1963. No details are known regarding the exact date and find location of the 1930s hoard, but coins acquired by the NMS in 1994, indicate it certainly contained billon coins from the reigns of James IV, V and Mary. The 1963 hoard was never fully published, but is known to have comprised ten silver and 368 billon coins from the reigns of James III, IV and V (Holmes 2006, p. 48). With both hoards containing billon coins of these kings, it is uncertain from which the two coins derive. Their acquisition together a few years after the discovery of the 1963 hoard suggests they may derive from the more recent find (Metcalf 1977, hoard 208, p. 50), rather than the 1930s hoard.

163, 475.

Mauchline (Netherplace House), Ayrshire

Deposited *c.* 1520, this hoard contained English (45 groats and half-groats the latest of Henry VIII) and Scottish silver coins (49 coins the latest of James IV), as well as a small group of billon coins, the latest a plack of James V. Five coins are stated to derive from this find, all coins of James IV: a plack, three type IV pence and a counterfeit type IV penny (Metcalf 1977, hoard 205, p. 49).

98, 295, 296, 297, 324.

Nederhemert, Netherlands (1966)

Found in early June 1966 by some children playing with a ball near a recently demolished house below Nederhemert (in the parish of Kerkwijk). The hoard contained 37 gold coins in a small pot which broke on recovery. The coins dated from the end of the fifteenth century to the mid-sixteenth, the latest to 1569. The hoard contained one Scottish coin, with the remainder being from the Spanish Netherlands (11); France (4); German Empire (1); Switzerland (2); Italy (17); and Spain (1) (J. Schulman, 1965–6, pp. 60–2). The coins were dispersed in a Schulman sale in 1966. One coin derived from this hoard was acquired by Lord Stewartby with other coins from the estate of Joan Murray in 1997. It is not known how Joan Murray acquired this coin.

1.

Rigghead, Collin, Dumfriesshire, (1963)

Found by Eric Beck on 6 August 1963 in a sand quarry at Rigghead in the parish of Torthorwald, Dumfries (STE/2/3/10). The hoard was contained in a narrow-necked globular jug within which there were coins and a small horn which may have acted as a purse. It comprised 10 gold, 134 silver and in excess of 374 billon coins predominantly of James V and Mary (Metcalf 1977, hoard 210, p. 50).

A detailed listing of the content of the Rigghead hoard is also given in Lord Stewartby's typescript paper on 'Medieval coin finds in Dumfries and Galloway' (STE/2/3/10) in the Lord Stewartby Scottish Numismatic Archive. This notes that it contained 14 gold coins (1 Mary, 13 French); 132 silver (Henry VIII, 89 groats and 21 half groats; James V, 19 groats and 5 third-groats); and 360 billon coins (23 placks, James III to V; 336 bawbees - James V, 127, Mary, Edinburgh, 197; Mary, Stirling, 12; and one half-bawbee of Mary).

13 James V bawbees in the Stewartby collection derive from this hoard, along with 16 Mary bawbees (no halves). The latest Mary bawbee is a group 4, and no Stirling bawbees in the Stewartby collection derive from this hoard. All coins listed from this hoard were acquired by Lord Stewartby in 1965 from an unspecified source. It seems likely he may have acquired a parcel of coins from the Rigghead hoard at this time.

491, 492, 493, 494, 504, 506, 513, 518, 519, 521, 529, 530, 532, 627, 628, 632, 633, 637, 638, 639, 660, 663, 696, 697, 710, 711, 713, 717, 774.

'*c.* 1972, Spink Hoard'

A James IV plack is noted as having been acquired '*c.* 1972, ex Spink hoard.' This suggests Spink acquired a hoard, or a parcel of coins from a hoard, containing billon coins at around this time and that Lord Stewartby acquired this coin through them. No other details are known.

66.

ABBREVIATIONS AND BIBLIOGRAPHY

ABBREVIATIONS

Acq.	Acquired.
B.	Burns reference number by type and variety from E. Burns, *The Coinage of Scotland*, 3 vols. (Edinburgh, 1887). B. references are stated by illustrated type example followed by the variety the coin matches e.g. B.775.4, is the type illustrated at fig. 775, and the variety the coin matches number 4 as itemised in his catalogue (vol. 2).
BNJ	*British Numismatic Journal.*
Bt	Bought.
cts	carats.
C-P	Cochran-Patrick 1876.
g.	grams.
gr.	grains.
HSAN	Hunterian Stewartby Accession Number, the unique reference number assigned by the Hunterian. Coins from the Stewartby collection are ordered and stored according to these numbers. Numbering of the silver and billon up to 2223 (James III) was undertaken by Lord Stewartby himself. Numbering from James IV onwards and the gold was undertaken by the Hunterian. Lord Stewartby's numbering of the earlier coins has been retained by the Hunterian and extended across the later silver, billon and copper as well as the gold. The resulting HSAN is noted against each coin in this Sylloge where the ordering starts at 1. Attribution errors in the HSAN sequencing means that the ordering of this Sylloge does not run parallel with the HSAN sequencing.
i.m.	initial mark, a symbol that usually appears at the start of the legend.
NC	Numismatic Chronicle.
NCirc	Spink's Numismatic Circular.
NMAS	National Museum of Antiquities of Scotland.
NNP	Newman Numismatic Portal (nnp.wustl.edu), Washington University in St Louis, USA.
PSAS	*Proceedings of the Society of Antiquaries of Scotland.*
Q	a quarter as defined by the arms of a cross, where q1 is upper left; q2 is upper right; q3 is lower right; q4 is lower left.

S.	Spink Standard catalogue reference number from *Standard Catalogue of British Coins. Volume 2: Coins of Scotland, Ireland and the Islands*, 3rd ed., (London, 2015).
SCBI	Sylloge of Coins of the British Isles.
STE	The Achival title by which the Lord Stewartby Scottish Numismatic Archive is arranged at the Hunterian Museum.

BIBLIOGRAPHY

Archibald and Cook 2020 — M. Archibald and B. Cook, 'The palm-tree ryal of Mary Queen of Scots revisited,' *BNJ* 90 (2020), 165–82.

Bateson and Mayhew 1987 — J. D. Bateson and N. J. Mayhew, *Scottish Coins in the Ashmolean Museum Oxford and Hunterian Museum, Glasgow*, SCBI 35 (London, 1987).

Bateson 1997 — J. D. Bateson, *Coinage in Scotland* (London, 1997).

Bateson 2019 — J. D. Bateson, 'Ian Stewart', *Biographical Memoirs of Fellows of the British Academy* XVIII (London, 2019), 217–49.

Burns 1887 — E. Burns, *The Coinage of Scotland*, 3 vols. (Edinburgh, 1887).

Cochran-Patrick 1876 — R. W. Cochran-Patrick, *Records of the Coinage of Scotland*, 2 vols (Edinburgh, 1876).

Eaglen, Pagan and Mitchell 2001 — R. J. Eaglen, H. E. Pagan and P. D. Mitchell, 'Coin tickets in the British hammered series', *BNJ* 71 (2001), 136–57.

Holmes 1998a — N. M. McQ. Holmes, *Scottish Coins: a History of small change in Scotland* (Edinburgh, 1998).

Holmes 1998b — N. M. McQ. Holmes, 'Scottish coin hoards, 1996–7' *BNJ* 68 (1998), 77–94.

Holmes 2006 — N. M. McQ. Holmes, *Scottish Coins in the National Museums of Scotland, Edinburgh, part I, 1526–1603*, SCBI 58 (London, 2006).

Kerr 1948 — R. Kerr, 'The forty-shilling piece of James VI of Scotland', *NC*, 6th series, 8 (1948), 104

Manville and Robertson 1986 — H. E. Manville and T. J. Robertson, *British Numismatic Auction Catalogues 1710–1984* (Oxford, 1986).

Manville 2009 — H. E. Manville, *Biographical Dictionary of British and Irish Numismatics* (London, 2009).

Metcalf 1977 — D. M. Metcalf, 'The evidence of Scottish coin hoards for monetary history', in *Coinage in Medieval Scotland*, ed. D. M. Metcalf, British Archaeological Reports, British Series 45 (Oxford, 1977), 1–59.

Murray, J. E. L. 1971 — J. E. L. Murray, 'The Early Unicorns and heavy groats of James III and IV' *BNJ* 40 (1971), 62–96.

Murray, J. E. L. 1972 — 'The Mauchline (Ayrshire) hoard', unpublished paper read to the British Numismatic Society, 25 January 1972.

Murray, J. E. L. 1979 — J. E. L. Murray, 'The first gold coinage of Mary, Queen of Scots', *BNJ* 49 (1979), 82–6.

Murray, J. E. L. 1987 — J. E. L. Murray, 'The coinage of the Marians in Edinburgh Castle in 1572', *BNJ* 57 (1987), 47–52.

Murray and Murray 1980 — J. E. L. Murray and J. K. R. Murray, 'Notes on the *Vicit Leo* testoons of Mary, Queen of Scots', *BNJ* 50 (1980), 81–91.

Murray, J. K. R. 1966a — J. K. R. Murray, 'The Stirling bawbees of Mary, Queen of Scots', *NCirc* Dec. 1966, 306.

Murray, J. K. R. 1966b — J. K. R. Murray, 'Two Scottish re-used dies', *NCirc* April 1966, 94.

Murray, J. K. R. 1967 — J. K. R. Murray, 'The Scottish Coinage of 1560–61', *NCirc* April 1967, 95–6.

Murray, J. K. R. 1968a — J. K. R. Murray, 'The Scottish Coinage of 1553', *BNJ* 37 (1968), 98–109.

Murray, J. K. R. 1968b — J. K. R. Murray, 'A further note on the forty-shilling piece of James VI of Scotland', *NC* 128 (1968), 161–7.

Murray, J. K. R. 1968c — J. K. R. Murray, 'The Stirling bawbees of Mary, Queen of Scots', *NCirc* Sept. 1968, 265.

Murray, J. K. R. 1969 — J. K. R. Murray, 'The gold forty-shilling piece of James VI of Scotland', *BNJ* 38 (1969), 193–4.

Murray, J. K. R. 1972 — J. K. R. Murray, 'The billon coinages of James VI of Scotland', *NC* 132 (1972), 177–82.

Murray, J. K. R. 1979 — J. K. R. Murray, 'The Scottish gold coinage of 1555–8', *NC* 139 (1979), 155–64.

Murray, J. K. R. 1981 — J. K. R. Murray, 'The Scottish testoons', *NCirc* 89 (December 1981), 397.

Rampling and Murray 1989 — D. J. Rampling and J. E. L. Murray, 'The coinage of the Marians in Edinburgh Castle in 1572 – an addendum', *BNJ* 59 (1989), 213.

Spencer 2002 — P. D. Spencer, 'The source for the portrait on the 1561–62 testoons and half-testoons of Mary, Queen of Scots', *NCirc* 110 (February 2002), 14–17.

Spink and Son — *Standard Catalogue of British Coins. Volume 2: Coins of Scotland, Ireland and the Islands*, 3rd ed., (London, 2015).

STE — The Lord Stewartby Scottish Numismatic Archive (at the Hunterian, University of Glasgow).

Stevenson 1989 — R. B. K. Stevenson, 'The bawbee issues of James V and Mary', *BNJ* 59 (1989), 120–56.

Stevenson 1991 — R. B. K. Stevenson, 'The groat coinage of James V', *BNJ* 61 (1991), 37–56.

Stewart 1953 — I. H. Stewart, 'The heavy silver Coinage of James III and James IV', *BNJ* 27 (1953), 182–94.

Stewart 1962 — I. H. Stewart, 'The maundy of King James IV', *The Stewarts* 9 (1962), 138–41.

Stewart 1966 — I. H. Stewart, 'Some Scottish ceremonial coins', *PSAS* 98 (1964–6), 254–75.

Stewart 1967 — I. H. Stewart, *The Scottish Coinage,* rev. ed. (London, 1967).

Stewart 1982 — I. H. Stewart, 'Two centuries of Scottish numismatics', in *The Scottish Antiquarian Tradition*, ed. A.S.Bell (Edinburgh, 1982), 227–65.

Stewart 1983 — I. H. Stewart, 'Coinage and propaganda: an interpretation of the coin types of James VI', in *The Stone Age to the Forty-Five: Studies Presented to R. B. K. Stevenson*, ed. A. O. Connor and D. V. Clarke (Edinburgh, 1983), 452–64.

Stewart 1986 — I. H. Stewart, 'Obituary of Lieutenant-Colonel J. K. R. Murray with list of published works', *BNJ* 56 (1986), 202–4.

Stewartby 1992	Lord Stewartby, 'The Wingate sale of 1875', *BNJ* 62 (1992), 175–84.
Stewartby 1995	Lord Stewartby, 'Robert B. K. Stevenson, 1913–1993: a numismatic appreciation', *BNJ* 65 (1995), 202–13.
Stewartby 1996	Lord Stewartby, 'Scottish coin collectors', *BNJ* 66 (1996), pp. 87–117.
Stewartby 1997a	Lord Stewartby, 'The Scottish thirty shilling piece dated 1581', *NC* 157 (1997), 209–11.
Stewartby 1997b	Lord Stewartby, 'Obituary of Mrs J. E. L. Murray', *BNJ* 67 (1997), 162–7.
Stewartby 2003	Lord Stewartby, 'John Gloag Murdoch, 1830–1902', *BNJ* 73 (2003), 186–90.
Stewartby and Stewartby 2007	Lord Stewartby and Lady Stewartby, 'Mary Stuart, the tortoise and the palm-tree,' *The Stewarts* 22.4 (2007), 224–8.
Stewartby and Holmes 2008	Lord Stewartby and N. M. McQ. Holmes, 'The 1533 issue of James V Placks', *BNJ* 78 (2008), 246–7.
Wingate 1868	J. Wingate, *Illustrations of the Coinage of Scotland* (Glasgow, 1868).

ARRANGEMENT AND ORDERING OF THE CATALOGUE

The coinages of James IV, V and VI are ordered here by metal: gold, silver and billon, arranged by chronological sequence of issue and then by denomination in descending value. The coinages of James VI from before and after his English accession are listed separately. The coinage of Mary is ordered using the traditional divisions, as used in other SCBI volumes, into the five periods that reflect her marital status: first period, before marriage (1542–58); second period, marriage to Francis (1558–60); third period, first widowhood (1560–5); fourth period, marriage to Darnley (1565–7); and fifth period, second widowhood (1567). Within each period coins are ordered by metal, gold, silver and billon, and within each metal by denomination in descending order of value and by date in chronological sequence.

Coins are arranged by Stewart (1967) types and varieties. Subdivisions reflecting those of Stevenson are applied for the bawbees of Mary, as noted by Lord Stewartby. Each gold and silver coin is referenced according to Burns, but the Burns reference is noted only against the type or denomination for the billon and copper, as typological attribution of each billon coin is not possible given their varied preservation. The relevant entry in the readily accessible *Standard Catalogue of British Coins* (London, 2015) is given for each coin type or, where applicable, variety.

Each entry uses a standard format. The first four columns from left to right, state the number of the coin in the Sylloge ordering; the weight of the coin in grams; the weight of the coin in grains, and the die axis. Where an issue carries several dates, the year appearing on the coin is noted in a fifth column. Instances of the date differing between obverse and reverse (as on first and second period testoons) are noted where necessary. A date is not stated if the issue was only struck in one year.

Any variations in initial marks, legends and stops from the description at the head of each type, variety or section, are noted. The description notes any references for the coin, along with information on acquisition, and any previously known provenance. Provenances are those noted by Lord Stewartby with the coin. These have been verified, with corrections or deletions where appropriate. For each coin the Hunterian Stewartby Accession Number (HSAN) is noted at the end of the description. This number is the sequence in which the coins are arranged at the Hunterian. One sequence covers all the gold (4744 to 4863) and another (1 to 4743), the silver, billon and copper coins, Alexander III to William and Mary, 1280–1694. The crescent and pellet coins of William I, as the sole surviving part of the pre-1280 holdings not lost to the burglaries, are arranged according to a different scheme, numbered 4865–5007 (included within this portion is a single *Short Cross* penny of Henry II of England).

PLATES

JAMES IV (1488–1513)

GOLD COINAGE

Unicorn

Theoretical weight 3.82g, 59 gr: value 18 shillings Scots, struck at 21 cts or less.

i.m. lis both sides. Obv. **IACOBVS . DEI . GRACIA : REX : SCOTORV**, chained unicorn left, crown on neck, grasping shield bearing lion rampant. Rev. **EXVRGAT DEVS ET DISSIPENTVR INIMICI EIVS**, six-point radiant star extending from central pellet over long-cross fleury.

Note: the symbol / within the obverse legend denotes the point at which the legend in broken by the horn of the unicorn.

Transitional James III/IV. Obv. crown with three lis as James IV type Ib. Rev. as James III Ia.

	Weight g.	gr.	Die Axis	
1	3.41	52.6	270	i.m. lis. Obv. six-point star stops, **IACOBVS : DEI . GRACIA : REX : S ./ COTR**, three lis crown. Rev. five-point star stops, **EXVRGAT : DE : ET : DISIPENT . NIMICI E :**, roman **N** (Stewart James III I/II; B. - / B.632.10 var.; Murray James IV Ib/James III Ia; S.5362/3515). Acq. 1998, ex J. E. L. Murray; ex Nederhemert (HSAN 4780).

Type I. *c. 1488–c. 1496*

i.m. lis both sides. Obv. crown with three lis on neck of unicorn, lombardic N.

Ic, with broken five-point or six-point star stops.

2	3.74	57.7	180	Five-point broken star stops. Obv. **ICOBVS : DEI : GRACIA : REX : SCO / TOV**. Rev. **EXVRGAT : DS : ET : DISIPENT . INIMICI : ES**, lombardic **N** (Stewart Ib; B.-; Murray Ic; S.5315). Acq. 1998, ex J. E. L. Murray (HSAN 4782).
3	3.77	58.2	180	Six-point star stops. Obv. **IACOBVS : DEI : GRACIA : REX : S . / . COTR**. Rev. **EXVRGAT : DES : ET : DIPENT : NIMICI EI**, lombardic **N** (Stewart James III, I: B.627.5; Murray Ic; S.5315). Bt Spink, 12 May 1961 (HSAN 4788).

Id, with v shaped stops.

4	3.68	57.1	360	Obv. **IACOBVS : DEI : GRACIA : REX : SCT / ORV**. Rev. **EXVRGAT : DES : ET : DISIPENT . INI**, lombardic **N** (Stewart Ia; B.659.1; Murray Id; S.5315). Bt Baldwin, 1963 (HSAN 4781).

Type II, *c. 1496–c. 1512*

i.m. cross potent. Obv. crown with five lis on neck of unicorn.

IIa, with pellet stops.

5	3.71	57.3	180	Obv. **IACOBVS : DEI : GRACIA : REX : SCOTORV**. Rev. **EXVRGAT : DEVS . DISIPENTVR** [..]**INI**[.]**I EIVS** (Stewart IIa; B.680.5; S.5317). Acq. 1998, ex J. E. L. Murray; noted ex Sotheby, 20 February 1974, evidence of mounting (HSAN 4783).

IId, with lis stops one or both sides.

6	3.78	58.4	90	Pellet stops. Obv. **IACOBVS : DEI . GRACIA : REX . SCOTORV**. Rev. lis stops, **EXVRGA . T . DEVS . DISSIPET . INIMICI . EI, T** in **EXVRGAT** over-struck with lis to left of vertical, pellet above stop after **DISSIPET** (Stewart IIb; B.688.8a; S.5317). Acq. 1998, ex J. E. L. Murray; ex Dundee lot 86, a IIa/ IId mule (HSAN 4784).
7	3.47	53.6	360	Lis stops both sides. Obv. **IACOBVS . DEI . GRA . REX . SCOTORVM, E** in **REX** struck over an uncertain symbol. Rev. i.m. cross fleury, **EXVRGAT . DEVS . DISSIPENT . IIMICI . EIV** (Stewart IId; B.687 .7b; S.5317). Acq. 1998, ex J. E. L. Murray, acq. 1980 (HSAN 4785).

PLATE 1

1 2 3 4 5

6 7 8 9 10

11 12 13 13a 14 15

	Weight g.	gr.	Die Axis	
8	3.83	59.1	270	Lis stops both sides. Obv. IACOBVS . DEI . GRA . REX . SCOTORVM. Rev. EXVRGAT . DEVS . DISSIPET . INIMICI . E. Bt. Spink, March 1990; ex Davidson (Stewart IId; B.687.7a; S.5317). Same reverse die as Lockett II lot 872 (HSAN 4786).

Type III, *c. 1512–13*

i.m. crown obverse only. Obv. crown with five lis on neck of unicorn, without chain, roman letters, 4 after IACOBVS, pellet and five-point star stops.

9	3.79	58.5	180	Obv. * IACOBVS 4 : DEI * GRA * REX * SCOTO / RVM .. Rev. two joined broken stars before legend, *EXVRGAT * DEVS Z DISIPENT . INIMICI * EIV * (B.699 .11; S.5319). Ex Butterfield, lot 12; ex Hird lot 48; ex Bearman; ex Murdoch lot 155; ex Richardson; ex Addington; ex Wingate lot 192 (HSAN 4787).

Half-unicorn

Theoretical weight 1.91 g, 29.5 gr: value 9 shillings Scots.

As type I unicorn.

Type Ia.

i.m. lis, no stops both sides or star stops, with roman letter N.

10	1.90	29.9	90	No stops both sides. Obv. IACOBVS DEI GRCIA REX S / COTOR. Rev. EXVRGAT DE Z DISIPENT NIMICI (Stewart James III, II; B.635.5; Murray Ib; S.5321). Acq. 1998, ex J. E. L. Murray; ex Glendining, 30 March 1983, lot 9 (HSAN 4789).
11	1.71	26.4	160	No stops. [..]COBVS DEI GRACI[..]. Rev. six-point star stops, EXVRGAT. DISIPENTVR[..]IMICI : E ˙ (Stewart James III, II; B. -; Murray Ib; S.5321). Acq. 9 December 1957; ex Cochran-Patrick (1957) lot 142. Same dies as Murdoch, lot 145 (now NMAS) (HSAN 4790).

i.m. cross potent/lis, v-shaped stops, with lombardic letter N.

12	1.76	27.1	270	i.m. cross potent /lis, v stops both sides, Obv. IACOBVS : DEI . GRACIA : R / EX : SCT. Rev. EXVRGAT . D . S . ET . DISIPENTVR IN (Stewart Ia; B.660.1; Murray Id; S.5322). Acq. 1998, ex J. E. L. Murray. Holed. Obverse die type Id with altered i.m. (?) (HSAN 4793).

Type Ib

With lombardic letter N, i.m. lis, no stops or star stops

13	1.44	22.2	360	No stops both sides. Obv. IACOBVS DIE GRACIA REX SC / OTR. Rev. EXVRGAT DEVS ET DISIPENTV IN, inverted N (B.- ; Murray Ib; Stewart -; S.5322). Acq. 1998, ex J. E. L. Murray (HSAN 4791).
13A	1.70	26.3	180	Six point star stops both sides. Obv. IACOBVS . DEI . GRACIAS : RE / X : SCOT, large ring on chain, rev. EXVRGAT . DE : ET : DISIPENT[..]N . E. Acq. 1998, ex J. E. L Murray. Ex Bute, lot 162 (B.633 (2); Murray Ib; S.5322) (HSAN 4794).

Type Ic

With lombardic letter N. i.m. colon of two broken stars, no stops.

14	1.82	28.1	30	i.m. two broken stars, no stops both sides. Obv. IACOBVS DEI GRACIA REX / SCO. Rev. EXVRGAT DS ET DISIPT INIMI E (Stewart, James IV Ic; B.663.4; Murray Ic; S.5322). Bt Baldwin, 1960 (HSAN 4792).

Type III, *c. 1512–13*

James IV/V

i.m. crown both sides, roman letters. Obv. without chain, three points on crown at unicorn's neck, annulet below unicorn.

15	1.90	29.3	340	Obv. . IACOBVS DEI : GRACIA . REX . SCOTOR / VM : * :, inverted S in IACOBVS, pellet stops. Rev. . FXVGAT : DFVS . FT . DISIPPNT . INIMICI . FIVS * (B.735.1; S.5324). Acq. 1998, ex J. E. L. Murray; ex Stack, 29 April–1 May 1987, lot 1864; ex Bute, lot 174 (HSAN 4795).

GOLD *(cont.)*

Lion or crown, after c. 1496

Theoretical weight 3.39 g, 52.25 gr: value 13 shillings and 4 pence Scots.

Type II.

i.m. crown both sides, star stops both sides, lombardic-lettering. Obv. IACOBVS DEI GRA REX SCOTTORVM IIII, crowned shield bearing lion rampant, lis each side. Rev. SALVVM FAC POPVLVM TVVM DOMINE, St Andrew facing crucified on saltire cross, lis each side.

	Weight g.	gr.	Die Axis	
16	3.28	50.6	270	Rev. SA | LVVM . FAC| PPLV |V . TVVM DNE' . (Stewart II; B.673.1; S.5326). Ex Douglas lot 275; ex Hird lot 56; ex Brand (HSAN 4796).

SILVER COINAGE

Heavy coinage, *c. 1488–c. 1496*

Groat

Type I, *c. 1489–90*

Theoretical weight 3.05 g, 47.12 gr: value 1 shilling and 2 pence Scots.

i.m. cross fleury, rarely cross patonce with cross pattée, annulet colon stops both sides. Obv. facing crowned bust with bare shoulders, small crown with five fleurs, within unbroken tressure of twelve arcs, a lis on cusps at sides and above bust, IACOBVS : Q : DI : GRA : REX : SCOTOR, old Arabic numeral 4 after name. Rev. outer-circle, DNS : PROTECTOR : MEVM : ET MEVOR, this abbreviated, and VIL | LAE | DIN | BRVG, long-cross, crown and trefoil of pellets with added annulet, in alternate angles.

Type Ib, *With unbroken tressure, annulet stops*

17	2.89	44.6	45	i.m. cross pattée with cross patonce/cross fleury. Rev. DNS : P | ROTECT | OR MEO .: | [.]VMTO, crown q1 and 3 (Stewart Ib; B. 652 var. ; Murray B; S.5331). Ex Glendining 16–17 May 1973, lot 576 (part) (HSAN 2424).
18	3.08	47.5	225	i.m. cross fleury both sides. Rev. [D]NS : P | ROCTO : | RMEVM | ET MEV, crown q2 and 4 (Stewart Ib; B.652 var.; Murray B; S.5331). Bt Spink, 24 July 1987; ex Davidson; ex Dakers, lot 426; ex Cochran-Patrick (1936), lot 226 (HSAN 2425).

Type II. *c. 1490–c. 1496*

Theoretical weight 3.08 g, 47.5 gr: value 1 shilling and 2 pence Scots.

i.m. cross fleury, six-point star stops. Obv. facing crowned bust within tressure, IACOBVS : DEI : GRACIA : REX SCOT :. Rev. i.m. DOMINVS PROTECTOR MEVS ET LIBERATOR MEVS abbreviated, i.m. VILLA EDINBRVG, pellets with annulet in two quarters, a crown and a lis in the others.

IIa. *With unbroken tressure*

Obv. Crown with five fleurs, as type I, tressure of twelve arcs unbroken by bare shoulders, thin cheeks, trefoils on cusps at sides and above bust, with annulet on breast.

19	2.96	45.7	180	Obv. REX : COT :. Rev. DNS : P | ROTOR M | EVM ET | MEVOR :, E : | DIN | BRVG, pellets q1 and 3, lis q2, crown, q4 (B.62; S.5332). Bt Baldwin, 1976; ex F. Baldwin (HSAN 2428).
20	3.03	46.8	290	Obv. REX : COT :. Rev. DNS : P | ROTOR M | EVM ET | MEVOR :, E . | DIN | BRVG, pellets q2 and 4, lis q1, crown q3 (B.623; S.5332). Acq. 14 April 1955; ex Bute, lot 230 (HSAN 2431).

IIb. *With broken tressure*

Obv. Crown with three fleurs, tressure broken by draped shoulders, without annulet on breast, six-point star stops (S.5333).

PLATE 2

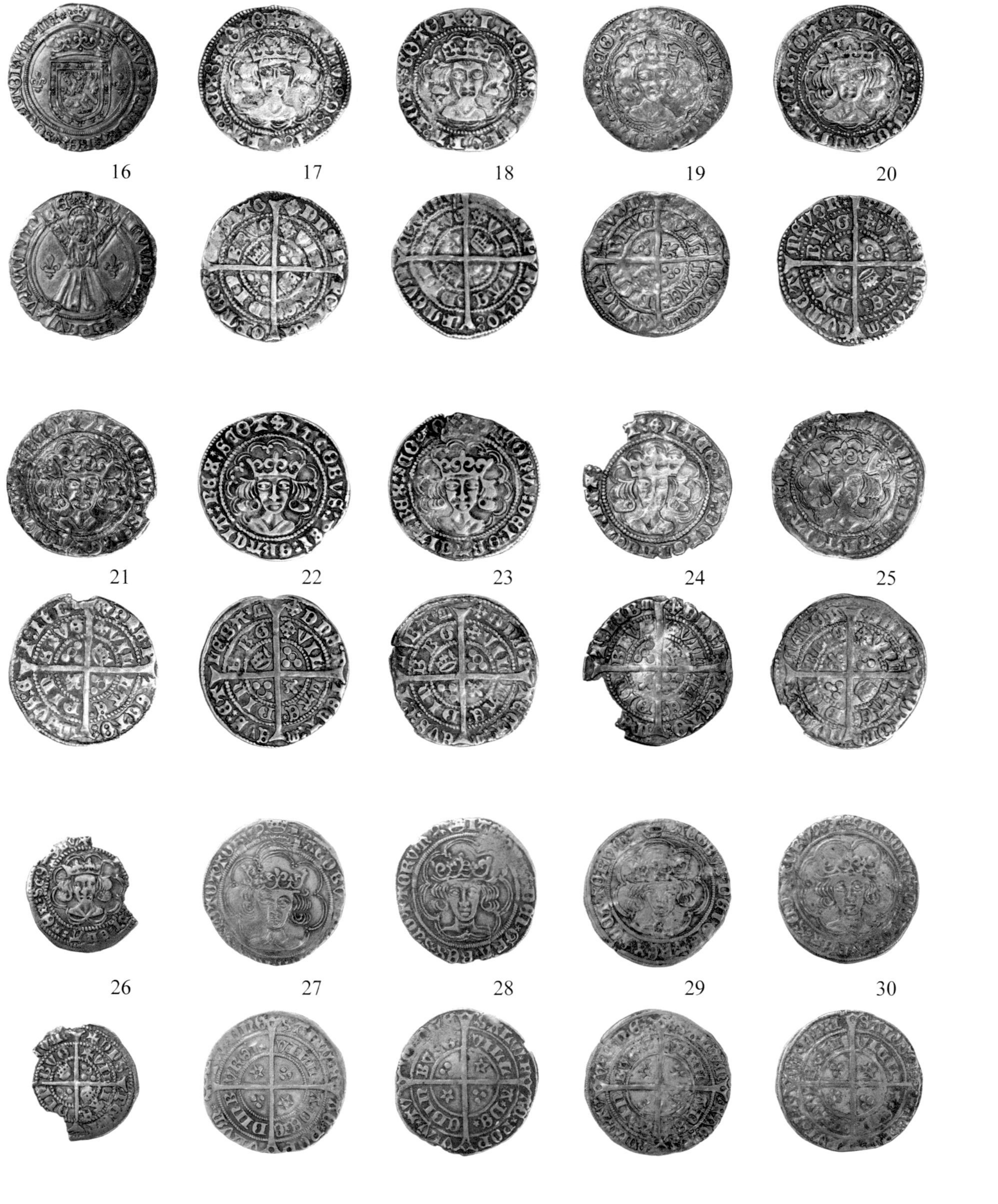

16 17 18 19 20 21 22 23 24 25 26 27 28 29 30

Plate 2 (*cont.*)

Obv. tressure of twelve arcs, trefoil on cusps above and at sides.

	Weight g.	gr.	Die Axis	
21	2.91	44.9	270	Rev. DNS : P | TECTO : | MEVS : E | T : LEB ., E . | DIN | BRVG, pellets q1 and 3, crown q2, lis q4 (B.624; S.5333). Bt. Spink, 1965; ex Marr (HSAN 2432).
22	3.04	46.9	225	Rev. DNS . P | TECT : M | EVS : ET | LEBA . M, pellets, q2 and 4, lis q3, crown q1, E . | DIN | BRG (cf. B.624; S.5333). Bt. Spink, 24 July 1987; ex Davidson); ex *NCirc.* August 1936, item 54516a; ex Cochran-Patrick (1936), lot 219 (HSAN 2433).

Obv. tressure of twelve arcs, lis on cusp each side of crown, star on two cusps by hair.

23	2.64	40.7	100	Obv. REX : SCOTO :. Rev. DNS : P | TECT : M | EVS : ET | LIBA . M, pellets q2 and 4, crown q1, lis q3, VIL | LA E . | DIN | BRG (B.626; S.5333). Ex Macfarlan (HSAN 2429).

Obv. tressure of ten arcs, plain cusps.

24	2.66	41.0	200	Obv. GRACEA, REX : [SCO]T :. Rev. DNS : P | TECTO : | ME[.] | T : LEB M, pellets q1 and 3, lis q4, crown q2 (B.626A; S.5333). Acq. 18 September 1970; ex Cochran-Patrick (1957), lot 143 (part) (HSAN 2427).

Obv. tressure of ten arcs, lis on cusp each side of crown, star on two cusps each side of hair.

25	2.82	43.5	140	Obv. IACOBVS : DEI . GRACIA : REX : SCOT :. Rev. DNS . P | ROTOR M | EVM ET | MEVOR, E : | DIN | BRVG, pellets q2 and 4, crown, q3, lis q1 (B.626; S.5334). Acq. 26 March 1956 (HSAN 2430).

Half-groat

Theoretical weight 1.52 g, 23.5 gr: value 7 pence Scots.

i.m. cross pattée/cross pattée, pellet stops. Obv. crowned facing bust with draped shoulders, crown with four fleurs, within unbroken tressure, nine arcs, IACOBVS : DI : GRA : REX : SCOTORV : with or without numeral **4** or Q at end of legend. Rev. DNS : PROTECTOR : MEVM : ET MEVOR, this abbreviated.

Type Ib, *c. 1489–90*

Obv. tressure of nine arcs, without numeral at end of obverse legend.

26	1.15	17.7	20	Obv. pellet stops. Rev. no stops, DNS | PROT | [....]EVM, E | DIN | BVG, crowns q1 and 3 (Stewart -; B.653; S.5336). Acq. 12 June 1956; ex R. C. Carlyon-Britton; ex Thorburn; ex Brushfield, lot 50 (HSAN 2426).

Light coinage, *c. 1496–1513*

Groat

Theoretical weight 2.53 g, 39.12 gr: value 12 pence Scots.

Type III.

i.m. crown obverse only. Obv. crowned facing bust within unbroken tressure, IACOBVS : DEI : GRA : REX : SCOTORVM :, with or without numeral. Rev. SALVVM . FAC . POPVLVM . TVVM . DOMINE . legend abbreviated, long-cross, pellets and mullets in alternate quarters, VILLA EDINBVRG.

Type IIIa. *With old Arabic* 4 *at end of obverse legend*

Obv. IACOBVS DEI GRA REX SCOTTORVM 4, without stars by neck, small trefoil on all cusps. Rev. VILLA DE EDINBVRG.

Six-point star stops. Obv. tressure of seven arcs.

27	2.47	38.1	330	Obv. no stops, SCOTOTORV 4. Rev. SALVV . F | AC . POP | VLVM . | TVV . DNE, DE . E | DINB | VRGI ., pellets, q2 and 4, mullets q1 and 3 (Stewart IIIa; cf. B. 657A; S.5338). Acq. 1998, ex J. E. L. Murray; acq. Spink, November 1977; ex Chown. Double struck on obverse, noted by Lord Stewartby as with early style hair (HSAN 2447).

Five-point star stops. Obv. tressure of seven arcs.

	Weight g.	gr.	Die Axis	
28	2.26	34.9	350	Rev. : **SALVV . F | AC . POP | VLV . TV | VM . DNE**, pellets q1 and 3, mullets q2 and 4 (Stewart IIIa; B.657A; S.5338). Bt. Spink, 1965; ex Marr (HSAN 2448).
29	2.50	38.6	210	Rev. . **SALVVM | . FAC . PO | PVLV . TV | V . DNE .**, **DE : | EDIN | BVRG**, pellets q2 and 4, mullets q1 and 3 (Stewart IIIa; B.657A; S.5338). Acq. 18 August 1967. Same dies as DNW 7 October 2004, lot 796 (HSAN 2449).

Five-point star stops. Obv. tressure of eight arcs, small trefoil on cusps at sides and below only. Rev. **VILLA EDINBVRG**.

30	2.39	36.9	280	Obv. **REX . SCOTTORV 4 .**. Rev. **SALVVM . | FAC . PO | PVLV . T | V . DNE**, pellets q1 and 3, mullets q2 and 4, **VILL | A . EDI | NBVV | RGII** (Stewart IIIa; B. 657: S.5338). Acq. 1998, ex J. E. L. Murray (HSAN 2450).

SILVER. Light coinage *(cont.)*

Groats. Type III (cont.)

Type IIIb. *Without* QRT, QT, QR, IIII *or old Arabic* 4, *without stars by neck*

v stops. Obv. tressure of nine arcs, lis on cusps.

	Weight g.	gr.	Die Axis	
31	2.27	35.0	90	Obv. . IACOBVS :, SCOTTORVM :. Rev. SALVV . | FAC . P. | OPVL. | TVV . D :, pellets q1 and 3, mullets q2 and 4, ED. | IN . B | V . RG . (Stewart IIIb; B.658.5 - same rev. die; S.5337). Bt Spink, 28 July 1987; ex Davidson; ex Lockett II, lot 876; ex Dakers, lot 429 (part) (HSAN 2434).

Six-point star stops. Obv. tressure of seven arcs, small trefoil on cusps and within arc above central fleur of crown. Rev. VILLA DE EDINBVRG.

32	2.35	36.3	170	Obv. SCOTTORVM. Rev. . SALVVM | . FAC . PO | PVLV . TV | V . DNE .., pellets q2 and 4, mullets q1 and 3, .VILL | A . DE . | EDIN | BVRG (Stewart IIIb; B. -; S.5337). Exchange with J. E. L Murray, no date stated, with old French dealers ticket (HSAN 2451).

Type IIIc. *With* QRA

Six-point star stops both sides. Obv. tressure of seven arcs, small trefoils on cusps at sides and below, without stars by neck, IACOBVS . DEI . GRA . REX . SCOTTORV . QRA (or QRT). Rev. VILLA EDINBVRGE.

33	2.56	39.5	150	Obv. . QRA. Rev. SALVV | FAC : PO | PVLVT | VV. DNE, stop after FAC a semi-colon. Rev. . ED | INBV | RGE ., pellets q1 and 3, mullets q2 and 4 (Stewart IIIc; B. 665.8; S.5340). Acq. 1976; ex Walters, lot 647 (HSAN 2435).
34	2.38	36.7	150	Obv. . QRA. Rev. SALVV . | FAC . PO | PVLV : T | VV . DNE, semi-colon after PVLV and before DNE, . ED | INBV | RGE ., pellets q1 and 3, mullets q2, and4 (Stewart IIIc; B.665.8; S.5340). Acq. 1976; ex Walters, lot 646. Same obverse die as **35** and **36** (HSAN 2436).
35	2.20	33.9	160	Obv. . QRA. Rev. five-point star stops, SALVVM | FAC . PPV | LVVM T | VVDNE, VILL | A . EDI | N . BV . | RGI ., pellets q1, and 3, mullets q2 and 4 (Stewart IIIc; B.665.7; S.5340). Bt Baldwin, 1976; ex F. Baldwin. Same obverse die as **34** and **36** (HSAN 2437).
36	2.45	37.8	50	Obv. . QRA. Rev. v stops, SALVV | . FAC . PO | PVLV T | VVDNE, VILL | A . ED | INBV | RGE ., pellets q2 and 4, mullets q1 and 3 (Stewart IIIc; B.664.6; S.5340). Acq. 4 April 1957; ex Dakers, lot 428 (part). Same obverse die as **34** and **35** (HSAN 2438).

As last, but five-point star stops, tressure of seven arcs, large five-point star each side of neck.

37	2.27	35.0	280	Obv. REX SCOTTORV : QRA. Rev. colon stops with comma and five-point star, SALVV . | FAC . PO | PVLIT | VV : DNE, VILL | A . ED | INBV | RGE ., pellets q2 and 4, mullets q1 and 3 (Stewart IIIc var.; B.666.9; S.5341). Bt Spink, 14 January 1957 (HSAN 2439).
38	2.39	36.4	100	Obv. REX SCOTTORV QRA. Rev. colon stops with comma and six-point star, SALVV | FAC . PO | PVLV . T | VV DNE., pellets q1 and 3, mullets q2 and 4, VILL | A ED | INBV | RGE . (Stewart IIIc var.; B.666.9; S.5341). Bt. Spink, 1965; ex Marr; ex Mann, lot 434 (HSAN 2440).

Type IIIe. *With roman* IIII *at end of the obverse legend*

Usually no stops / five-point star stops. Obv. tressure of nine arcs, small trefoil on each cusp, with small five-point stars by neck, IACOBVS DEI GRA REX SCOTTORVM IIII. Rev. VILLA EDENBEOVRGE.

39	2.55	39.3	120	Obv. no stops. Rev. . SALVVM | . FAC . PPIT | VVM TV | VM DNE ., . VILL | A . EDE | NBEO | VRGE, pellets q1 and 3, mullets q2 and 4 (Stewart IIIe; cf. B.675.15; S.5342). Acq. 1965; ex Parsons, lot 726 (part). Same obverse die as **40** and **41** (HSAN 2441).

31 32 33 34 35

36 37 38 39 40

41 42 43 44 45

	Weight g.	gr.	Die Axis	
40	2.22	34.3	10	Obv. no stops. Rev. . SALVVM | FAC POP | VVM TV | VM . DNE, . VILL | A . EDE | NBEOR | VRGE ., pellets q1 and 3, mullets q2 and 4 (Stewart IIIe; B.675.15a; S.5342). Bt Spink, 15 August 1955. Same obverse die as **39** and **41** (HSAN 2442).
41	2.48	38.3	100	Obv. no stops. Rev. SALVVM | FAC . PPL | VVM . TV | VM . DNE, VILL | A . EDE | NBEO | VRGE, pellets q1 and 3, mullets, q2 and 4 (Stewart IIIe; cf. B.675.15a; S.5342). Bt. Spink, 1965; ex Marr. Same obverse die as last **39** and **40** (HSAN 2443).
42	1.97	30.4	25	Obv. no stops. Rev. SALVVM . | FAC . PPL | VVM TV | VM[.DNE], VILL | A . EDE | NBEOR | VRGE ., pellets q1 and 3, mullets q2 and 4 (Stewart IIIe; B.675.15a; S.5342). Bt Seaby, 29 April 1955 (HSAN 2444).
43	2.36	36.4	100	Star stops both sides. Obv. SCOTTORVM . IIII. Rev. . SALVVM | . FAC PPL | VVM . TV | VM DNE ., VILL | A . EDE | NBEO | VRGE, pellets q1 and 3, mullets q2 and 4 (Stewart IIIe; cf. B.675A.15b; S.5342). Acq. 1976; ex Parsons, lot 726 (part) (HSAN 2445).
44	2.49	38.4	20	Star stops both sides. Obv. SCOTTORVM IIII. Rev. SALVVM | FAC . PPL | VVL . TV | VM DNE, VILL | A . EDE | NBEO | VRGE, pellets q2 and 4, mullets q1 and 3 (Stewart IIIe; cf. B.675A.15b; S.5342). Bt Baldwin, 1976; ex F. Baldwin (HSAN 2446).

The light coinage groat Stewart type IIId (with QT) is not represented in the collection.

Type IV. *'Maundy groat' 1512*

Weight standard *c.* 2.10 g, *c.* 33 gr: value 12d Scots.

i.m. crown/trefoil, roman letters, pellet stops both sides. Obv. bearded facing draped bust with jewelled crown, shoulders breaking tressure, nine arcs, IACOBVS : 4 : DEI : GRA : REX : SCOTTORV .. Rev. EXVRGAT DEVS ET DISSIPENTVR INIMICI EIVS, VILLA : EDINBVRG : I, long-cross, mullet and trefoils in alternate angles.

Referred to as the 'Maundy groat', these were struck by order of James IV as Maundy money from 11lbs 1½oz of silver for the Cena Domini in 1512 (Stewart 1966, p. 265).

45	2.32	35.8	20	Rev. EXVRG | AT : DEV | S Z : DISSI | . PENT : I, triple stop between T and I, .VILL | A : EDI | NBVR | G : I Z :, pellets q2 and 4, mullets q1 and 3 (Stewart IV; B.698A; S.5343). Acq. 1998, ex J. E. L. Murray (with her ticket, acq. January 1989); ex Trampitsch. Different dies to the other two known examples; signs of die flip in legend left above crown (HSAN 2455).

SILVER. Light coinage *(cont.)*

Half-groats

Theoretical weight 1.26 g, 19.5 gr: value 6 pence Scots.

Type IIIa. *Without numeral*

Similar to type IIIb groat, pellet stops both sides. Obv. tressure of seven arcs, trefoil on cusps by hair and neck only.

	Weight g.	gr.	Die Axis	
46	1.29	19.9	215	Rev. SALVV . | FAC . PO | PVLVV . | TVDNE ˙ , VIL | LA EI | INB | VRGE, pellets q1 and 3, mullets q2 and 4 (Stewart IIIa; cf. B.671.1b; S.5344). Acq. 1998, ex J. E. L. Murray; ex Dunbar, lot 102; ex Dundee, lot 94; ex Lockett I, lot 276; ex Bearman; ex Murdoch, lot 152; ex Richardson; ex Ford, lot 847 (HSAN 2452).

Type IIIb. *With numeral*

Similar to type IIIe groat, five-point star stops. Obv. tressure of nine arcs, trefoil on each cusp. Rev. EDENBEOVRGE.

47	1.06	16.4	300	Obv. SCOTTORV IIII. Rev. SALVV ’. | FAC . PP | LVV[..] | V . DNE ., VILL | A EDE | INEO | VRGE, pellets q1 and 3, mullets q2 and 4 (Stewart IIIb; B.676a: S.5346). Ex Villeneuve, lot 49 (HSAN 2453).
48	0.91	14.0	250	Obv. SCOTTORV [IIII]. Rev. SALVV . | FAC . PP | [..].TV. | V . DNE ., VILL | A EDE | NBEO | VRGE., pellets q1 and 3, mullets q2 and 4 (Stewart IIIb; B.676; S.5346). Acq. 24 August 1955; ex Dakers (HSAN 2454).

BILLON COINAGE

Plack

Value 4d Scots.

Obv. shield bearing lion rampant, crown above and at sides, within a tressure of three arcs, legend around. Rev. plain saltire within lozenge with curving sides from which extend cruciform limbs terminating in a floriated cross fourchée, a crown in each angle, legend around.

Classification as Stewart 1967, pp. 145–6.

Possible dating; placks with i.m. cross fleury, 1488–90; i.m. cross potent, *c.* 1490–*c.* 1496; i.m. crown, with lombardic letters after *c.* 1496; i.m. crown, with roman letters, *c.* 1512–13.

(Type I — reading SCOTORVM QRA *not represented)*

Type II — *lombardic-lettering both sides, obverse legend without* QRA *at end of obverse legend*

i.m. cross fleury or cross potent. Obv. IACOBVS . DEI . GRACIA . REX . SCOTTO, lombardic-lettering, lis in upper spandrels of shield surround only. Rev. VILL | A . DE . | EDIN | BVRG often larger neater lombardic-lettering (B.667.1a, 682b.4a–5a, 689.6–7d, 690.8–11h, 690a.11i–11k, 692.12–13, 693.14–23; S.5349).

Type IIa

i.m. cross potent (not cross pattée as noted by Stewart), with pellet stops both sides (Stewart IIa)

i.m. cross potent, cross of pellets or crown, pellet stops both sides.

49	2.12	32.7	210	Obv. pellet stops, colon after SCOTORVM. Rev. trefoil stop after DE. Acq. 1998, ex J. E. L. Murray (HSAN 2600).
50	1.71	26.4	200	Pellets stops both sides. Obv. GRA. Rev. VIL | LA. Unprovenanced (HSAN 2612).
51	1.58	24.4	330	Obv. pellet stops/no stops, colon after SCOTORVM. Acq. October 1991 (HSAN 2641).
52	1.46	22.5	110	i.m. uncertain, pellet stops. Obv. GRA. Rev. VILL | A . DE . E | DINB | VRG .. Acq. November 1991 (HSAN 2642).

46 47 48 49 50

51 52 53 54 55

56 57 58 59 60

	Weight g.	gr.	Die Axis	
53	1.64	25.3	140	i.m. uncertain, pellet stops. Obv. lis in spandrels uncertain. Rev. VIL | LA . D | [...]GI. Unprovenanced (HSAN 2643).

i.m. cross potent/crown, as last, pellet stops. Obv. with four pellets cruciform after IACOBVS and DEI, pellet in one or more spandrels (B.667.1b, 682A.4c; S.5349).

54	1.36	21.0	70	Obv. SCTORVR, pellet in lower spandrels. Rev. VIL | LA . D | E : EDI | NBVRG. Acq. October 1991 (HSAN 2596).
55	1.78	27.5	100	Obv. SCTORVM, pellet in lower spandrels. Rev. VIL | LA : D | E : EDI | NBVRG, colon stops. Acq. 1998, ex J. E. L. Murray (HSAN 2597).
56	1.63	25.2	100	i.m. uncertain/crown,. Obv. pellet in lower spandrels. Rev. VIL | LA : DE | EDIN | BVRG, colon stops. Bt Spink, 1965; ex Marr (HSAN 2599).
57	1.85	28.5	50	i.m. ?cross potent/crown. Obv. colon stops, SCOTORV, pellet in lower spandrels. Rev. no stops (?), VILL | A : DE : E | DINB | VRGHI. Acq. October 1991 (HSAN 2601).

i.m. one or four pellets cruciform/crown or cross potent. Obv. pellet in upper spandrels of shield surround only (B.682, B.-; S.5349).

58	1.97	30.4	200	i.m. four pellets cruciform/crown, colon/pellet stops. Obv. no pellets in spandrels, SCOTORV. Rev. VIL | LA . ED | INBV | RTH .. Bt Baldwin, 1976 (HSAN 2592).
59	2.15	33.2	200	i.m. pellet/cross potent, colon stops. Obv. SCOTORV. Rev. VILL | A . DE . E | DINBV | RGHT .. Acq. 1998, ex J. E. L. Murray; acq. Spink, January 1978; ex Chown (HSAN 2593).
60	1.61	24.8	20	i.m. uncertain/crown, colon pellet stops. Obv. pellet in top left spandrel,. Rev. [VILL A . DE] EDIN[.]. Lord Stewartby notes 'probably Linlithgow but reads Edinburgh.' Acq. November 1991 (HSAN 2594).

BILLON *(cont.)*

Placks. Type IIa (cont.)

i.m. crown, obv. or rev. Obv. **IACOBVS DEI GRACIA REX SCOTORVM**, no lis in spandrels on obverse. Rev. **VIL | LA DE | EDIN | BVRG** (B. -; S.5349).

	Weight g.	gr.	Die Axis	
61	1.89	29.2	350	i.m. crown/cross potent. Obv. pellet stops, **SCOTORV**. Rev. uncertain stops, **EDINB | VRGH**. Bt Spink, June 1989; ex Davidson (HSAN 2591).
62	1.47	22.7	280	i.m. crown/uncertain. Obv. colon/trefoil stops, **SCOTORV**, **EDIN | BVRGI**, inked number 6358 on rev. bt Spink, June 1989; ex Davidson (HSAN 2595).
63	1.79	27.6	360	Obv. i.m. two crowns after **SCOTORVM**, colon stops, **EDI**[..]. Unprovenanced (HSAN 2598).
64	1.93	29.8	140	Obv. i.m. ?crown/uncertain. Obv. four pellets cruciform after **SCOTORVM**. Rev. ?no stops. Bt Baldwin, 1976 (HSAN 2602).

Type IIb

i.m. cross potent (not cross patteé as noted by Stewart for IIb); usually lis stops obverse, pellet stops reverse (Stewart IIb)

65	2.25	34.7	330	Lis stops/pellet stops. Rev. **VILL | A . DE . | EDIN | BVRG**. Bt Baldwin, 1976; ex F. Baldwin (HSAN 2639).
66	1.25	19.3	20	Lis stops/pellet stops. Obv. **GRA**, **SCOTORV**. Rev. **VIL | LA . DE .** |. Bt Spink, *c.*1972; ex 'Spink hoard' (HSAN 2640).
67	1.57	24.2	190	i.m. cross potent/uncertain, pellet quatrefoil stops. Obv. lis in all spandrels. Rev. lis stops, **VIL | LA . DE . | EDIN | BVRG**. Unprovenanced (HSAN 2662).

Type IIc

i.m. cross potent (not cross pattée as noted by Stewart for IIb); lis stops both sides (Stewart IIc).

68	1.58	24.4	70	Obv. four pellets cruciform after **IACOBVS**, stop after **SCOTORVM**. Unprovenanced (HSAN 2606).
69	1.90	29.3	90	i.m. uncertain both sides. Bt Spink; June 1989; ex Davidson (HSAN 2603).
70	2.00	30.9	30	Obv. **SCOTORV**. Rev. **VIL | LA . D | E . EDI | BVRG**. Acq. 1960 (HSAN 2604).
71	1.90	29.3	200	Rev. **VIL | LA**. Acq. Bt Spink, June 1989, ex Davidson (HSAN 2605).
72	2.07	31.9	190	Rev. unclear, ?**VIL | LA**. Acq. October 1991 (HSAN 2607).
73	1.70	26.2	360	Obv. **GRA**, **SCOTORVV**. Bt Baldwin, 1976 (HSAN 2613).
74	1.60	24.7	220	Rev. **VIL | LA . D | E . EIN | BVRG**. Bt Spink, June 1989; ex Davidson (HSAN 2614).
75	1.43	22.1	20	i.m. uncertain/cross potent. Rev. **VIL | LA . D | E . EIN | BVRG**. Acq. October 1991 (HSAN 2615).

61 62 63 64 65

66 67 68 69 70

71 72 73 74 75

BILLON (cont.)

Placks. Type IIc (cont.)

	Weight g.	gr.	Die Axis	
76	1.38	21.3	140	i.m. cross potent/uncertain. Obv. lis in all spandrels. Rev. pellet to left of central saltire, VIL | LA . D | E. EDI | NBVRG (B.690.9). Bt Spink, June 1989; ex Davidson (HSAN 2616).
77	1.85	28.5	320	i.m. uncertain. Rev. VIL | LA . D | E . EDI | NBVRG (B.690.11a). Bt Spink, June 1989; ex Davidson (HSAN 2617).
78	2.07	31.9	60	i.m. uncertain/cross potent. Obv. trefoil after SCOTORV. Rev. VIL | LA . D | E . EDI | NBVR. Bt Spink, 1965; ex Marr (HSAN 2618).
79	1.90	29.3	30	Rev. VIL | LA . DE | EDIN | BVRG .. Bt Baldwin, 1976; ex F. Baldwin (HSAN 2619).
80	1.93	29.8	340	Obv. GRA, lis in all spandrels. Rev. VIL | LA . DE | . EDIN | BVRG. Bt Baldwin, 1976; ex F. Baldwin (HSAN 2620).
81	2.28	35.2	20	i.m. uncertain/cross potent. Obv. GRA, lis in all spandrels. Rev. VIL | LA . DE |. Unprovenanced (HSAN 2621).
82	2.51	38.7	330	i.m. uncertain/cross potent. Rev. VIL | LA . D | [E . ED..]. Acq. November 1991. Pierced from reverse at crown (HSAN 2622).
83	1.72	26.5	20	Obv. SCOTORV. Bt Spink, June 1989; ex Davidson (HSAN 2623).
84	1.25	19.3	200	i.m. uncertain/cross potent. Obv. no lis in spandrels. Rev. VIL | LA. Bt Spink, June 1989; ex Davidson (HSAN 2624).
85	1.16	17.9	100	i.m. cross potent/uncertain, stops uncertain. Obv. SCOTOR. Unprovenanced (HSAN 2625).
86	1.57	24.2	225	Lis stops/no stops. Obv. GRA (B.690.11). Bt Spink, June 1989; ex Davidson (HSAN 2626).
87	1.48	22.8	340	Obv. GRA. Bt Spink, June 1989; ex Davidson. Kirkcudbrightshire find, with 19th-century ticket (HSAN 2627).
88	1.52	23.5	220	Obv. GRA, SCOTTORVM. Rev. VIL | LA . D | E . ED | INBVR, inked number 6359 on rev. Bt Spink, June 1989; ex Davidson (HSAN 2628).
89	1.91	29.5	40	Obv. GRA, rev. VIL | LA . D | E . EDI | NBVR. Unprovenanced (HSAN 2629).
90	2.04	31.5	45	i.m. cross potent/uncertain. Rev. VIL | LA . DE . | EDIN | BVRG. Bt Spink, June 1989; ex Davidson (HSAN 2630).

PLATE 6

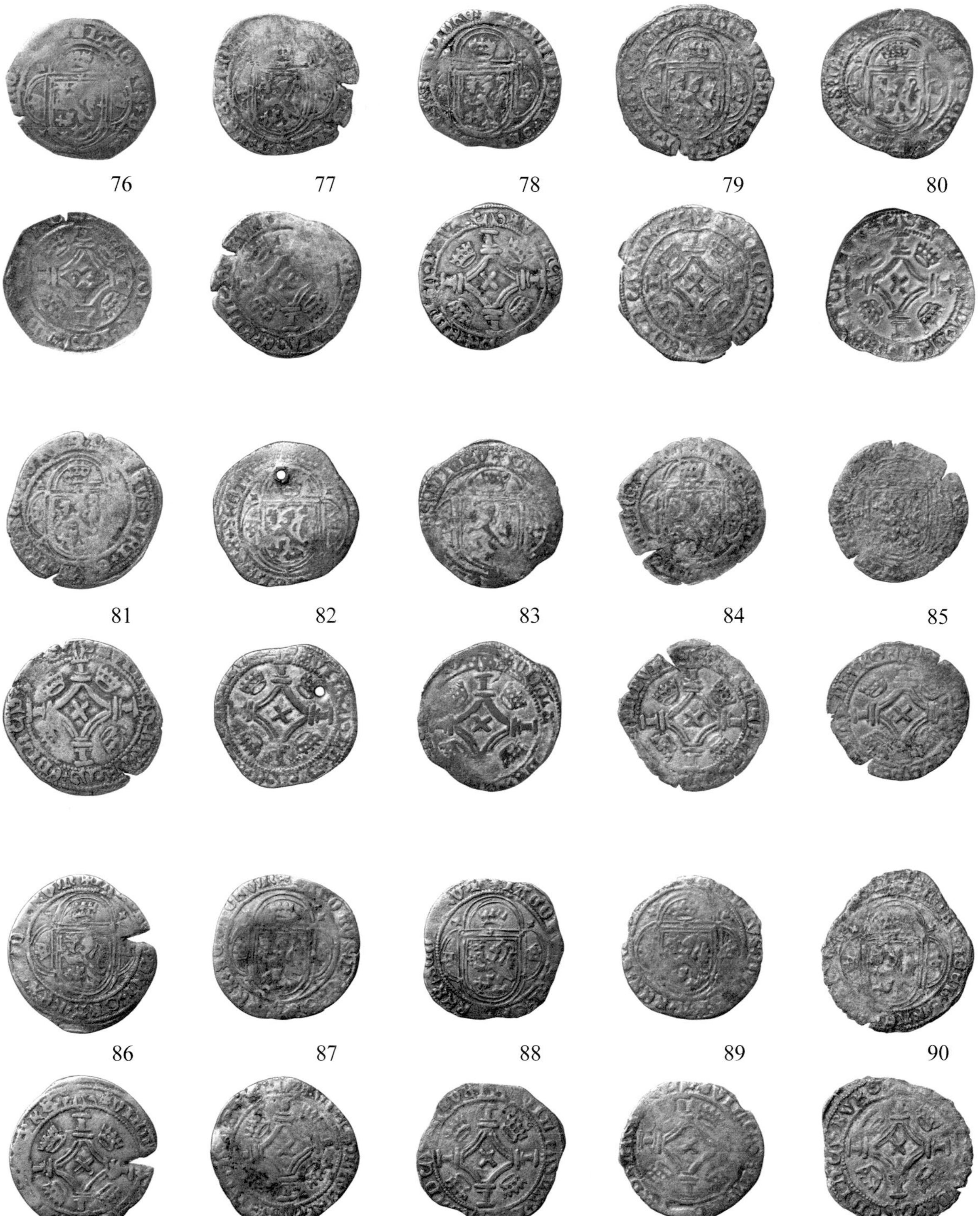

BILLON *(cont.)*

Placks. Type IIc (cont.)

	Weight g.	gr.	Die Axis	
91	1.54	23.8	250	Rev. VIL | LA . D | E . EDI | NBVG. Acq. October 1991 (HSAN 2631).
92	1.80	27.8	225	Lis stops/uncertain. Rev. VIL | LA . D | E . EDI | BVR. Acq. 14 June 1995 (HSAN 2632).
93	1.83	28.2	100	Obv. GRA. Bt Spink, June 1989; ex Davidson (HSAN 2633).
94	2.14	33.0	210	i.m. cross potent/uncertain. Rev. VIL | LA . D | E . EDE | [..]R. Unprovenanced (HSAN 2634).
95	1.85	28.5	180	Rev. VIL | LA . DE |. Acq. 1976; ex Winstanley (HSAN 2635).
96	1.92	29.9	360	Obv. GRA. Rev. VIL | LA . D | E . EDI | NBVRG. Bt Spink, June 1989; ex Davidson (HSAN 2636).
97	2.30	35.5	313	i.m. cross potent/uncertain. Bt Spink, June 1989; ex Davidson. Kirkcudbrightshire find (HSAN 2637).
98	2.51	38.7	120	i.m. uncertain/cross potent. Obv. GRA. Rev. VILL | A . DE . | EDEN | BVRG. Ex Mauchline (HSAN 2638).
99	2.05	31.6	120	Rev. stops uncertain. Unprovenanced (HSAN 2659).
100	2.20	33.9	100	Lis stops. Rev. uncertain stops. Unprovenanced (HSAN 2695).
101	2.10	32.4	190	i.m. cross potent/uncertain. Rev. VILL | A . DE | [...]. Unprovenanced (HSAN 2727).
102	0.52	8.0	45	i.m. and stops uncertain. Rev. cross potent between VIL | LA and DE. Bt Spink, *c.* 1972; ex 'Spink hoard'. Corroded, not illustrated (HSAN 2697).

Type II — unclassified.

i.m. cross potent, without stops either obverse or reverse (Stewart -)

103	1.70	26.2	60	i.m. small crown (?)/cross fleury, no stops (?). Obv. SCOTOR. Unprovenanced (HSAN 2608).
104	2.07	31.9	200	i.m. small cross fleury both sides, no stops (?). Rev. no stops (Stewart —). Bt Spink, June 1989; ex Davidson (HSAN 2689).
105	1.43	22.1	320	Star stops. Rev. no stops, VIL | LA, (Stewart -). Unprovenanced (HSAN 2728).
106	1.58	24.4	360	i.m. uncertain, no stops. Rev. ?[VILLA] DE (Stewart -). Unprovenanced (HSAN 2610).

PLATE 7

91 92 93 94 95

96 97 98 99 100

101 103 104 105 106

BILLON *(cont.)*

Placks. Type IIc (cont.)

	Weight g.	gr.	Die Axis	
107	1.38	21.3	160	i.m. uncertain/cross potent, pellets stops/no stops. Unprovenanced (Stewart —) (HSAN 2611).
108	1.98	30.6	30	Uncertain stops. Rev. no stops, VIL | LA . DE | EDIN | BVRG. Unprovenanced (Stewart —). Corroded, not illustrated (HSAN 2694).

Type IId

i.m. cross fleury. Obv. lis stops. Rev. star stops (Stewart IId).

109	2.24	34.6	100	Lis stops/no stops. Obv. lis in all spandrels (cf. B.693.16ff, 692.12). Acq. 1998, ex J. E. L. Murray (HSAN 2652).

Type IIe

i.m. cross fleury, forked stops both sides (Stewart IIe).

110	1.45	22.4	350	Obv. SCOTTORV (cf. B.692.12a). Bt Spink, June 1989; ex Davidson (HSAN 2651).

Type IIf

i.m. cross fleury, star stops both sides (Stewart IIf)

111	1.68	25.9	90	i.m. uncertain/cross fleury. Obv. star stops. Rev. uncertain. Unprovenanced (HSAN 2609).
112	1.41	21.8	30	i.m. cross fleury/uncertain. Obv. lis in all spandrels. Bt Spink, June 1989; ex Davidson (HSAN 2644).
113	1.75	27.0	100	Obv. lis in all spandrels. Bt Spink, June 1989; ex Davidson (HSAN 2645).
114	2.14	33.0	360	Obv. lis in all spandrels. Rev. VIL | LA . DE |. Acq. October 1991 (HSAN 2646).
115	2.18	33.6	160	Obv. Lis in all spandrels. Bt Spink, June 1989; ex Davidson (HSAN 2647).
116	1.57	24.2	315	Obv. lis in all spandrels (cf. B.693.17). Bt Spink, June 1989; ex Davidson (HSAN 2648).
117	1.78	27.5	330	i.m. cross fleury/uncertain, Obv. lis in all spandrels. Bt Spink, 1965; ex Marr (HSAN 2649).
118	2.12	32.7	360	Obv. SCOTT. Bt Baldwin, 1976 (HSAN 2650).
119	2.12	32.7	180	Obv. SCOTT, lis in spandrels uncertain. Bt Baldwin, 1976 (HSAN 2653).
120	1.58	24.4	280	Obv. SCOTT. Bt Spink, June 1989; ex Davidson (HSAN 2654).
121	1.84	28.4	220	Bt Spink, June 1989; ex Davidson. Kirkcudbrightshire find, noted on old ticket 24 July 1924 (HSAN 2655).
122	2.82	43.5	180	Obv. Lis in all spandrels. Acq. 29 September 1959; ex Mcfarlan (HSAN 2656).

107 109 110 111 112

113 114 115 116 117

118 119 120 121 122

BILLON *(cont.)*

Placks. Type IIf (cont.)

	Weight g.	gr.	Die Axis	
123	1.94	29.9	130	Rev. stops uncertain. Unprovenanced (HSAN 2657).
124	2.46	38.0	40	Unprovenanced (HSAN 2658).
125	2.45	37.8	210	Obv. lis in all spandrels. Unprovenanced (HSAN 2660).
126	1.85	28.5	180	i.m. uncertain both sides, Obv. lis in all spandrels. Unprovenanced (HSAN 2661).
127	1.20	18.5	270	i.m. cross fleury/uncertain, Obv. no lis in spandrels. Rev. VIL | LA .. Unprovenanced (HSAN 2663).
128	1.56	24.1	190	i.m. four (?) pellets cruciform/cross fleury. Obv. SCOTTOR, stops uncertain. Rev. star stops. Unprovenanced (HSAN 2664).
129	1.62	25.0	220	Stops uncertain. Obv. no lis in spandrels. Rev. star stops. Unprovenanced (HSAN 2665).
130	2.14	33.0	50	i.m. uncertain both sides, star stops. Obv. no lis in spandrels. Unprovenanced (HSAN 2666).
131	1.16	17.9	190	i.m. uncertain/cross fleury, uncertain stops. Obv. no lis in spandrels, Rev. star stops. Unprovenanced (HSAN 2667).
132	1.73	26.7	350	i.m. cross fleury and plain-cross (?)/plain-cross (?). Unprovenanced (HSAN 2668).
133	1.57	24.2	190	Obv. no lis in spandrels. Rev. uncertain stops. Unprovenanced (HSAN 2669).
134	1.91	29.5	40	i.m. cross fleury/uncertain. Obv. no lis in spandrels. Rev. VILL | A . DE. E | DINB | VRGH. Bt Spink, June 1989; ex Davidson (HSAN 2670).
135	2.02	31.2	320	i.m. cross fleury/uncertain. Obv. lis in first spandrel only. Unprovenanced (HSAN 2671).
136	2.63	40.6	250	Bt Baldwin, 1976; ex F. Baldwin (HSAN 2672).
137	1.66	25.6	50	Rev. uncertain stops, VIL | LA. Bt Baldwin, 1976; ex F. Baldwin (HSAN 2673).

PLATE 9

123 124 125 126 127

128 129 130 131 132

133 134 135 136 137

BILLON *(cont.)*

Placks. Type IIf (cont.)

	Weight g.	gr.	Die Axis	
138	1.88	29.0	260	i.m. cross fleury/uncertain. Obv. lis in upper right spandrel only. Rev. VIL | LA. Bt Spink, June 1989; ex Davidson (HSAN 2674).
139	2.31	35.6	280	Obv. lis in upper and lower right spandrels, SCOTTOR. Bt Spink, June 1989; ex Davidson (HSAN 2675).
140	1.75	27.0	100	i.m. uncertain/cross fleury. Obv. SCOT[TOR]. Rev. VIL | LA. Bt Baldwin, 1976 (HSAN 2676).
141	2.24	34.6	190	i.m. uncertain/cross fleury. Obv. SCOTTORV. Bt Spink, June 1989; ex Davidson (HSAN 2677).
142	2.16	33.3	300	Obv. SCOTTORV. Ex Macfarlan (HSAN 2678).
143	2.38	36.7	20	i.m. uncertain/cross fleury. Obv. ?SCOTTORV. Unprovenanced (HSAN 2679).
144	1.87	28.9	290	Bt Spink, June 1989; ex Davidson (HSAN 2680).
145	1.80	27.8	220	Obv. lis in all spandrels. Rev. VIL | LA . D | E . EDI | NBVR. Bt Baldwin, 1976; ex F. Baldwin (HSAN 2681).
146	2.03	31.3	230	i.m. uncertain/cross fleury. Obv. lis in all spandrels. Rev. VIL | LA . DE | EIN | BVRG. Bt Spink, June 1989; ex Davidson (HSAN 2682).
147	1.50	23.1	180	Obv. SCOTT. Bt. Spink, June 1989; ex Davidson (HSAN 2683).
148	2.18	33.6	100	Obv. SCOTT. Rev. VILL | A . DE E | DINB | VRGT. Bt Baldwin, 1976; ex F. Baldwin; ex Bearman, acq. 4 March 1909 (HSAN 2684).
149	2.65	40.9	20	Obv. SCOTT. Bt Spink, June 1989; ex Davidson (HSAN 2685).
150	2.13	32.9	120	Obv. SCOTT. Rev. VILL | A . DE E | DINB | VRGT. Bt Spink, June 1989; ex Davidson (HSAN 2686).
151	1.62	25.0	190	Bt Spink, June 1989; ex Davidson (HSAN 2687).
152	2.12	32.7	230	Bt Spink, June 1989; ex Davidson (HSAN 2688).

PLATE 10

138 139 140 141 142

143 144 145 146 147

148 149 150 151 152

BILLON *(cont.)*

Placks. Type IIf (cont.)

	Weight g.	gr.	Die Axis	
153	1.68	25.9	360	Ex R. C. Carlyon-Britton (HSAN 2690).
154	2.04	31.5	20	Obv. SCOTTORV. Rev. VILL | A . DE E | DIN | BVRG. Bt Baldwin, 1967 (HSAN 2691).
155	1.72	26.5	180	i.m. cross fleury/cross potent, star stops. Obv. SCOTTORVM (?). Rev. lis stops (?), VIL | LA . DE | EDIN | BVRG. Unprovenanced (HSAN 2692).
156	1.73	26.7	10	Ex Glendining 14 June 1995, lot 450 (part) (HSAN 2724).
157	2.59	40.0	320	Lis in all spandrels Ex Glendining, 14 June 1995, lot 450 (part) (HSAN 2729).
158	2.08	32.1	140	i.m. cross fleury/uncertain. Unprovenanced (HSAN 2730).
159	1.57	24.2	60	i.m. cross fleury/uncertain. Rev. VIL | LA. Unprovenanced (HSAN 2731).
160	1.48	22.8	200	i.m. and stops uncertain. Rev. ?cross potent. Unprovenanced (HSAN 2696).
161	2.31	35.6	300	Obv. [SCOTTOR]VM. Rev. lis stops, lis after EDIN | BVRG. Unprovenanced. A IIe/IIf mule (HSAN 2693).

Type II/Type IV mule (Stewart IIIa)

With roman-lettering on the reverse (A type IIf obverse muled with a type IV reverse) (B. 697.24–24a; S.5350).

162	1.85	28.5	135	i.m. cross fleury/-, lombardic letters, star stops. Obv. GRACIA . REX . SCOTTO. Rev. roman letters, trefoil stops, . VILL | A : DE | . EDIN | BVRG (B. 697.24a). Bt Seaby, 14 August 1980. Noted by Lord Stewartby as RRRR (HSAN 2703).

Type IV. *With numeral* 4, *roman-lettering*

Type IVa

With trefoil stops both sides. Not represented in the collection.

Type IVb

i.m. crown/trefoil. Obv. IACOBVS 4 DEI GRA REX SCOTORVM, pellet stops, lis in all spandrels. Rev. trefoil stops, VILL | A . DE . | EDIN | BVRG (Stewart IVb; B. 700.26–704.30e; S.5351).

163	2.03	31.2	100	Obv. . IACOBVS 4 : DEI . GRA . REX . SCOTORV, lis in upper spandrels only. Rev. VILL : | A : E : | : EDIN | BVRG. Acq. 31 May 1970. Linlithgow hoard (HSAN 2704).
164	1.95	30.1	230	Pellet colon stops. Obv. IACOBVS[.] DEI : GRA . REX . SCOTORVM. Bt Baldwin, 1975 (HSAN 2705).
165	2.11	32.6	100	Obv. IACO[BVS : 4 : DE]I : GRA . REX . SCOTORVM. Rev. VILL | A : D[E : ED]IN | BVRG. Bt Baldwin, 1975 (HSAN 2706).
166	1.93	29.8	290	i.m. crown both sides. Obv. **4** obscured, lis in upper spandrels only. Bt Baldwin, 1975; ex F. Baldwin (HSAN 2707).
167	2.16	33.3	270	Obv. . IACOBVS 4 . DEI [G]RA : REX . SCOTORVM. Rev. trefoil after EDINBVRG. Acq. 1998, ex J. E. L. Murray (HSAN 2708).

PLATE 11

153 154 155 156 157

158 159 160 161 162

163 164 165 166 167

BILLON *(cont.)*

Placks. Type IVb (cont.)

	Weight g.	gr.	Die Axis	
168	2.38	36.7	120	Obv. IACOBVS . 4. Rev. round G. Acq. 1998, ex J. E. L. Murray (HSAN 2709).
169	1.82	28.1	260	Obv. IACOBVS 4 : DEI:[..]. Rev. VILL | A[..] VRG, trefoil after VRG, round G. Unprovenanced (HSAN 2710).
170	2.19	33.8	250	Rev. VILL[…] BVRG, round G. Unprovenanced (HSAN 2711).
171	1.86	28.7	60	Obv. IACOBVS . 4. Unprovenanced (HSAN 2712).
172	2.22	34.3	110	Obv. IACOBVS . 4. Rev. VILL | A . DE | . EDIN | BVRG, round G. Unprovenanced (HSAN 2713).
173	1.65	25.5	360	Obv. . IACOBVS. 4. Rev. . VILL | A . DE |, round G. Unprovenanced (HSAN 2714).
174	1.49	23.0	320	Obv. trefoil before IACOBVS : 4. Rev. VILL | A DE | EDIN | BVIG ., round G. Bt Spink, June 1989; ex Davidson (HSAN 2715).
175	1.56	24.1	20	Obv. trefoil before IACOBVS : 4. Rev. trefoil after EDIN | BVRG. Bt Spink, 1965; ex Marr (HSAN 2716).
176	1.85	28.5	300	Obv. trefoil before IACOBVS 4 :, trefoil after SCOTORVM. Rev. trefoil colon after EDIN | BVRG. Bt Baldwin, 1975; ex F. Baldwin (HSAN 2717).
177	1.71	26.4	200	Obv. trefoil before IACOBVS : 4. Rev. trefoil colon after EDIN | BVRG. Bt Baldwin, 1975; ex F. Baldwin (HSAN 2718).
178	2.06	31.8	350	Obv. . IACOBVS 4 :, SCOTORVM :. Rev. trefoil before VILLA:, round G. Unprovenanced (HSAN 2719).
179	2.73	42.1	340	Obv. IACOBVS : 4, trefoil colon after SCOTORVM. Rev. . VIL | LA : DE . | . EDIN | BVRG :. Bt Baldwin, 1975 (HSAN 2720).
180	2.84	43.8	340	i.m. uncertain. Rev. trefoil before VILL[A], round G. Bt Baldwin, 1975 (HSAN 2721).
181	2.14	33.0	360	Pellet stops. Rev. lis stops, : VILL | A, lis before EDIN | BVRG, R overstruck, round G. Acq. 29 September 1959. Lord Stewartby notes very rare with lis stops on the reverse (HSAN 2722).
182	1.63	25.2	360	Obv. IACOBVS 4.. Rev. four pellets lozenge before VILL | A, double pellet colon after EDIN | BVRG, round G. Unprovenanced (HSAN 2732).

PLATE 12

168 169 170 171 172

173 174 175 176 177

178 179 180 181 182

BILLON *(cont.)*

Placks. Type IVb (cont.)

	Weight g.	gr.	Die Axis	
183	1.48	22.8	10	Obv. trefoil colon after SCOTORVM. Rev. . VILLA. Unprovenanced (HSAN 2733).
184	1.83	28.2	260	Obv. IACOBVS . 4 DEI, trefoil in all spandrels, trefoil colon after SCOTORVM. Rev. no i.m., trefoil stops, trefoil before VILL | A . DE . | . EDIN | BVRG, round G. Unprovenanced (HSAN 2734).
185	1.97	30.4	270	Obv. IACOBVS . 4 DEI, trefoil after SCOTORVM. Rev. trefoil before VILLA. Unprovenanced (HSAN 2735).

Type V

As last, but with star stops (Stewart Va-c; B.705.30j-g; S.5352).

186	1.82	28.1	290	i.m. crown, pellet stops. Obv. pellet before IACOBVS 4, lis in all spans, SCOTORV. Rev. no i.m., star stops, EDINBVRG, open G. Bt Spink, June 1989; ex Davidson (Stewart Va) (HSAN 2725).
187	1.92	29.6	50	i.m. crown, star stops. Obv. star before IACOBVS, lis in all spandrels. Rev. no i.m., star stops, open G. Bt Spink, 1965; ex Marr; ex R. C. Carlyon-Britton (Stewart Vc) (HSAN 2723).
188	2.04	31.5	10	i.m. uncertain, star stops, lis (?) trefoil, in all spandrels. Rev. no i.m., star stops. Acq. 1998, ex J. E. L. Murray; acq. Spink 1978; ex Chown (Stewart Vc) (HSAN 2726).

Half-plack

Value 2d Scots

As plack.

Type I. *With* QR

i.m. cross potent both sides, pellet stops. Obv. no lis in spandrels, IACOBVS . DEI . GRA . REX SCOTORVM QR (or QRA). Rev. VIL | LADE | EDIN | BVRG, lombardic-lettering, similar to type I Plack (cf. Stewart IIa; B. -; S.5353).

189	0.74	11.4	360	Obv. [SCOTORV Q]R, no lis in spandrels. Rev. neat letters, VIL | [LADE] | EDIN | BVRG. Ex Sotheby 24 June 1970, lot 81 (part) (HSAN 2700).

Type II. *Without* QR

i.m. cross potent, similar to type II plack, but without QR (or QRA) at end of obverse legend, lombardic-lettering (cf. Stewart IIa; B.- ; S.5354).

i.m. cross potent/crown, pellets stops, similar to type IIa plack.

190	0.91	14.0	315	i.m. cross potent/crown, pellet colon stops. Obv. IACOBVS : DEI : GRA : REX : SCO, no lis in spandrels. Rev. no stops, VIL | LAE | DINV | RGH. Bt Spink, June 1989; ex Davidson (HSAN 2699).

i.m. cross potent, lis stops. Obv. lis instead of crowns by shield, similar to type IIc plack (Stewart IIc; B. 691.1; S.5356)

191	1.18	18.2	10	Obv. IACOBVS . DEI . GRA . REX . SCOT, lis in lower spandrels. Rev. VIL | LA .. | DE . ED | INBV, two lis between VILLA and DE, 12 December 1956, ex R. C. Carlyon-Britton (HSAN 2701).
192	0.98	15.1	200	Obv. IACOBVS . DEI . GRA . REX . SCOTOR, lis in lower spandrels. Rev. VIL | LA . E | DINB | VRG ., lis after BVRG. Bt Seaby, 15 September 1951; ex Whitton; ex Cochran-Patrick (1936), lot 225 (part) (HSAN 2702).

PLATE 13

183 184 185 186 187

188 189 190 191 192 193

194 195 196 197 198 199 200

Type III. *With Arabic numeral* 4

i.m. cross potent. Obv. pellet stops, lombardic-lettering with distinctive thin E with curved back and R with sinuous curving arc and tail to right side of letter, **IACOBVS . DEI . GRA . REX . SCOTORVM . 4**. Rev. no stops (Stewart -; B. —; S. —).

Stated by Lord Stewartby to be a unique example of a James IV half-plack with an Arabic numeral 4 appearing in the obverse legend.

	Weight g.	gr.	Die Axis	
193	1.15	17.7	45	Rev. **VIL | LA DE | EDIN | BVRGI**. Ex Mcfarlan; ex Napier, lot 221 (part) (HSAN 2698).

Penny

First issue. *Pellets reverse*

i.m. plain-cross with indented arms both sides. Obv. tall bust with crown of five fleurs, **IACOBVS DEI GRA REX**. Rev. cross and pellets, **VI | LLA E | DIN | BVR**.

Type 1

With annulets by neck, with annulet stops (Stewart 1; B.655.2–3a; S.5357).

194	0.60	9.3	300	Obv. **DIE GRA**, annulet stop after **GRA**, saltire stop after **IACOBVS**. Rev. annulet before **BVR**. Acq. 1975; ex Drabble II, lot 1195 (part); ex Bearman. His ticket notes 'bt. A H Baldwin Nov 16 1914' (HSAN 2580).
195	0.27	4.2	20	Obv. **DEI GRA**, annulet stop after **IACOBVS**. Rev. annulet before **BVR**. Bt Seaby, 14 January 1954 (HSAN 2581).

Type 2

As Type I, without annulets by neck, without annulet stops (Stewart 2; B.654.1–1b; S.5358).

196	0.60	9.3	20	Acq. 13 March 1974; ex Rose, lot 373 (part); ex R. C. Carlyon-Britton (HSAN 2469).
197	0.63	9.7	30	Obv. **DIE GRA**. Rev. saltire stops **VIL | . A E**[..]. Ex Bearman, acq. Spink 8 February 1909; ex Pollexfen, lot 314 (part) (HSAN 2470).
198	0.43	6.6	110	Rev. added pellet in q1, 3 and 4. Bt Spink, 1965; ex Marr (HSAN 2579).
199	0.58	8.9	360	Saltire stops/no stops. Bt Baldwin, 16 September 1953; ex Dakers (HSAN 2582).
200	0.41	6.3	Uncertain	Obv. **RIX**. Bt Spink, 1965; ex Marr; ex R. C. Carlyon-Britton (HSAN 2583).

BILLON *(cont.)*

Pennies. First Issue. Type 2 (cont.)

	Weight g.	gr.	Die Axis	
201	0.42	6.5	120	Saltire stops both sides both sides. Rev. VI . | . LLA E | . DIN[.]. Bt Baldwin, 16 September 1953; ex Dakers (HSAN 2584).
202	0.42	6.5	270	Annulet stops/saltire stops. Obv. DIE GRA. Bt Spink; 1965; ex Marr (HSAN 2585).
203	1.06	16.4	200	Rev. saltire stops. Bt Baldwin, 1975; ex F. Baldwin. A thick and heavy flan, anomalous (HSAN 2586).
204	0.62	9.6	20	Pellet stops/saltire stops, Obv. DIE GRA. Bt Baldwin, 15 September 1953; ex Dakers (HSAN 2587).
205	0.37	5.7	110	Rev. saltire stops, EDIN BVRG. Acq. 1975 (HSAN 2588).
206	0.33	5.1	200	Rev. saltire stops. Acq. 1975 (HSAN 2589).
207	0.42	6.5	Uncertain	Obv. saltire stops. Acq. 1975; ex Hurley (HSAN 2590).

Second issue. *Lis and Crowns reverse*

Type I. *with* SALVVM *reverse*

i.m. crown obverse only, no stops. Obv. small neat bust with crown of five fleurs, IACOBVS DEI GRA REX SCOTTO. Rev. SALVM FAC POPVLVM TVVM DOMINE, this abbreviated, long-cross, crown and lis in alternate angles, lis usually q1 and 3 (Stewart I; B.678.5f; S.5359).

208	0.56	8.6	100	Acq. 1 October 1956 (HSAN 2456).
209	0.61	9.4	135	Rev. SAL[..]VV DNE. Ex Parsons, lot 727; ex R. C. Carlyon-Britton (HSAN 4864).

Type II. *Edinburgh, mint named on reverse, i.m. crown*

i.m. crown both sides. Obv. IACOBVS DEI GRA REX SCOTTOR. Rev. VI \| LLA ED \| INBV \| RGH, lis usually q2 and 4 (Stewart II; B. 678.5–6f; S.5360).

210	0.65	10.9	110	Star stops both sides. Obv. REX:. Rev. VIL | LA : |EDIN | RVG :. Bt Baldwin, 1976 (HSAN 2457).
211	0.50	7.7	110	No stops, lis q1 and 3. Bt Seaby, December 1972 (HSAN 2458).
212	0.61	9.4	220	Obv. pellet stops, IACOBVS : DEI : GRACIA : REX. Rev. no stops, VIL | LA | EDIN | BVR. Bt Baldwin, 1976 (HSAN 2459).
213	0.85	13.1	220	Star stops/pellet stops. Obv. IACOBVS . DEI . GRACIA : REX. Rev. VIL | LA . ED | INBR | VGH .. Bt Baldwin, 1976; ex F. Baldwin (HSAN 2460).
214	0.51	7.9	90	Pellet stops. Obv. IACOBVS . DEI . GRACIA : REX. Rev. […]B| VRG. Bt Baldwin, 1976; ex F. Baldwin (HSAN 2461).
215	0.33	5.1	190	i.m. obv. uncertain/omitted on rev. Rev. VILL | A[ ]| VRG, lis q1 and 3. Acq. 1975; ex Bearman, acq. Spink 24 February 1909; ex Pollexfen, lot 314 (part) (HSAN 2462).
216	0.79	12.2	170	Rev. ED | INB | VGH. Acq. 1975; ex Dakers (HSAN 2463).
217	0.60	9.3	120	Rev. star stops, ED | INBV | RGH :. Bt Baldwin, 1975; ex F. Baldwin (HSAN 2464).
218	0.39	6.0	210	Acq. 18 April 1955 (HSAN 2465).
219	0.54	8.3	120	Bt Baldwin, 1976 (HSAN 2466).
220	0.80	12.3	350	Star stops both sides. Obv. DEI GRACIA : REX. Rev. VIL | LA : E | DINB | RVG:. Bt Spink, October 1989; ex Davidson (HSAN 2467).
221	0.60	9.3	30	Lis stops. Obv. DIE : GRACIA : REX. Rev. EDIN | BVRG. Acq. 5 April 1966 (HSAN 2472).
222	0.60	9.3	260	No stops. Obv. SCOTTO. Bt Baldwin, 1976 (HSAN 2473).
223	0.50	7.7	210	Obv. star stops, DEI . GRACIA . REX. Bt Senior, March 2003 (HSAN 2474).

PLATE 14

201 202 203 204 205 206 207

208 209 210 211 212 213 214

215 216 217 218 219 220 221

222 223 224 225 226 227 228

Type III. *Edinburgh, mint named on reverse, i.m. cross potent both sides or cross potent/crown*

i.m. cross potent both sides or cross potent/crown. Obv. larger bust with long face, IACOBVS DEI GRA REX SCOT. Rev. with mint name usually, VIL | LA E | DINB | VRG, lis usually q2 and 4 (Stewart III; B.682D.6g – 683E.9d; S.5361).

	Weight g.	gr.	Die Axis	
224	0.58	8.9	30	i.m. cross potent both sides. Obv. RE SCOT, broken hair. Rev. lis q1 and 3. Bt. Senior, February 2001 (HSAN 2468).
225	0.54	8.3	40	i.m. cross potent/uncertain. Obv. no stops. Bt Spink, 1965, ex Marr (HSAN 2475).
226	0.75	11.6	350	i.m. cross potent/crown. Obv. pellet stops. Bt Spink, 1965; ex Marr (HSAN 2476).
227	0.77	11.9	280	i.m. cross potent/crown. Rev. i.m. uncertain, EDINB | VRGH. Unprovenanced (HSAN 2477).
228	0.79	12.2	225	i.m. cross potent/uncertain. Rev. . EDIN | BVR. Bt Spink; 1965; ex Marr (HSAN 2478).

BILLON *(cont.)*

Pennies. Type III (cont.)

	Weight g.	gr.	Die Axis	
229	0.68	10.5	280	i.m. cross potent/crown. Rev. E | DINB | VRGH. Bt Baldwin, 16 September 1953; ex Dakers (HSAN 2479).
230	0.54	8.3	100	i.m. cross potent/uncertain. Obv. SCOTTOR. Rev. lis q1 and 3. Bt Spink, October 1989; ex Davidson (HSAN 2480).
231	0.66	10.2	230	i.m. uncertain both sides. Rev. lis q1 and 3. Ex Blunt; ex Shirley-Fox bequest 1939 (HSAN 2481).
232	0.75	11.6	360	i.m. uncertain/crown. Rev. E | DINB | VRGI, pellet colon after VIL | LA. Acq. 8 April 1961; ex Hurley (HSAN 2482).
233	0.60	9.3	200	i.m. uncertain/crown. Rev. E | DINB | VRGH. Bt Spink, October 1989; ex Davidson (HSAN 2483).
234	0.81	12.5	190	i.m. cross potent/two pellets. Bt Spink, 1965; ex Marr (HSAN 2484).
235	0.45	6.9	100	Unprovenanced, corroded, not illustrated (HSAN 2485).
236	0.59	9.1	100	Unprovenanced, corroded, not illustrated (HSAN 2486).
237	0.60	9.3	200	Unprovenanced, corroded, not illustrated (HSAN 2487).
238	0.65	10	120	i.m. cross potent/crown. Bt Baldwin, 1976; ex F. Baldwin (HSAN 2488).
239	0.67	10.3	20	i.m. cross potent/crown. Rev. lis q1 and 3. Bt Baldwin, 1976; ex F. Baldwin. Ticket (written by Bearman?) reads 'March 4th 1909' (HSAN 2489).
240	0.58	8.9	180	i.m. cross potent both sides. Bt Baldwin, 1976; ex F. Baldwin (HSAN 2490).
241	0.82	12.7	10	i.m. cross potent/crown. Rev. lis q1 and 3. Bt Baldwin, 1976; ex F. Baldwin (HSAN 2491).
242	0.68	10.5	360	i.m. uncertain both sides. Bt Baldwin, 1976; ex F. Baldwin (HSAN 2492).
243	0.87	13.4	100	i.m. cross potent both sides. Rev. pellet colon after VILLA. Bt Baldwin, 1976; ex F. Baldwin (HSAN 2493).
244	0.70	10.8	45	i.m. cross potent both sides, broken star stops. Rev. VIL | LA . DE . | . EDIN | BVRG, lis q1 and 3. Bt Baldwin, 1976 ex F. Baldwin (HSAN 2520).
245	0.73	11.3	260	i.m. cross potent uncertain. Obv. REX SCO. Rev. E | DINB | VRGI. Bt Baldwin, 1976 (HSAN 2494).
246	0.70	10.8	310	i.m. cross potent/crown. Obv. SCO. Rev. E | DIN | BVRG. Bt Baldwin, 1976. Holed at 11 o'clock (HSAN 2495).
247	0.63	9.7	Uncertain	i.m. uncertain both sides, very base. Bt Baldwin, 1976; ex F. Baldwin. Corroded, not illustrated (HSAN 2496).
248	0.67	10.3	20	i.m. uncertain both sides. Rev. lis q1 and 3. Bt Baldwin, 1976; ex F. Baldwin (HSAN 2497).
249	0.60	9.3	190	i.m. uncertain both sides. Obv. broken hair punches. Unprovenanced. Corroded, not illustrated (HSAN 2498).
250	0.40	6.2	260	i.m. uncertain/crown. Unprovenanced. Corroded, not illustrated (HSAN 2499).
251	0.34	5.2	250	i.m. uncertain/two pellets. Unprovenanced. Corroded, not illustrated (HSAN 2500).
252	0.52	8.0	210	i.m. uncertain/crown. Unprovenanced. Corroded, not illustrated (HSAN 2501).
253	0.48	7.4	Uncertain	i.m. uncertain/crown. Unprovenanced. Corroded, not illustrated (HSAN 2502).
254	0.47	7.3	270	i.m. uncertain/crown. Unprovenanced. Corroded, not illustrated (HSAN 2503).
255	0.57	8.8	220	i.m. cross potent both sides. Rev. lis q1 and 3. Ex Cairncross, lot 450 (part) (HSAN 2529).
256	0.43	6.6	110	i.m. cross potent/uncertain. Rev. VIL | LA . ED | INB | [..], trefoil stops. Unprovenanced (HSAN 2556).
257	0.62	9.6	190	i.m. uncertain both sides. Rev. VIL | LA E | [..]N | BVRG. Bt Baldwin, 1976; ex F. Baldwin (HSAN 2566).
258	1.14	17.6	100	i.m. cross potent/crown. Bt Spink, October 1989; ex Davidson. Bust as type IV, unusually heavy, on thick irregular flan (HSAN 2527).

229 230 231 232 233 234 238

239 240 241 242 243 244 245

246 248 255 256 257 258 259

260 261 262 264 265 266 267

Type IV. *i.m. small cross, Edinburgh, mint named on reverse*

i.m. small pattée cross both sides. Obv. bust with rounded features, **IACOBVS DEI GRA REX SCOT**. Rev. **VILL | A DE | EDIN | BVRG**, crown and lis in alternate angles, lis usually q2 and 4; of very base-metal, many occur on a smaller thicker module (Stewart IV; B.684.12–685.22; S.5362- type IV).

Stops noted: IVa, pellet; IVb, saltire; IVc, trefoil; IVd, none; IVe, star. These are noted here where it has been possible to determine that used.

	Weight g.	gr.	Die Axis	
259	0.78	12.0	340	i.m. small cross potent both sides. Rev. **VIL	LA E	DNB	VRG**. Bt Baldwin, 1976; ex F. Baldwin. Neat style (IVd) (HSAN 2569).
260	0.64	9.9	110	i.m. uncertain. Unprovenanced (IVa) (HSAN 2504).
261	0.83	12.8	150	i.m. -/pellet, pellet stops. Unprovenanced (IVa) (HSAN 2505).
262	0.90	13.9	350	i.m. small cross/trefoil (?), lis q1 and 3. Ex Sotheby, 24 June 1970, lot 81 (part) (IVd) (HSAN 2506).
263	0.52	8.0	Uncertain	i.m. uncertain both sides. Unprovenanced. Corroded, not illustrated (HSAN 2507).
264	0.52	8.0	100	i.m pellet/small cross (?), **[EDIN]	BVRH**. Unprovenanced (HSAN 2508).
265	0.46	7.1	220	Bt Spink, October 1989; ex Davidson (HSAN 2509).
266	0.95	14.7	100	i.m. small cross/uncertain. Bt Spink, October 1989; ex Davidson (HSAN 2510).
267	0.59	9.1	190	Bt Spink, October 1989; ex Davidson (HSAN 2511).

BILLON *(cont.)*

Pennies. Type IV (cont.)

	Weight g.	gr.	Die Axis	
268	1.28	19.8	100	Bt Spink, October 1989; ex Davidson (IVd) (HSAN 2512).
269	0.39	6.0	360	i.m. uncertain both sides. Unprovenanced. Pierced (HSAN 2513).
270	0.63	9.7	340	i.m. uncertain. ?small cross, star stops. Bt Spink, 1965; ex Marr (IVb) (HSAN 2514).
271	0.72	11.1	90	i.m. small cross/uncertain. Acq. 1966 (IVd) (HSAN 2515).
272	0.76	11.7	140	i.m. small cross/small cross above (?). Bt Spink, 1965; ex Marr (HSAN 2516).
273	0.74	11.4	290	i.m. small cross/small cross (?). Bt Spink, 1965; ex Marr (HSAN 2517).
274	0.64	9.9	350	i.m. uncertain. Obv. star stops. Bt Baldwin, 1976; ex F. Baldwin, (IVb) (HSAN 2518).
275	0.61	9.4	225	i.m. small cross/small cross. Obv. SCOTO. Bt Baldwin, 1976; ex F. Baldwin; ex Bearman, acq.. Spink 15 March 1909; ex Pollexfen, lot 314 (IVd) (HSAN 2519).
276	0.64	9.9	125	Trefoil stops. Acq. 1976; ex Dakers (IVc) (HSAN 2521).
277	0.70	10.8	360	Unprovenanced (HSAN 2522).
278	0.34	5.2	230	i.m. uncertain/small cross. Unprovenanced. Corroded, not illustrated (HSAN 2523).
279	0.34	5.2	110	i.m. uncertain/small cross. Unprovenanced (HSAN 2524).
280	0.69	10.6	190	i.m uncertain both sides. Unprovenanced (HSAN 2525).
281	0.30	3.6	Uncertain	i.m. uncertain. Unprovenanced. Corroded, not illustrated (HSAN 2526).
282	1.06	16.4	315	i.m. uncertain both sides. Ex Cairncross, lot 450 (part) (HSAN 2528).
283	0.72	11.1	150	Ex Cairncross lot 450 (part) (HSAN 2530).
284	0.48	7.4	280	Bt Spink, October 1989; ex Davidson (HSAN 2531).
285	0.42	6.5	20	i.m. uncertain both sides. Unprovenanced. Thin flan (HSAN 2532).
286	0.56	8.6	225	i.m. uncertain both sides. Unprovenanced (HSAN 2533).
287	0.52	8.0	270	Uncertain/small cross. Unprovenanced. Corroded, not illustrated (HSAN 2534).
288	0.17	2.6	Uncertain	i.m. uncertain both sides. Unprovenanced. Corroded, not illustrated (HSAN 2535).
289	0.44	6.8	270	i.m. uncertain both sides. Unprovenanced. Corroded, not illustrated (HSAN 2536).
290	0.52	8.0	290	i.m. uncertain. Unprovenanced. Corroded, not illustrated (HSAN 2537).
291	0.79	12.2	110	i.m. uncertain/small cross, pellet stops. Unprovenanced (IVa) (HSAN 2538).
292	0.54	8.3	30	Obv. pellets stops. Unprovenanced (IVa) (HSAN 2540).
293	0.50	7.7	110	Obv. SCOTO. Unprovenanced (HSAN 2541).
294	0.73	11.3	360	Unprovenanced (HSAN 2542).
295	0.69	10.6	250	Ex Mauchline (IVd) (HSAN 2543).
296	0.78	12.0	140	Rev. VIL	LA E	DIN	BVRG. Ex Mauchline (IVd) (HSAN 2544).
297	0.56	8.6	120	Ex Mauchline (IVd) (HSAN 2545).
298	0.46	7.1	200	i.m. uncertain/?small cross, trefoil (?) stops. Rev. lis q1 and 3. Bt Spink, October 1989; ex Davidson (HSAN 2546).
299	0.77	11.9	120	No stops both sides. Rev. VIL	LA E	DIN	BVRG. Unprovenanced (IVd) (HSAN 2547).
300	0.57	8.8	130	Bt Spink, 1965; ex Marr (IVd) (HSAN 2548).
301	0.78	12.0	320	i.m. small cross/uncertain. Acq. 8 April 1961; ex Hurley (HSAN 2549).

PLATE 16

268 269 270 271 272 273 274

275 276 277 279 280 282 283

284 285 286 291 292 293 294

295 296 297 298 299 300 301

BILLON *(cont.)*

Pennies. Type IV (cont.)

	Weight g.	gr.	Die Axis	
302	0.80	12.3	200	i.m. small cross (?)/small cross. Acq. 8 April 1961; ex Hurley (HSAN 2550).
303	0.61	9.4	60	i.m. uncertain/small cross, no stops both sides. Acq. 16 September 1953; ex Dakers (IVd) (HSAN 2551).
304	0.65	10.0	260	Trefoil stops both sides. Bt Spink, 1965; ex Marr (IVc) (HSAN 2552).
305	0.50	7.7	340	i.m. small cross/uncertain, pellet stops both sides. Acq. 8 April 1961; ex Hurley (IVa) (HSAN 2553).
306	0.53	8.2	200	Rev. VIL | LA E | DIN | BVRG. Acq. 8 April 1961; ex Hurley (HSAN 2554).
307	0.95	14.7	60	i.m. uncertain/small cross. Unprovenanced (IVd) (HSAN 2555).
308	0.57	8.8	270	i.m. small cross/uncertain. Rev. VIL | LA . E | D[..], trefoil stops. Bt Baldwin, 1976; ex F. Baldwin (IVc) (HSAN 2557).
309	0.81	12.5	90	i.m. uncertain both sides. Rev. VIL | LA . E | D[..], trefoil stops. Acq. 1976; ex Dakers (IVc) (HSAN 2558).
310	0.55	8.5	140	Bt Baldwin, 1976; ex F. Baldwin (HSAN 2559).
311	0.81	12.5	220	No stops both sides. Obv. SCO. Bt Baldwin, 1976; ex F. Baldwin (IVd) (HSAN 2560).
312	0.73	11.3	210	i.m. small cross both sides. Obv. pellet stops. Bt Baldwin, 1976 (IVa) (HSAN 2561).
313	0.61	9.4	225	Rev. pellet stops. Bt Baldwin, 1976 (IVa) (HSAN 2562).
314	0.71	11.0	220	Bt Baldwin, 1976 (IVd) (HSAN 2563).
315	0.55	8.5	80	i.m. small cross/uncertain, no stops. Obv. SCOTO. Bt Baldwin, 1976 (IVd) (HSAN 2564).
316	0.39	6.0	10	Obv. SCOTO. Bt Baldwin, 1976; ex F. Baldwin (IVd) (HSAN 2565).
317	0.63	9.7	170	i.m. large pellet (?)/small cross (?), no stops on either side. Bt Baldwin, 1976; ex F. Baldwin (IVd) (HSAN 2567).
318	0.75	11.6	260	i.m. pellet (?)/uncertain. Obv. SCOTO. Bt Baldwin, 1976; ex F. Baldwin (IVd) (HSAN 2568).
319	0.81	12.5	350	Bt Spink, May 1976 (HSAN 2570).
320	0.81	12.5	160	Rev. EDI | NBVR. Bt Baldwin 1976; ex F. Baldwin (HSAN 2571).
321	0.78	12.0	135	Acq. 1976; ex Drabble II, lot 1195 (part) (IVd) (HSAN 2572).
322	0.52	8.0	120	i.m. star (?)/small cross both sides, star stops/lis stops (?). Bt Seaby, December 1972 (IVe – not noted by Stewart) (HSAN 2573).

Type IV. Contemporary counterfeits, as last (S.5362)

323	0.67	10.3	110	Rev. lis q1 and 3. bt Spink, October 1989; ex Davidson, noted as counterfeit by Seaby (HSAN 2471).
324	0.78	12.0	Uncertain	Blundered legends both sides. Ex Mauchline (HSAN 2539).
325	0.51	7.9	Uncertain	i.m. small cross/uncertain, legends largely off flan. Bt Baldwin, 1976; ex F. Baldwin (HSAN 2574).
326	0.78	12.0	200	i.m. cross both sides. Rev. lis q1 and 3. Bt Baldwin, 1976; ex F. Baldwin (HSAN 2575).
327	0.47	7.3	180	i.m. uncertain both sides. Rev. lis q1 and 3. Bt Baldwin, 1976; ex F. Baldwin (HSAN 2576).
328	0.62	9.6	180	i.m. uncertain both sides. Bt Baldwin, 1976; ex F. Baldwin (HSAN 2577).
329	0.63	9.7	180	i.m. uncertain both sides. Bt Baldwin, 1976; ex F. Baldwin (HSAN 2578).

PLATE 17

302 303 304 305 306 307 308

309 310 311 312 313 314 315

316 317 318 319 320 321 322

323 324 325 326 327 328 329

JAMES V (1513–42)

GOLD COINAGE

First coinage, *c.* 1518–26

Unicorn
Theoretical weight 3.82 g, 59 gr, 21 ct.: value 20 shillings Scots.

i.m. crown, trefoil/pellet stops, roman-lettering. Obv. chained unicorn left grasping shield bearing lion rampant, crown on neck, X below, IACOBVS . DEI . GRA : REX . SCOTORVM. Rev. EXVRGAT . DEVS : ET DISSIPENTVR . INIMICI : EIVS, six-point radiant star, extending from central mullet, over long-cross fleury.

Type I

Reverse with cinquefoil countermark.

	Weight g.	gr.	Die Axis	
330	3.82	59.0	0	Obv. SCOTOR / VM, ground line below unicorn. Rev. DISIPENT . NIMICI : EI, countermark to right of upper arm of cross (Stewart Ia; B.727.2; S.5364). Acq. 1998, ex J. E. L. Murray; ex Hird, lot 58; ex Shand, lot 239 (HSAN 4798)
331	3.84	59.3	90	Trefoil stops both sides. Obv. A in IACOBVS recut, SCOTOR / VM, ?broken annulet beneath legs of unicorn. Rev. DISIPENT . NMICI . E, countermark between first and second arm of cross (Stewart Ia; B.730.3; S.5364). Ex Glendining 26 May 1977, lot 9. Same dies as Lockett I lot 280 (HSAN 4801).

Type I.

Base-metal contemporary counterfeit.

332	3.41	52.6	270	Obv. X above end of chain, flan flaw above unicorn. Rev. countermark above second arm of cross. Acq. 1971; Baldwin (gift from P. Mitchell) (HSAN 4802).

Type II.

As Type I, reverse without cinquefoil countermark.

333	3.77	58.2	40	Obv. SCOTOR / VM :. Rev. DISIPENT . NIMICI : E : (Stewart II; B.733.5; S.5365). Bt Spink, 14 January 1957; ex O'Hagan, lot 614. Same dies as Lockett II, lot 879 (HSAN 4799).
334	3.80	58.7	180	Trefoil stops both sides. Obv. SCOTOR \ VM :. Rev. DISIPENT . INIMICI . (Stewart II; B.727.2; S.5365). Acq. 1998, ex J. E. L. Murray; ex Beresford-Jones, lot 486; ex Bute lot 173 (HSAN 4800).

Half-unicorn

Theoretical weight 1.91 g, 29.50 gr: value 10 Shillings Scots

Similar to the unicorn

335	1.91	29.5	220	Trefoil and pellet stops, ground line below unicorn. Obv. . IACOBVS ⁂ DEI . GRA . REX . SCOTORVM : ∵ .∵ ∴ ¤:. Rev. EXVRGAT ⁂ DEVS ⁂ ET ⁂ DISIPENT ⁂ NIMICI . EI : (B.736.1a; S.5366). Ex Douglas, lot 277; ex Hird, lot 65; ex Gantz II, lot 1540; acq. by Gantz, 31 May 1928 (HSAN 4803).

Second coinage, 1526–39

Crown

Theoretical weight 3.39 g, 52.25 gr, 21.5 ct.: value 20 shillings Scots.

i.m. radiant sun/crown Obv. crowned shield bearing lion rampant, a saltire each side, IACOBVS : 5 : DEI : GRA : REX : SCOTORVM. Rev. triple-stranded cross fleury, a thistle head in each angle.

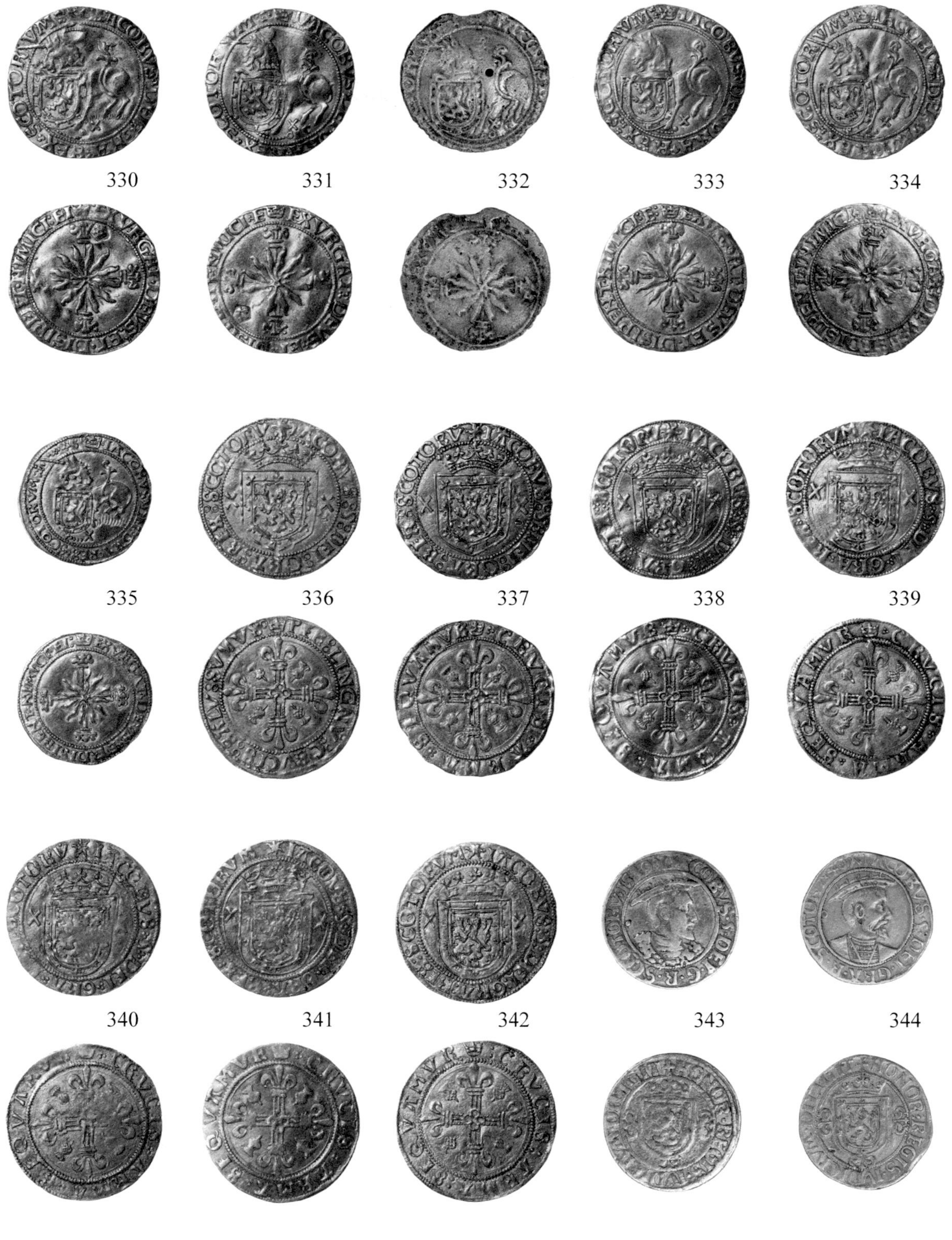

330 331 332 333 334

335 336 337 338 339

340 341 342 343 344

Type II.

Obv. Open crown, shield with pointed base. Rev. CRVCIS . ΛRMΛ . SEQVΛMVR.

	Weight g.	gr.	Die Axis	
336	3.38	52.2	180	Annulet colon stops. Obv. SCOTORV, annulet in V, bar below right saltire. Rev. PER : LINGNV : CRVCIS : SALV: SVMVS ., annulet in V in LINGV, a II/I mule (Stewart II/I; B.746.9; S.5369/5368). Ex Butterfield, lot 15; ex Hird, lot 66; ex Sotheby 15 October 1953, lot 18 (HSAN 4804).
337	3.41	52.6	30	Obv. annulet colon stops, SCOTORV, annulet in V, smaller open crown, bar below right saltire. Rev. trefoil stops, . CRVCIS . ΛRMΛ . SEQVΛMVR, a II/III mule (Stewart II/III; B.747.10; S.5369/5370). Ex Westfälische Auktions 26, 13–16 April 2004, lot 4256; ex Hird, lot 67; ex Lockett II, lot 880; ex Bearman; ex Murdoch, lot 177 (HSAN 4806).

Type III.

Trefoil stops. Obv. smaller open crown, shield with rounded base. Rev. CRVCIS ΛRMΛ SEQVΛMVR.

338	3.35	51.7	200	Colon trefoil stops. Obv. SCOTORV, large open crown. Rev. trefoil stops (Stewart III; B. -: S.5370). Ex DNW 67, 29 September 2005, lot 1156; ex Dundee, lot 101(HSAN 4805).
339	3.35	51.7	310	Crested and barred A both sides. Obv. SCOTORVM (Stewart III; B.737.1a; S.5370). Ex DNW 67, 29 September 2005, lot 1155; ex Dundee, lot 100; ex Glendining, 12–13 July 1966, lot 5. Same rev. dies as Lockett I, lot 284 (HSAN 4807).
340	3.40	52.5	110	Obv. SCOTORV, annulet in V, interior of crown frosted (Stewart III; B.740.3; S.5370). Acq. 1 June 1962; ex Lorimer (HSAN 4808).
341	3.31	51.1	160	Obv. IACOVS . 5 ., SCOTORVM, crown with corded lines (Stewart III; B.744.7; S.5370). Acq. October 1997; ex Elsen list 194, autumn 1997, item 1126 (HSAN 4809).

Type IV.

As Type III but with pellet colon stops

342	3.41	52.6	240	(Stewart IV; B.742.4a - this coin; S.5371) Acq. 7 October 2003; ex Davidson I, lot 883; ex Lornie lot 77 (HSAN 4810).

Third coinage, 1538–42

Ducat or 'Bonnet piece' (1539–40)

Theoretical weight 3.82 g, 88.3 gr: value 40 shillings Scots.

i.m. saltire/plain-cross, pellet stops. Obv. bearded profile bust to right wearing bonnet, IACOBVS . 5 . DEI . GRA . R . SCOTORVM, date after SCOTORVM. Rev. HONOR . REGIS . IVDICIVM . DILIGIT, crowned shield bearing lion rampant over short-cross fleury.

	Weight g.	gr.	Die Axis	Date	
343	5.70	88.0	0	1539	Obv. bust wearing collar of the Order of the Thistle, pellet by inner-circle at 9 o'clock between O and R, DEI . G . R . SCOTORV . **1539** (B.752.2; S.5373). Acq. 21 May 1999; ex Lockett I, lot 289; ex Bearman; ex Foster, lot 275 (HSAN 4811).
344	5.48	84.6	200	1540	Obv. SCOTOR . **1540**, annulet by inner-circle at 9 o'clock between T and O. Rev. stop after HONOR a pellet with wedge above and below (B.753.4; S.5373). Ex Spink auction 16, 9–10 July 1981, lot 800 (HSAN 4812).

GOLD *(cont.)*

Third coinage (cont.)

Two-thirds ducat (1540)

Theoretical weight 5.72 g, 58.9 gr: value 26 shillings and 8 pence Scots.
i.m. lis/plain-cross, similar to ducat. Obv. IACOBVS . D . G . R . SCOTORVM . **1540**. Rev. crowned shield bearing lion rampant on plain ground, I to left, **5** to right of shield.

	Weight g.	gr.	Die Axis	
345	3.81	58.8	270	Obv. IACOBVS . D . G . R . SCOTORVM . **1.5.4.0.** (B.755.1; S.5374). Bt Baldwin, 1973 (HSAN 4813).

One-third ducat (1540)

Theoretical weight 1.91 g, 29.5 grns: value 13 shillings and 4 pence Scots.

Similar to two-thirds ducat.

346	1.83	28.3	90	Obv. IACOBVS . D . G . R . SCOTOR : **1540**. Rev. HONO . REGIS . IVDICIV DILICIT, abbreviation pellet below second O in HONO. Unprovenanced (B.756.1; S.5375) (HSAN 4814).

SILVER COINAGE

Second coinage, 1526–38

Groat

Classification follows Stevenson 1991.

Theoretical weight 2.72 g, 42.0 gr: value 18 pence Scots.

i.m., cross/-. Obv. +IACOBVS : 5 : DEI : GRA : REX : SCOTOR, crowned bust right. Rev. shield bearing lion rampant over long-cross with foliate ends.

Type I. *With reverse* VILLA EDINBRVGH

i.m. plain-cross, colon annulet stops both sides, roman G. Obv. double-arched crown, closed mantle. Rev. : VILL | A : ED | INBR | VGh X, shield with pointed base (Stewart I).

347	2.56	39.5	90	(B.724.24; Stevenson Ia; S.5376). Ex Dakers, lot 439 (part); bt Baldwin 1925. Same obv. die as **348**, **351**, **352** and **354** (HSAN 2736).
348	2.63	40.6	90	(B.724.24; Stevenson Ia; S.5376). Acq. 17 December 1965; ex Dakers, lot 439 (part); acq. Lincoln, no date stated. Same obv. die as **347**, **351**, **352** and **354** (HSAN 2737).
349	2.67	41.2	250	(B.724.24; Stevenson Ia; S.5376). Bt Baldwin; ex F. Baldwin, with old ticket (HSAN 2738).
350	2.66	41.0	320	(B.724.24; Stevenson Ia; S.5376). Bt Baldwin, 1976; ex F. Baldwin. Same rev. die as **357** (HSAN 2739).
351	2.55	39.4	320	(B.724.24; Stevenson Ib; S.5376). Bt Spink, 1975. Same obv. die as **347**, **348**, **352** and **354** (HSAN 2740).
352	2.60	40.1	90	(B.724.24; Stevenson Ib; S.5376). Ex Dakers, lot 439 (part); acq. from Lincoln 1930. Same obv. die as **347**, **348**, **351** and **354** (HSAN 2741).
353	2.58	39.8	120	(B.724.24; Stevenson Ib; S.5376). Bt Baldwin, 1978; ex F. Baldwin (HSAN 2742).
354	2.52	38.9	360	(B.724.24; Stevenson Ib; S.5376). Bt Spink, 1965; ex Marr. Same obv. die as **347**, **348**, **351** and **352** (HSAN 2743).
355	2.54	39.2	180	Obv. numeral **5** omitted, SCOTORV, contraction mark above V (B.723.22; Stevenson Ib; S.5376). Bt Spink, 24 July 1987; ex Davidson; acq. Spink, 9 October 1970 (HSAN 2744).
356	2.63	40.6	80	(B.724.24; Stevenson Ib; S.5376). Ex Cochran-Patrick (1936), lot 235 (part) (HSAN 2745).
357	2.59	40.0	240	(B.724.24; Stevenson Ib; S.5376). Bt Spink, 1965; ex Marr; acq. Seaby, 14 May 1957. Same rev. die as **350** (HSAN 2746).

345 346 347 348 349

350 351 352 353 354

355 356 357 358 359

Type II. *With reverse* OPPIDVM EDINBVRGI

i.m. plain-cross/-, colon annulet stops both sides, roman G both sides. Obv. SCOTOR, crown with single arch, closed mantle. Rev. : OPPI | DVM : E | DINB | VRGI, shield with pointed base (Stewart II).

358	2.46	38.0	360	Obv. crown band with twelve pellets (B.720.19: Stevenson IIa(i); S.5377). Ex Walters, lot 653 (part) (HSAN 2747).
359	2.48	38.3	135	Obv. crown band with twelve pellets, SCOTORV, annulet above V (B.720.19; Stevenson IIa(ii); S.5377). Ex Walters, lot 653 (part) (HSAN 2748).

SILVER. Second coinage *(cont.)*

Groats (cont.)

Type II/III Mules

Obv. as type II, trefoil by inner-circle behind head, roman G. Rev. as type III, with single trefoil stops, curled G, **:** **OPPI | DV : E | DINB | VRGI**, usually pellet above **V** in **DV**, shield with rounded base (Stewart II/IV; S.5377/5378).

	Weight			
	g.	gr.	Die Axis	
360	2.63	40.6	340	Obv. trefoil by **S**. Rev. double trefoil stops (B.722.21/712.18; Stevenson IIa(i)/IIb(ii)). Bt Baldwin, 1978; ex F. Baldwin. Same obv. die as **361**, **362** and **363** (HSAN 2749).
361	2.37	36.6	45	Obv. trefoil by **S** (B.722.21/712.8; Stevenson IIa(ii)/IIb(ii)). Ex Caladon, lot 104 (part). Same obv. die as **360**, **362** and **363** (HSAN 2750).
362	2.72	42.0	90	Obv. trefoil by **S**, clear annulet above **R** of **OR** (B.722.21/712.8; Stevenson IIa(ii)/IIb(iii)). Ex Cochran-Patrick (1936), lot 235 (part). Same obv. die as **360**, **361** and **363** (HSAN 2751).
363	2.41	37.2	120	Obv. trefoil by **S**, clear annulet above **R** of **OR** (B.722.21/712.8; Stevenson IIa(ii)/IIb(iii)). Bt Seaby, 1 October 1971. Same obv. die as **360**, **361** and **362** (HSAN 2752).

Type III. *With reverse* **OPPIDV EDINBVRGI**

i.m. plain-cross /-, single trefoil stops both sides, curled G. Obv. crown with single arch, open mantle, usually **SCOTORV**. Rev. **. OPPI | DV . E | DINB | VRGI**, usually pellet above **V** in **DV**, shield with rounded base (Stewart IV).

364	2.55	39.4	90	Obv. **SCOTORVM**, trefoil by inner-circle behind head by **O** (B.716.15; Stevenson IIIa(ii); S.5378). Bt Spink, 24 July 1987; ex Davidson (HSAN 2764).
365	2.65	40.9	320	Obv. **SCOTOR**, trefoil by inner-circle behind head by **S** (B.717.17; Stevenson IIIa(ii); S.5378). Bt Spink, 1965; ex Marr. Same obv. die as **366** (HSAN 2770).
366	2.68	41.4	340	Obv. **SCOTOR**, trefoil by inner-circle behind head by **S** (B.717.17; Stevenson IIIa(ii); S.5378). Unprovenanced. Same obv. die as **365** (HSAN 2771).
367	2.71	41.8	350	Obv. **SCOTOR** (B.714.12; Stevenson IIIa(ii); S.5378). Ex Walters lot 652 (part) (HSAN 2772).
368	2.61	40.3	180	Obv. trefoil by inner-circle behind head by **O**. Rev. no pellet in **V** in **DV** (B.717.15; Stevenson IIIa(ii); S.5378). Ex Brushfield, lot 53 (part); ex Banes, lot 377 (part). Same obv. die as **369**, **370** and **371** (HSAN 2773).
369	2.52	38.9	340	Obv. trefoil by inner-circle behind head by **O** (B.717.15; Stevenson IIIa(ii); S.5378). Ex Walters, lot 653 (part). Same obv. die as **368**, **370** and **371** (HSAN 2774).
370	1.85	28.6	340	Obv. trefoil by inner-circle behind head by **O** (B.717.15; Stevenson IIIa(ii); S.5378). Bt Baldwin. Same obv. die as **368**, **369** and **371** (HSAN 2775).
371	2.64	40.7	340	Obv. trefoil by inner-circle behind head by **O** (B.717.15; Stevenson IIIa(ii); S.5378). Bt Spink, 1965; ex Marr. Same obv. die as **368**, **369** and **370** (HSAN 2776).
372	2.52	38.9	190	Obv. pellet in **V** in **SCOTORV**, trefoil by inner-circle behind head between **SC** (B.718.16a; Stevenson IIIa(ii); S.5378). Bt Baldwin; ex F. Baldwin (HSAN 2777).
373	2.72	42.0	20	Obv. numeral **5** omitted (B.713.10; Stevenson IIIb(i); S.5378). Bt Baldwin; ex F. Baldwin (HSAN 2778).
374	2.61	40.3	140	Obv. **SCOTOR** (B.718.17; Stevenson IIIb(i); S.5378). Bt Baldwin; ex F. Baldwin; ex Brushfield, lot 53 (part). Ticket carries note 'Mure bequest 1 July 1930' (HSAN 2779).

PLATE 20

360 361 362 363 364

365 366 367 368 369

370 371 372 373 374

SILVER. Second coinage *(cont.)*

Groats (cont.)

	Weight g.	gr.	Die Axis	
375	2.35	36.3	320	Obv. trefoil by inner-circle behind head by O (B.717.15; Stevenson IIIb(iii); S.5378). Bt Spink, 24 July 1987; ex Davidson; ex Bruun, lot 927 (part) (HSAN 2759).
376	2.52	38.9	200	Obv. SCOTORVM (B.718.16; Stevenson IIIb(iii); S.5378). Bt Baldwin, 1962 (HSAN 2760).
377	2.44	37.7	180	(B.714.11; Stevenson IIIb(iv); S.5378). Bt Spink, 24 July 1987; ex Davidson (HSAN 2780).
378	2.63	40.6	80	(cf. B.712.8; Stevenson IIIb(iv); S.5378). Bt Baldwin; ex F. Baldwin (HSAN 2781).
379	2.60	40.1	340	Obv. SCOTORVM, pellet above V, trefoil by inner-circle behind head by O (B.716.14; Stevenson IIIb(iv); S.5378). Ex Cochran-Patrick (1936), lot 234 (part) (HSAN 2761).
380	2.70	41.7	280	Obv. SCOTORVM, VM ligate, trefoil by inner-circle behind head between SC (cf. B.716.4; Stevenson IIIb(iv); S.5378). Bt Baldwin; ex F. Baldwin. Same obv. die as **381** (HSAN 2762).
381	2.56	39.5	330	Obv. SCOTORVM, VM ligate, trefoil by inner-circle behind head between SC (cf. B.716.14; Stevenson IIIb(iv); S.5378). Bt Baldwin, 14 May 1968. Same obv. die as **380** (HSAN 2763).
382	2.45	37.8	45	(B.712.8; Stevenson IIIb(v); S.5378). Bt Baldwin; ex F. Baldwin. Holed (HSAN 2782).
383	2.72	42.0	210	(B.712.8; Stevenson IIIb(v); S.5378). Ex Walters, lot 652 (part) (HSAN 2783).
384	2.69	41.5	90	Obv. pellet above V in SCOTORV, trefoil by inner-circle behind head by C. Rev. inverse barred N (B.712.9; Stevenson IIIb(v); S.5378). Ex Brushfield, lot 53 (part); ex Banes, lot 377 (part) (HSAN 2784).
385	2.61	40.3	320	Obv. pellet above V in SCOTORV, trefoil by inner-circle behind head by C (cf. B.712.9; Stevenson IIIb(v); S.5378). Bt Spink, 24 July 1987; ex Davidson; Mackenzie, lot 281 (part) (HSAN 2785)
386	2.59	40.0	280	Obv. SCOTORVM, trefoil by inner-circle behind bust by C (B.-; Stevenson IIIc(i); S.5378). Bt Seaby, 10 August 1953. Same obv. die as **387** (HSAN 2786).
387	2.79	43.1	225	Obv. SCOTORVM, trefoil by inner-circle behind head by C (B.716.14; Stevenson IIIc(i); S.5378). Bt Baldwin; ex F. Baldwin. Same obv. die as **386** (HSAN 2787).
388	2.77	42.8	45	(B.712.8; Stevenson IIIc(i); S.5378). Bt Baldwin, 26 June 1969. Same obv. die as **391** (HSAN 2788).
389	2.25	34.8	180	(B.712.8; Stevenson IIIc(ii); S.5378). Bt Baldwin, 1976 (HSAN 2766).

PLATE 21

375 376 377 378 379

380 381 382 383 384

385 386 387 388 389

SILVER. Second coinage *(cont.)*

Groats (cont.)

	Weight g.	gr.	Die Axis	
390	2.64	40.8	150	Obv. pellet inside inner-circle by X in REX (B. -; Stevenson IIIc(ii); S.5378). Bt Baldwin, 1976 (HSAN 2767).
391	2.45	37.8	210	(B.706.3; Stevenson IIIc(ii); S.5378). Bt Seaby, May 1966; ex R. C. Carlyon-Britton. Same obv. die as **388**. Holed behind hair (HSAN 2789).
392	2.71	41.8	180	(B.712.8/706.1; Stevenson IIIc(ii)/IIIc(iii); S.5378). Bt Baldwin, 1978 (HSAN 2768).
393	2.65	40.9	250	(B.706.3; Stevenson IIIc(iii); S.5378). Obv. pellet above V in SCOTORV. Acq. 21 January 1987 (HSAN 2769).
394	2.61	40.3	70	Crested A (cf. B.706.3; Stevenson IIIc(iii); S.5378). Ex Brushfield, lot 53 (part), with erroneous ticket stating ex 'Glendining 24 April 1924 lot 32'. Same obv. die as **395** (HSAN 2790).
395	2.61	40.3	225	Crested A (cf. B.706.3; Stevenson IIIc(iii); S.5378). Bt Spink, 1965; ex Marr. Same obv. die as **394** (HSAN 2791).
396	2.49	38.4	170	(cf. B.706.3; Stevenson IIIc(iv); S.5378). Bt Baldwin, 28 June 1969 (HSAN 2753).
397	2.64	40.7	300	Obv. SCOTORV . (cf. B.706.3; Stevenson IIIc(iv); S.5378). Ex Walters, lot 652 (part). Same obv. die as **398** and **399** (HSAN 2754).
398	2.16	33.3	300	Obv. SCOTORV . (cf. B.706.3; Stevenson IIIc(iv); S.5378). Bt Baldwin. 1978. Same obv. die as **397** and **399** (HSAN 2755).
399	2.61	40.3	225	Obv. SCOTORV . (cf. B.706.3; Stevenson IIIc(iv); S.5378). Acq. 1987; ex Blunt. Same obv. die as **397** and **398** (HSAN 2756).
400	2.55	39.4	180	Obv. SCOTOR (B.706.1; Stevenson IIIc(iv); S.5378). Bt Baldwin; ex F. Baldwin (HSAN 2792).
401	2.65	40.9	160	Rev. DV .. (B. -; Stevenson IIIc(iv); S.5378). Ex Ryan II, lot 1359 (part). Same obv. die as **402**, **403** and **404** (HSAN 2793).
402	2.72	42.0	90	(B.706.3; Stevenson IIIc(iv); S.5378). Acq. 1978; bt Baldwin; ex F. Baldwin. Same obv. die as **401**, **403** and **404** (HSAN 2794).
403	2.50	38.6	90	(B.706.3; Stevenson III c(iv); S.5378). Ex Brushfield, lot 53 (part); ex Banes, lot 377 (part). Same obv. die as **401**, **402** and **404** (HSAN 2795).
404	2.56	39.5	360	(B.706.3; Stevenson IIIc(iv); S.5378). Bt Baldwin, 14 May 1968. Same obv. die as **401**, **402** and **403** (HSAN 2796).

390

391

392

393

394

395

396

397

398

399

400

401

402

403

404

SILVER. Second coinage *(cont.)*

Groats (cont.)

	Weight g.	gr.	Die Axis	
405	2.67	41.2	260	Obv. SCOTOR (B.706.1; Stevenson IIIc(iv); S.5378). Ex Walters, lot 652 (part) (HSAN 2797).
406	2.77	42.8	135	Obv. SCOTORM, RM ligate (B.706.2; Stevenson IIIc(iv); S.5378). Bt *c.* 1950 (HSAN 2798).
407	2.71	41.8	170	Obv. SCOTOR (B.706.1; Stevenson IIIc(iv); S.5378). Ex Walters, lot 652 (part). Same obv. die as **412** (HSAN 2799).
408	2.67	41.2	45	Obv. pellet above V in SCOTORV. Rev. pellet in V in BVRGI (B.706.3; Stevenson IIIc(iv); S.5378). Bt Baldwin; ex F. Baldwin (HSAN 2802).
409	2.75	42.4	360	With hollow mouth (cf. B.707.4; Stevenson IIIc(v); S.5378). Bt Spink, 1965; ex Marr; ex R. C. Carlyon-Britton (HSAN 2757).
410	2.59	40.0	360	(cf. B.707.4; Stevenson IIIc(v); S.5378). Bt Baldwin, 14 May 1968 (HSAN 2758).
411	2.53	39.0	260	(B.707.5; Stevenson IIIc(v); S.5378). Bt Baldwin, 14 May 1968 (HSAN 2765).
412	2.62	40.4	170	Obv. SCOTOR (B.707.5; Stevenson IIIc(v); S.5378). Ex Walters lot 652 (part). Same obv. die as **407** (HSAN 2800).
413	2.46	38.0	225	Obv. SCOTOR (B.707.5; Stevenson IIIc(v); S.5378). Bt Baldwin, 1972 (HSAN 2801).
414	2.64	40.7	315	Obv. SCOTOR (B.707.5; Stevenson IIIc(v); S.5378). Bt Baldwin, 1976; ex Lockett II, lot 887 or 888 (part); ex Bearman; ex Pollexfen lot 316 (HSAN 2803).

Type IV

As type III, i.m. plain-cross/- or lis, lis tipped points on central finial of crown, trefoil or colon pellet stops both sides (Stewart III).

415	2.45	37.8	330	Obv. SCOTORV, RV ligate, trefoil stops. Rev. as type III (B.709.7; Stevenson IVa; S.5379). Bt Spink, July 1987; ex J. K. R. Murray, lot 177. Same dies as Christies 24 February 1988, lot 23 (HSAN 2804).
416	2.52	38.9	260	IVb, i.m. cross/lis, pellet colon stops both sides. Obv. SCOTORV, pellet above V. Rev. i.m. lis (B.709.7; Stevenson IVb; S.5379). Bt Spink, 12 August 1955 (HSAN 2805).

One-third groat

Theoretical weight 0.90 g,14.0 gr: value 6 pence Scots.

Classification follows Stevenson 1991.

As type III groat, i.m. plain-cross/-, pellet stops both sides. Obv. IACOBVS : 5 : DEI : GRA : R : SCOTOR, bust usually without chain on breast, tunic sometimes low set. Rev. : OPPI | DV : E | DINB | VRGI, pellet within V of DV.

417	0.91	14.0	210	Obv. with chain, SCOTO (B.710.1; Stevenson IVc(i); S.5380). Acq. 1976; ex Cochran-Patrick (1936), lot 234 (part) (HSAN 2819).
418	0.78	12.0	200	Obv. with chain, SCOTO (B.710.1; Stevenson IVc(ii; S.5380). Bt Baldwin, 1976; ex F. Baldwin (HSAN 2817).
419	0.89	13.8	40	Obv. with chain, low set tunic, GRΛ (B.711.3; Stevenson IVc(ii); S.5380). Bt Baldwin, September 1990 (HSAN 2818).

PLATE 23

405 406 407 408 409

410 411 412 413 414

415 416 417 418 419

SILVER. Second coinage *(cont.)*

One third groats (cont.)

	Weight g.	gr.	Die Axis	
420	0.89	13.8	60	Obv. low set tunic, SCOTORV, GRΛ (B.711.4; Stevenson IVc(iii); S.5380). Bt Baldwin, 1976; ex F. Baldwin (HSAN 2815).
421	0.92	14.2	30	Obv. low set tunic, SCOTOR, GRΛ (B.711.3; Stevenson IVc(iii); S.5380). Bt Baldwin, 1976; ex F. Baldwin (HSAN 2816).
422	0.78	12.0	315	Obv. without central bar in crown (B.711.3; Stevenson IVd(i); S.5380). Acq. 30 September 1957; ex Bute, lot 238 (part). Holed behind crown (HSAN 2807).
423	0.89	13.7	90	Obv. with chain (B.711.3; Stevenson IVd(i); S.5380). Bt Baldwin; ex F. Baldwin (HSAN 2811).
424	0.81	12.5	100	Obv. with chain (B.711.3; Stevenson IVd(i); S.5380). Unprovenanced. Holed above crown (HSAN 2813).
425	0.89	13.7	110	Obv. with chain, SCOTOR, OR ligate, GRΛ (B.-; Stevenson IVd(i); S.5380). Bt Spink, 1965; ex Marr; ex Hurley (HSAN 2814).
426	0.88	13.6	45	Obv. SCOTO. Rev. inverse barred N (B.711.2; Stevenson IVd(ii); S.5380). Acq. 30 September 1957; ex Bute, lot 238 (part) (HSAN 2806).
427	0.88	13.6	315	Obv. IACORVS. Rev. inverse barred N (B.711.2; Stevenson IVd(ii); S.5380). Bt Seaby, September 1966 (HSAN 2808).
428	0.80	12.3	340	Pellet behind head, A without bar. Rev. inverse barred N (B.711.2; Stevenson IVd(ii); S.5380). Bt Baldwin; ex F. Baldwin; ex Lockett II, lot 887 or 888 (part) (HSAN 2809).
429	0.78	12.0	360	Obv. SCOTORV (B.711.4; Stevenson IVd(ii); S.5380). Bt Baldwin; ex F. Baldwin (HSAN 2810).
430	0.78	12.0	190	Obv. low set tunic, GRΛ, SCOTORV (B.711.4; Stevenson IVd(ii); S.5380). Acq. 30 September 1957; ex Bute, lot 238 (part) (HSAN 2812).
431	0.85	13.1	360	Obv. SOTORV (B.-; Stevenson IVd(ii); S.5380). Acq. 23 March 1968; ex Thorburn (HSAN 2820).
432	0.88	13.6	320	Obv. SOTORV, IΛC. Rev. inverse barred N (B. -; Stevenson IVd(ii); S.5380). Ex Pollexfen, lot 318 (part); Beaufoy lot 85 (part) (HSAN 2821).

BILLON COINAGE

First coinage 1513–26

Plack

Value 4 pence Scots.

i.m. crown/-, roman letters. Obv. : IACOBVS . DEI . GRA . REX . SCOTORVM, crowned shield bearing lion rampant, crown at each side, sat within a tressure of three arcs, legend around. Rev. : VILL | A . DE : | : EDIN | BVRG :, a five-point mullet (sometimes appears to be a star) at centre within lozenge with curving sides from which extend cruciform limbs terminating in a floriated cross fourchée, a crown and a plain-cross in alternate angles, legend around.

Classification follows Stewart 1967, p. 147. Varieties based on stops, as below:

Stewart var.	Stops, obv/rev	Sylloge annotation
Ia	Star/star	i/i
Ib	Star/trefoil	i/ii
IIa	Pellet/pellet	iii/iii
IIb	Trefoil/trefoil	ii/ii
IIc	Pellet/trefoil	iii/ii

PLATE 24

420 421 422 423 424 425

426 427 428 429 430 431

432 433 434 435 436 437

Type I. *With plain roman-lettering*

Transitional types – *James IV/James V.*

Obv. as James IV type II. Rev. as James V type I (mule James IV type II obverse with James V reverse) (B.-; S.5350/5381).

	Weight g.	gr.	Die Axis	
433	1.83	28.2	190	Obv. (James IV type II), i.m. cross fleury, stops i/i, **SCOTT**, lis in upper spans. Rev. (James V), **: VILL[..]N | BVRG:**, crown q1 and 3. Acq. 14 June 1958; ex Spufford (Stewart Ia) (HSAN 2827).
434	2.44	37.7	360	Obv. (James IV type II), i.m. cross fleury, stops i/i, **SCOTT**, lis in upper spans. Rev. (James V) [..]**A : [.] : EDIN | BVRG :**, inverse barred N, crown q1 and 3. Bt Spink, June 1989; ex Davidson; bt Daniels (Stewart Ia) (HSAN 2828).

Obv. as James IV type IV. Rev. as James V type I (mule James IV type IV obverse with James V reverse) (B.757.1–758.1b; S.5352/5381).

435	1.96	30.2	30	Obv. (James IV type IV), i.m. crown, stops i/i, **SCOTORVM**, pellet colon after **4**, lis in all spans. Rev. (James V), **: VILL | A : DE: | : EDIN | BVRG :**, crown q2 and 4. Bt Spink; 1965; ex Marr; acq. Seaby 1957 (Stewart Ia) (HSAN 2829).
436	1.46	22.5	120	Obv. (James IV type IV), i.m. crown, stops i/i star, **SCOTORVM**, no colon after **4**, lis in upper spans. Rev. (James V), [..]**A | . DE : | : EDIN | BVRG :**, crown q1 and 3. Bt Spink, 7 May 1978 (Stewart Ia) (HSAN 2830).

Type I – *James V*

With James V obverse and reverse, stops i/i, i/ii (Stewart var Ia, Ib) (B.760.3–4,–761.5–5a; S.5381).

437	1.64	25.3	320	Stops i/i. Obv. **. IACOBVS**, slipped-trefoil in upper spandrels, lis in lower. Rev. **: VILL | A : DE : |**, crown q2 and 4. Bt Baldwin, 1976. Cracked rev. die (Stewart Ia) (HSAN 2835).

BILLON. First coinage *(cont.)*

Placks (cont.)

	Weight g.	gr.	Die Axis	
438	1.44	22.22	290	Stops i/ii,. Obv. trefoil in upper spandrels. Rev. . VILL | [ ] | . EDIN | BVRG :, crown q2 and 4. Bt Spink, 1965; ex Marr; ex Parsons (Stewart Ib) (HSAN 2831).
439	1.87	28.9	60	Stops i/ii. Obv. . IACOBVS, star in upper spandrels, lis in lower. Rev. DE ., crown q2 and 4. Acq. 1976; ex Winstanley (Stewart Ib) (HSAN 2832).
440	1.70	26.2	270	Stops i/ii. Obv. . IACOBVS, star in upper spandrels, ?lis in lower. Rev. .VILL | A. DE . | . EDIN | BVRG, crown q2 and 4. Bt Baldwin, 1976; ex F. Baldwin (Stewart Ib) (HSAN 2833).
441	1.69	26.1	360	Stops i/ii. Obv. star in all spandrels. Rev. crown q2 and 4. Acq. November 1991 (Stewart Ib) (HSAN 2834).

Type II - *James V*

With James V obverse and reverse, stops iii/iii, ii/ii, iii/ii (Stewart vars, IIa, IIb, IIc) (B.762.6–8a; 764.9a; 765.9b–11b; 766.11c–11e; 767.12–12e; 768.13–17; 770/71.18–26); S.5381).

442	2.19	33.8	350	Stops iii/iii. Obv. IACOBVS : DEI :, lis in upper spandrels. Rev. . VILL | A :, : EDIN | BVRG, crown q1 and 3. Bt Baldwin, 1976 (Stewart IIa) (HSAN 2867).
443	1.82	28.1	330	Stops iii/iii. Obv. IACOBVS . DEI GRA ., pellet in right upper spandrels only. Rev. : VILL | A :, crown q1 and 3. Bt Baldwin, 1976 ex F. Baldwin (Stewart IIa) (HSAN 2868).
444	2.55	39.4	190	Stops iii/iii. Obv. . IAC[.], curled G, star in right upper spandrel only. Rev. : VILL | A :, crown q1 and 3. Bt Spink, June 1989; ex Davidson (Stewart IIa) (HSAN 2869).
445	2.13	32.8	225	Stops iii/iii. Obv. . IACOBVS . , [.]X :. lis in upper spandrels. Rev. crown q2 and 4. Acq. 1998, ex J. E. L. Murray (Stewart IIa) (HSAN 2871).
446	2.01	31.0	20	Stops ii/ii. Rev. . VILL | A . DE . | . EDIN | BVRG :, crown q2 and 4. Bt Spink, 26 March 1956 (Stewart IIb) (HSAN 2823).
447	1.72	26.5	360	Stops ii/ii. Obv. trefoil in upper spandrels. Rev. : VILL | A . DE . | : EDIN | BVRG:, crown q1 and 3. Bt Spink, 1948 (Stewart IIb) (HSAN 2824).
448	2.47	38.1	360	Stops ii/ii Obv. trefoil in upper spandrels. Rev. : VILL | A . DE : | : EDIN | BVRG :, crown q1 and 3. Bt Spink, June 1989; ex Davidson (Stewart IIb) (HSAN 2825).
449	1.43	22.1	110	Stops ii/ii. Obv. trefoil in upper spandrels. Rev. : VILL | A . DE . | : EDIN | BVRG :, crown q1 and 3. Bt. Spink, June 1989; ex Davidson (Stewart IIb) (HSAN 2826).
450	1.41	21.8	250	Stops ii/ii. Obv. DEI :, star in upper spandrels, lis in lower. Rev. crown q2 and 4. Bt Seaby, 1964; acquired to stock 1954 (Stewart IIb) (HSAN 2836).
451	2.16	33.3	90	Stops ii/ii. Obv. IACOBVS, DEI :, lis in all spandrels. Rev. : VILL | A : DE : |, crown q1 and 3. Bt Baldwin, 1976 (Stewart IIb) (HSAN 2837).
452	1.69	26.1	210	Stops ii/ii. Obv. IACOBVS, DEI :, lis in all spandrels. Rev. VILL |A :, crown q1 and 3. Bt Spink, 1965; ex Marr; ex Whitton (Stewart IIb) (HSAN 2838).

438 439 440 441 442

443 444 445 446 447

448 449 450 451 452

BILLON. First coinage *(cont.)*

Placks (cont.)

	Weight g.	gr.	Die Axis	
453	1.58	24.4	360	Stops ii/ii. Obv. IACOBVS : DEI :, lis in all spandrels. Rev. : VILL | A :, crown q2 and 4. Bt Spink, June 1989; ex Davidson (Stewart IIb) (HSAN 2839).
454	1.31	20.2	190	Stops ii/ii. Obv. . IACOBVS . DEI :, SCOTORVM :, lis in upper spandrels. Rev. : VILL | A : DE : | . EDIN | BVRG, crown q1 and 3. Bt Baldwin, 1976; ex F. Baldwin (Stewart IIb) (HSAN 2840).
455	1.73	26.7	220	Stops ii/ii. Obv. IACOBVS :, lis in upper spandrels. Rev. [.]LL | A : DE : |, crown q1 and 3. Bt Spink, 1965; ex Marr; ex R. C. Carlyon-Britton (Stewart IIb) (HSAN 2841).
456	2.11	32.6	300	Stops ii/ii. Obv. . IACOBVS, SCOTORV :, lis in upper spandrels. Rev. crown q1 and 3. Bt Spink, June 1989; ex Davidson (Stewart IIb) (HSAN 2842).
457	1.65	25.5	180	Stops ii/ii. Obv. lis in upper spandrels. Rev. : VILLA :, curled G, crown, q2 and 4. Bt Spink, June 1989; ex Davidson (Stewart IIb) (HSAN 2843).
458	2.05	31.6	200	Stops ii/ii. Obv. [.]OBVS :, small lis in upper spandrels. Rev. : EDEN | BVRG, crown, q1 and 3. Bt Baldwin, 1962 (Stewart IIb) (HSAN 2844).
459	1.84	28.4	180	Stops ii/ii. Obv. : IACOBVS : DEI :, trefoil in upper spandrels. Rev. : VILL | A ., crown q1 and 3. Acq. 1998, ex J. E. L. Murray (Stewart IIb) (HSAN 2846).
460	2.04	31.5	220	Stops ii/ii. Obv. : IA[..]S :, SCOTORV :, small lis in upper spandrels. Rev. crown q1 and 3. Acq. 1989 (Stewart IIb) (HSAN 2847).
461	2.30	35.5	210	Stops ii/ii. Obv. trefoil in upper spandrels. Rev. crown q1 and 3. Bt Spink, 26 March 1956 (Stewart IIb) (HSAN 2848).
462	1.73	26.7	10	Stops ii/ii. Obv. SCOTORVM :, trefoil in upper spandrels. Rev. crown q1 and 3, flan flaw on rev. in q3. Bt Seaby, 1966 (Stewart IIb) (HSAN 2849).
463	1.85	28.6	220	Stops ii/ii. Obv. . IACOBVS : DEI :, [..]ORVM ., trefoil in upper spandrels, curled G, rev. crown, q2 and 4. Bt Baldwin, 1976; ex F. Baldwin (Stewart IIb) (HSAN 2850).
464	2.04	31.5	120	Stops ii/ii,. Obv. trefoil in upper spandrels. Rev. : VILL | A :, crown q1 and 3. Bt Seaby, 1966 (Stewart IIb) (HSAN 2851).
465	2.33	36.0	50	Stops ii/ii. Obv. trefoil in upper spandrels. Rev. curled G, crown q2 and 4. Acq. 2 January 1956; bt Spink (Stewart IIb) (HSAN 2852).
466	1.78	27.5	200	Stops ii/ii. Obv. SCOTORVM ., trefoil in upper spandrels. Rev. crown q1 and 3. Bt Spink, June 1989; ex Davidson (Stewart IIb) (HSAN 2853).
467	1.43	22.1	80	Stops ii/ii Obv. trefoil in upper spandrels. Rev. : VILL | . DE :, crown q1 and 3. Bt Spink, June 1989; ex Davidson (Stewart IIb) (HSAN 2854).

453 454 455 456 457

458 459 460 461 462

463 464 465 466 467

BILLON. First coinage *(cont.)*

Placks (cont.)

	Weight g.	gr.	Die Axis	
468	2.26	34.9	250	Stops ii/ii. Obv. trefoil in upper spandrels, curled G. Rev. [..]LL | [..]E : |, crown q1 and 3. Bt Spink, June 1989; ex Davidson (Stewart IIb) (HSAN 2855).
469	1.24	19.1	280	Stops ii/ii. Obv. small lis in upper spandrels. Rev. crown q1 and 3. Bt Spink, June 1989; ex Davidson (Stewart IIb) (HSAN 2873).
470	2.08	32.1	20	Stops iii/ii. Obv. IACOBVS : DEI : GRA : REX . SCOTORV :, trefoil colon after SCOTORV, lis in upper spandrels. Rev. : VILL | A : DE : |, crown q2 and 4. Acq. 1966; ex R. C. Carlyon-Britton (Stewart IIc) (HSAN 2845).
471	2.06	31.8	190	Stops iii/ii. Obv. GRA :, trefoil in upper spandrels. Rev. curled G, crown q1 and 3. Bt Spink, 1965; ex Marr; acq. Seaby 1962 (Stewart IIc) (HSAN 2856).
472	1.51	23.3	90	Stops iii/ii. Obv. : IACOBVS :, SCOTORVM :, nil in upper spandrels. Rev. : VILL | A :, crown q1 and 3. Bt Spink, June 1989; ex Davidson (Stewart IIc) (HSAN 2857).
473	1.58	24.4	110	Stops iii/ii. Obv. IACOBVS . DEI :, SCOTORVM :, lis in upper spandrels. Rev. : VILL | A :, crown q1 and 3. Bt Spink, 1965; ex Marr; ex Parsons, lot 730 (part) (Stewart IIc) (HSAN 2858).
474	1.68	25.9	10	Stops iii/ii. Obv. IACOBVS : DEI :, [.]OTORVM :, lis in upper spandrels. Rev. crown q2 and 4. Bt Spink, 2 January 1956 (Stewart IIc) (HSAN 2859).
475	2.06	31.8	190	Stops iii/ii. Obv. IAO[BVS], small lis in upper spandrels. Rev. crown q2 and 4. Acq. 31 May 1970; ex Linlithgow hoard (Stewart IIc) (HSAN 2860).
476	1.70	26.2	360	Stops iii/ii. Obv. GRA :, small lis in upper spandrels. Rev. [.]LL | A :, crown q2 and 4. Bt Spink; 1965; ex Marr (Stewart IIc) (HSAN 2861).
477	1.92	29.6	190	Stops iii/ii. Obv. small lis in upper spandrels. Rev. . VILL | A ., crown q2 and 4. Bt Spink, June 1989; ex Davidson (Stewart IIc) (HSAN 2862).
478	1.60	24.7	290	Stops iii/ii. Obv. IACOBVS, lis in upper spandrels. Rev. crown q2 and 4. Bt Spink, June 1989; ex Davidson (Stewart IIc) (HSAN 2863).
479	1.54	23.8	220	Stops iii/ii. Obv. IACOBVS :, lis in upper spandrels. Rev. crown q1 and 3 (B.768.13). Bt Spink, June 1989; ex Davidson (Stewart IIc) (HSAN 2864).
480	1.25	19.3	360	Stops iii/ii, curled G both sides. Obv. . IACOBVS : DEI :, SCOTORVM :, pellet in upper spandrels. Rev. crown q2 and 4. Acq. 1998, ex J. E. L. Murray (Stewart IIc) (HSAN 2865).
481	2.14	33.0	20	Stops iii/ii. Obv. . IACOBVS : DEI :, curled G, pellet in upper spandrels. Rev. crown q1 and 3. Bt Spink, June 1989; ex Davidson (Stewart IIc) (HSAN 2866).
482	1.78	27.5	110	Stops - / iii. Obv. star in upper spandrels. Rev. crown q1 and 3. Bt Baldwin, 1976; ex F. Baldwin (HSAN 2870).

PLATE 27

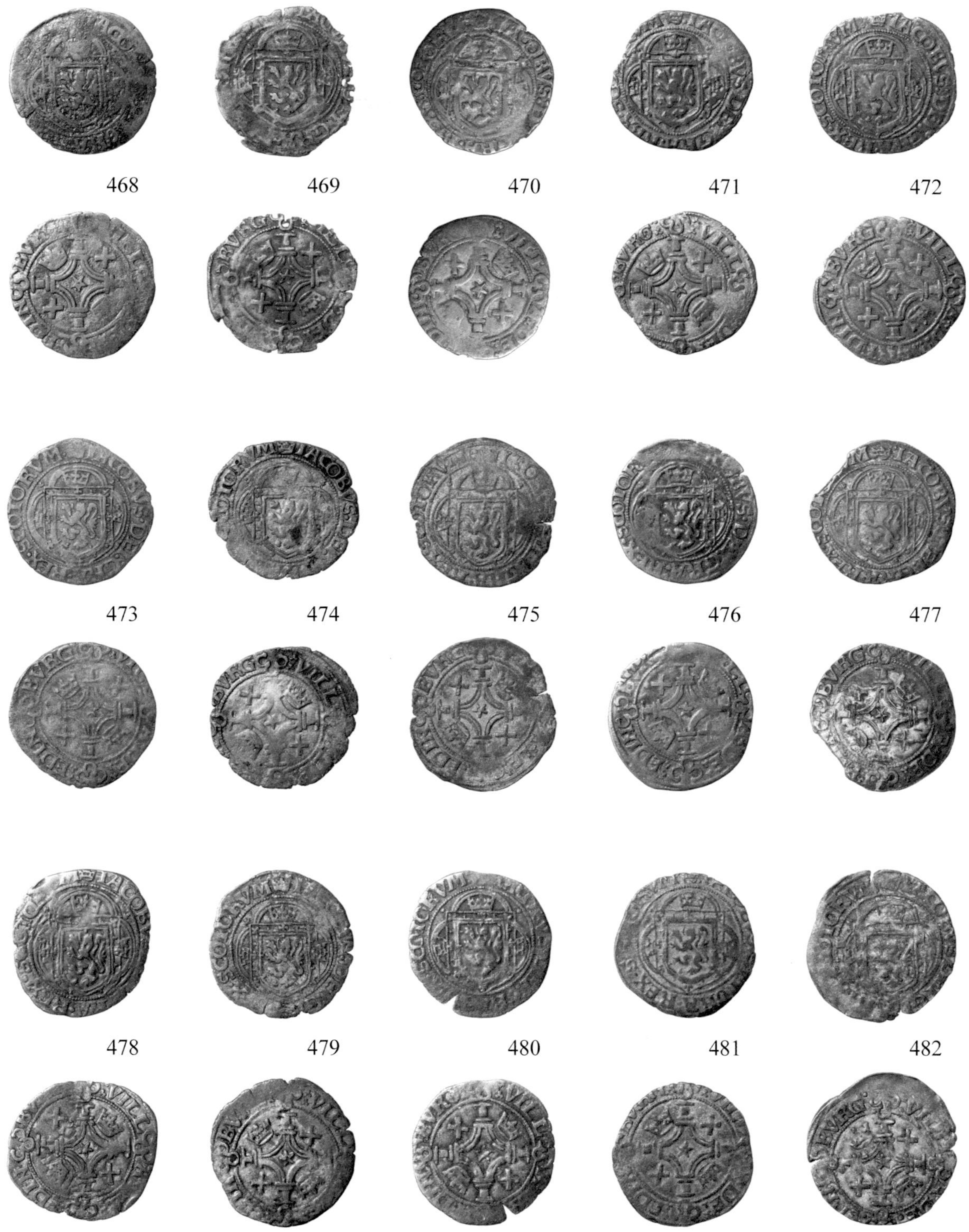

468 469 470 471 472

473 474 475 476 477

478 479 480 481 482

BILLON. First coinage *(cont.)*

Placks (cont.)

	Weight g.	gr.	Die Axis	
483	1.57	24.2	20	Stops iii/ii. Obv. [..]COTORV :, ?small lis in upper spandrels, curled G. Rev. . VILL | A ., crown q1 and 3. Bt Spink, 1965; ex Marr; acq. Seaby 1962 (Stewart IIc) (HSAN 2872).
484	1.46	22.5	10	Stops iii/ii. Obv. IACOBVS, small lis in upper spandrels. Rev. : VILL | A :, crown q1 and 3. Bt Seaby, 1966; ex R. C. Carlyon-Britton (Stewart IIc) (HSAN 2874).
485	1.65	25.5	30	Stops iii/ii. Obv. lis in upper spandrels. Rev. crown q1 and 3. Bt Spink, 1965; ex Marr; acq. Seaby 1957 (Stewart IIc) (HSAN 2875).
486	1.64	25.3	30	Stops iii/ii. Obv. small lis in upper spandrels. Rev. . VILL | A., pellet colon before EDIN, crown q2 and 4. Bt Spink, June 1989; ex Davidson (Stewart IIc) (HSAN 2876).
487	1.66	25.6	280	Stops iii/ii. Obv. IACOBVS ., [.]TORVM :, small lis in upper spandrels. Rev. crown q1 and 3. Bt Spink, 1965; ex Marr; acq. Seaby 1954 (Stewart IIc) (HSAN 2878).
488	1.50	23.2	20	Stops iii/ trefoil and pellet. Obv. IACOBVS . DEI : GRA :, trefoil in upper spandrels. Rev. : VILL | A ∵ DE ∵ | ∵ EDIN | BVRG :, crown q1 and 3. Bt Baldwin, 1976; ex F. Baldwin (Stewart -) (HSAN 2877).

Second coinage, 1526–38

Plack - Issue of 1533.

i.m. cross/-, similar to first coinage type I, but with more elegant roman-lettering. Rev. crown in all angles (B. -; S.5382).

489	2.06	31.8	320	Stops iii/iii, curled G both sides. Obv. IACOBVS :, GRA : REX :, large annulet in upper spandrels. Rev. : VILL | A :. Bt Spink, 1965; ex Marr (see Stewartby and Holmes, 2008, illus. fig 1) (HSAN 2879).

Third coinage, 1538–42

Bawbee

Theoretical weight 1.88 g, 29.00 gr: value 6d Scots.

James V bawbees have been ordered using the traditional typology that differentiates coins with and without an annulet on the reverse. Classification follows Stevenson 1989, with five types, Ja-Je, some of which have sub-classes denoted with a lower-case roman numeral, as follows:

— Ja, obv. crown without pellets, two varieties, rev. trefoil stops.
— Jb, obv. as Ja, rev. single pellet stops.
— Jc, obv. as Ja, cusps of crown with added pellets, rev. single pellet stops.
— Jd, obv. crown interiors not indicated, letter N two varieties, rev. single pellet stops.
— Je, as Jd(ii), letter R as on gold ducat.

i.m. plain-cross/lis, Obv. crowned thistle dividing I and **5**, i.m. IACOBVS . D . G . REX . SCOTORVM. Rev. OPPIDVM . EDINBVRGI, crown over saltire cross dividing two thistles.

Stops obv./rev. :

i. Pellet/trefoil.
ii. Pellet/pellet.

Obv. without annulet over I or **5** or by inner-circle (B.775.4–776.5; S.5383).

490	1.83	28.2	180	Stops i. Obv. IACOBVS . **5** . D . G . REX . SCOTORV(Ja(i)). Acq. 1987; gift from Blunt (HSAN 2880).
491	1.74	26.9	60	Stops i (Ja(i)). Acq. 1965. Rigghead hoard. Same rev. die as *BNJ* 59, pl. 12, 3 and 4 – this coin rev. illustrated. Rusty dies (HSAN 2884).
492	2.15	33.2	180	Stops i (Ja(ii)). Acq. 1965. Rigghead hoard (HSAN 2882).

483 484 485 486 487

488 489 490 491 492

493 494 495 496 497

	Weight			
	g.	gr.	Die Axis	
493	1.63	25.2	90	Stops i (Ja(ii)). Acq. 1965. Rigghead hoard (HSAN 2883).
494	1.73	26.7	360	Stops i (Ja(ii)). Acq. 1965. Rigghead hoard (HSAN 2885).
495	1.39	21.5	190	Stops i (Ja(ii)). Unprovenanced (HSAN 2886).
496	1.72	26.5	90	Stops i (Ja(ii)). Unprovenanced (HSAN 2887).
497	0.96	14.8	360	Stops i (Ja(ii)). Bt Spink, 25 October 1988; ex Davidson (HSAN 2888).

BILLON. Third coinage *(cont.)*

Bawbees (cont.)

	Weight g.	gr.	Die Axis	
498	1.21	18.7	190	Stops i. Rev. B over D in EDINBVRGI (Ja(ii)). Unprovenanced (HSAN 2889).
499	1.74	26.9	270	Stops i. Obv. R in OR re-cut (Ja(ii)). Ex R. C. Carlyon-Britton (HSAN 2890).
500	1.80	27.8	30	Stops i (Ja(ii)). Unprovenanced (HSAN 2891).
501	1.65	25.5	30	Stops i (Jb). Bt Baldwin, 1968. *BNJ* 59, pl. 12, 7 and 8 – Obv. and Rev. of this coin illustrated (HSAN 2892).
502	1.68	25.9	330	Stops ii (Jb). Unprovenanced (HSAN 2893).
503	1.80	27.8	220	Stops ii (Jd(i)). Acq. 1980, given by Spink. Same obv. die as *BNJ* 59, pl. 12, 28. Holed at centre and at 5 o'clock (HSAN 2881).
504	2.02	31.2	280	Stops ii (Jd(i)). Acq. 1965. Rigghead hoard (HSAN 2897).
505	1.46	22.5	250	Stops ii (Jd(i)). Bt Baldwin, 1976; ex F. Baldwin (HSAN 2901).
506	1.45	22.4	200	Stops ii (Jd(ii)). Acq. 1965. Rigghead hoard (HSAN 2899).
507	1.91	29.5	20	Stops ii (Jd(ii)). Unprovenanced (HSAN 2911).
508	1.99	30.7	210	Stops ii (Jd(ii)). Unprovenanced (HSAN 2914).
509	1.60	24.7	340	Stops ii (Jd(ii)). Rev. EDINBVVRG. Unprovenanced (HSAN 2917).

Obv., with annulet above I to left of thistle or by inner-circle (B.772.1–774.3; S.5384).

510	1.27	19.6	340	Stops ii. Obv. annulet on inner-circle at O in OR (Jc). Ex J. K. R. Murray, lot 180 (part) (HSAN 2894).
511	1.58	24.4	170	Stops i. Obv. annulet on inner-circle between R and V (Jc). Unprovenanced (HSAN 2895).
512	1.54	23.8	300	Stops ii. Obv. 5 omitted, annulet left of crown (Jd(i)). Ex R. C. Carlyon-Britton (HSAN 2900).
513	1.57	24.2	110	Stops ii (Jd(i)). Acq. 1965. Rigghead hoard (HSAN 2902).
514	1.91	29.5	360	Stops ii (Jd(i)). Bt Spink, 1988; ex Davidson (HSAN 2822).
515	1.81	27.9	180	Stops ii (Jd(i)). Acq. 30 September 1957; ex Bute, lot 238 (part) (HSAN 2905).

498 499 500 501 502 503

504 505 506 507 508 509

510 511 512 513 514 515

BILLON. Third coinage *(cont.)*

Bawbees (cont.)

	Weight g.	gr.	Die Axis	
516	1.82	28.1	230	Stops ii (Jd(i)). Unprovenanced (HSAN 2922).
517	1.48	22.8	220	Stops ii (Jd(ii)). Ex R. C. Carlyon-Britton (HSAN 2898).
518	1.37	21.1	160	Stops ii (Jd(ii)). Acq. 1965. Rigghead hoard (HSAN 2903).
519	1.78	27.5	190	Stops ii. Obv. i.m. horizontal bar of cross omitted (Jd(ii)). Acq. 1965. Rigghead hoard (HSAN 2904).
520	1.63	25.2	90	Stops ii (Jd(ii)). Acq. 1976; ex Walters, lot 656 (part) (HSAN 2906).
521	1.87	28.9	340	Stops ii (Jd(ii)). Acq. 1965. Rigghead hoard (HSAN 2907).
522	2.02	31.2	30	Stops ii (Jd(ii)). Bt Spink, 26 March 1956 (HSAN 2908).
523	1.56	24.1	220	Stops ii (Jd(ii)). Unprovenanced (HSAN 2912).
524	1.75	27.0	210	Stops ii (Jd(ii)). Bt Spink; ex Davidson, acq. 1924, Kirkcudbright hoard (HSAN 2913).
525	1.76	27.2	200	Stops ii (Jd(ii)). Unprovenanced (HSAN 2915).
526	1.66	25.6	315	Stops ii (Jd(ii)). Unprovenanced (HSAN 2916).
527	2.03	31.3	140	Stops ii (Jd(ii)). Ex R. C. Carlyon-Britton (HSAN 2918).
528	1.80	27.8	180	Stops ii (Jd(ii)). Unprovenanced (HSAN 2919).
529	1.75	27.0	10	Stops ii (Jd(ii)). Rigghead hoard (HSAN 2920).
530	1.83	28.2	90	Stops ii (Jd(ii)). Rigghead hoard (HSAN 2921).
531	1.76	27.2	170	Stops ii (Je/Jd(ii)). Bt Spink; ex Davidson; acq. 1924, Kirkcudbright hoard (HSAN 2924).
532	1.87	28.9	30	Stops ii (Je). Acq. 1965. Rigghead hoard (HSAN 2909).
533	1.70	26.2	190	Stops ii. Obv. **5** omitted (Je). Ex R. C. Carlyon-Britton (HSAN 2923).

PLATE 30

516 517 518 519 520 521

522 523 524 525 526 527

528 529 530 531 532 533

BILLON. Third coinage *(cont.)*

Bawbees (cont.)

Obv., with annulet above **5** to right of thistle (B. -; S.5384A).

	Weight g.	gr.	Die Axis	
534	1.58	24.4	190	Stops ii (Jd(i)). Bt Baldwin, 1976 (HSAN 2896).
535	1.78	27.5	280	Stops ii (Jd(ii)). Ex R. C. Carlyon-Britton (HSAN 2910).

Half-bawbee

Theoretical weight 0.94 g, 14.50 gr: value 6d Scots

Half-bawbees have been ordered using the traditional typology that differentiates coins with an annulet above the **I** or **5** on the reverse from those without. The Stevenson 1989 classification with two types JA, JB is noted where
— JA, obverse with narrow initial cross and interior of the crown usually shown;
— JB, obverse with wide initial cross and interior of the crown not indicated.

i.m. plain-cross/lis, pellet stops, as bawbee. Obv. **IACOBVS . D . G . R . SCOTORVM**. Rev. lis by crown omitted.

Obv. without annulet above **I** or **5** (Stewart 1c; B.778.2; S.5386).

536	0.71	11.0	30	(JA). Bt Baldwin, 1985 (HSAN 2925).
537	0.89	13.7	280	Obv. **B . SCOTORVM** (JA). Acq. 17 December 1965; ex Dakers, lot 441 (part) (HSAN 2929).

Obv. with annulet above **I** (Stewart 1a; B.777.1; S.5387)

538	0.75	11.6	180	(JA). Acq. 17 December 1965; ex Dakers, lot 441 (part) (HSAN 2927).
539	1.15	17.7	330	(JA). Bt Baldwin, 1976 (HSAN 2928).
540	0.65	10.0	80	(JA). Bt Baldwin, 1968 (HSAN 2931).
541	0.83	12.8	45	(JB). Bt Baldwin, 1976; ex F. Baldwin (HSAN 2930).

Obv. with annulet above **5** (Stewart 1b; B.779.2a; S.5388)

542	0.78	12.0	230	(JB). Bt Spink, 1965; ex Marr; ex R. C. Carlyon-Britton (HSAN 2926).

MARY (1542–67)

FIRST PERIOD, 1542–58. BEFORE MARRIAGE TO FRANCIS

GOLD COINAGE

Crown

Theoretical weight 3.39 g, 52.25 gr, issued at value 20 shillings Scots in 1542, which was raised to 22 shillings and 10 pence in 1543.

i.m. radiant star/crown, single pellet stops. Obv. crowned shield bearing lion rampant, cinquefoil at sides, **MΛRIΛ . DEI . GRΛ . REGINΛ . SCOTORVM**. Rev. **. CRVCIS . ΛRMΛ . SEQVΛMVR**, triple-stranded cross fleury, thistle head in each angle.

543	3.39	52.3	320	(B.808.2; Stewart fig. 165; S.5390). Acq. 21 February 1970 (HSAN 4815)
544	3.34	51.5	250	Rev. A with bar, second A in **ARMA** inserted above a stop (B.808.2/808.1; Stewart fig. 169; S.5390). Ex Beresford-Jones, lot 490; ex Basmadjieff, lot 147; ex Ryan I, lot 571; ex Scott Plummer, lot 365. Noted by Lord Stewartby as 'a mule with the reverse of the second-issue.' (HSAN 4816).

Twenty-Shilling Piece (1543)

Theoretical weight, 2.86 g, 44.17 gr, issued 1543: value 20 shillings Scots.

i.m. plain-cross/radiant star, single pellet stops. Obv. crowned shield bearing lion rampant, **MARIA . D . G . R . SCOTORVM . 1.5.4.3**. Rev. **ECCE . ANCILLA . DOMINI**, MR monogram, crown above, cinquefoil below.

545	2.83	43.7	270	(B.809.1; Stewart fig. 168; S.5391). Ex Butterfield, lot 21; ex Dundee, lot 114; ex Hird, lot 80 (HSAN 4817).

PLATE 31

534 535 536 537 538 539

540 541 542 543 544

545 546 547 548 549

Forty-Four Shilling Piece (1553)

Theoretical weight 5.09 g, 78.5 gr, first issue, 1553: value 44 shillings Scots.

Type III

i.m. cross, pellet stops. Obv. crowned shield bearing lion rampant dividing I G, MARIA . D . G . SCOTORVM . REGINA. Rev. DILIGITE . IVSTICIAM . 1553, crown above monogram of MARIA REGINA, a cinquefoil each side.

	Weight g.	gr.	Die Axis	
546	5.12	79.0	30	Trefoil stop after REGINA (cf. B.811.1; Stewart 172; S.5394). Acq. 4 April 1997, ex Format, postal auction, item 1 (HSAN 4818).
547	5.09	78.5	40	MARIA . DEI . GRA . R . SCOTORVM (B.812.3; Stewart 172; S.5394). Acq. 7 June 1961 (HSAN 4819).

Twenty-Two Shilling Piece (1553)

Theoretical weight 2.55 g, 39.25 gr, issued 1553: value 22 shillings Scots.

i.m. -/cross, crowned shield bearing lion rampant. Obv. crown breaking legend, MARIA . D . G . R . SCOTORVM. Rev. DILIGITE . IVSTICIAM . 1553, MR monogram, a cinquefoil each side.

548	2.50	38.6	180	Obv. no stops. Rev. trefoil stop after DILIGITE (B.-/817.4; S.5396). Bt Baldwin; ex Michison (HSAN 4820).

Three-Pound Piece or Gold Ryal (1555, 1557–8)

Theoretical weight 7.63 g, 117.75 gr : value 3 pounds or 60 shillings Scots.

No i.m., pellets stops, Obv. bust left, MARIA . DEI . G . SCOTOR : REGINA. Rev. . IVSTVS . FIDE . VIVIT . 1555, crowned shield bearing lion rampant.

	Weight g.	gr.	Die Axis	Date	
549	7.43	114.6	40	1555	Rev. Interior of crown shaded (B.819.1; Stewart 169; S.5397). Ex Glendining 30 March 1983, lot 14 (HSAN 4821).

First Period. GOLD *(cont.)*

Thirty-Shilling Piece or Gold Half-Ryal (1555, 1557/8)

Theoretical weight 3.81 g, 58.8 gr : value 30 shillings Scots

As Three-Pounds

	Weight		Die		
	g.	gr.	Axis	Date	
550	3.72	57.4	140	1555	Obv. . MARIA . DEI . G . SCOTOR . REGINA ., trefoil stop after REGINA. Rev. interior of crown shaded (cf. B.822.8; S.5398). Ex Douglas, lot 288; ex Lockett II, lot 893; ex Huth, lot 658; ex Murdoch, lot 217; ex Marsham, lot 920 (HSAN 4824).

SILVER COINAGE

GROUP I

Testoon (1553)

Theoretical weight 78.5 gr, 5.08 g, 0.916 fine: value 4 shillings Scots.

i.m. star/cross. Obv. crowned bust right within double-inner circle, MARIA . DEI . GRA . R . SCOTORVM. Rev. . DA . PACEM . DOMINE . 1553 ., crowned shield bearing lion rampant, a cinquefoil at sides.

	Weight			
	g.	gr.	Die Axis	
551	4.48	67.6	350	(B.780.1; Stewart 166; Murray 4; S.5401). Acq. April 1965; ex Parsons, lot 731 (HSAN 2932).

GROUP II

Testoon (1555)

Theoretical weight 7.63 g, 117.75 gr, 0.725 fine: value 5 shillings Scots.

i.m. cross potent/-. Obv. crown above initial M, small crown above thistle head each side, MARIA . DEI . G . SCOTOR . REGINA . 1555 .. Rev. DILICI | E . DNI . | COR . HV | MILE, crowned shield bearing lion rampant over long-cross potent.

552	6.29	97.1	100	Obv. wedge in q2 and 3 of i.m. (cf. B.783.6; S.5402). Bt Baldwin, 1975; ex F. Baldwin (HSAN 2933).
553	6.62	102.2	180	Obv. wedge in q2 and 4 of i.m. (cf. B.783.6; S.5402). Bt Baldwin, 1975; ex F. Baldwin (HSAN 2934).
554	7.45	115.0	340	Obv. wedge in q3 and by end of left arm of i.m. after date. Rev. DILICI . | DNI . C | OR . HV | MILE, space between MI and LE (B. -; S.5402). Bt Baldwin, 13 March 1969 (HSAN 2935).
555	7.03	108.5	340	Rev. annulet above top arm of cross, trefoil to left of lower arm (B.783.5; S.5402). Bt. Spink, 28 July 1987; ex Davidson (HSAN 2937).

Similar, Obv. with annulet above over left crown above thistle head.

556	7.22	111.4	80	Obv. small trefoil at centre base of crowned M. Rev. trefoil to left of lower arm of cross (B.-; S.5403). Acq. October 1967; ex Hurley (HSAN 2936).

Half-testoon (1555)

Similar to Group II testoon

Theoretical weight 3.81 g, 58.90 gr: value 2 shillings and 6 pence Scots.

557	3.74	57.7	210	Rev. CORIIV MILE, last stop a wedge (B.785.3; S.5410). Bt Baldwin, 1975; ex F. Baldwin (HSAN 2938).
558	3.70	57.1	140	Rev, wedge after COR, trefoil to right of lower arm of cross (B.785.2; S.5410). Ex Davidson II, lot 450 (HSAN 2939).
559	3.34	51.5	230	Obv. trefoil at centre base of crowned M, small crowns surmounted with a cross. Rev. trefoil to right of lower arm of cross (B.784; S.5410). Bt Spink; 1965; ex Marr (HSAN 2940).

550 551 552 553 554

555 556 557 558 559

560 561 562 563 564

	Weight g.	gr.	Die Axis	
560	3.71	57.3	10	Obv. small crowns surmounted with cross. Rev. annulet above top arm (B.785.3; S.5410). Bt Baldwin, 13 March 1969 (HSAN 2941).
561	3.84	59.8	270	Obv. small crowns surmounted with cross. Rev. annulet above top arm, trefoil to right of lower arm, struck off-centre (B.785.3; S.5410). Acq. 2 October 2000; ex Cochran-Patrick (1936), lot 238 (part) (HSAN 2942).

GROUP III 1556–8

Testoon (1556–8)

Theoretical weight 6.11 g, 94.25 gr, 0.916 fine, dated 1556, 1557, 1558: value 5 shillings Scots, countermarked coins revalued at 7 shillings and 4 pence in 1578.

i.m., small cross potent/crown. Obv. crowned shield bearing lion rampant dividing M, left, R right, MARIA . DEI . G . SCOTOR . REGINA ., date after REGINA. Rev. IN . VIRTVTE . TVA . LIBERA . ME ., date after ME ., short cross potent, a small cross in each angle.

First variety (1556–7)

Obv. narrow, small high-arched crown, with annulet below M and R by shield, dated 1556, 1557.

	Weight g.	gr.	Die Axis	Date	
562	5.83	90.0	20	1556./1556	Rev. i.m. cross potent (B.786.7; S.5404). Acq. 1975; ex Cochran-Patrick (1936), lot 241 (part) (HSAN 3024).
563	5.95	91.8	10	1556/1556	(B.788.10; S.5404). Bt Baldwin, 1975; ex F. Baldwin (HSAN 3025).
564	5.71	88.1	30	1556/1556	Rev. crowned thistle countermark q1 (cf. B.788.11; S.5404). Bt Baldwin, 1975; ex F. Baldwin (HSAN 3026).

First Period. SILVER *(cont.)*

Testoons. Group III *(cont.)*

	Weight g.	gr.	Die Axis	Date	
565	6.10	94.1	320	1556/1556.	Obv. MARIA . D . G . (B.788.12; S.5404). Bt Spink, 24 July 1987; ex Davidson; ex Ready, lot 832 (part) (HSAN 3028).
566	5.94	91.7	50	1556/1556	Rev. crowned thistle countermark q3 (B.789.13; S.5404). Bt Spink, 24 July 1987; ex Davidson; ex Roth, lot 371 (part) (HSAN 3029).
567	6.01	92.7	330	1556/1556	No stops both sides, Rev. LIBER, VTE over VAE, (B.788.13/- ; S.5404). Acq. 25 May 1992; ex Dolphin list 2, item 1425; ex J. K. R. Murray, lot 188 (part) (HSAN 3030).
568	6.00	92.6	210	1556./1556.	Rev. crowned thistle countermark to left of q1 (B.798.8; S.5404). Acq. 25 March 1992; ex Seaby/CNA auction, lot 1411 (HSAN 3031).
569	6.26	96.6	350	1556/1556	Obv. no stops (B.790.14; S.5404). Acq. 26 May 1992; ex Dolphin list 2, item 1426 (HSAN 3032).
570	6.07	93.7	40	1556./1556	MARIA . D . G . (B.788.12; S.5404). Bt Baldwin, February 2004 (HSAN 3033).
571	5.97	92.1	350	1556./1556.	Rev. i.m. cross potent, stop before VIR over V (B.787.8; S.5404). Bt Spink, 24 July 1987; ex Davidson. Kirkcudbright hoard (HSAN 3034).
572	5.56	85.8	40	1556/1557.	Obv. no stops. Rev. crowned thistle countermark q1 (B.786.7/792.17; S.5404). Bt Spink, 1965; ex Marr; ex R. C. Carlyon-Britton; ex Parsons, lot 733 (part). Same obverse die as **573** (HSAN 3035).
573	6.01	92.7	350	1556/1557.	Obv. no stops (B.786.7/792.17; S.5404). Acq. 1975; ex Ryan II, lot 1362 (part). Same obverse die as **572** (HSAN 3036).
574	5.97	92.1	90	1557./1556	Rev. crowned thistle countermark to left q4 (cf. B.789.13; S.5404). Acq. 1969 (HSAN 3037).
575	6.04	93.2	30	1557/1557	(cf. B.792.17; S.5404). Acq. 1975; ex Dakers, lot 447 (part); ticket notes ex 'Laing 1923' (HSAN 3039).
576	6.03	93.0	10	1557/1557	Rev. crowned thistle countermark q1 (cf. B.789.13/-; S.5404). Bt Baldwin, 1975; ex F. Baldwin (HSAN 3041).
577	5.70	88.0	360	1557/1557	Obv. no stops. Rev. . LIBERA ME . (B.789.14/-; S.5404). Bt Baldwin, 1975; ex F. Baldwin (HSAN 3042).
578	5.86	90.4	340	1557/1557	Obv. no i.m. Rev. no stops, crowned thistle countermark q1 (B. 792.17; S.5404). Bt Baldwin, 1975; ex F. Baldwin (HSAN 3044).

As last. Obv. without annulet below M and R by shield, dated 1556, 1557

579	5.71	88.1	340	1556/1556	(B.794.15; S.5405). Acq. 29 September 1954 (HSAN 3027).

PLATE 33

565 566 567 568 569

570 571 572 573 574

575 576 577 578 579

First Period. SILVER *(CONT.)*

Testoons. Group III *(cont.)*

	Weight g.	gr.	Die Axis	Date	
580	6.03	93.0	360	1557/1556.	Obv. MARIA . D . G . (B.-; S.5405). Bt Spink, 24 July 1987; ex Davidson (HSAN 3038).
581	6.19	95.5	20	1557/1557	Obv. MARIA . D . G . (B.-; S.5405). Acq. 1975; ex Parsons, lot 733 (part) (HSAN 3040).

Second variety (1557–8)

As first variety, but Obv. large low-arched crown, usually without annulets below M and R by shield, dated 1557, 1558.

582	6.01	92.7	10	1557./1557	Rev. no stops (cf. B.793.18; S.5406). Acq. 1975; ex Parsons, lot 733 (part) (HSAN 3046).
583	5.99	92.4	360	1557/1557	(B.793.18; S.5406). Ex J. K. R. Murray, lot 191 (part); ex Hird, lot 147 (HSAN 3048).
584	5.71	88.1	320	1557/1558.	Rev. Crowned thistle countermark over left arm of cross (cf. B.974.19; S.5406). Acq. 1975; ex Parsons, lot 733 (part) (HSAN 3049).
585	6.15	94.9	340	1557/1558	(B.794.19; S.5406). Acq. 1975; ex Parsons lot 733 (part) (HSAN 3050).
586	6.10	94.1	360	1557/1558	Obv. no stops. Rev. VERTVTE (cf. B.794.14; S.5406). Bt Baldwin, 1975; ex F. Baldwin (HSAN 3051).
587	6.02	92.9	10	1557/1558	Rev. VERTVTE (B.794.19; S.5406). Bt Spink, 1965; ex Marr (HSAN 3052).
588	6.04	93.2	10	1558./1557	Obv. no i.m.. Rev. no stops (B.798.23; S.5406). Bt Baldwin, 1975; ex F. Baldwin (HSAN 3053).
589	5.93	91.5	340	1558./1558	Obv. no i.m. (cf. B.798.24; S.5406). Acq. 1975; ex Parsons, lot 733 (part). Same obverse die as **592** (HSAN 3054).
590	5.55	85.6	350	1558./1558.	Obv. no i.m. (?) (B.798.24; S.5406). Acq. 1 April 1967 (HSAN 3055).
591	5.98	92.3	10	1558./1558	Obv. . MARIA. Rev. B over E in ME (B.-; S.5406). Acq. *c.* 1950 (HSAN 3056).
592	6.03	93.0	80	1558./1558	Obv. no i.m.. Rev. VERTVTE, crowned thistle countermark q1 (B.798.24; S.5406). Bt Baldwin, 1975; ex F. Baldwin. Same obverse die as **589** (HSAN 3057).
593	6.02	92.9	20	1558./1558	Rev. VERTVTE (B.798.25; S.5406). Acq. 1975; ex Parsons, lot 733 (part) (HSAN 3058).
594	6.06	93.5	250	155[8]./1558.	Obv. no i.m. (?) (B.798.24; S.5406). Acq. 1975; ex Cochran-Patrick (1936), lot 243 (part) (HSAN 3059)

PLATE 34

580

581

582

583

584

585

586

587

588

589

590

591

592

593

594

First Period. SILVER *(cont.)*

Testoons. Group III (*cont.*)

	Weight g.	gr.	Die Axis	Date	
595	5.83	90.0	350	1558./1558.	Rev. VERTVTE, crowned thistle countermark q1 (B.798.26; S.5406). Bt Baldwin, 1975; ex F. Baldwin (HSAN 3060).
596	5.86	90.4	10	1558./1558.	Obv. no i.m., SCOTOR (cf. B.798.24; S.5406). Bt Baldwin, 1975; ex F. Baldwin (HSAN 3061).
597	5.79	89.3	340	1558/1558	(B.798.24; S.5406). Bt Baldwin, 1975 (HSAN 3062).
598	6.09	94.0	150	1558/1558.	(cf. B.798.24; S.5406). Bt Baldwin, February 2004 (HSAN 3070).
599	5.98	92.3	220	1558./1558	(cf. B.798.24; S.5406). Bt Baldwin, February 2004 (HSAN 3071).
600	6.18	95.4	160	1558./1558.	(cf. B.798.24; S.5406). Unprovenanced (HSAN 3074).

Obv. an A in field below R to right of shield, dated 1558.

601	5.93	91.5	210	1558./1558	(B.795.20; S.5408). Bt Baldwin, 1975; ex F. Baldwin, ex Dakers (HSAN 3063).
602	6.01	92.7	350	1558. /1558.	Rev. LIBER . A ME . (cf. B.795.20.S.5408). Bt Spink, 1965; ex Marr (HSAN 3064).
603	5.99	92.4	210	1558./1558.	(cf. B.795.20; S.5408). Acq. October 1967; ex Hurley (HSAN 3065).

Obv. with annulet below M and R by shield, dated 1557, 1558.

604	5.90	91.0	30	1557/1557	Rev. no stops, crowned thistle countermark over left arm of cross (cf. B.797.22; S.5407). Bt Baldwin, 1975; ex F. Baldwin (HSAN 3043).
605	5.52	85.2	350	1557/1557	Rev. no stops, crowned thistle countermark q1 (cf. B.797.22; 5407). Acq. 1975; ex Winstanley (HSAN 3045).
606	6.07	93.7	20	1557/1557	(cf. B.797.22; S.5407). Ex J. K. R. Murray, lot 191 (part) (HSAN 3047).
607	6.04	93.2	40	1558./1558.	Rev. crowned thistle countermark q1 (B.797.22; S.5407). Acq. 1975; ex Parsons, lot 733 (part) (HSAN 3066).
608	6.10	94.1	10	1558./1558	(B.797.24; S.5407). Acq. 1975; ex Parsons, lot 733 (part) (HSAN 3067).
609	6.44	99.4	350	1558./1558	Rev. VERTVTE (B.798.25; S.5407). Acq. 1975; ex Cochran-Patrick (1936), lot 243 (part) (HSAN 3068).

PLATE 35

595 596 597 598 599

600 601 602 603 604

605 606 607 608 609

First Period. SILVER *(cont.)*

Testoons. Group III *(cont.)*

	Weight g.	gr.	Die Axis	Date	
610	5.99	92.4	40	1558./1558	(cf. B.797.23; S.5407). Bt Baldwin, 1975. Same reverse die as **611**. Holed above crown right (HSAN 3069).
611	6.03	93.0	10	1558./1558	Obv. large annulets (cf. B.797.23; S.5407). Bt Spink, 24 July 1987; ex Davidson. Same reverse die as **610** (HSAN 3072).
612	5.76	88.9	40	1558./1558	Obv. large annulets (B.797.22; S.5407). Acq. 10 June 1992; Dolphin list 2, item 1437; ex J. K. R. Murray, not in sale (HSAN 3073).

Half-testoon (1556–8)

Theoretical weight 3.06 g, 47.12 gr, 0.916 fine, dated 1556, 1557, 1558: value 2 shillings and 6 pence Scots, countermarked coins revalued at 3 shillings and 8 pence in 1578.

Similar to first variety testoon.

i.m., -/crown, Obv. small high-arched crown, annulet below M and R (1556–7).

613	2.83	43.7	100	1557/1556,	Obv. no stops. Rev. small plain-crosses (B.803.10/801.6; S.5411). Acq. 4 February 1992; ex Dolphin, list 2, item 1442 (HSAN 3081).
614	2.65	40.9	120	.1557. /1557	Rev. small plain-crosses (B.803.10; S.5411). Acq. 13 March 1969 (HSAN 3082).

No annulets by M and R (1556–8)

615	2.90	44.8	190	1556./.1556	Obv. MARIA . D . G . (cf. B.800.5; S.5413). Bt Spink 1975 (HSAN 3075).
616	2.97	45.8	320	.1556/1556	Obv. MARIA . D . G .. Rev. small plain-crosses (cf. B.800.5; S.5413). Bt Baldwin, 1975; ex F. Baldwin (HSAN 3076).
617	2.90	44.8	110	1556/1556.	Obv. no stops. Rev. crowned thistle countermark q1 (cf. B.801.8a; S.5413). Acq. *c.* 1965 (HSAN 3077).
618	3.03	46.8	10	1556/.1556	Obv. no stops, MARIA D G (B.800.8a; S.5413). Acq. 1967; ex Hurley (HSAN 3078).
619	3.01	46.4	130	1556/1556	MARIA . D . G . SCOTOR REGINA. Rev. small plain-crosses (B.800.8a; S.5413), 26 May 1992, Dolphin list 2, item 1443, ex J. K. R. Murray lot 197; ex Marr (HSAN 3079).
620	2.85	44.0	360	1556/1556	Obv. no stops. Rev. i.m. cross potent, small plain-crosses (B.800.8a; S.5413). Ex Parsons, lot 734; ex R. C. Carlyon-Britton. Holed below shield (HSAN 3080).
621	2.96	45.7	320	.1557./.1557.	Rev. large plain-crosses (B.800.11; S.5413). Acq. 4 February 1992; ex Dolphin, list 2, item 1445; ex J. K. R. Murray, lot 198; ex Marr; ex Lockett II, lot 896; ex Bearman; ex Murdoch, lot 198 (HSAN 3083).
622	2.77	42.7	190	.1557./.1558.	Rev. small plain-crosses (B.805.12; S.5413). Bt Baldwin, 1975; ex F. Baldwin. Holed left above crown (HSAN 3084).
623	2.92	45.1	280	1558/.1558.	Obv. no stops (?). Rev. small plain-crosses (B.-; S.5413). Acq. 1975; ex Cochran-Patrick (1936), lot 243 (part); ex Wigan (HSAN 3085).

As last, date on reverse only (1558 only).

624	3.02	46.6	360	-/.1558.	Obv. no stops, MARIA D G. Rev. LBERA, small plain-crosses, (B.806.15; S.5414). Bt Baldwin, 1972 (HSAN 3086).
625	2.92	45.1	260	-/.1558	Obv. MARIA . D . G .. Rev. crowned thistle countermark q1 (cf. B.806.15; S.5414). Bt Baldwin, 1975; ex F. Baldwin (HSAN 3087).

As last, Obv. A in field below M, date on reverse only (1558).

626	2.75	42.4	310	-/.1558.	Obv. MARIA . D . G .. Rev. LIBER, small crosses plain-cross (B.-, noted p. 282; S.5415). Acq. *c.* 1950s; ex Thorburn; ex Mackenzie, lot 293 (HSAN 3088).

PLATE 36

610 611 612 613 614

615 616 617 618 619 620

621 622 623 624 625 626

First Period. BILLON.
Bawbees. Group 1 (Edinburgh).

BILLON COINAGE

Bawbee 1543-c.1553–4 (undated)

Theoretical weight 1.91 g, 29.5 gr: value 6 pence Scots.

Classification follows Stevenson 1989, with 4 groups and eight types, with each type divided into one or more sub-classes:

Edinburgh, with solid saltire, B.823.1–839.40; Stevenson groups 1, 2 and 3, class Vb; S.5432;
Edinburgh, with voided saltire, B.845.41–859.73; Stevenson groups 3 and 4; S.5433;
Stirling, B.860.74–861.78; Stevenson groups I, Is(i) to Is(v); S.5434.

The Stirling issued bawbees are included within Group I. Some coins are worn or corroded and classification for these is based on the crown on the obverse and lettering as may be best determined from examination.

i.m. cross (cross potent)/lis, Obv. crowned thistle dividing M R, MARIA . D(EI). G(RA) . R(EGINA) . SCOTOR(VM). Rev. OPPIDVM . EDINBVRGI, saltire cross through an open crown, a cinquefoil each side.

GROUP 1. Edinburgh 1543–4

Reverse with solid saltire, open A (Classes Ia, Ib(i) and (ii))

Obv. MΛRIA . D . G . REGINΛ . SCOTORV(M). Rev. solid saltire with graining.

	Weight g.	gr.	Die Axis	
627	1.93	29.8	180	(Ia(i)). Acq. 1965. Rigghead hoard (HSAN 3214).
628	1.67	25.8	150	Obv. SCOTORVM (Ia(i)). Acq. 1965. Rigghead hoard (HSAN 3246).
629	1.54	23.8	320	(Ia(i)). Bt Spink, 25 October 1988 (HSAN 3247).
630	1.41	21.8	140	Obv. ORV pellet in V (Ia(ii)). Bt Baldwin, 1989 (HSAN 3150).
631	2.07	31.9	260	(Ia(ii)). Acq. 26 March 1956 (HSAN 3208).
632	2.07	31.9	260	Obv. ORV pellet in V (Ib(i)). Acq. 1965. Rigghead hoard (HSAN 3151).
633	1.76	27.2	10	Obv. ORV pellet in V (Ib(i)). Acq. 1965. Rigghead hoard (HSAN 3152).
634	1.78	27.5	160	(Ib(i)). Bt Spink, 25 October 1988; ex Davidson (HSAN 3153).
635	1.86	28.7	100	Obv. ORV, pellet in V. Rev. inverted crown (Ib(ii)). Acq. 13 February 1965. Holed from reverse at D . G (HSAN 3148).
636	1.38	21.3	270	(Ib(ii)). Unprovenanced. Reverse double struck (HSAN 3253).
637	1.42	21.9	360	Obv. ORV pellet in V. Rev. OPPIDVM .. EDINBVRGI (Ib(ii)). Acq. 1965. Rigghead hoard (HSAN 3254).
638	1.69	26.1	270	(Ib(ii)). Acq. 1965. Rigghead hoard (HSAN 3255)
639	1.43	22.1	360	Obv. ORV pellet in V (Ib(ii)). Acq. 1965. Rigghead hoard (HSAN 3256).
640	1.45	22.4	190	(Ib(ii)). Acq. 1989 (HSAN 3275).
641	1.85	28.6	140	Rev. pellet to right of upper left arm of saltire (Ib(iii)). Acq. 1957 (HSAN 3143).

GROUP 1, Stirling (Summer-Autumn 1544)

i.m. plain-cross/crown. Obv. crowned thistle dividing M R, MARIA . D . G . REGINA . SCOTORV. Rev. OPPIDVM . STIRLINGI, large cross potent, a plain-cross in each angle.

Stevenson classification, Group 1, type I (Stirling), classes Is(i) to (v).
- Λ : Is(i) to (ii)
- Barred and lob-topped A: Is(iii) to (v)

642	1.71	26.4	340	(Is(i)). Ex Dakers, lot 458 (part) (HSAN 3319).
643	2.29	35.3	20	Obv. ORV pellet in V (Stevenson Is(ii)). Ex Dakers, lot 458 (part) (HSAN 3320).
644	1.60	24.7	350	(Is(iii)). Bt Spink, 25 October 1988; ex Davidson; ex Thorburn (HSAN 3321).

627 628 629 630 631 632

633 634 635 636 637 638

639 640 641 642 643 644

First Period. BILLON *(cont.)*
Bawbees. Group 1 (Stirling) *(cont.)*

	Weight g.	gr.	Die Axis	
645	1.70	26.2	280	(Is(iii)). Bt Spink, 1965; ex Marr (HSAN 3322).
646	1.30	20.1	340	Obv. ORV pellet in V (Is(iii)). bt Spink, 25 October 1988; ex Davidson. Corroded (HSAN 3323).
647	1.32	20.4	310	Obv. ORV pellet in V (Is(iv)/Is(i-iii)). Bt Spink, 25 October 1988; ex Davidson. Same obv. as **648** (HSAN 3324).
648	1.87	28.9	10	(Is(iv)/Is(iii)). Unprovenanced. Same obv. as **647** (HSAN 3325).
649	1.87	28.9	80	(Is(iv)). Bt Baldwin, 1968 (HSAN 3326).
650	1.98	30.6	260	(Is(iv)). Bt Spink, 25 October 1988; ex Davidson (HSAN 3336).
651	1.74	26.9	110	Obv. ORV pellet in V (Is(v)/Is(ii-iii)). Bt Baldwin, 1968 (HSAN 3327).
652	1.63	25.3	350	Obv. RV ligate (Is(v)). Ex Lockett I, lot 326 (part); ex Bearman; ex F. G. Lawrence, lot 197 (HSAN 3328).
653	1.80	27.8	350	Obv. ORV pellet in V (Is(v)). Bt Spink, 25 October 1988; ex Davidson (HSAN 3329).
654	1.69	26.1	10	(Is(v)). Ex Dakers lot 458 (part). Same obv. as *SCBI* 35, 1056–7 (HSAN 3330).
655	1.63	25.2	30	Obv. ORV pellet in V (Is(v)). Bt Spink, 25 October 1988 (HSAN 3331).

GROUP 1 Edinburgh (from autumn 1544)

Obv. MARIA . D . G . REGINA . SCOTOR. Rev. with solid saltire (Stevenson classes Ib(iii), mules, Ib(iv), Ic(i-ii)).

656	1.35	20.8	180	Obv. SCOTORVM (Ib(iii)). Bt Baldwin, 1989 (HSAN 3144).
657	1.79	27.6	20	Obv. ORV pellet in V (Stevenson Ib(iii)). Acq. 1950 (HSAN 3145).
658	1.93	29.8	100	(Ib(iii)). Acq. 1953; ex Thorburn; acq. Perth, September 1948 (HSAN 3146).
659	1.84	28.4	70	Obv. MΛRIΛ, REGINA (Ib(iii)). Acq. 13 February 1965 (HSAN 3147).
660	1.66	25.6	120	(Ib(iii)). Acq. 1965. Rigghead hoard (HSAN 3149).
661	1.62	25.0	90	(Ib(iii)). Acq. 1953; ex Thorburn; acq. Seaby (HSAN 3154).
662	1.71	26.4	210	(Ib(iii)). Bt Baldwin (HSAN 3155).

PLATE 38

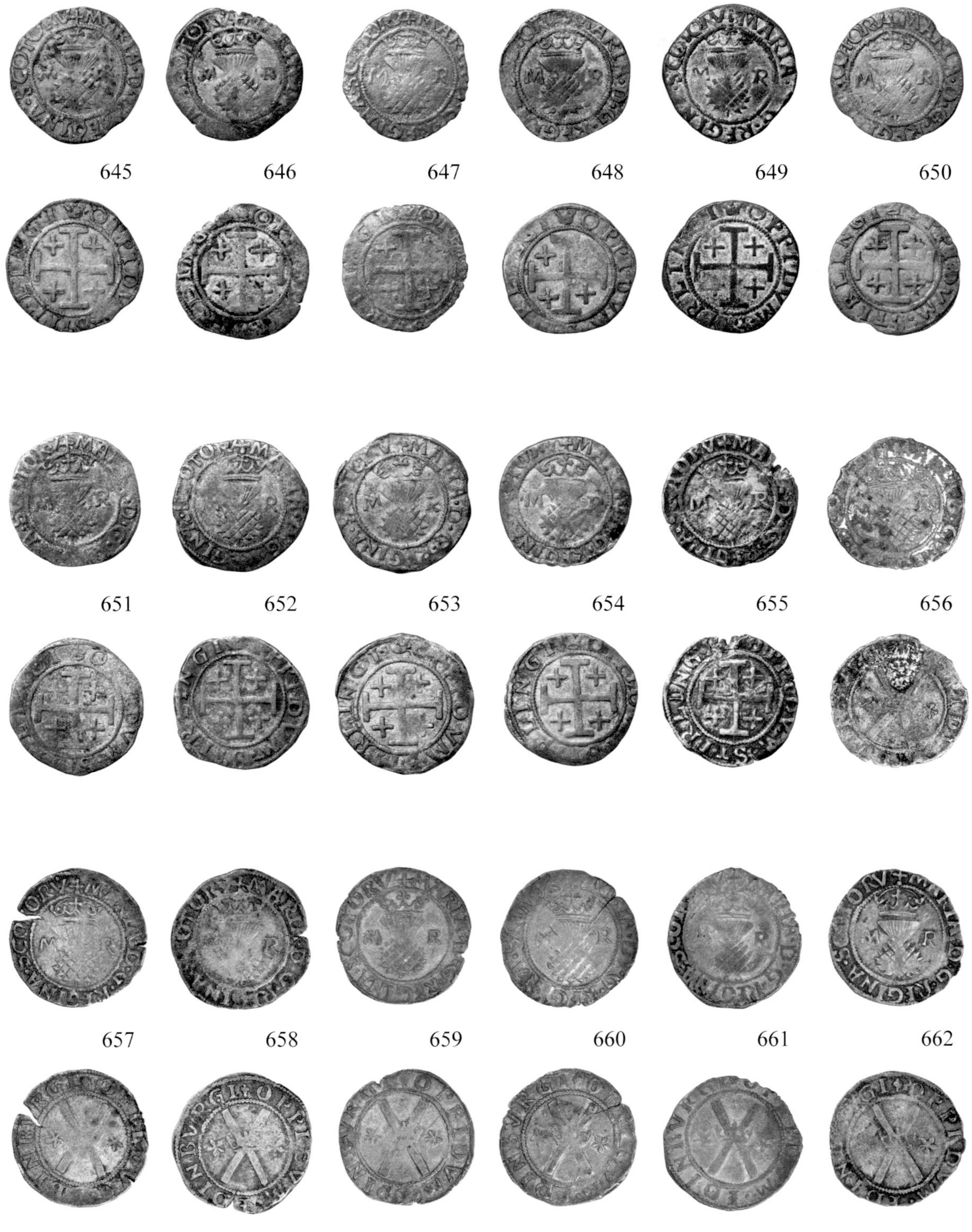

645 646 647 648 649 650

651 652 653 654 655 656

657 658 659 660 661 662

First Period. BILLON *(cont.)*
Bawbees. Group 1 *(cont.)*

	Weight g.	gr.	Die Axis	
663	1.60	24.7	360	Obv. SCOTORV (Stevenson Ib(iii)). Acq. 1965. Rigghead hoard (HSAN 3245).
664	1.39	21.5	170	(Ib(iii)). Acq. 1989 (HSAN 3248).
665	1.92	29.6	40	Obv. ORV pellet in V (Ib(iii)). Acq. 1989 (HSAN 3249).
666	1.50	23.2	90	(Ib(iii)). Bt Spink, 25 October 1988; ex Davidson (HSAN 3156).
667	1.89	29.2	120	(Ib(iv)). Bt Spink, 25 October 1988; ex Davidson (HSAN 3332).
668	1.57	24.2	20	(Ic(i)). Unprovenanced (HSAN 3157).

GROUPS 2 TO 4, ALL EDINBURGH

GROUP 2

Obv. MARIA . D . G . REGINA . SCOTORV. Rev. plain solid saltire (Stevenson classes ii, iii, iv, va).

On some coins the i.m. appears to be slipped-cross, i.e. with tapered lower arm, rather than the more usual plain-cross. Where this appears to be the case this is noted.

669	2.10	32.4	300	Obv. SCOTOR (IIa(i)). Bt Spink, 25 October 1988; ex Davidson (HSAN 3158).
670	1.71	26.4	140	Rev. EDINBVR.GI. (IIa(i)), 13 February 1965 (HSAN 3159).
671	1.73	26.9	140	Obv. SCOTORV, RV compressed, M with short centre. Rev. EDINBVRGI . (IIa(i)). Bt Spink, 25 October 1988; ex Davidson. Kirkcudbright hoard 1924. Obv. as *SCBI* 35, 1034 (HSAN 3163).
672	1.52	23.5	260	i.m. slipped-cross. Obv. SCOTOR. Rev. EDINBVRGI (IIa(ii)). Bt Baldwin, 16 July 1993; ex Plumbridge (HSAN 3160).
673	2.03	31.3	60	i.m. slipped-cross. Rev. EDINBVRGI . (IIa(ii)). Bt Spink, 25 October 1988 (HSAN 3164).
674	1.70	26.2	100	Obv. SCOTOR. Rev. . OPPIDVM . EDINBVRGI ., uncertain letter between N and B (IIa(ii)). Acq. 13 February 1965 (HSAN 3337).
675	1.79	27.6	140	i.m. slipped-cross. Rev. EDINBVRGI . (IIb). Unprovenanced (HSAN 3165).
676	1.79	27.6	270	i.m. slipped-cross (IIc). Bt Baldwin, 16 July 1993; ex Plumbridge (HSAN 3166).
677	1.69	26.1	330	i.m. slipped-cross. Rev. EDINBVRGI . (IIc). Acq. 1976; ex Dakers, lot 458 (part) (HSAN 3167).
678	1.76	27.2	320	Obv. RV ligate (IIc). Bt Spink, 1965; ex Marr (HSAN 3168).
679	1.69	28.1	120	(IIc). Bt Spink, 25 October 1988 (HSAN 3170).
680	2.22	34.3	210	(IIc). Bt Spink, 25 October 1988; ex Davidson; ex *NCirc* 2 February 1906, item 24385 (HSAN 3171).

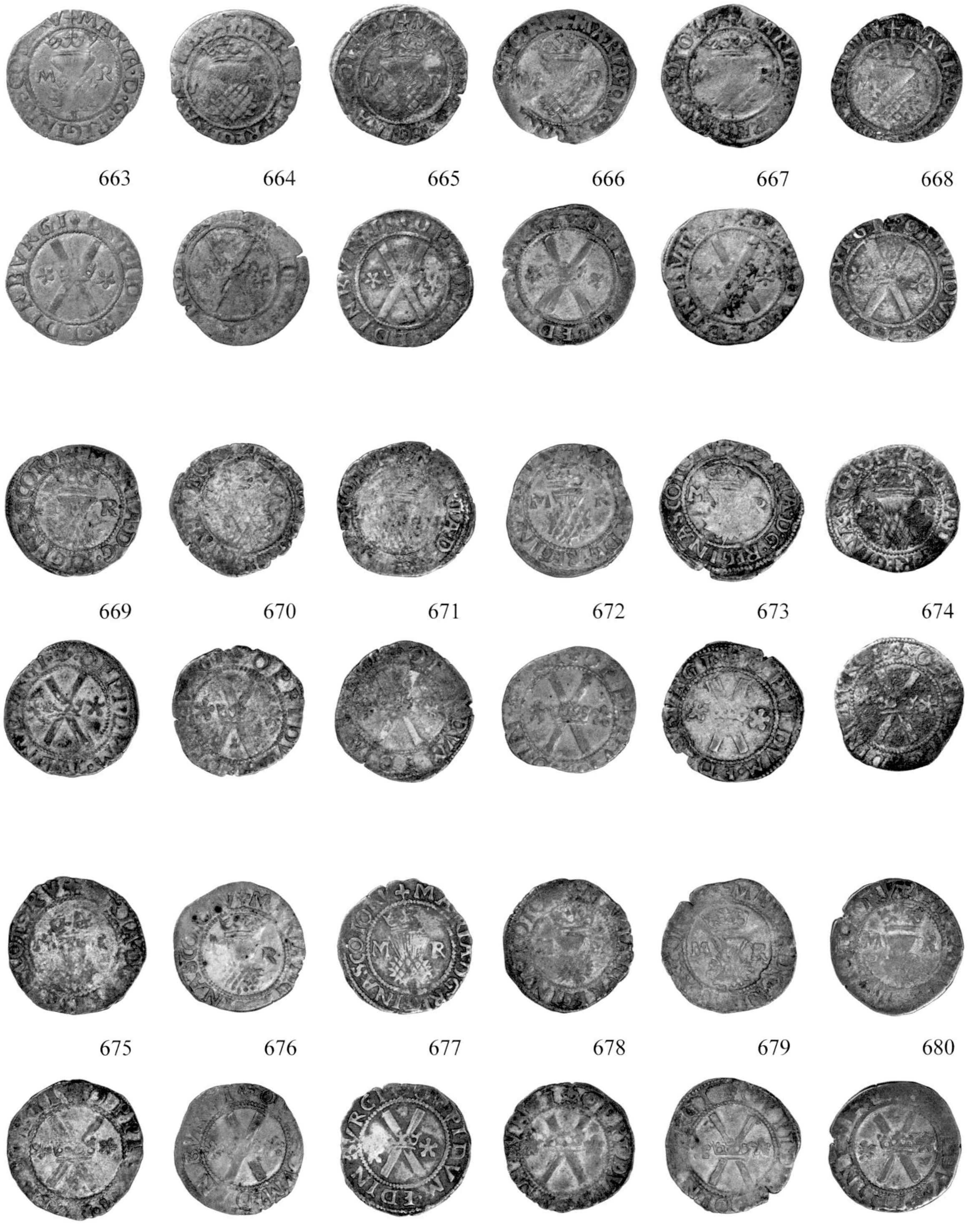

663 664 665 666 667 668

669 670 671 672 673 674

675 676 677 678 679 680

First Period. BILLON *(cont.)*
Bawbees. Group 2 *(cont.)*

	Weight g.	gr.	Die Axis	
681	1.81	27.9	210	(IIc). Acq. 1987; ex Blunt; ex Shirley-Fox bequest 1939 (HSAN 3172).
682	1.65	25.5	270	Rev. EDINBVRG . I (IIIa). Bt Baldwin, 16 July 1993; ex Plumbridge (HSAN 3161).
683	1.71	26.4	360	(IIIa). Acq. 13 February 1965 (HSAN 3176).
684	1.93	29.8	200	(IIIa). Bt Baldwin (HSAN 3180).
685	1.71	26.4	170	i.m. slipped-cross (IIIa). Bt Spink, 25 October 1988 (HSAN 3187).
686	1.88	29.0	190	Obv. SCOTORV .. Rev. curled G (IIIa). Bt Spink, 25 October 1988; ex Davidson (HSAN 3188).
687	1.92	29.6	360	i.m. slipped-cross. Obv. SCO ORV . (IIIa). Bt Baldwin, 1968 (HSAN 3189).
688	1.39	21.5	360	Obv. SCOTOR (IIIa). Bt Baldwin (HSAN 3190).
689	1.72	26.5	30	i.m. slipped-cross (IIIa). Bt Baldwin (HSAN 3191).
690	2.07	31.9	90	(IIIa). Rev. EDINBVRGI .. Bt Baldwin, 24 April 1985 (HSAN 3192).
691	1.87	28.9	90	i.m. slipped-cross. Rev. fluted saltire, normal N (IIIa). Acq. 1953; ex Thorburn; acq. Seaby, December 1948 (HSAN 3194).
692	2.34	36.1	270	Obv. SCOTORV . (IIIa). Bt. Spink, 25 October 1988; ex Davidson (HSAN 3215).
693	1.75	27.0	270	i.m. slipped-cross (IIIa). Bt Spink, 25 October 1988; ex Davidson (HSAN 3216).
694	1.84	28.4	240	Curled G. Rev. EDINBVRGI . (IIIa). Bt Spink, 25 October 1988; ex Davidson (HSAN 3242).
695	2.23	34.4	180	(IIIb). Bt Baldwin (HSAN 3186).
696	1.36	21.0	180	Obv. SCOTORVM (Stevenson IIIb). Acq. 1965. Rigghead hoard (HSAN 3270).
697	2.26	34.9	90	(IIIc). Acq. 1965. Rigghead hoard (HSAN 3243).
698	2.00	30.9	90	i.m. slipped-cross (IIIc). Acq. 1976; ex Dakers, lot 458 (part) (HSAN 3244).

681 682 683 684 685 686

687 688 689 690 691 692

693 694 695 696 697 698

First Period. BILLON *(cont.)*
Bawbees. Group 2 *(cont.)*

	Weight g.	gr.	Die Axis	
699	1.75	27.0	250	(IIIc). Bt Baldwin (HSAN 3193).
700	1.95	30.1	180	(Stevenson IIId). Unprovenanced (HSAN 3209).
701	1.58	24.4	30	Obv. SCOTORVM (Vb(i)). Ex Lockett I, lot 326 (part); ex Mackenzie lot 312 (part) (HSAN 3169).
702	2.13	32.9	150	Obv. SCOTOR (IVa). Bt Spink, 25 October 1988 (HSAN 3213).
703	1.55	23.9	360	Rev. EDINBVRGI . (IVb,). Unprovenanced (HSAN 3211).
704	1.70	26.2	200	Obv. SCOTORVM. Rev. curled G (IVb). Unprovenanced (HSAN 3271).
705	1.75	27.0	210	(IVb). Bt Baldwin, 1968 (HSAN 3272).
706	1.77	27.3	170	(IVb). Acq. 13 February 1965 (HSAN 3273).
707	1.96	30.2	70	i.m. slipped-cross (Va(i)). Acq. 1953; ex Thorburn (HSAN 3210).
708	2.14	33.0	190	(Va(i)). Acq. 13 February 1965 (HSAN 3212).
709	1.92	29.6	340	i.m. slipped-cross (Va(ii)). bt Baldwin, 1976; ex F. Baldwin (HSAN 3195).
710	1.89	29.2	210	i.m. slipped-cross (Va(ii)). Acq. 1965. Rigghead hoard (HSAN 3196).
711	1.86	28.7	150	Rev. EDINBVRGI . (Va(ii)). Acq. 1965. Rigghead hoard (HSAN 3197).
712	1.74	26.9	310	i.m. slipped-cross. Rev. EDINBVRGI . (Va(ii)). Acq. 13 February 1965 (HSAN 3198).
713	1.61	24.8	220	i.m. slipped-cross. Rev. EDINBVRG (Va(ii)). Acq. 1965. Rigghead hoard (HSAN 3199).
714	2.12	32.7	180	i.m. slipped-cross. Rev. curled G (Va(ii)). Bt Spink, 25 October 1988 (HSAN 3200).
715	1.82	28.1	30	Obv. KEGINA (Va(ii)). Bt Spink, 1988 (HSAN 3201).
716	1.79	27.6	190	(Va(ii)). Bt Baldwin. Corroded, not illustrated (HSAN 3202).
717	1.59	24.5	260	i.m. slipped-cross (Va(iii)). Acq. 1965. Rigghead hoard (HSAN 3204).

PLATE 41

699 700 701 702 703 704

705 706 707 708 709 710

711 712 713 714 715 717

First Period. BILLON *(cont.)*
Bawbees. Group 3

GROUP 3

i.m. plain-cross, Obv. MARIA . D . G . R . SCOTORVM. Rev. voided saltire, usually with И, inverted N (Stevenson classes Vb, Vc, Vd, VI, VIIa).

On some coins the i.m. appears to be a thin-cross (with narrower arms) or a slipped-cross (with tapered lower arm), rather than the more usual plain-cross. This is noted where appropriate.

Stevenson varieties of rev. voided saltire include classes Vb(i), Vc(ii) to Vc(iv), Vd(i) to Vd(ii), VIa(i) to VIa(iii), VIb (i) to VIb(v), VIc (i) to VIc(iii), VId, VIIa(i) to VIIa(ii).

	Weight g.	gr.	Die Axis	
718	1.58	24.4	50	(Vb). Acq. 13 February 1965 (HSAN 3203).
719	1.86	28.7	310	Obv. SCOTORVM .. Rev. . OPPIDVM . EDINBVRGI . (Vb(i)). Acq. 1976; ex Dakers, lot 458 (part) (HSAN 3162).
720	1.80	27.80	220	Rev. : OPPIDV[M . EDIN]BVRGI . (Vb(i)). Acq. 13 February 1965 (HSAN 3205).
721	1.31	20.2	310	(Vb(i)/Vc(i)). Bt Baldwin, 1968 (HSAN 3177).
722	1.64	25.3	70	i.m. thin-cross. Rev. . OPPIDVM . EDIIDVRGI ., ?E/R (Vc(ii)). Bt Baldwin, 1968 (HSAN 3217).
723	1.77	27.3	260	i.m. thin-cross. Rev. EDINBVRGI . (Vc(ii)). Bt Baldwin, 1976; ex F. Baldwin (HSAN 3218).
724	1.68	25.9	90	i.m. thin-cross, Rev. . OPPIDVM . EDINBVRGI . (Vc(ii)). Ex Lockett I, lot 326 (part); ex Mackenzie, lot 312 or 313 (part) (HSAN 3219).
725	1.24	19.1	140	Rev.. OPPIDVM . EDINBVRGI . (Vc(ii)). Bt Spink, 25 October 1988; ex Davidson (HSAN 3220).
726	1.94	29.9	260	i.m. thin-cross (Vc(ii)). Acq. 13 February 1965 (HSAN 3221).
727	1.72	26.5	30	Curled G. Rev. EDINBVRGI . (Vd(i)). Ex Lockett I, lot 326 (part); ex Bearman, acq. Baldwin, 29 December 1910; ex F. G. Lawrence, lot 197 (part) (HSAN 3222).
728	1.45	22.4	270	(Vd(ii)). Unprovenanced (HSAN 3223).
729	1.98	30.6	110	Obv. . MARIA . Rev. . OPPIDVM . EDINBVRGI . (Stevenson VIa(i)). Ex F. Baldwin (HSAN 3224).
730	2.04	31.5	310	Obv. . MARIA, SCOTORVM . (VIa(i)). Acq. 13 February 1965 (HSAN 3225).
731	1.84	28.4	170	Rev. inverted crown (VIa(i)). Bt Spink, 25 October 1988; ex Davidson (HSAN 3226).
732	1.54	23.8	220	i.m. thin-cross (VIa(i)). Unprovenanced (HSAN 3227).
733	2.07	31.9	340	Obv. SCOTORVM .. Rev. . OPPIDVM . EDINBVRGI (VIa(i)). Unprovenanced (HSAN 3228).
734	1.91	29.5	30	i.m. thin-cross. Rev. . OPPIDVM . EDINBVRGI . (VIa(ii)). Bt Spink, 25 October 1988; ex Davidson (HSAN 3229).
735	1.47	22.7	170	i.m. thin-cross, . OPPIDVM . ED[INBVRGI] (VIa(ii)). Unprovenanced (HSAN 3230).

PLATE 42

718 719 720 721 722 723

724 725 726 727 728 729

730 731 732 733 734 735

First Period. BILLON *(cont.)*
Bawbees. Group 3 *(cont.)*

	Weight g.	gr.	Die Axis	
736	2.12	32.7	90	Obv. SCOTORVM **.** (VIa(ii)/VIb(i-iii)). Acq. 13 February 1965 (HSAN 3231).
737	1.78	27.5	230	i.m. thin-cross (VIa(iii)). Bt Spink, 25 October 1988; ex Davidson (HSAN 3232).
738	1.95	30.1	110	i.m. thin-cross. Rev. inverted crown (VIa(iv)). Ex Dakers 458 (part) (HSAN 3233).
739	1.72	26.5	330	(VIb(ii)). Bt Spink, 25 October 1988; ex Davidson (HSAN 3173).
740	1.27	19.6	320	(VIb(ii)). Bt Baldwin (HSAN 3174).
741	1.66	25.6	280	(VIb(ii)). Acq. 1953; ex Thorburn (HSAN 3175).
742	1.56	24.1	350	(VIb(ii)). Bt Baldwin (HSAN 3181).
743	2.16	33.3	350	(VIb(ii)/VIb(iv)). Acq. 13 February 1965 (HSAN 3182).
744	1.64	25.3	90	(VIb(iii)). Bt Baldwin, 16 July 1993; ex Plumbridge (HSAN 3183).
745	1.55	23.9	210	i.m. thin-cross (VIb(iii)). Bt Spink, 25 October 1988; ex Davidson (HSAN 3234).
746	1.35	20.8	160	i.m. thin-cross (Stevenson VIb(iii)). Acq. 13 February 1965 (HSAN 3235).
747	1.44	22.2	340	i.m. thin-cross (VIb(iii)/VIb(iv)). Bt Spink, 25 October 1988; ex Davidson (HSAN 3236).
748	1.79	27.6	360	(VIc(i)). Acq. 1947 (HSAN 3178).
749	1.83	28.2	10	(VIc(i)). Acq. 1976; ex Dakers, lot 458 (part) (HSAN 3184).
750	1.84	28.4	270	i.m. ?slipped-cross (VIc(i)). Acq. 13 February 1965 (HSAN 3185).
751	1.90	29.3	220	(VIc(iii)). Acq. 1976; ex Dakers, lot 458 (part) (HSAN 3179).
752	1.78	27.5	280	i.m. thin-cross (VIb(iv)). Acq. 1976; ex Dakers, lot 458 (part) (HSAN 3238).
753	1.70	26.2	190	i.m. thin-cross (VIb(iv)/VIb(i-ii)). Acq. 13 February 1965 (HSAN 3237).

736 737 738 739 740 741

742 743 744 745 746 747

748 749 750 751 752 753

First Period. BILLON *(cont.)*
Bawbees. Group 3 *(cont.)*

	Weight g.	gr.	Die Axis	
754	2.72	42.0	40	(VIb(v)). Bt Spink, 25 October 1988; ex Davidson (HSAN 3239).
755	2.12	32.7	40	Obv. MARIA, second A over G (VIb(v)). Acq. 13 February 1965 (HSAN 3240).
756	1.63	25.2	180	i.m. thin-cross (VIc(i)). Acq. 13 February 1965 (HSAN 3241).
757	1.56	24.1	50	Rev. EDIN with D/И and I/E (VIc(i)). Acq. 1976; ex Dakers, lot 458 (part) (HSAN 3250).
758	2.64	40.7	200	i.m. thin-cross. Rev. EDIN reads DD with D recut (VIc(i)). Acq. 1957 (HSAN 3251).
759	1.93	29.8	270	i.m. thin-cross (VIc(i)). Bt Baldwin (HSAN 3252).
760	1.71	26.4	60	(VIc(i)). Bt Spink, 25 October 1988; ex Davidson (HSAN 3257).
761	1.96	30.2	310	(VIc(i)). Unprovenanced (HSAN 3285).
762	1.52	23.5	180	i.m. thin-cross (VIc(i)). Unprovenanced (HSAN 3286).
763	2.04	31.5	360	(VIc(i)). Unprovenanced (HSAN 3289).
764	2.24	34.6	180	i.m. thin-cross (VIc(i)/VIb(ii)). Bt Spink, 25 October 1988; ex Davidson (HSAN 3258).
765	2.13	32.9	320	i.m. thin-cross (VIc(i)/VIc(ii)). Unprovenanced (HSAN 3259).
766	1.98	30.6	30	(VIc(ii)). Bt Spink, 25 October 1988; ex Davidson (HSAN 3260).
767	1.79	27.6	360	i.m. thin-cross (VIc(ii)). Unprovenanced (HSAN 3261).
768	2.64	40.7	190	i.m. thin-cross (VIc(ii)). Bt Spink, 25 October 1988; ex Davidson (HSAN 3262).
769	1.95	30.1	90	i.m. thin-cross (VIc(ii)). Acq. 1989 (HSAN 3263).
770	1.43	22.1	50	i.m. slipped-cross (VIc(ii)). Acq. 1976; ex Dakers, lot 458 (part) (HSAN 3264).
771	2.03	31.3	270	i.m. thin-cross (VIc(ii)). Bt Baldwin, 1968 (HSAN 3265).

PLATE 44

754 755 756 757 758 759

760 761 762 763 764 765

766 767 768 769 770 771

First Period. BILLON *(cont.)*
Bawbees. Group 3 *(cont.)*

	Weight g.	gr.	Die Axis	
772	1.59	24.5	270	(VIc(ii)). Acq. 1976; ex Dakers, lot 458 (part) (HSAN 3266).
773	2.20	34.0	280	(VIc(ii)). Unprovenanced (HSAN 3287).
774	1.21	18.7	140	i.m. thin-cross (VIc(ii)). Acq. 1965. Rigghead hoard (HSAN 3267).
775	2.30	35.5	200	i.m. thin-cross (VIc(ii)). Unprovenanced (HSAN 3290).
776	2.09	32.3	140	i.m. thin-cross (VIc(ii)). Unprovenanced. Holed to lower left of i.m. (HSAN 3291).
777	1.90	29.3	30	i.m. slipped-cross (VIc(ii)). Unprovenanced (HSAN 3292).
778	1.53	23.6	280	(VIc(ii)). Bt Spink, 25 October 1988; ex Davidson. Kirkcudbright hoard. Corroded, not illustrated (HSAN 3333).
779	2.26	34.9	270	(VIc(iii)). Acq. 13 February 1965 (HSAN 3288).
780	1.77	27.3	90	i.m. thin-cross (VIc(iii)/VId). Acq. 1953; ex Thorburn, acq. Seaby, December 1948 (HSAN 3268).
781	1.78	27.5	260	(VId). Bt Spink, 25 October 1988; ex Davidson (HSAN 3206).
782	2.06	31.8	230	i.m. long-cross (VId). Unprovenanced (HSAN 3207).
783	1.97	30.4	300	i.m. thin-cross (VId/VIIa(ii)). Unprovenanced (HSAN 3269).
784	1.87	28.9	360	i.m. thin-cross (VIIa). Acq. 13 February 1965 (HSAN 3281).
785	2.12	32.7	90	i.m. thin-cross. Rev. EDIИBVRGI (VIIa(i)). Acq. 1976; ex Dakers, lot 458 (part) (HSAN 3276).
786	1.57	24.2	160	i.m. thin-cross (VIIa(i)). Acq. 13 February 1965 (HSAN 3277).
787	2.43	37.5	350	Obv. SCOTORVM . (VIIa(i)). Ex Dakers, lot 458 (part) (HSAN 3278).
788	1.82	28.1	300	(VIIa(i)). Acq. 4 February 1989; ex Lockett I, lot 326 (part); ex Bearman, acq. Baldwin, 4 February 1899 (HSAN 3279).
789	1.76	27.2	180	(VIIa(i)). Acq. 1976; ex Dakers, lot 458 (part) (HSAN 3280).
790	1.61	24.8	130	(VIIa(i)). Unprovenanced (HSAN 3282).
791	1.76	27.2	170	i.m. thin-cross (VIIa(i)). Bt Spink, 25 October 1988; ex Davidson (HSAN 3283).

772 773 774 775 776 777 779

780 781 782 783 784 785

786 787 788 789 790 791

First Period. BILLON *(cont.)*
Bawbees. Group 3 *(cont.)*

	Weight g.	gr.	Die Axis	
792	2.18	33.6	180	i.m. thin-cross (VIIa(i)). Bt Spink, 25 October 1988; ex Davidson (HSAN 3284).
793	1.90	29.3	50	(VIIa(i)/VId). Acq. 1953; ex Thorburn (HSAN 3274).
794	1.65	25.5	340	i.m. thin-cross (VIIa(ii)). Unprovenanced (HSAN 3293).
795	1.92	29.6	230	i.m. thin-cross (VIIa(ii)/VIIb(i)). Acq. 13 February 1965 (HSAN 3294).
796	1.65	25.5	320	Rev. D in EDINBVRGI recut, normal N (VIIa/(Group 4) VIIb(i)). Bt Baldwin, 1968 (HSAN 3295).

GROUP 4, 1553–4

Obv. i.m. cross potent/lis, MARIA . D(EI) . G . R . SCOTORVM. Rev. usually normal N (Stevenson classes VIIb, VIII).

797	2.26	34.9	120	(VIIb(i)). Bt Baldwin; ex F. Baldwin (HSAN 3296).
798	1.76	27.2	160	(VIIb(ii)). Ex Lockett I, lot 326 (part); ex Mackenzie, lot 312 or 313 (part) (HSAN 3297).
799	2.42	37.3	100	Rev. i.m. cross potent (VIIb(ii)). Acq. 1953; ex Thorburn (HSAN 3298).
800	1.61	24.8	220	Rev. wire-line inner-circle (VIIb(iii)). Ex Dakers, lot 458 (part) (HSAN 3299).
801	2.01	31.0	70	Rev. wire-line inner-circle (VIIb(iii)). Ex Dakers, lot 458 (part) (HSAN 3300).
802	1.83	28.2	270	No inner-circles. Rev. OPPIDVM EDINBVRGI (VIIb(iv)). Ex Dakers, lot 458 (part) (HSAN 3301).
803	1.96	30.2	240	Obv. no inner-circle. Rev. wire-line inner-circle (VIIb(iv)). Ex Lockett I, lot 326 (part); ex Mackenzie, lot 312 or 313 (part) (HSAN 3302).
804	1.54	23.8	170	Obv. no inner-circle. Rev. traces of wire-line inner-circle (VIIb(iv)). Acq. 1953; ex Thorburn, acq. Baldwin (HSAN 3303).
805	1.88	29.0	180	Obv. no inner-circle. Rev. traces of wire-line inner-circle (VIIb(iv)). Acq. 23 January 1968; ex Harris (HSAN 3304).
806	1.83	28.2	290	Wire-line inner circles. Rev. OPPIDVM EDINBVRGI (VIIb(iv)). Bt Spink, 25 October 1988; ex Davidson (HSAN 3305).
807	1.77	27.3	250	Obv. no inner-circle. Rev. OPPIDVM EDINBVRGI (VIIb(v)/VIIb(iii)). Ex Dakers, lot 458 (part) (HSAN 3306).
808	2.00	30.9	300	(VIIb(v)), no stops, traces of wire-line inner-circle. Bt Spink, 25 October 1988; ex Davidson (HSAN 3334).
809	1.44	22.2	170	Obv. space after SCOTORVM. Rev. OPPIDVM EDINBVRGI, wire-line inner-circles (VIIb(v)). Ex Dakers, lot 458 (part) (HSAN 3307).

PLATE 46

792 793 794 795 796 797

798 799 800 801 802 803

804 805 806 807 808 809

First Period. BILLON *(cont.)*
Bawbees. Group 4 *(cont.)*

Weight				
	g.	gr.	Die Axis	
810	1.82	28.1	220	Obv. no inner-circle, A recut. Rev. OPPIDVM EDINBVRGI, wire-line inner-circle (VIIb(v)). Bt Baldwin; ex F. Baldwin (HSAN 3308).
811	1.48	22.8	210	Obv. DEI. Rev. i.m. cinquefoil, . OPPIDVM . (VIIIa). Bt Baldwin; ex F. Baldwin (HSAN 3309).
812	1.75	27.0	100	Obv. DEI. Rev. EDINBVRGI . (VIIIb). Ex Lockett I, lot 326 (part); ex Bearman, acq. Verity, 16 November 1899 (HSAN 3311).
813	1.78	27.5	60	Obv. DEI. Rev. i.m. cinquefoil without one petal (VIIIb(i)). Ex F. Baldwin (HSAN 3310).
814	1.98	30.6	360	Obv. . DEI G R .. Rev. . OPPIDVM . EDINBVRGI . (VIIIb(i)). Ex Dakers, lot 458 (part) (HSAN 3312).
815	1.42	21.9	280	Obv. MARIA . D . G . R . SCOTORVM (VIIIb(i)). Unprovenanced (HSAN 3313).
816	1.74	26.9	40	Obv. DEI (VIIIb(i)). Bt Baldwin (HSAN 3314).
817	1.95	30.1	320	Obv. DEI. Rev. . OPPIDVM . EDINBVRGI . (VIIIb(i)). Bt Spink, 25 October 1988; ex Davidson (HSAN 3335).
818	1.76	27.2	50	Obv. DEI (VIIIb(iii)). Bt Baldwin, 1968 (HSAN 3315).
819	1.70	26.2	270	Obv. MARIA DEI G . (VIIIb(iii)). Acq. 1953; ex Thorburn, acq. Seaby, December 1948 (HSAN 3316).
820	2.20	34.0	10	Obv. DEI (VIIIb(iii)). Bt Spink, 25 October 1988; ex Davidson (HSAN 3317).

Contemporary Counterfeit

821	2.09	32.25	170	Garbled legend, copper flan, a contemporary counterfeit. Bt Seaby, 10 August 1953 (HSAN 3318).

Half-bawbee (undated)

Theoretical weight 0.95 g, 14.73 gr : value 3 pence Scots.

i.m. plain-cross/lis. Obv. as bawbee, MARIA . D . G . R . SCOTORVM. Rev. as bawbee but with a single cinquefoil in lower angle of saltire.

References:
Solid saltire; B.862.1–2; Stevenson (1989), type A and B; S.5435.
Fluted saltire; B.863.3; Stevenson (1989) type C and D; S.5436.

Variations in letters and the obverse crown determine Stevenson classes and sub-classes.

Types A and B.

Rev. plain saltire

822	0.97	15.0	40	(Aa). Bt Baldwin, 1976; ex F. Baldwin (HSAN 3341).
823	0.93	14.4	160	(Ab(i)). Ex Dakers, lot 458 (part) (HSAN 3340).
824	1.04	16.1	90	(Ab). Bt Spink, 25 October 1988; ex Davidson (HSAN 3338).
825	1.18	18.2	330	(Ab(ii)). Bt Spink, 1965; ex Marr; ex R. C. Carlyon-Britton; ex Parsons (HSAN 3342).
826	1.08	16.7	160	(Ab(ii)). Acq. 1953; ex Thorburn, acq. Seaby (HSAN 3343).
827	0.95	14.7	210	(Ab(iii)). Bt Spink, 1965; ex Marr; ex R. C. Carlyon-Britton; ex Parsons (HSAN 3344).
828	0.74	11.4	250	(B). Bt Baldwin, 1976; ex F. Baldwin (HSAN 3345).
829	0.84	13.0	190	(B). Acq. 13 February 1965. Corroded (HSAN 3346).

810 811 812 813 814 815

816 817 818 819 820 821

822 823 824 825 826 827 828 829

First Period. BILLON *(cont.)*
Half-bawbees (cont.)

Types C and D

Rev. With fluted saltire, inverted N usual (S.5436; B.863.3).

	Weight g.	gr.	Die Axis	
830	1.19	18.4	160	(Cb(ii)). Bt Spink, 25 October 1988; ex Davidson (HSAN 3339).
831	0.80	12.3	270	(Ca(ii)). Bt Baldwin, 1976; ex F. Baldwin (HSAN 3347).
832	0.83	12.8	170	(Cb(ii)). Bt Baldwin, 1976; ex F. Baldwin. Corroded, not illustrated (HSAN 3348).
833	1.09	16.8	280	(Cb(ii)). Acq. 1953; ex Thorburn, acq. Seaby (HSAN 3349).
834	0.99	15.3	90	(Cb(ii)). Acq. 1959 (HSAN 3350).
835	0.88	13.6	280	(Cb(ii)). Unprovenanced (HSAN 3351).
836	1.07	16.5	60	(Cb(ii)) (B.863). Bt Baldwin, 1976; ex F. Baldwin (HSAN 3352).
837	0.67	10.3	160	(Cb(ii)/Cb(ii)). Ex Dakers, lot 458 (part) (HSAN 3353).
838	0.84	13.0	280	(Cb(iii)). Bt Baldwin, 1985 (HSAN 3354).
839	0.87	13.4	290	(Da(i)). Bt Baldwin, 1976; ex F. Baldwin (HSAN 3355).
840	0.93	14.4	60	(Da(ii)). Ex Dakers, lot 458 (part) (HSAN 3357).
841	0.86	13.3	190	Obv. crown with no arch (Da(ii)). Ex Dakers, lot 458 (part) (HSAN 3356).
842	0.74	11.4	90	(Da(ii)). Ex Dakers, lot 458 (part) (HSAN 3358).
843	0.72	11.1	190	Rev. small cinquefoil (Da(iii)). Ex Dakers, lot 458 (part) (HSAN 3359).
844	0.99	15.3	260	(Db). Unprovenanced. Noted by Lord Stewartby as the only example of which he knew with Db dies both sides (HSAN 3360).
845	0.68	10.5	90	Rev. **GI** ligate (Db/Dc), see J. K. R. Murray 1968c, fig. 31, 32. Acq. 1953; ex Thorburn, acq. Seaby, 1949 (HSAN 3361).
846	0.74	11.4	10	Obv. M R reversed, no inner-circle (Dc/Da(ii)). Ex Dakers, lot 458 (part) (HSAN 3362).

Penny, 1547–56/7

Theoretical weight 0.73 g, 11.27 gr: value 1 penny Scots.

First issue

i.m. plain-cross/-. Obv. crowned facing bust, **MARIA . D . G . R . SCOTORVM**

Type Ia (*c.* 1547)

i.m. plain-cross/-. Obv. 'baby' face, crown with single arch. Rev. **OPI | DVM | EDN | BVR**, foliated long-cross, crown or cinquefoil in alternate angles, undated (B.864.1–2; Stewart 1967, fig. 162; S.5440).

847	0.43	6.6	350	Rev. crowns q2 and 4. Bt Spink, 1965; ex Marr, acq. Seaby 1962 (HSAN 3137).
848	0.67	10.3	330	Rev. crowns q1 and 3. Acq. 24 August 1955 (HSAN 3138).
849	0.64	9.9	80	Obv. no stops. Rev. crowns q2 and 4. Bt Baldwin, 1976; ex F. Baldwin (HSAN 3363).
850	0.62	9.6	280	Rev. crowns q1 and 3. Bt Baldwin, 1976; ex F. Baldwin (HSAN 3364).
851	0.49	7.6	300	Rev. crowns q2 and 4. Ex Sotheby, 24 June 1970, lot 81 (part) (HSAN 3365).
852	0.70	10.8	90	Obv. no stops. Rev. crowns q1 and 3. Bt Spink, July 1987; ex Davidson (HSAN 3367).

Type Ib, as Ia, but Obv. bust with open crown (B.864.4; S.5441) not represented in the collection.

Type II

i.m. Cinquefoil or cross/-. Obv. facing child's bust with open crown, **MARIA . D . G . R . SCOTORVM**. Rev. **OPI | DV . E | EDINB | VRGI**, pellet in first V, long-cross fourchée, crown or cinquefoil in alternate angles, undated (B.865.5–6; S.5442).

830 831 833 834 835 836 837 838

839 840 841 842 843 844 845 846

847 848 849 850 851 852 853 854 855

856 857 858 859 860 861 862 863 864

	Weight g.	gr.	Die Axis	
853	0.88	13.6	180	i.m. cinquefoil/-. Rev. crowns q1 and 3. Bt Spink, 3 June 1989; ex Davidson. Found at Lincluden Abbey, Dumfries (HSAN 3366).
854	0.88	13.6	190	i.m. uncertain. Rev. **. OPI**, crowns q1 and 3. Unprovenanced (HSAN 3369).

Type III

Struck under license by Monsieur D'Oysel, December-January 1554–5 (Holmes 1998, p. 41).

i.m. small lis/-, without inner-circles. Obv. facing child's bust with double arched crown, **MARIA . D . G . R . SCOTORVM**. Rev. **OPPI | DVM | EDIN | BVRG**, foliated long-cross, a crown or lis in alternate angles, undated (B.867.7–8; S.5443).

855	0.69	10.7	220	Rev. crowns q2 and 4. Bt Baldwin, 1976; ex F Baldwin (HSAN 3370).
856	0.50	7.7	150	Rev. crowns q1 and 3. Bt Baldwin, 1976; ex F Baldwin (HSAN 3371).
857	0.60	9.3	50	Rev. crowns q1 and 3. Bt Baldwin, 1976; ex F Baldwin (HSAN 3372).
858	0.61	9.4	190	Rev. crowns q1 and 3. Bt Baldwin, 1976; ex F Baldwin (HSAN 3373).

Second issue (dated 1556), mostly struck in 1557

i.m. cross potent/-. Obv. **MARIA D G SCOTOR REGINA**, large cross potent with a small cross potent in each angle. Rev. **. VICIT . / VERITAS . / . 1556 . / .**, crown, pellet each side, above (B.869.1–2; Stewart 1967, fig. 164; S.5444).

859	0.69	10.7	250	Unprovenanced (HSAN 3139).
860	0.60	9.3	340	Bt Baldwin, 1976; ex F. Baldwin (HSAN 3374).
861	0.66	10.2	210	Bt Spink, June 1989; ex Davidson (HSAN 3375).
862	0.68	10.5	90	Bt Spink, June 1989; ex Davidson (HSAN 3376).
863	0.57	8.8	160	Rev. crown omitted. Bt Baldwin, 1976; ex F. Baldwin (HSAN 3377).
864	0.56	8.6	140	Bt Spink, 1955 (HSAN 3378).

First Period. BILLON *(cont.)*

Hardheads or Lions

Hardheads or Lions (1555–8)

Theoretical weight 0.95 g, 14.72 gr: value 1 penny halfpenny Scots.

i.m. cross potent both sides. Obv. crowned M, sometimes with pellet in central angle, MARIA . D . G . SCOTOR . REGINA. Rev. . VICIT . VERITAS . (date) . , crowned lion rampant left, dated 1555, 1556, 1558.

Countermarked, 1575, with star in heart (mark of James Douglas, Earl of Morton, regent to James VI), with the intention of distinguishing counterfeit from true coins.

First issue (1555, 1556), struck at one denier fine.

Type I (1556)

Obv. with an annulet each side of the crowned M; arched crown (B.867.1–3; Stewart fig. 160; S.5438).

	Weight g.	gr.	Die Axis	Date	
865	0.86	13.3	40	1556	Obv. no stops, pellet in M. Ex Dakers, lot 459 (part) (HSAN 3385).
866	1.20	18.5	50	1556	Rev. wire-line inner-circle. Bt Spink, 1965; ex Marr (HSAN 3386).
867	0.86	13.3	360	1556	Ex J. K. R. Murray, lot 246 (part); ex Thorburn; ex Pollexfen, lot 364b (part) (HSAN 3387).

Type II (1555, 1556)

Obv. usually arched crown, sometimes open crown, without annulets on either side of the crowned M, dated 1555, 1556 (B.868.4–5; Stewart 1967, fig. 160; S.5439).

868	0.94	14.5	200	1555	Rev. VERIAS, countermark before lion. Bt Spink, 1965; ex Marr; ex R. C. Carlyon-Britton; ex Parsons, lot 734 (part) (HSAN 3379).
869	0.67	10.3	100	1555	Rev. trefoil stops, countermark in legend at 7 o'clock. Bt Baldwin, 1976; ex F. Baldwin (HSAN 3380).
870	0.86	13.3	280	1555	Obv. open crown, no stops, pellet in M, REGINAA. Rev. countermark on shoulder of lion. Ex J. K. R. Murray, lot 246 (part) (HSAN 3381).
871	1.10	17.0	190	1555	Obv. MARIA DEI . G .. Noted 'ex Richardson lot 172.' Unprovenanced (HSAN 3382).
872	0.83	12.8	150	1555	Obv. open crown, with pellet in M. Rev. VECIT. Ex R. C. Carlyon-Britton; ex Parsons, lot 734 (part) (HSAN 3383).
873	0.91	14.0	270	1555	Wire-line inner-circle both sides. Obv. open crown, pellet in M. Bt Baldwin, 1976; ex F. Baldwin (HSAN 3384).
874	0.76	11.7	270	1555	Rev. countermark before lion. Ex Davidson (no date) (HSAN 3391).

Second issue (1558), struck at a half denier fine

As first issue, dated 1558. Obv. with arched crown (B.873.1–876.9; Stewart 1967, fig. 160; S.5445).

	Weight g.	gr.	Die Axis	
875	0.79	12.2	70	Obv. no stops, pellet in M, N without bar. Acq. 1976; ex Dakers, lot 459 (part) (HSAN 3388).
876	0.90	13.9	340	Bt Baldwin, 1976; ex F. Baldwin (HSAN 3389).
877	1.26	19.4	180	Obv. arched crown, pellet in M. Bt Baldwin, 1976; ex F. Baldwin (HSAN 3390).
878	1.42	21.9	360	Obv. pellet in M. Rev. traces of wire-line inner-circle. Bt Baldwin, 1976; ex F. Baldwin (HSAN 3392).
879	1.0	15.4	360	Ex Walters lot 660 (part) (HSAN 3393).
880	0.96	14.8	280	Rev. countermark before lion. Acq. 1966. Corroded, not illustrated (HSAN 3394).

865 866 867 868 869 870 871 872

873 874 875 876 877 878 879

881 882 883 884 885 886 887 888

889 890 891 892 893 894

	Weight g.	gr.	Die Axis	
881	0.74	11.4	340	Obv. pellet in M. Rev. annulet stops. Bt Baldwin, 1976; ex F. Baldwin (HSAN 3395).
882	0.90	13.9	170	Obv. pellet in M. Rev. wire-line inner-circle. Bt Baldwin, 1976; ex F. Baldwin (HSAN 3396).
883	0.79	12.2	310	Obv. pellet in M. Rev. open crown on lion, countermark before lion. Bt Baldwin, 1976; ex F. Baldwin (HSAN 3397).
884	1.10	17.0	200	Obv. pellet in M, Rev. open crown with interior detail above lion. Unprovenanced (HSAN 3398).
885	1.06	16.4	180	Rev. arched crown above lion. Unprovenanced (HSAN 3399).
886	1.20	18.5	280	Obv. pellet in M, N mis-formed without bar. Rev. arched crown above lion, wire-line inner-circle. Bt Spink, 1965; ex Marr (HSAN 3400).
887	0.81	12.5	170	Obv. pellet in M. Rev. arched crown above lion, countermark by lion's chest. Ex J. K. R. Murray, lot 246 (part) (HSAN 3401).
888	0.96	14.8	360	Obv. pellet in M. Rev. wire-line inner-circle formed of tiny pellets, arched crown above lion. Bt Baldwin, 1976; ex F. Baldwin (HSAN 3402).

Plack (1557)

Theoretical weight 1.91 g, 29.50 gr: value 4 pence Scots.

i.m. small cross potent/lis. Obv. crowned shield bearing rampant lion dividing M R, MARIA . DEI . G . SCOTOR . REGINA . 1557. Rev. . SERVIO . ET . VSV . TEROR . 1557, ornate cross with lozenge centre containing a plain-cross, with a crown in each angle (B.871.5–872.8; Stewart fig. 157; S.5437).

Countermarked, 1575, with star in heart (mark of James Douglas, Earl of Morton, regent to James VI), with the intention of distinguishing counterfeit from true coins.

The typology follows the unpublished classification by Stevenson, as in *SCBI* 58.

Type A

Rev. crowns with beaded arch.

889	2.69	41.5	210	(Stevenson M1/A). Acq. 1976; ex Dakers, lot 459 (part) (HSAN 3104).
890	2.07	31.9	270	Obv. wide crown (Stevenson M1/A). Bt Spink, 25 October 1988; ex Davidson (HSAN 3105).
891	2.00	30.9	180	Obv. wide crown (Stevenson M1/A). bt Spink, 1990; ex Davidson (HSAN 3106).
892	2.09	32.3	180	Obv. small crown. no stop before date (Stevenson M1/A). Ex Dakers, lot 459 (part) (HSAN 3107).
893	1.23	19.0	360	Obv. small crown, countermark left of shield (Stevenson M1/A). Acq. 1976; ex Dakers, lot 459 (part) (HSAN 3108).
894	1.47	22.7	90	Obv. no stop before date (Stevenson M1/A). Unprovenanced (HSAN 3109).

FIRST PERIOD. BILLON *(cont.)*
Placks (cont.)

	Weight g.	gr.	Die Axis	
895	1.72	26.5	360	Obv. small crown, **57** struck over i.m., countermark left of shield (Stevenson M1/A). Unprovenanced (HSAN 3110).
896	2.22	34.3	90	Obv. no stops, small crown, rev. **1557.** (Stevenson M2/A). Ex J. K. R. Murray, lot 246 (part) (HSAN 3111).
897	2.45	37.8	180	Obv. no stop before date, small crown, countermark lower left of shield (Stevenson M2/A). Unprovenanced (HSAN 3112).
898	2.32	35.8	270	Obv. small crown, rev. **1557.** (Stevenson M2/A). Bt Spink, 1990; ex Davidson (HSAN 3113).
899	1.86	28.7	160	Obv. no stop before date, small crown (Stevenson M2/A). Bt Spink, 1990; ex Davidson (HSAN 3114).
900	1.72	26.5	30	Obv. no stops, countermark left of shield. Rev. **1557.** (Stevenson M2/A). Ex J. K. R. Murray, lot 246 (part) (HSAN 3115).
901	2.01	31.0	100	Obv. no stops, small crown, REGIN . A, countermark top left of shield. Rev. **1557.** (Stevenson M2/A). Bt Spink, 25 October 1988; ex Davidson (HSAN 3116).
902	1.68	25.9	130	Obv. small crown. Rev. **1557.** (Stevenson M2/A). Bt Baldwin, 1976; ex F. Baldwin (HSAN 3117).
903	1.64	25.3	90	Obv. wide crown. Rev. **1557.** (Stevenson M2/A). Bt Spink, 1990; ex Davidson (HSAN 3118).
904	1.73	26.7	50	Obv. small crown, no stop before date. Rev. **1557.** (Stevenson M2/A). Ex J. K. R. Murray, lot 246 (part) (HSAN 3119).

Type b.

Rev. crowns with plain arch.

905	1.92	29.6	170	Obv. large pellet below i.m., no stop before date, small crown. Rev. **1557.** (Stevenson M3/B). Ex Dakers, lot 459 (part) (HSAN 3120).
906	1.68	25.9	200	Obv. small crown, **1557.** both sides (Stevenson M3/B). Unprovenanced (HSAN 3121).
907	2.13	32.9	340	Obv. small crown, no stop before date. Rev. **1557.** (Stevenson M3/B). Bt Spink, 1965; ex Marr; acq. Seaby 1962 (HSAN 3122).
908	2.00	30.9	100	Obv. small crown, no stop before date. Rev. no stops except **1557.** (Stevenson M4/B). Bt Baldwin, 1976; ex F. Baldwin (HSAN 3123).
909	2.21	34.1	10	No stops both sides. Obv. small crown (Stevenson M4/B). Bt Spink, 25 October 1988; ex Davidson (HSAN 3124).
910	1.88	29.0	50	Obv. small crown, rev. **1557.** (Stevenson M4/B). Acq. before 1960 (HSAN 3125).
911	1.69	26.1	190	No stops both sides. Obv. small crown, countermark left of shield (Stevenson M5/B). Ex J. K. R. Murray, lot 246 (part) (HSAN 3126).

Type c.

Rev. crowns with plain arch disconnected from outer fleurs.

912	2.00	30.9	190	Obv. no stops, small crown (Stevenson M5/C). Bt Spink, 25 October 1988; ex Davidson (HSAN 3127).

PLATE 50

895 896 897 898 899 900

901 902 903 904 905 906

907 908 909 910 911 912

First Period. BILLON *(cont.)*
Placks (cont.)

	Weight g.	gr.	Die Axis	
913	1.54	23.8	90	Obv. **. DEI G ., . REGINA 1557**, small crown. Rev. **1557.** (Stevenson M6/C). Bt Spink, 25 October 1988; ex Davidson (HSAN 3128).

Type d.

As last, but Rev. crowns with recut arch connected to outer fleurs.

914	1.69	26.0	170	Obv. small crown, countermark left of shield. Rev. **1557.** (Stevenson M6/D). Ex J. K. R. Murray, lot 246 (part) (HSAN 3129).
915	2.03	31.3	220	Obv. small crown, no stops, countermark left of shield. Rev. **1557.** (Stevenson M6/D). Ex R. C. Carlyon-Britton (HSAN 3130).
916	1.70	26.2	340	Obv. small crown, shield with large lis (Stevenson M7/D). Bt Baldwin, 1968 (HSAN 3131).
917	2.13	32.9	270	Obv. small crown. Rev. **1557.** (Stevenson M7/D). Bt Baldwin, 1976; ex F. Baldwin (HSAN 3132).
918	1.58	24.4	170	Obv. small crown, no stops. Rev. **1557.** (Stevenson M7/D). Ex J. K. R. Murray, lot 246 (part) (HSAN 3133).
919	1.21	18.7	80	Obv. small crown. Rev. **1557.** (Stevenson M7/D). Unprovenanced (HSAN 3134).

Contemporary Counterfeits.

920	1.28	19.8	350	Counterfeit on a thin flan in style of type d but with inner-circle added. Bt Spink, 25 October 1988; ex Davidson (HSAN 3135).
921	1.60	24.7	190	Copper counterfeit in style of type b but with inner-circle added. Bt Baldwin, 1976; ex F. Baldwin (HSAN 3136).

SECOND PERIOD, 1558–60. MARRIAGE TO FRANCIS

GOLD COINAGE

Ducat (1558)

Theoretical weight 7.63 g, 117.80 gr, issue dated 1558: value 60 shillings Scots.

i.m. cross. Obv. crown above tête à tête busts of Francis, left, and Mary, right, **. FRAN . ET . MARIA . D . G . R R SCOTOR . DELPHIN . VIEN**. Rev. **. HORVM . TVTA . FIDES . 1558**, eight interlinked dolphins forming a cross, a crown above each limb, with cross of Lorraine in each angle (B.888A-B, 1a–1b; Stewart 1967, fig. 170; S.5399).

Represented in this collection by a base yellow metal, 19th-century electrotype of the NMAS example. See non-contemporary copies and forgeries, **1462**.

SILVER COINAGE

First Issue (1558–9)

Testoon (1558–9)

Theoretical weight 6.10 g, 94.20 gr, 0.916 fine: value 5 shillings Scots, countermarked (crowned thistle) coins revalued at 7 shillings and 4 pence in 1578.

i.m. crown/cross potent. Obv. crowned halved shield bearing arms of the Dauphin, left, and Scotland, right, over cross potent, **. FRAN . ET . MA . D . G . R . R . SCOTOR . D . D . VIEN .**. Rev. **. FECIT . VTRAQVE . VNVM . 1558 .**, dated 1558 or 1559, crown above FM monogram, Lorraine cross each side (Stewart 1967, fig. 176)

913 914 915 916 917

918 919 920 921 922

923 924 925 926

	Weight g.	gr.	Die Axis	Date	
922	6.06	93.5	30	1558	(B.877.1; S.5416). Unprovenanced (HSAN 2943).
923	5.65	87.2	340	1558	Obv. **. DEI . G .**. Rev. **WNVM** (cf. B.878.2; S.5416). Unprovenanced (HSAN 2944).
924	5.91	91.2	140	1558	(B.877.1; S.5416). Bt Baldwin, 1975; ex F. Baldwin (HSAN 2945).
925	5.53	85.3	220	1558	Rev. countermark over left Lorraine cross (B.877.1; S.5416). Acq. 1975; ex Walters, lot 662 (part) (HSAN 2946).
926	5.82	89.8	210	1558	Rev. countermark over left Lorraine cross (B.877.2; S.5416). Bt Baldwin, 1975 (HSAN 2947).

Second Period. SILVER *(cont.)*
Testoons. First Issue *(cont.)*

	Weight g.	gr.	Die Axis	Date	
927	6.09	94.0	280	1558	Obv. stop before FRAN omitted, . DEI . G . (B.877.1 var.; S.5416). Bt Baldwin, 1975; ex F. Baldwin (HSAN 2948).
928	6.15	94.9	10	1558	(B.878.2; S.5416). Acq. 1975; ex Cochran-Patrick (1936), lot 248 (part) (HSAN 2949).
929	6.16	95.1	130	1559	Obv. stop before FRAN omitted, . DEI . G ., SCOTO .. Rev. countermark over left Lorraine cross (B.879.6; S.5416). Bt Spink, 1965; ex Marr (HSAN 2950).
930	5.76	88.9	350	1559	Obv. FAN for FRAN, stop before omitted, MRA for MA, . DEI . G . (B. -; S.5416). Bt Baldwin, 1975; ex F. Baldwin (HSAN 2951).
931	5.91	91.2	350	1559	Obv. stop before FRAN omitted, . DEI . G ., large lis in dauphiny arms. Rev. no i.m., countermark part over left Lorraine cross (cf. B.879.7; S.5416). Acq. 1975; ex Winstanley (HSAN 2952).

Half-testoon (1558–9)

Theoretical weight 3.06 g, 47.13 gr: value 2 shillings and 6 pence Scots, countermarked (crowned thistle) coins revalued at 3 shillings and 8 pence in 1578.

As testoon. Obv. FRAN . ET . MA . D . G . R . R . SCOTOR . D . D . VIEN, dated 1558, 1559.

932	2.77	42.7	220	1558	Obv. No stops. Rev. with stops (B.880.1; S.5419). Acq. 1967; ex Hurley (HSAN 2953).
933	3.00	45.3	350	1558	(B.880.1; S.5419). Bt Baldwin, 1972 (HSAN 2954).
934	3.05	47.1	320	1559	Obv. SCOTO (B. -; S.5419). Acq. 2 June 1973; ex Glendining 11 March 1953, lot 174 (HSAN 2955).

Second Issue (1560–1)

Testoon (1560–1)

Theoretical weight 6.10 g, 94.20 gr: value 5 shillings Scots, countermarked (crowned thistle) coins revalued at 7 shillings and 4 pence in 1578.

i.m. plain-cross/plain-cross. Obv. . FRAN . ET . MAR . D . G . R . R . FRANCO . SCOTOR *B* (or Q), crowned halved shield bearing arms of France, left, and Scotland, right, a plain-cross to left and saltire to right. Rev. . VICIT . LEO . DE . TRIBV . IVDA . 1560., crowned FM monogram, lis to left and thistle head to right both with small crown above.

Type 1 (1560 only)

Obv. . FRAN . ET . MAR . D . G . R . R . FRANCO . SCOTOR *B*, narrow and tall Scottish crown above shields both sides, dated 1560 (Stewart 1967, fig. 177).

	Weight g.	gr.	Die Axis	
935	6.06	93.5	160	Obv. . SCOTOR B .. Rev. i.m. cross potent, small crowns surmounted with cross potent (B.881.8; J. K. R. Murray (1967), 1; S.5417). Ex Glendining, 5 October 1987, lot 498 (HSAN 2956).
936	5.91	91.2	320	Obv. SCTTOR. Rev. i.m. saltire, small crowns surmounted with plain-cross (cf. B.882.11; J. K. R. Murray (1967), 1; S.5417). Bt Baldwin, 1975; ex F. Baldwin (HSAN 2957).
937	6.22	96.0	30	Obv. . SCOTOR *B* .. Rev. i.m. saltire, small crowns surmounted with plain-cross (B.882.11; J. K. R. Murray (1967), 1; S.5417). Bt Baldwin, 1975; ex F. Baldwin (HSAN 2958).
938	5.47	84.4	170	Rev. i.m. saltire, small crowns surmounted with plain-cross, countermark over left small crown (cf. B.882.11; J. K. R. Murray (1967), 1; S.5417). Acq. 1975; ex Walters, lot 662 (part) (HSAN 2959).
939	6.12	94.4	330	Obv. . SCOTOR . *B*. Rev. small crowns surmounted with plain-cross (B.881.8; J. K. R. Murray (1967), 1; S.5417). Bt Baldwin, 1975; ex F. Baldwin (HSAN 2960).

927 928 929 930

931 932 933 934 935

936 937 938 939

Second Period. SILVER *(cont.)*
Testoons. Second Issue *Type 1 (cont.)*

	Weight g.	gr.	Die Axis	
940	5.94	91.7	60	Obv. . SCOTOR *B* .. Rev. small crowns surmounted with plain-cross, (B.881.8; J. K. R. Murray (1967), 1; S.5417). Bt Baldwin, 1975; ex F. Baldwin (HSAN 2961).
941	5.65	87.2	260	Obv. . SCOTOR *B* .. Rev. i.m. cross potent, small crowns surmounted with cross potent, countermark over lis (B. -; J. K. R. Murray (1967) 1; S.5417). Ex J. K. R. Murray, lot 211 (HSAN 2962).
942	6.05	93.4	50	Obv. No pellet before FRAN. Rev. i.m. saltire, small crowns surmounted with plain-cross (B.882.11; J. K. R. Murray (1967), 1; S.5417). Acq. 1975; ex Cochran-Patrick (1936), lot 251 (part) (HSAN 2963).
943	5.89	90.9	60	Obv. . SCOTOR . *B*. Rev. small crowns surmounted with plain-cross (B.881.8; J. K. R. Murray (1967), 1; S.5417). Acq. 1972; ex Dakers, lot 450 (part) (HSAN 2964).
944	6.03	93.0	350	Obv. . SCOTOR . *B* .. Rev. VICIT . small crowns surmounted with plain-cross (B. -; J. K. R. Murray (1967), 1; S.5417). Acq. 1975; ex Cochran-Patrick (1936), lot 252 (part) (HSAN 2965).
945	5.94	91.7	100	Obv. . SCOTOR . *B*. Rev. VICIT ., small crowns surmounted with plain-cross, coarse, unofficial (?), countermark over lis (cf. B.881.9; J. K. R. Murray (1967), 1; S.5417). Acq. 1975; ex Marshall, lot 177 (part); ex Brushfield, lot 64 (part) (HSAN 2966).

Type 2 (1560–1)

Obv. FRAN . ET . MAR . D . G . R . R . FRANCO . SCOTOR ☾, wide crown with five lis on obverse. Rev. .VICIT . LEO . DE . TRIBV . IVDA . **1560** ., dated 1560 or 1561 (Stewart 1967, fig. 178).

	Weight g.	gr.	Die Axis	Date	
946	6.03	93.0	10	1560	Obv. . SCO.TOR ☾. Rev. no stop before VICIT ., small crowns without cross (cf. B.884.14; S.5418). Bt Baldwin, 1975; ex F. Baldwin (HSAN 2969).
947	6.14	94.7	350	1560	Rev. no stop before VICIT ., small crowns without cross (B.884.13; S.5418). Acq. 1975; ex Marshall, lot 177 (part); ex Brushfield, lot 64 (part) (HSAN 2970).
948	5.69	87.8	80	1560	Obv. . SCOTOR ☾ .. Rev. small crowns without cross (B.884.13; S.5418). Acq. 1975; ex Walters, lot 662 (part) (HSAN 2971).
949	5.62	86.7	10	1560	SCOTOR ☾. Rev. no stop before VICIT ., small crowns without cross, **5** over V and **6** over D in date, countermark over lis (cf. B.885.13; S.5418). Bt Baldwin, 1975; ex F. Baldwin (HSAN 2972).
950	5.81	89.7	350	1560	Obv. . DEI ., FRNCO . SCOTOR ☾ .. Rev. small crowns without cross, **0** in date over an inverted **5** (B. -; S.5418). Ex J. K. R. Murray, lot 215 (HSAN 2973).
951	5.90	91.0	270	1560	Obv. . FRAN, . SCOTOR ☾ .. Rev. small crowns surmounted with cross potent (B.884.12; J. K. R. Murray 1967, 3; S.5418). Ex J. K. R. Murray, lot 213 (HSAN 2974).

940 941 942 943

944 945 946 947

948 949 950 951

Second Period. SILVER *(cont.)*
Testoons. Second Issue. *Type 2 (cont.)*

	Weight g.	gr.	Die Axis	Date	
952	6.08	93.8	290	1560	Obv. i.m. cross potent, . SCOTOR . Q .. Rev. i.m. plain-cross, O in LEO recut, small crowns surmounted with plain-cross (B. -; J. K. R. Murray 1967, 2; S.5418). Bt Spink, 24 July 1987; ex Davidson (HSAN 2975).
953	6.26	96.6	230	1560.	Obv. SCOTOR . Q. Rev. .VICIT., small crowns without cross (B. 884.14; J. K. R. Murray 1967, 2; S.5418). Acq. 1975; ex Murdoch, lot 224 (HSAN 2976).
954	6.16	95.1	160	1560	Obv. . SCOTOR . Q. Rev. i.m. cross potent, small crowns surmounted with cross potent (cf. B.883.12; J. K. R. Murray 1967, 3; S.5418). Acq. 15 May 1990 (HSAN 2977).
955	5.87	90.6	20	1560.	Obv. . SCOTOR . Q, small N. Rev. no stop before VICIT, small crowns without cross (B.884.14; J. K. R. Murray 1967, 2; S.5418). Acq. 1975; ex Walters, lot 662 (part) (HSAN 2978).
956	6.07	93.7	170	1560	Obv. . SCOTOR . Q, small N. Rev. small crowns without cross, no stop after date, holed to left of shield (B.883.12; J. K. R. Murray 1967, 2; S.5418). Acq. 2 January 1956 (HSAN 2979).
957	6.20	95.7	260	1560	Obv. . SCOTOR . Q .. Rev. small crowns without cross (B.883.14; J. K. R. Murray 1967, 2; S.5418). Bt Baldwin, 1975 (HSAN 2980).
958	6.01	92.7	90	1561	Obv. . SCOTOR . Q. Rev. small crowns without cross (B.885.15; S.5418). Bt Baldwin, 1975; ex F. Baldwin (HSAN 2981).

Half-testoon (1560)

Theoretical weight 3.06 g, 47.13 gr: value 2 shillings and 6 pence Scots; coins countermarked with crowned thistle in 1578, and revalued at 3 shillings and 8 pence.

Type 1

As type 1 testoon, i.m. plain-cross. Obv. SCOTOR *B*, dated 1560.

	Weight g.	gr.	Die Axis	
959	2.75	42.4	90	Rev. small crowns surmounted with plain-cross (B.886.3; S.5420). 1975; ex Cochran-Patrick (1936), lot 251 (part) (HSAN 2987).
960	3.01	46.4	350	Obv. SCOTOR B.. Rev. small crowns surmounted by plain-cross (B.886.3; S.5420). Acq. October 1967; ex Hurley (HSAN 2988).

Type 2

As type 2 testoon, i.m. plain-cross. Obv. SCOTOR Q, dated 1560

961	2.69	41.5	330	Rev. + . VICIT, crowned thistle countermark left of F in monogram (B. -; S.5421). Acq. 1956; ex Parsons, lot 736 (part); ex Dakers, lot 450 (part) (HSAN 2989).
962	2.88	44.4	30	Rev. small crowns surmounted by plain-cross (B.887.5; S.5421). Acq. 1956 (HSAN 2990).
963	2.96	45.7	320	Obv. SCOTOR Q. Rev. small crowns surmounted by plain-cross (B.887.5; S.5421). Acq. 1975; ex Marshall, lot 177 (part); ex Brushfield, lot 64 (part) (HSAN 2991).
964	3.04	46.9	140	Obv. SCOTOR Q. Rev. small crowns surmounted by plain-cross (B.887.5; S.5421). Bt Baldwin, 1972. Obv. double struck (HSAN 2992).

952 953 954 955

956 957 958 959

960 961 962 963 964

Second Period. BILLON
Twelve-penny groats.

BILLON COINAGE

Twelve-penny groat, 'Nonsunt' (1558–9)

Theoretical weight 1.70 g, 26.20 gr: value 12 pence Scots.

i.m. cross potent. Obv. crowned **FM** monogram, with small crown above the dolphin, left, and small crown above thistle head, right, **FRAN . ET . MA . D . G . R . R . SCOTOR . D . D . VIEN**. Rev. i.m. / **IAM . NON / SVNT . DVO / SED . VNA / . CARO .**, in four lines within square panel, Lorraine cross at sides, dated 1558, 1559, a pellet before and after the date.

Type 1 (1558–9)

Obv. dolphin looking right, dated 1558 or 1559 (B.889.1–890.7; Stewart 1; S.5447).

	Weight		Die		
	g.	gr.	Axis	Date	
965	1.62	25.0	140	1558	Acq. 9 April 1957 (HSAN 3089).
966	1.83	28.2	270	1558	Rev. **SED VNA.**. Bt Baldwin, 1975; ex F. Baldwin (HSAN 3090).
967	1.78	27.5	360	1558	Acq. 1975; ex Dakers, lot 459 (part) (HSAN 3091).
968	1.67	25.8	270	1558	Acq. 1975; ex Dakers, lot 459 (part) (HSAN 3092).
969	1.46	22.5	210	1559	Crowns with small cross. Rev. no stops in **IAM NON SVNT DVO SED VNA CARO**. Bt Baldwin, 1975; ex F. Baldwin (HSAN 3093).
970	1.66	25.6	350	1559	Obv. crowns with small cross. Acq. 1975; ex Dakers, lot 459 (part) (HSAN 3094).
971	1.73	26.7	160	1559	Obv. crowns with small cross. Acq. 1975; ex Dakers, lot 459 (part) (HSAN 3095).
972	1.52	23.5	30	1559	Rev. **. DVO SED .**. Acq. 1956 (HSAN 3096).

Type 2 (1559)

Obv. dolphin looking left, **SCOTO**. Rev. small crowns surmounted with small cross, dated 1559 only (B.891.8–891.12; Stewart 2; S.5448).

	Weight			
	g.	gr.	Die Axis	
973	1.58	24.4	50	Acq. 1975; ex Dakers, lot 459 (part) (HSAN 3097).
974	1.50	23.2	40	Acq. 1975; ex Dakers, lot 459 (part) (HSAN 3098).
975	1.43	22.1	40	Obv. **SCOT**. Rev. **. DVO SED VNA .**. Bt Baldwin, 1975; ex F. Baldwin (HSAN 3099).
976	1.40	21.6	50	Rev. **X** over **N** in **SVNT**. Bt Spink, 1965; ex Marr (HSAN 3100).
977	1.41	21.8	100	Rev. panel with double lines. Bt *c.* 1946 (HSAN 3101).
978	1.84	28.4	360	Rev. panel with double lines. Bt Baldwin, 1975; ex F. Baldwin (HSAN 3102).
Contemporary Counterfeit				
979	1.38	22.0	360	An undated contemporary counterfeit. Acq. 1975; ex Dakers, lot 459 (part) (HSAN 3103).

PLATE 55

965 966 967 968 969

970 971 972 973 974

975 976 977 978 979

Second Period. BILLON *(cont.)*

Hardheads or lion

Hardhead or lion (1559–60)

Theoretical weight 0.95 g, 14.7 gr: value 1½ penny.

i.m. cross potent. Obv. crown with interior detail both sides, FRA . ET . MA . D . G . R . R . SCOT . D . D . VIEN, arched crown above FM monogram, dolphin each side. Rev. . VICIT . VERITAS . (date) ., crowned lion rampant left, sometimes with wire-line inner-circles.

Countermarked in 1575, with star in heart (mark of James Douglas, Earl of Morton, regent to James VI), with the intention of distinguishing counterfeit from true coins.

Type 1 (1559)

Obv. dolphins looking right (B.893.3–5; Stewart 1; S.5449).

	Weight			
	g.	gr.	Die Axis	
980	0.82	12.7	320	Bt Spink, 1965; ex Marr (HSAN 3141).
981	0.93	14.4	350	Rev. wire-line inner-circle. Unprovenanced (HSAN 3414).
982	0.85	13.1	200	Rev. VEIRTAS, wire-line inner-circle. Unprovenanced (HSAN 3415).
983	0.95	14.7	180	Bt. Spink, June 1989; ex Davidson. Corroded, not illustrated (HSAN 3416).
984	1.18	18.2	330	Acq. 1975; ex Dakers, lot 459 (part) (HSAN 3417).
985	1.13	17.4	360	Obv. no stops. Bt Baldwin, 1975; ex F. Baldwin (HSAN 3418).
986	0.80	12.3	170	Rev. countermark on lion's body. Bt Baldwin, 1975; ex F. Baldwin (HSAN 3419).
987	0.71	11.0	180	Bt Baldwin, 1975; ex F. Baldwin (HSAN 3420).
988	1.16	17.9	180	Rev. wire-line inner-circle. Bt Baldwin, 1975; ex F. Baldwin (HSAN 3421).
Contemporary counterfeit.				
989	1.12	17.3	360	Garbled legends, crude style. Ex J. K. R. Murray, lot 246 (part) (HSAN 3432).

Type 2 (1559–60)

Obv. dolphins looking left, arched crown both sides, sometimes with interior detail (B.894.6–10, 895.11; Stewart 2; S.5450).

	Weight		Die		
	g.	gr.	Axis	Date	
990	0.68	10.5	300	1559	Unprovenanced (HSAN 3142).
991	0.97	15.0	20	1559	Acq. June 1985; ex Davidson. Surfaces with appearance of silvering (HSAN 3403).
992	0.77	11.9	90	1559	Obv. SCOTO, pellet in M, ex Longstaffe, lot 343 (part) (HSAN 3404).
993	1.27	19.6	100	1559	Obv. Pellet in M. Rev. crown with interior detail. Bt Spink, June 1989, ex Davidson, corroded, not illustrated (HSAN 3405).
994	0.76	11.7	140	1559	Obv. SCOTO, crown with interior detail, pellet in M (B.894.9). Bt Baldwin, 1975; ex F. Baldwin (HSAN 3406).
995	0.88	13.6	180	1559	Obv. crown with interior detail, pellet in M. Bt Baldwin, 1976; ex Ryan, lot 1362 (part) (HSAN 3407).
996	1.07	16.5	50	1559	Crown with interior detail both sides. Obv. pellet in M. Bt Baldwin, 1975 (HSAN 3408).
997	0.70	10.8	270	1559	Crown with interior detail both sides. Obv. pellet in M. Bt Baldwin, 1975 (HSAN 3409).
998	0.78	12.0	30	1559	Pellet in M. Rev. crown only with interior detail. Bt Baldwin, 1975; ex F. Baldwin (HSAN 3410).
999	0.95	14.7	270	1559	Crown with interior detail both sides. Obv. COTO, pellet in M. Bt Spink, June 1989, ex Davidson (HSAN 3411).
1000	0.84	13.0	280	1559	Crown with interior detail both sides. Obv. FRA reads FA with F/R. Bt Spink, June 1989; ex Davidson (HSAN 3412).

980 981 982 984 985 986 987 988

989 990 991 992 994 995 996 997

998 999 1000 1002 1003 1004 1005 1006

1007 1008 1009 1010 1011 1012 1013

	Weight g.	gr.	Die Axis	Date	
1001	0.80	12.3	350	1559	Bt Spink, June 1989; ex Davidson. Corroded, not illustrated (HSAN 3413).
1002	0.55	8.5	250	1560	Crown with interior detail both sides. Obv. SCOTO. Rev. countermark below lion at 7 o'clock. Unprovenanced (HSAN 3422).
1003	0.93	14.4	40	1560	Crown with interior detail both sides. Ex Bearman, acq. Spink, 1 October 1900 (HSAN 3423).
1004	1.38	21.3	10	1560	Rev. crown with interior detail. Acq. 1975; ex Dakers, lot 459 (part) (HSAN 3424).
1005	0.67	10.3	280	1560	Crown with interior detail both sides. Bt Baldwin, 1975, ex F. Baldwin (HSAN 3425).

Contemporary counterfeit.

Obv. crown above dolphins with prominent central fleur tipped with three pellets, **.** ET **.** MA **.** D **:** G **.** R **.** SCCT[. D **.** D **.** VIEN .]. Rev. VICI[T **.** VERITA **. 58** .], wire-line inner-circle.

	Weight g.	gr.	Die Axis	
1006	0.71	11.0	20	Unprovenanced (HSAN 3140).
1007	0.97	15.0	40	Acq. 1975; ex Dakers, lot 459 (part) (HSAN 3426).
1008	0.82	12.7	350	Bt *c.* 1950 (HSAN 3427).
1009	0.63	9.8	90	Bt Baldwin, 1975; ex F. Baldwin (HSAN 3428).
1010	0.96	14.8	40	Unprovenanced (HSAN 3429).
1011	0.91	14.0	110	Unprovenanced (HSAN 3430).
1012	1.29	19.9	180	Unprovenanced (HSAN 3431).
1013	0.87	13.4	170	Acq. 1975; ex Dakers, lot 459 (part) (HSAN 3433).

THIRD PERIOD, 1560–5. FIRST WIDOWHOOD

SILVER COINAGE

Testoon (1561–2)

Theoretical weight 6.10 g, 94.20 gr: value 5 shillings Scots, countermarked with crowned thistle in 1578 and revalued at 7 shillings and 4 pence.

i.m. -/plain-cross. Obv. bust left wearing bonnet, date in panel below, legend commencing at 7 o'clock, **. MARIA . DEI . GRA . SCOTORVM . REGINA .**. Rev. **. SALVVM . FAC . POPVLVM . TVVM . DOMINE .**, crowned halved shield with arms of France, left, and Scotland, right, crowned M each side. Dated 1561 or 1562 (Stewart 1967, fig. 180).

	Weight g.	gr.	Die Axis	Date	
1014	5.83	90.0	350	1561	(B.897.2; S.5422). Bt Spink, 14 October 1970. Holed above head (HSAN 2982).
1015	5.70	88.0	190	1561	Rev. i.m. cross potent (B.899.4; S.5422). Acq. 30 March 1957; ticket states 'ex Boyd' (HSAN 2983).
1016	5.93	91.5	180	1561	(B.897.2; S.5422). Bt Baldwin, 1961 (HSAN 2984).
1017	5.86	90.4	200	1561	Obv. Countermark before face. Rev. i.m. small cross potent (cf. B.899.4; S.5422). Bt Baldwin, 1975; ex F. Baldwin (HSAN 2985).
1018	5.80	89.5	90	1561	Rev. small crowns with single arch (B.896.2; S.5422). Ex Glendining, 5 October 1987, lot 499 (HSAN 2986).
1019	6.09	94.0	300	1562	Rev. i.m. cross potent (B.899.5; S.5422). Bt Baldwin, 1975; ex F. Baldwin (HSAN 2995).

Half-testoon (1561–2)

Theoretical weight 3.08 g, 47.10 gr: value 2 shillings and 6 pence Scots, countermarked with crowned thistle in 1578 and revalued at 3 shillings and 8 pence.

i.m. -/cross potent, as testoon, dated 1561 or 1562.

1020	2.76	42.59	350	1561	Rev. i.m. cross potent (B.902.2; S.5423). Bt Spink, 2 February 1962 (HSAN 2993).
1021	2.97	45.83	40	1562	Rev. i.m. cross potent (B.903.3; S.5423). Acq. 1975; ex Dakers, lot 453 (HSAN 2994).

1014

1015

1016

1017

1018

1019

1020

1021

FOURTH PERIOD, 1565–67. MARRIAGE TO HENRY DARNLEY

SILVER COINAGE

The first issue 'marriage' ryal of 1565 is not represented in the collection.

Second Issue 1565–7

Ryal (1565–7)

Theoretical weight 30.54 g, 471.20 gr: value 30 shillings Scots, countermarked with crowned thistle in 1578 and revalued at 36 shillings and 9 pence.

i.m. plain-cross/thistle head. Obv. crowned shield bearing lion rampant, with thistle head each side, **. MARIA . & . HENRIC' . DEI . GRA . R . & . R . SCOTORV .**, contraction bar over **V**. Rev. **EXVRGAT . DEVS . & . DISSIPENTR . INIMICI . EI' .**, crown above palm tree, with tortoise climbing the trunk, **DAT GLORIA VIRES**, on banner above tortoise, date, divided, below. Dated 1565, 1566 and 1567.

	Weight g.	gr.	Die Axis	Date	
1022	30.19	465.8	220	1565	Obv. **HENRC**. Rev. **DISCIPENTR** (cf. B.904.3; S.5425). Ex Davidson II, lot 458 (HSAN 3007).
1023	29.34	452.7	360	1565	Obv. no bar in **V** in **SCOTORV**. Rev. **R** with truncated top, countermark to left of palm branches (cf. B.904.2; S.5425). Bt Baldwin, 1976 (HSAN 3008).
1024	29.96	462.3	100	1566	Obv. no bar in **V** in **SCOTORV**. Rev. crowned thistle countermark to left of palm branches (B.905.6; S.5425). Acq. 24 December 1954 (HSAN 3009).
1025	29.68	458.0	30	1566	Rev. **E'**, countermark to left of palm branches (B.905.6; S.5425). Bt Spink, November 1994. Tooled on obverse (HSAN 3010).
1026	30.23	466.5	300	1566	Rev. **E'** (B.905.6; S.5425). Ex Glendining, 28 July 1999, lot 450 (HSAN 3011).
1027	30.50	470.6	170	1567	Obv. **V** with contraction bar (B.906.7, this coin noted Wingate 1868, pl. XXI, 2, die as B.905.5 with 906.7; S.5425). Ex J. K. R. Murray, lot 227 (HSAN 3017).

1022 1023 1024

1025 1026 1027

Fourth Period. SILVER *(cont.)*

Two-thirds ryals.

Two-thirds ryal (1565–7)

Theoretical weight 20.36 g, 314.10 gr: value 20 shillings, countermarked with crowned thistle in 1578 and revalued at 24 shillings and 6 pence.

As ryal. Dated 1565, 1566 and 1567.

	Weight g.	gr.	Die Axis	Date	
1028	19.78	305.21	170	Undated	Undated. Rev. countermark left of palm branches (cf. B.907.9 - same reverse die but without date, 1565, J. K. R. Murray (1966b), 3, date omitted; S.5426). Ex Dundee, lot 216; ex Asherson; ex Parsons, lot 742 (HSAN 3019).
1029	20.53	316.8	140	1565	Obv. reads MARA. Rev. INIMMICI, DISSIPENTR:, T in PENT re-cut (B. -; S.5426). Acq. 1975; ex Dakers, lot 455 (part) (HSAN 3001).
1030	20.25	312.5	220	1565	Rev. countermark left of palm branches (B.907.12; S.5426). Acq. 1975; ex Cochran-Patrick (1936), lot 258 (part) (HSAN 3002).
1031	20.21	311.8	340	1565	Rev. countermark left of palm branches (B.907.12; S.5426). Acq. 1975; ex Walters, lot 665 (part) (HSAN 3003).
1032	20.26	312.6	360	1565	Rev. countermark left of palm branches (B.907.12; S.5426). 1975; ex Dakers, lot 455 (part) (HSAN 3004).
1033	20.19	311.5	320	1566	Rev. second I re-cut in INI, I in MIC over C (cf. B.908.13; S.5426). Acq. 1975; ex Walters, lot 665 (part). Same rev. die as **1042** (HSAN 3005).

One-third ryal (1565–6)

Theoretical weight 10.18 g, 157.10 gr: value 10 shillings Scots, countermarked with crowned thistle in 1578 and revalued at 12 shillings and 3 pence.

As ryal. Dated 1565 and 1566.

1034	9.15	141.2	70	1565	Obv. R . ET . R . SCOTORVM. Rev. ET . DISSIP[ENTR]., EIVS ., E in EIVS recut over small E, unofficial countermark, centre left, with a trefoil of three pellets within crown (B.910.16; S.5427). Bt Baldwin, 1975; ex F. Baldwin (HSAN 2996).

1028 1029 1030

1031 1032 1033 1034

Fourth Period. SILVER *(cont.)*
One-third ryals (cont.)

	Weight g.	gr.	Die Axis	Date	
1035	9.35	144.3	280	1565	Obv. R . ET . R. SCOTORVM. Rev. ET . DISSIPENTR ., EIVS., countermark left of palm branches (B.910.16; S.5427). Acq. 1975; ex Winstanley (HSAN 2997).
1036	9.30	143.5	10	1565	Obv. R . ET . R . SCOTORVM, E in HENRIC re-cut, large V. Rev. ET . DISSIPENTR ., EIVS ., countermark left of palm branches (B.910.17; S.5427). Bt Baldwin, 1975; ex F. Baldwin (HSAN 2998).
1037	9.84	151.8	280	1565	Large letter V both sides. Obv. MARIA . ET . HENRICVS . DEI . GR.A . R . ET . R . SCOTORVM. Rev. ET . DISSIPENTR., EIVS., countermark left of palm branches (obv. B.910.19/rev. 910.17; S.5427). Ex J. K. R. Murray, lot 233. Tooled in reverse field. A 1566 obverse die paired with a 1565 reverse die (HSAN 2999).
1038	9.77	150.8	10	1566	R . ET . R . SCOTORVM. Rev. ET . DISSIPENTVR, countermark to left of palm branches (B.911.20; S.5427). Bt Seaby, 21 September 1988; *SCMB* September 1988, item SH10 (HSAN 3000).

FIFTH PERIOD, 1567. SECOND WIDOWHOOD

SILVER COINAGE

Ryal (1567)

Theoretical weight 30.54 g, 471.20 gr: value 30 shillings Scots, countermarked with crowned thistle in 1578 and revalued at 36 shillings and 9 pence.

i.m. plain-cross/thistle head. Obv. crowned shield bearing lion rampant, thistle head each side, . MARIA . DEI . GRA . SCOTORVM . REGINA .. Rev. EXVRGAT . DEVS . & . DISSIPENTR . INIMICI . EI'., crown above palm tree, with tortoise climbing the trunk, DAT GLORIA VIRES on banner above tortoise, date below (divided). Dated 1567 only.

1039	29.72	458.6	120	1567	Rev. DISSIPENTR, T over R, countermark left of palm branches, MIC over MCC (B.912.2; S.5429). Acq. 1975; ex Walters, lot 666 (part) (HSAN 3015).
1040	31.04	479.0	150	1567	Rev. VERIS, countermark left of palm branches (cf. B.912.2; S.5429). Bt Baldwin, 1975; ex F. Baldwin (HSAN 3016).
1041	29.52	455.5	150	1567	Rev. IC over CI, thistle countermark left of palm branches (cf. B.912.2; S.5429). Bt Spink, 1965; ex Marr (HSAN 3018).

1035 1036 1037 1038

1039 1040 1041

Fifth Period. SILVER *(cont.)*
Two-thirds ryals

Two-thirds ryal (1567)

Theoretical weight 20.36 g, 314.10 gr: value 20 shillings, countermarked with crowned thistle in 1578 and revalued at 24 shillings and 6 pence.

As Ryal, dated 1567 only.

	Weight g.	gr.	Die Axis	Date	
1042	19.47	300.4	320	1566	Obv. SCOTORV no contraction bar in V. Rev. DISSIPENT, recut in INI, I in MIC over C (B.913.3/908.13; S.5430/5426), a mule of a fifth period obverse with a fourth period reverse. Ex Scaife, lot 1255. Same rev. die as **1033** (HSAN 3006).
1043	19.65	303.2	360	1567	Obv. REG with widely spaced letters. Rev. DISSIPENTR, small R, no stop before INIMICI, countermark left of palm branches (B.913.4; S.5430). Acq. April 1965; ex Hurley (HSAN 3014).

One-third ryal (1567)

Theoretical weight 10.18 g, 157.10 gr: value 10 shillings Scots, countermarked with crowned thistle in 1578 and revalued at 12 shillings and 3 pence.

As Ryal, dated, 1566 or 1567 (S.5431)

1044	9.82	151.5	160	1567	Rev. ET . DISSIPENTVR ., . EIVS, countermark left of palm branches (B.915.7; S.5431). Ex J. K. R. Murray, lot 238 (part); ex Dundee, lot 225; ex Lockett I, lot 344 (part) (HSAN 3012).
1045	9.53	147.1	240	1567	Rev. ET . DISSPENTVR . EI'., countermark left of palm branches (cf. B.915.6; S.5431). Bt Baldwin, 1975; ex F. Baldwin (HSAN 3013).

JAMES VI (1567–1625)

BEFORE ACCESSION TO THE ENGLISH THRONE, 1567–1603

GOLD COINAGE

First coinage, 1567–71.

No gold issued

Second Coinage, 1571–80

Twenty-pound piece (1575–6)

Theoretical weight 29.89 g, 461.2 gr: issued at value 20 pounds Scots, 1575 and 1576. 22 cts fine.

Obv. IACOBVS . 6 . DEI . GRA . REX . SCOTOR, half-length standing figure of youthful James VI in profile, crowned and armoured, holding sword to shoulder in right hand, and extending olive branch in left, IN . VTRVNQVE . / . PARATVS . / . **1575** ., below in panel. Rev. PARCERE SVBIECTIS . & DEBELLARE SVPERBOS, crowned shield bearing lion rampant (Stewart 1967, fig. 186).

	Weight g.	gr.	Die Axis	Date	
1046	30.11	464.7	90	1575	Obv. device after SCOTOR, VTRVN QVE (B.947- 1576; S.5451). Ex Pye, lot 170 (HSAN 4826).

1042 1043 1044 1045

1046 1047 1048 1049 1050

Third Coinage, 1580–1

Ducat or four-pound piece (1580)

Theoretical weight 6.10 g, 94.2 gr: value 4 pounds or 80 shillings Scots. 21 cts fine.

i.m. crown/plain-cross. Obv. **. IACOBVS 6 . DEI . GRA . REX . SCOTORVM .**, bareheaded youthful bust left wearing ruff. Rev. **. EXVRGAT . DE'. ET . DISSIP . INIMICI . EIVS.**, crowned shield bearing lion rampant dividing date (Stewart 1967, fig. 188).

	Weight g.	gr.	Die Axis	
1047	6.11	94.3	340	Obv. **D . EI** (cf. B.948.1; S.5452). Ex Pye, lot 171; ex Brand; ex Glendining, 7–8 July 1948, lot 37 (HSAN 4827).

Fourth Coinage, 1582–8

Lion noble (1584–6, 1588)

Theoretical weight 5.09 g, 78.5 gr: value 75 shillings Scots. 21.5 cts fine.

i.m. quatrefoil/quatrefoil. Obv. **POST . 5 . & . 100 . PROA'. INVICTA . MANENT . HEC**, crowned lion sejant, holding sword, left, and sceptre, right. Rev. **DEVS . IVDICIVM . TVVM . REGI . DA** (date), four crowned **IR** monograms arranged saltire around central **S** (Stewart 1967, fig. 187).

	Weight g.	gr.	Die Axis	Date	
1048	5.08	78.4	310	1586	(B.949.3; S.5453). Ex Butterfield, lot 29; ex Hird, lot 96; ex Lockett II, lot 916; ex Cochran-Patrick (1936), lot 68; ex Wingate (Wingate 1868, this coin illustrated pl. 34, 7) (HSAN 4828).

Two-thirds lion noble (1584–5, 1587)

Theoretical weight 3.39 g, 52.30 gr: value 50 shillings Scots.

As lion noble.

1049	3.38	52.0	290	1584	Obv. single pellet stops, **MANET**. Rev. no stops, annulet by inner-circle, below, at 12 o'clock (cf. B.950.1; S.5454). Ex Strauss, lot 125; ex Lockett I, lot 348; ex Bruun, lot 917 (HSAN 4829).

One-third lion noble (1584)

Theoretical weight 1.70 g, 26.2 gr: value 25 shillings Scots.

As lion noble.

	Weight g.	gr.	Die Axis	
1050	1.65	25.5	90	Obv. **POS .T** (cf. B.950A.1a; S.5455). Ex Strauss, lot 126; ex Ryan I, lot 575; ex Scott Plummer, lot 369. Reverse flan flaw (HSAN 4830).

Before English Accession. GOLD *(cont.)*

Fifth Coinage, 1588–90

Thistle Noble (1588 - undated)

Theoretical weight 7.63 g, 117.8 gr: value 146 shillings and 8 pence Scots. 23 cts fine.

i.m. quatrefoil/quatrefoil. Obv, crowned shield bearing lion rampant within ship, flags at bow with letter I and at stern with number 6, **. IACOBVS . 6 . DEI . GRATIA . REX . SCOTORVM .** (i.m) .. Rev. **. FLORENT . SCEPT'. PIIS . REGNA . HIS . IOVA . DAT . NVMERATQ .**, tressure of four arcs each containing a lion alternating with four angles each containing a crown, thistle plant over crossed sceptres at centre, and thistle head in spandrels (Stewart 1967, fig. 191).

	Weight			
	g.	gr.	Die Axis	
1051	7.58	116.9	330	Rev. no stops, **SCEPTRA**, **NVMERAQ**, **ME** ligate, quatrefoil partially over **Q** (B.951.5; S.5456). Acq. 15 March 2007; bt Spink; ex Finn list 18, 2000, item 22; ex Thellusson, lot 162 (HSAN 4831).
1052	7.46	115.1	240	Obv. no stop after **SCOTORVM**. Rev. **SCEPT .** (B.951.1; S.5456). Acq. 25 September 1967; ex *SCMB* (HSAN 4832).

Sixth Coinage, 1591–3

Hat piece (1591–3)

Theoretical weight 4.52 g, 69.80 gr: value 4 pounds or 80 shillings Scots. 22 cts fine.

i.m. cinquefoil/cinquefoil. Obv. bust right wearing tall hat, thistle head behind, **. IACOBVS . 6 . D . G . R . SCOTORVM ..** Rev. **. TE . SOLVM . VEREOR .** (date) **.**, crowned lion, within inner-circle at lower right, sejant to left, holding sceptre upright before, cloud above with 'Jehovah' in Hebrew letters (Stewart 1967, fig. 193).

	Weight		Die		
	g.	gr.	Axis	Date	
1053	4.49	69.3	90	1592	(B.952.2; S.5457). Bt Baldwin, 3 August 1973 (HSAN 4833).

Seventh Coinage, 1594–1601

Rider (1593–5, 1598–9, 1601)

Theoretical weight 5.08 g, 78.50 gr: value 5 pounds or 100 shillings Scots, re-valued in 1598 to 106 shillings and 8 pence. 22 cts fine.

i.m. quatrefoil/quatrefoil. Obv. king, armoured and brandishing sword, riding right on caparisoned horse, date, pellet before and after, in exergue below, **. IACOBVS . 6 . D . G . R . SCOTORVM ..** Rev. **. SPERO . MELIORA .**, crowned shield bearing lion rampant (Stewart 1967, fig. 196).

1054	5.02	77.5	0	1593	Early style dies (B.953.1; S.5458). Ex Glendining, 24 November 1976, lot 17 (HSAN 4834).
1055	4.97	76.7	20	1599	Date without pellet each side (B.954.9; S.5458). Bt Seaby, 1984 (HSAN 4835).
1056	4.94	76.3	320	1601	(B. -, noted; S.5458). Ex Davidson I, lot 906; acq. Spink, 17 June 1971 (HSAN 4836).

Half-rider (1593–5, 1598–9, 1601)

Theoretical weight 2.55 g, 39.3 gr: value 50 shillings Scots, revalued in 1598 to 53 shillings and 4 pence.

As Rider.

1057	2.50	38.5	240	1599	(B.955.4; S.5459). Bt Baldwin, 1962 (HSAN 4837).

1051 1052 1053 1054

1055 1056 1057 1058 1059

Eighth Coinage, 1601–4

Sword and sceptre piece (1601–4)

Theoretical weight 5.09 g, 78.5 gr: value 6 pounds or 120 shillings Scots.

i.m. quatrefoil/quatrefoil. Obv. crowned shield bearing lion rampant, **. IACOBVS . 6 . D . G . R . SCOTORVM .**. Rev. **. SALVS . POPVLI . SVPREMA . LEX .**, crossed sword and sceptre saltire, thistle head each side, crown above, date, a pellet before and after, below (Stewart 1967, fig. 197).

	Weight g.	gr.	Die Axis	Date	
1058	5.05	78.0	260	1604	Obv. no stop after **IACOBVS** (B. -, noted; S.5460). Bt Baldwin. 3 August 1973 (HSAN 4838).

Half sword and sceptre piece (1601–04)

Theoretical weight 2.55 g, 39.30 gr: value 3 pounds or 60 shillings Scots, 22 cts fine.

As sword and sceptre piece.

1059	2.50	38.6	220	1601	(B.957.2; S.5462). Acq. 21 February 1970; ex Rockley; ex Cowley (HSAN 4839).

Before English Accession. SILVER
First coinage. *Ryals*

SILVER COINAGE

First Coinage, 1567–71

Ryal (1567–7)

Theoretical weight 30.53 g, 471.2 grns: value 30 shillings Scots, countermarked with crowned thistle in 1578 and revalued at 36 shillings and 9 pence.

i.m. none. Obv. shield bearing lion rampant dividing I and R both crowned, IACOBVS . 6 . DEI . GRATIA . REX SCOTORVM ., a small trefoil at start of legend, crown with jewelled band. Rev. PRO . ME . SI . MEREOR . IN . ME, a small trefoil at start and end of legend, crowned sword vertical dividing date, hand pointing upper left, mark of value, XXX, upper right (Stewartby 1967, fig. 183; S.5472).

	Weight g.	gr.	Die Axis	Date	
1060	29.68	458.0	40	1567	Obv. trefoil after SCOTORVM. Rev. countermark left of sword hilt guard (B.921.2; S.5472). Bt Baldwin, 16 January 1971 (HSAN 3434).
1061	30.66	473.1	20	1567	Obv. trefoil after SCOTORVM. Rev. small 5 (B.921.1; S.5472). Bt Baldwin, 1976; ex F. Baldwin (HSAN 3435).
1062	30.50	470.6	225	1568	Obv. . IACOBVS. Rev. no trefoil at end of legend. ME ., countermark left of sword hilt guard (B.921.3; S.5472). Ex Dakers, lot 474 (part) (HSAN 3436).
1063	29.57	456.3	60	1568	Rev. no trefoil at end of legend. ME ., countermark left of sword hilt guard (B.921.3; S.5472). Bt Baldwin; ex F. Baldwin; ex Glendining, 14 December 1928, lot 300. Extensive tooling on both sides (18th century?) (HSAN 3437).
1064	29.86	460.7	90	1569	Obv. no trefoil, . IACOBVS, SCOTORVM . (B.921.3; S.5472). Ex Cairncross, lot 459 (part) (HSAN 3438).
1065	29.26	451.5	30	1569	Obv. trefoil at start and end of legend. Rev. countermark left of sword hilt guard (B.921.4; S.5472). Bt Baldwin, 1969 (HSAN 3439).

1060 1061 1062

1063 1064 1065

Before English Accession. SILVER *(cont.)*
First coinage *(cont.)*. *Ryals (cont.)*

	Weight g.	gr.	Die Axis	Date	
1066	30.45	469.8	360	1570	Obv. trefoil at start and end of legend, crown with plain band. Rev. countermark left of sword hilt (B.921.5; S.5472). Bt Spink, 14 January 1957 (HSAN 3440).
1067	30.40	469.1	180	1570	Obv. trefoil at start and end of legend, crown with plain band (B.921.5; S.5472). Acq. 1969; ex Parsons, lot 748 (part) (HSAN 3441).
1068	30.32	467.8	90	1570	Obv. trefoil at start and end of legend, crown with plain band (B.921.5; S.5472). Ex Ryan II, lot 1365 (part). Plugged (HSAN 3442).
1069	30.29	467.4	20	1571	Obv. trefoil at start and end of legend, A in TIA recut, crown with plain band. Rev. countermark left of sword hilt guard (B.921.7; S.5472). Bt Baldwin, 1970 (HSAN 3443).
1070	29.67	457.8	130	1571	Obv. trefoil at start and end of legend, crown with plain band. Rev. countermark left of sword hilt guard (B.921.6; S.5472). Acq. 24 December 1954; ex Thorburn (HSAN 3444).
1071	30.39	468.9	100	1571	Obv. trefoil at start and end of legend, crown with plain band. Rev. last ME with mis-cut M (B.921.6; S.5472). Acq. 1960; ex Parsons, lot 748 (part) (HSAN 3445).

1066 1067 1068

1069 1070 1071

Before English Accession. SILVER *(cont.)*
First coinage *(cont.)* *Two-thirds ryals*

Two-thirds ryal (1567–71)

Theoretical weight 20.36 g, 314.1 gr: value 20 shillings Scots, countermarked with crowned thistle in 1578 and revalued at 24 shillings and 6 pence.

As ryal, but with value given on reverse as **XX**.

	Weight g.	gr.	Die Axis	Date	
1072	19.98	308.3	280	1561 error	Erroneous date, **1561** for 1571. Obv. trefoil at start and end of legend. Rev. no stops or trefoils, countermark left of sword hilt guard (B.-; S.5474). Bt Spink, September 1967; ex Asherson; ex Lockett II, lot 927; ex Bearman; ex Kirke, lot 78 (HSAN 3446).
1073	19.89	306.9	330	1567	Obv. trefoil at start and end of legend. Rev. countermark left of sword hilt (B.922.2; S.5474). Bt Baldwin, 1976; ex F. Baldwin (HSAN 3447).
1074	20.27	312.8	30	1568	Obv. no trefoil, **. IACOBVS**, crown with plain band. Rev. no trefoil after last **ME**, value erased (B.922.3; S.5474). Acq. 1967; bt Baldwin; ex Bearman; ex Sotheby 'Gentleman' (1914), lot 117 (part) (HSAN 3448).
1075	20.21	311.8	170	1569	Obv. **IACOBV.S 6 .**, small **6**, trefoil at start and end of legend, crown with plain band. Rev. small date (cf. B.922.4; S.5474). Ex Pye, lot 193; ex Lingford II, lot 1140 (HSAN 3449).
1076	20.12	310.5	180	1570	Obv. trefoil at start and end of legend (B.922.5; S.5474). Ex Cochran-Patrick (1936), lot 269 (HSAN 3450).
1077	19.98	308.3	315	1571	Obv. no stop before **DEI** (cf. B.922.5; S.5474). Acq. 17 December 1965; ex Dakers, lot 476 (part) (HSAN 3451).

1072

1073

1074

1075

1076

1077

Before English Accession. SILVER *(cont.)*
First coinage *(cont.) One-third ryals*

One-third ryal (1567–71)

Theoretical weight 10.18 g, 157.10 gr: value 10 shillings Scots, countermarked with crowned thistle in 1578 and revalued at 12 shillings and 3 pence.

As ryal, but with value given on reverse as X (Stewart 1967, fig. 183).

	Weight g.	gr.	Die Axis	Date	
1078	9.74	150.3	15	1567	Obv. trefoil at start and end of legend (B.923.1; S.5476). Ex Bridgewater House, lot 506 (HSAN 3452).
1079	8.93	137.8	340	1568	Obv. i.m. plain-cross, no trefoil, **. IACOBVS**. Rev. pellet stop at end of legend, countermark left of sword hilt guard (B.923.2; S.5476). Acq. 18 December 1991; ex Dolphin list 2 (1992), item 1490 (HSAN 3453).
1080	9.64	148.8	210	1569	Obv. no trefoils, **IACOBVS**, **SCOTORVM** crown with plain band. Rev. small **N** in **IN**, large date (B.923.3; S.5476). Ex Duncan, lot 306 (HSAN 3454).
1081	9.27	143.0	20	1570	Obv. crown with plain band (B. 923.4). Acq. 19 December 1965; ex Dakers, lot 476 (part) (HSAN 3455).
1082	9.59	148.0	45	1571	Obv. trefoil at start and end of legend (B.923.5; S.5476). Bt Spink, September 1967; ex Asherson; ex Lockett I, lot 370 (part); ex Bearman, acq. Lincoln, 16 July 1906 (HSAN 3456).
1083	9.63	148.6	300	1571	Obv. trefoil at start and end of legend. Rev. countermark left of sword hilt guard (B.923.5; S.5476). Ex Walters, lot 667 (part) (HSAN 3457).

Second Coinage, 1571–80

Half-merk or noble (1572–7, 1580)

Theoretical weight 6.78 g, 104.7 gr: value 6 shillings and 8 pence Scots, 8 deniers fine.

i.m. plain-cross both sides, wire-line inner circles both sides. Obv. crowned shield bearing lion rampant dividing **6** and **8**, crown with jewelled band, **+ . IACOBVS . 6 . DEI . GRATIA . REX . SCOTORVM .**. Rev. **+ . SALVVM . FAC . POPVLVM . TVVM . DNE .** (date), foliate cross with infill of bars, extending from lozenge panel containing a star of five-points, thistle head and crown in alternate angles (Stewart 1967, fig. 184).

1084	6.70	103.4	80	1533 error	Erroneous date reading **1533**. Rev. date with **7/3**, crowns q1 and 3 (B.-; S.5478). Ex Walters, lot 669 (part) (HSAN 3458).
1085	6.74	104.0	85	1572	Rev. crowns q2 and 4 (B.924–26.2; S.5478). Acq. 1976; ex Cochran-Patrick (1936), lot 272 (part) (HSAN 3459).

1078 1079 1080 1081

1082 1083 1084 1085

Before English Accession. SILVER *(cont.)*
Second coinage *(cont.)* *Half-merks or nobles (cont.)*

	Weight g.	gr.	Die Axis	Date	
1086	6.66	102.8	220	1572	Rev. crowns q2 and 4 (B.924–26.2; S.5478). Bt Baldwin, 1976 (HSAN 3460).
1087	6.91	106.6	280	1572	Rev. pellets on cross, crowns q2 and 4 (B.924–6.2; S.5478). Bt Baldwin, 1976 (HSAN 3461).
1088	6.12	94.4	270	1572	Obv. crown with plain band. Rev. **: SALVVM**, crowns q2 and 4 (B.924–26.1; S.5478). Acq. 17 January 1996; ex Finn list 6, item 416 (HSAN 3462).
1089	6.11	94.2	280	1572	Obv. Initial cross linked to crown. Rev. small date, crowns q2 and 4 (B.924–26.6; S.5478). Acq. 1976; ex Ryan II, lot 1365 (part) (HSAN 3463).
1090	5.84	90.1	280	1572	Obv. Initial cross linked to crown, crown with plain band. Rev. crowns q2 and 4 (B.924–26.1; S.5478). Bt Baldwin, 1976 (HSAN 3464).
1091	6.49	100.1	360	1572	Initial cross linked to crown. Rev. crowns q2 and 4 (J. E. L. Murray, *BNJ* 1987, p. 53, illus. no. 4 - this coin; B.924–26.2; S.5478). Acq, 1998, ex J. E. L. Murray; ex Pye, lot 201 (part); ex Lingford II, lot 1146 (part) (HSAN 3465).
1092	6.42	99.1	40	1572	Obv. initial cross linked to crown. Rev. crowns q1 and 3 (B.924–26.2; S.5478). Bt Spink, 24 July 1987; ex Davidson (HSAN 3466).
1093	4.21	65.0	80	1572	Obv. Initial cross linked to crown. Rev. crowns q 2 and 4 (B.924–26.2; S.5478). Bt Baldwin, 1976. Same obv. die as **1096** (HSAN 3467).

1086 1087 1088 1089

1090 1091 1092 1093

Before English Accession. SILVER *(cont.)*
Second coinage *(cont.)* *Half-merks or nobles (cont.)*

	Weight g.	gr.	Die Axis	Date	
1094	6.62	102.2	350	1572	Obv. initial cross linked to crown. Rev. pellets on cross, crowns q2 and 4 (J. E. L. Murray, *BNJ* 1987, p. 53, illus. no. 1 - this coin; B.924–26.2; S.5478). Bt Spink, September 1967; ex Asherson; ex Lockett II, lot 929 (part). Attributed by Murray to the Marians at Edinburgh Castle (HSAN 3468).
1095	6.57	101.4	330	1572	Rev. pellets on cross, crowns q2 and 4 (B.924–26.2; S.5478). Acq. 19 October 1955 (HSAN 3469).
1096	5.91	91.2	260	1572	Initial cross linked to crown. Rev. crowns q2 and 4 (B.924–26.2; S.5478). Ex Cairncross, lot 459 (part). Same obv. die as **1093** (HSAN 3470).
1097	6.32	97.5	40	1572	Obv. initial cross linked to crown, no inner-circle. Rev. pellets on cross, crowns q2 and 4 (J. E. L. Murray, *BNJ* 1987, p. 53, illus. no. 2 – this coin; B.924–26.2; S.5478). Acq. 1998, ex J. E. L. Murray; ex Pye, lot 201 (part); ex Lingford II, lot 1146 (part). Attributed by Murray to the Marians at Edinburgh Castle (HSAN 3471).
1098	6.59	101.7	210	1573	Obv. initial cross linked to crown. Rev. crowns q2 and 4 (J. E. L. Murray, *BNJ* 1987, p. 53, illus. no. 5 - this coin; B.924–26.5; S.5478). Acq. 1998, ex J. E. L. Murray; ex Pye, lot 201 (part); ex Lingford II, lot 1146 (part) (HSAN 3472).
1099	6.45	99.5	350	1573	Obv. initial cross linked to crown. Rev. no stops, crowns q1 and 3 (B.924–25.4; S.5478). Ex Cochran-Patrick (1936), lot 272 (HSAN 3473).
1100	6.06	93.5	150	1573	Obv. initial cross linked to crown. Rev. no stops, crowns q1 and 3 (B.924–26.4; S.5478). Ex Cairncross, lot 459 (part). Same obv. die as **1103** (HSAN 3474).
1101	6.93	106.9	180	1573	Obv. initial cross linked to crown. Rev. crowns q1 and 3 (B.924–26.4; S.5478). Ex Walters, lot 669 (part) (HSAN 3475).

1094 1095 1096 1097

1098 1099 1100 1101

Before English Accession. SILVER *(cont.)*
Second coinage *(cont.)* *Half-merks or nobles (cont.)*

	Weight g.	gr.	Die Axis	Date	
1102	5.99	92.4	45	1573	Obv. initial cross linked to crown. Rev. crowns q1 and 3 (B.924–26.4; S.5478). Ex Cairncross, lot 459 (part) (HSAN 3476).
1103	6.65	102.6	340	1573	Obv. initial cross linked to crown. Rev. crowns q1 and 3 (B.924–26.4; S.5478). Bt Baldwin, 27 January 1987. Same obv. die as **1100** (HSAN 3477).
1104	6.77	104.5	180	1573	Obv. initial cross unclear. Rev. crowns q2 and 4, thistle in q1 punched over crown (B.924–26.5; S.5478). Bt Baldwin, 1976 (HSAN 3478).
1105	6.71	103.5	85	1573	Obv. **. IACOBVS DEI GRATIA REX SCOTORVM .**, initial cross linked to crown. Rev. crowns q2 and 4 (B.924–26.5; S.5478). Bt Spink, September 1967; ex Asherson (HSAN 3479).
1106	6.39	98.6	190	1574	Obv. Crown with plain band (?), initial cross linked to crown. Rev. **. SALVVM FAC .**, crowns q2 and 4 (B.924–26.6; S.5478). Ex Cairncross, lot 459 (part) (HSAN 3480).
1107	6.64	103.5	260	1574	Obv. crown with plain band, initial cross unclear. Rev. crowns q1 and 3 (B.924–26.6; S.5478). Ex Cairncross, lot 459 (part). Same obv. die as **1108** (HSAN 3481).
1108	6.09	94.0	320	1574	Obv. crown with plain band, initial cross linked to crown. Rev. crowns q1 and 3 (B.924–26.6; S.5478). Ex Cairncross, lot 459 (part). Same obv. die as **1107** (HSAN 3482).
1109	6.19	95.5	340	1574	Obv. crown with plain band, initial cross unclear, no wire-line inner-circle. Rev. stop after **FAC** over **O**, crowns q1 and 3 (B.924–26.7; S.5478). Bt *c.* 1950 (HSAN 3483).

1102 1103 1104 1105

1106 1107 1108 1109

Before English Accession. SILVER *(cont.)*
Second coinage *(cont.)* *Half-merks or nobles (cont.)*

	Weight g.	gr.	Die Axis	Date	
1110	6.35	98.0	240	1574	Obv. crown with plain band, initial cross linked to crown. Rev. crowns q1 and 3 (B.924–26.6; S.5478). Bt Baldwin, 1976 (HSAN 3484).
1111	6.77	104.5	320	1574	Obv. initial cross linked to crown. Rev. crowns q1 and 3 (B.924–26.5 var.; S.5478). Ex Cochran-Patrick (1936), lot 272 (part) (HSAN 3485).
1112	5.56	85.8	85	1575	Obv. SOTORVM, initial cross linked to crown. Rev. crowns q1 and 3 (B.924–26.8; S.5478). Ex Walters, lot 669 (part) (HSAN 3486).
1113	6.00	92.6	220	1575	Obv. initial cross linked to crown. Rev. crowns q1 and 3, with second wire-line inner-circle (B.924–26.8; S.5478). Ex Cairncross, lot 459 (part) (HSAN 3487).
1114	6.81	105.1	80	1575	Obv. crown with plain band, initial cross linked to crown. Rev. crowns q1 and 3 (B.924–26.9; S.5478). Ex Cairncross, lot 459 (part) (HSAN 3488).
1115	6.79	104.8	70	1575	Obv. initial cross linked to crown. Rev. crowns q1 and 3 (B.924–26.8; S.5478). Bt Baldwin, 1976 (HSAN 3489).
1116	6.04	93.2	220	1575	Obv. crown with plain band, initial cross linked to crown. Rev. crowns q1 and 3 (B.924–26.9; S.5478). Acq. 1974; ex Winstanley (HSAN 3490).
1117	6.64	102.5	270	1575	Obv. initial cross linked to crown. Rev. crowns q2 and 4 (B.924–26.8; S.5478). Ex Christie's, 24 February 1988, lot 242; ex Bearman; ex Beaufoy, lot 87 (HSAN 3491).

1110 1111 1112 1113

1114 1115 1116 1117

Before English Accession. SILVER *(cont.)*
Second coinage *(cont.)* *Half-merks or nobles (cont.)*

	Weight g.	gr.	Die Axis	Date	
1118	5.80	89.5	350	1576	Obv. crown with plain band, initial cross linked to crown, without wire-line inner-circle. Rev. crowns q1 and 3 (B.-, noted p. 356; S.5478). Bt Spink, November 1994; ex *NCirc* July/August 1994, item 4775 (HSAN 3492).
1119	6.59	101.7	10	1576	Obv. initial cross linked to crown. Rev. crowns q1 and 3 (B.-, noted p. 356; S.5478). Acq. 1 October 1971; ex R. C. Carlyon-Britton; ex Parsons, lot 753 (part) (HSAN 3493).
1120	6.03	93.0	360	1576	Obv. initial cross linked to crown. Rev. crowns q2 and 4 (B.-, noted p. 376; S.5478). Bt Seaby, 1 October 1971 (HSAN 3494).
1121	6.66	102.8	315	1576	Obv. GRATIA, second I over A, SCOTTORVM, crown with plain band, initial cross linked to crown. Rev. crowns q2 and 4 (B.-, noted, p. 356, similar; S.5478). Acq. 1 October 1971; ex R. C. Carlyon-Britton (HSAN 3495).
1122	5.69	87.8	330	1577	Obv. initial cross linked to crown, plain band. Rev. crowns q2 and 4 (B.924–26.10; S.5478). Bt Baldwin; ex F. Baldwin. Holed at centre (HSAN 3496).
1123	6.94	107.1	160	1577	Obv. initial cross linked to crown. Rev. crowns q1 and 3 (B.924–26.11; S.5478). Ex Cochran-Patrick (1936), lot 272 (part). Same obv. die as **1127** (HSAN 3497).
1124	6.25	96.4	360	1577	Obv. initial cross linked to crown. Rev. crowns q1 and 3 (B.924–26.11; S.5478). Bt Spink, 1965; ex Marr (HSAN 3498).
1125	6.12	94.4	360	1577	Obv. initial cross linked to crown. Rev. crowns q1 and 3 (B.924–26.11; S.5478). Ex Cairncross, lot 459 (part) (HSAN 3499).

1118 1119 1120 1121

1122 1123 1124 1125

Before English Accession. SILVER *(cont.)*
Second coinage *(cont.)* *Half-merks or nobles (cont.)*

	Weight g.	gr.	Die Axis	Date	
1126	6.93	106.9	190	1577	Obv. initial cross linked to crown, without wire-line inner-circle. Rev. crowns q1 and 3 (cf. B.924–26.11; S.5478). Bt Baldwin, 30 September 1994 (HSAN 3500).
1127	7.09	109.4	160	1577	Obv. initial cross linked to crown. Rev. crowns q2 and 4 (B.924–26.10; S.5478). Ex Cairncross, lot 459 (part). Same obv. die as **1123** (HSAN 3501).
1128	5.69	87.8	20	1580	Obv. initial cross linked to crown, without wire-line inner-circle. Rev. i.m. cross pattée, no stop before **SALVVM**, crowns q1 and 3 (B.924–26.12; S.5478). Ex Cairncross, lot 459 (part). Same obv. die as **1129** (HSAN 3502).
1129	6.80	104.9	280	1580	Obv. initial cross linked to crown, without wire-line inner-circle. Rev. i.m. cross pattée, no stop before **SALVVM**, **0** in date recut, crowns q1 and 3 (cf. B.924–26.12; S.5478). Acq. 26 May 1992; ex Dolphin list 2, item 1500; ex J. K. R. Murray, lot 267. Same obv. die as **1128**; same rev. die as **1131** (HSAN 3503).
1130	6.47	99.8	10	1580	Without wire-line inner-circle both sides. Obv. initial cross linked to crown. Rev. i.m. uncertain, first stop uncertain, crowns q2 and 4 (cf. B.924–26.13; S.5478). Bt Seaby, 16 December 1965; ex L. A. Lawrence (HSAN 3504).
1131	6.44	99.4	10	1580	Obv. initial cross linked to crown, without wire-line inner-circle. Rev. i.m. cross pattée, no stop before **SALVVM**, **0** in date recut, crown q1 and 3, same rev. die as **1129** (cf. B.924–26.12; S.5478). Acq. October 1967; ex J. K. R. Murray duplicates (HSAN 3505).

Quarter-merk or half-noble (1572–7, 1580)

Theoretical weight 3.39 g, 52.4 gr: value 3 shillings and 4 pence Scots.

As half merk. Obv. shield dividing **3** and **4**, crown with plain band.

1132	3.32	51.2	250	1572	Rev. pellets on cross, crowns q2 and 4 (J. E. L. Murray, *BNJ* 1987, p. 53, illus. no. 6 - this coin; B.927–29.1; S.5479). Acq. 1998, ex J. E. L. Murray; ex Pye, lot 206 (part); ex Lingford II, lot 1149 (part) (HSAN 3506).
1133	3.15	48.6	225	1572	Obv. no stops at start and end of legend. Rev. crowns q2 and 4 (B.927–29.1; S.5479). Acq. 1998, Ex J. E. L. Murray; ex Pye, lot 206 (part); ex Lingford II, lot 1149 (part) (HSAN 3507).
1134	3.30	50.9	310	1572	Obv. **SOTORVM**. Rev. crowns q2 and 4 (B.927–27.1; S.5479). Acq. 14 April 1984; ex J. K. R. Murray, (HSAN 3508).
1135	3.32	51.2	90	1572	Rev. crowns q2 and 4 (B.927–29.1; S.5479). Ex Cairncross, lot 459 (part) (HSAN 3509).
1136	3.25	50.2	315	1572	Rev. crowns q2 and 4 (B.927–29.1; S.5479). Acq. 1976; ex Cochran-Patrick (1936), lot 272 (part) (HSAN 3510).
1137	3.14	48.5	270	1572	Rev. crowns q2 and 4 (B.927–29.1; S.5479). Bt Spink, 10 December 1955 (HSAN 3511).
1138	3.19	49.2	10	1573	Rev. crowns q2 and 4 (cf. B.927–29.2; S.5479). Bt Spink, 24 July 1987; ex Davidson (HSAN 3512).
1139	3.24	50.0	170	1573	Obv. no stops. Rev. crowns q1 and 3 (B.927–29.2; S.5479). Acq. 1998, ex J. E. L. Murray; ex Pye, lot 206 (part); ex Lingford II, lot 1149 (part) (HSAN 3513).

1126 1127 1128 1129

1130 1131 1132 1133 1134

1135 1136 1137 1138 1139

Before English Accession. SILVER *(cont.)*
Second coinage *(cont.)* *Quarter-merks or half nobles (cont.)*

	Weight g.	gr.	Die Axis	Date	
1140	3.36	51.8	30	1573	Obv. no stops. Rev. POPVLV TVVM, crowns q1 and 3 (cf. B.927–29.2; S.5479). Ex Cairncross, lot 459 (part) (HSAN 3514).
1141	3.27	50.5	90	1573	No stops at start and end of legend both sides. Obv. IACOBVSS., SCOTOKVM, Rev. crowns q1 and 3 (cf. B.927–29.2; S.5479). Ex Cairncross, lot 459 (part). Same rev. die as **1144** (HSAN 3515).
1142	3.22	49.7	180	1573	Obv. initial mark not linked to crown. Rev. crowns q1 and 3 (B.927–29.2; S.5479). Ex Cochran-Patrick (1936), lot 272 (part) (HSAN 3516).
1143	3.53	54.5	225	1573	Rev. crowns q1 and3 (B.927–29.2; S.5479). Ex Cochran-Patrick (1936), lot 272 (part) (HSAN 3517).
1144	3.40	52.5	270	1573	Obv. no stops, right leaf of fleur on crown band broken. Rev. SALVVM . FAC . POPVLVM TVVM DNE 1573., crowns q1 and 3 (cf. B.927–29.2; S.5479). Acq. 1968, ex J. K. R. Murray. Same rev. die as **1141** (HSAN 3518).
1145	3.26	50.3	300	1574	Rev. crowns q1 and 3 (cf. B.927–29.3; S.5479). Bt Seaby, 16 December 1965; ex Dakers, lot 477 (part) (HSAN 3520).
1146	3.22	49.7	220	1574	Obv. no stop after SCOTORVM. Rev. no stop left or right of date, crowns q1 and 3 (cf. B.927–29.3; S.5479). Bt Spink, 1959 (HSAN 3521).
1147	3.31	51.1	160	1574	Rev. crowns q1 and 3 (B.927–29.3; S.5479). Ex Cairncross, lot 459 (part) (HSAN 3522).
1148	3.30	50.9	50	1577	Rev. no stop before date, wire-line inner-circle omitted, crowns q2 and 4 (B.927–29.7; S.5479). Bt Seaby, 1975 (HSAN 3523).
1149	3.16	48.8	140	1577	Wire-line inner-circles omitted both sides. Obv. IACOBVS . 6 . DEI . GRATIA . REX SCOTORVM, initial cross not linked to crown. Rev. no stop before SALVVM or date, crowns q2 and 4 (cf. B.927–29.7; S.5479). Ex Cochran-Patrick (1936), lot 272 (part) (HSAN 3524).
1150	3.37	52.0	315	1577	Obv. initial cross not linked to crown, wire-line inner-circle omitted, SOTORVM. Rev. . FAC POPVLUM T . VVM ., crowns q2 and 4 (cf. B.927–29.7; S.5479). Ex Cairncross, lot 459 (part) (HSAN 3525).
1151	3.48	53.7	10	1577	Rev. crowns q2 and 4 (B.927–29.7; S.5479). Ex Cairncross, lot 459 (part) (HSAN 3526).
1152	2.76	42.6	180	1580	Obv. no stop before IACOBVS, . SCOIORVM .. Rev. crowns q1 and 4 (cf. B.927–29.8; S.5479). Acq. 4 February 1992; ex Dolphin list 2, item 1503 (HSAN 3527).
1153	3.00	46.3	200	1580	Obv. no stop before IACOBVS. Rev. crowns q1 and 4 (cf. B.927–29.8; S.5479). Bt Spink, 1965; ex Marr; ex R. C. Carlyon-Britton; ex Parsons, lot 753 (part) (HSAN 3528).

Contemporary counterfeit, quarter-merk.

1154	2.24	34.6	270	1573	Contemporary counterfeit struck on plated flan. Rev. crowns q1 and 3. Bt Baldwin, 1976 (HSAN 3519).

PLATE 73

1140 1141 1142 1143 1144

1145 1146 1147 1148 1149

1150 1151 1152 1153 1154

Before English Accession. SILVER *(cont.)*
Second coinage *(cont.) Two merk pieces or 'thistle dollars'*

Two-merk piece or 'thistle dollar' (1578–80)

Theoretical weight 2.21 g, 342.75 gr: value 26 shillings and 8 pence Scots, 11 deniers fine.

i.m. plain-cross linked to crown/crown. Obv. . IACOBVS . 6 . DEI . G . REX . SCOTORVM ., crowned shield bearing lion rampant. Rev. . NEMO . ME . IMPVNE . LACESSET . (date), thistle plant with a flower and two leaves dividing I, left, R right (Stewart 1967, fig. 185).

	Weight g.	gr.	Die Axis	Date	
1155	21.51	331.9	220	1578	(B.930–30A.1a; S.5480). Bt Spink, 30 March 1957; ticketed 'ex Boyd' (HSAN 3529).
1156	21.34	329.3	180	1579	(B.930–30A.1a; S.5480). Bt Baldwin, 1976; ex Lingford, portion of collection acq. by Baldwin. Same dies as Lingford lot 1150 (HSAN 3530).
1157	22.45	346.4	190	1580	Obv. C in SCOTORVM over S (B.930–31A.2; S.5480). Ex LaRiviere, lot 171, acq. Spink, 3 May 1985; ex Dundee, lot 251; ex Lockett I, lot 373; stated to be 'ex Gordon' in Lockett (HSAN 3531).

Merk piece (1579–80)

Theoretical weight 11.10 g, 171.3 gr: value 13 shillings and 4 pence Scots.

As two-merk piece.

1158	10.67	164.6	310	1579	(B.930B.1a; S.5481). Bt Spink, September 1967; ex Asherson. Same dies as Lingford lot 451, Dakers and Cochran-Patrick specimens (HSAN 3532).
1159	11.20	172.8	300	1580	(B.930B.1b; S.5481). Ex Glendining, 21 July 1976, lot 661; ex Dundee, lot 252; ex Asherson; ex Lockett II, lot 931. Pierced on obverse left of shield; attempted piercing on reverse on thistle flower head (HSAN 3533).

Third Coinage, 1580–1

Sixteen-shilling piece (1581)

Theoretical weight 11.10 g, 171.3 gr: value 16 shillings Scots, 11 deniers fine.

i.m. cross linked to crown both sides. Obv. . IACOBVS . 6 . DEI . GRATIA . REX SCOTORVM ., crowned shield bearing lion rampant. Rev. . NEMO . ME . IMPVNE . LACESSET . **1581**, crowned thistle plant with two leaves and flower, annulet within root at base (Stewart 1967, fig. 189).

	Weight g.	gr.	Die Axis	
1160	10.67	164.6	200	Rev. no stop at start or end of legend, annulet by base of E in IMPVNE (cf. B.930C.1a; S.5482). Bt Spink, 3 November 1965; ex *NCirc.* November 1965, item 6515 (HSAN 3534).

Eight-shilling piece (1581)

Theoretical weight 5.55 g, 85.7 gr: value 8 shillings Scots.

As sixteen-shilling piece.

1161	5.21	80.4	180	Obv. . IACOBVS 6 DEI ., O/T in SCOT. Rev. no stop at start or end of legend (cf. B.930C.1a, p. 364.1a, not in plates; S.5483). Bt Spink, 23 February 1968 (HSAN 3535).

Four-shilling piece (1581)

Theoretical weight, 2.77 g, 42.8 gr: value 4 shillings Scots.

As sixteen-shilling piece except obv. reads SCOTOR for SCOTORVM, rev. IMPVИE.

1162	2.53	39.0	140	Rev. no stop at start and end of legend (B.930D.1a; S.5484). Ex LaRiviere, lot 177; ex Mackenzie, lot 327 (HSAN 3536).

PLATE 74

1155 1156 1157 1158

1159 1160 1161 1162

Before English Accession. SILVER *(cont.)*
Fourth coinage.

Fourth Coinage, 1582–8

Forty-shilling piece (1582)

Theoretical weight 30.53 g, 471.2 gr: value 40 shillings Scots, 11 deniers fine.

i.m. plain-cross both sides, on obv. linked to crown. Obv. **IACOBVS . 6 . DEI . GRATIA . REX . SCOTORVM .**, half-length armoured and crowned bust left, holding sword before. Rev. **HONOR . REGIS . IVDICIVM . DILIGIT .** (date) ., crowned shield bearing lion rampant dividing, left **I**, with **XL** below, and right **R**, **S** below (Stewart 1967, fig. 190).

	Weight g.	gr.	Die Axis	
1163	29.68	458.0	170	Rev. reads **HONOR ..**, double struck on **REGIS** (cf. B.931.1; S.5486). Bt. 1960; ex R. C. Carlyon-Britton; ex Parsons, lot 756; ex Bute, lot 256; noted in collection of Marquess of Bute in 1767. Dies not in Kerr (HSAN 3537).

Thirty-shilling piece (1581–6)

Theoretical weight 22.90 g, 353.4 gr: value 30 shillings Scots.

As forty-shilling piece, except reverse with **X / XX** in two lines.

	Weight g.	gr.	Die Axis	Date	
1164	22.88	353.0	200	1582	(B.933.1; S.5487). Ex Cochran-Patrick (1936), lot 279 (HSAN 3538).
1165	22.53	347.6	130	1582	Obv. **COTORVM ..** Rev. **DILIGT**, **8** in date part overstruck on the **5** (cf. B.933.2; S.5487). Bt Baldwin; ex F. Baldwin (HSAN 3539).
1166	22.94	354.0	30	1582	Obv. **. IACOBVS .**, undecorated armour. Rev. **XXX** on one line (cf. B.932.1; S.5488). Bt Spink, September 1967; ex Asherson; ex Lockett I, lot 377; ex Bearman (HSAN 3540).
1167	22.20	342.6	10	1582	Obv. **. IACOBVS ..** Rev. no stops, **. IVDICIVM .** over **DILIG** (cf. B.932.2; S.5487). Acq. 26 May 1992; ex Dolphin list 2, item 1506 (HSAN 3541).
1168	22.96	354.3	135	1583	Rev. first **O** in **HONOR** recut (cf. B.933.3; S.5487). Ex Walters, lot 667 (part) (HSAN 3542).

1163 1164 1165

1166 1167 1168

Before English Accession. SILVER *(cont.)*
Fourth coinage *(cont.)* *Thirty shilling pieces (cont.)*

	Weight g.	gr.	Die Axis	Date	
1169	21.43	330.7	280	1584	(B.933.5; S.5487). Bt Baldwin, 18 November 1967 (HSAN 3543).
1170	22.23	343.0	190	1584	Rev. . HONOR . (B.933.5; S.5487). Bt Spink, 23 February 2006; ex *NCirc* February 2006, item SCO 445 (ex P. Higginson); ex J. K. R. Murray, lot 276 (HSAN 3544).
1171	21.97	339.0	180	1585	(B.933.7; S.5487). Ex Clonterbrook, lot 336; ex Lockett II, lot 933; ex Bearman; ex Stoate, lot 288 (part). Same obv. die as **1172** (HSAN 3546).
1172	22.40	345.6	180	1586	(B.-; S.5487). Bt Spink, 1965; ex Marr. Same obv. die as **1171** (HSAN 3547).

Twenty-shilling piece (1582–4)

Theoretical weight 15.26 g, 235.6 gr: value 20 shillings Scots.

As forty-shilling piece except reverse with XX for XL.

1173	14.64	225.9	50	1582	Obv. . DEI .., I in DEI recut, small **6** (cf. B.934–35.1). Bt Baldwin, 1976 (HSAN 3548).
1174	15.23	235.0	110	1582	(B.934–35.1). Acq. 9 December 1968; ex Hurley. Obv. metal flaw at 5 o'clock (HSAN 3549).
1175	15.18	234.2	280	1582	Rev. IVDICVM, tall crown (cf. B.934–35.1). Bt Baldwin, 1976 (HSAN 3550).
1176	14.79	228.2	340	1582	Obv. . IACOBVS ., small **6**. Rev. no stops (cf. B.934–35.2). Bt Seaby, 1983; ex R. Kirton (HSAN 3551).

PLATE 76

1169 1170 1171 1172

1173 1174 1175 1176

Before English Accession. SILVER *(cont.)*
Fourth coinage *(cont.)* *Twenty shilling pieces (cont.)*

	Weight g.	gr.	Die Axis	Date	
1177	15.58	240.4	90	1583	Obv. . IACOBVS 6 DEI ., small **6** (cf. B.934–35.3). Unprovenanced (HSAN 3553).
1178	15.16	233.9	315	1583	Obv. . IACOBVS 6 DEI ., small **6** (cf. B.934–35.3). Acq. October 1967; ex Hurley (HSAN 3554).
1179	14.55	224.5	340	1584	Obv. . IACOBVS 6 DEI .. Rev. . HONOR . (B.-, noted p. 369). Acq. 28 May 1986; ex J. K. R. Murray; ex Bridgewater House, lot 509 (HSAN 3555).

Twenty-shilling piece - Counterfeit.

1180	10.14	156.5	360	1582	Obv. small **6**, a contemporary counterfeit, of base-metal and coarse style. Acq. 9 December 1968; given by Baldwin (HSAN 3552).

Ten-shilling piece (1582–4)

Theoretical weight 7.63 g, 117.8 gr: value 10 shillings Scots.

As forty-shilling piece, except reverse with X for XL.

1181	7.40	114.2	315	1582	Obv. reads GRAATIA. Rev. no stops, small X (cf. B.936.1; S.5490). Bt Spink, 1965; ex Marr (HSAN 3556).
1182	7.68	118.5	135	1582	Obv. no stop after SCOTORVM. Rev. large X (cf. B.936.1; S.5490). Acq. 13 March 1969; ex Hurley (HSAN 3557).
1183	7.17	110.6	40	1583	Obv. . IACOBVS . , no stop after SCOTORVM (B.936.2; S.5490). Acq. 28 May 1986; J. K. R. Murray; ex R. C. Carlyon-Britton (HSAN 3558).
1184	7.60	117.3	30	1584	Obv. no stop after SCOTORVM (B.-, noted p. 370; S.5490). Ex Lingford II, lot 1169 (HSAN 3559).

Fifth Coinage, 1588–90

No silver struck.

1177 1178 1179 1180

1181 1182 1183 1184

Before English Accession. SILVER *(cont.)*
Sixth coinage.

Sixth Coinage, 1591–3

Balance half-merk (1591–3)

Theoretical weight, 4.63 g, 71.4 gr: value 6 shillings and 8 pence Scots, 10.5 deniers fine.

i.m. cinquefoil both sides. Obv. **. IACOBVS . 6 . D . G . R . SCOTORVM .** (date) **.**, crowned shield bearing lion rampant, a thistle head each side. Rev. **. HIS . DIFFERT . REGE . TYRANNVS .**, composite **N**, a balance over a diagonally aligned upright sword (Stewart 1967, fig. 194).

	Weight g.	gr.	Die Axis	Date	
1185	4.61	71.1	280	1591	Rev. unbroken **N**s (B.937.1; S.5491). Bt Spink, August 1980. A specimen striking of fine work style (HSAN 3560).
1186	4.69	72.4	135	1591	(B.937.2; S.5491). Ex Dakers, lot 488 (part) (HSAN 3561).
1187	4.48	69.1	310	1591	(B.937.2; S.5491). Ex Dakers, lot 488 (part) (HSAN 3562).
1188	4.61	71.1	275	1591	Rev. date reads **15591** (cf. B.937.2; S.5491). Ex Cochran-Patrick (1936), lot 285 (part); ex Wigan (HSAN 3563).
1189	4.55	70.2	245	1591	(B.937.2; S.5491). Ex Marshall, lot 179; ex Grantley, lot 1791 (HSAN 3564).
1190	4.62	71.3	100	1591	(B.937.2; S.5491). Acq. 1951; ex Hurley (HSAN 3565).
1191	4.56	70.4	200	1591	(B.937.2; S.5491). Ex Dakers, lot 488 (part) (HSAN 3566).
1192	4.66	71.9	330	1592	(cf. B.937.4; S.5491). Rev. with wire-line inner-circle. Ex Cochran-Patrick (1936), lot 285 (part); ex Wigan (HSAN 3567).
1193	4.44	68.5	230	1592	(B.937.4; S.5491). Bt Spink, 1965; ex Marr (HSAN 3568).
1194	4.64	71.6	70	1593	(B.937.5; S.5491). Ex Dakers, lot 488 (part) (HSAN 3569).

Balance quarter-merk (1591)

Theoretical weight, 2.31 g, 35.7 gr: value 3 shillings and 4 pence.

As balance half-merk.

	Weight g.	gr.	Die Axis	
1195	2.16	33.3	40	Rev. no stop before **HIS .** (B.938.1; S.5492). Bt Spink, 1965; ex Marr (HSAN 3570).
1196	1.98	30.6	330	No stop after date (B.938.2; S.5492). Bt Seaby, 1 October 1971; ex R. C. Carlyon-Britton (HSAN 3571).

1185

1186

1187

1188

1189

1190

1191

1192

1193

1194

1195

1196

Before English Accession. SILVER *(cont.)*
Seventh coinage.

Seventh Coinage, 1594–1601

Ten-shilling piece (1593–5, 1598–1601)

Theoretical weight, 6.10 g, 94.2 gr: value 10 shillings Scots, revalued at 10 shillings and 8 pence in 1598; 11 deniers fine.

i.m. quatrefoil both sides. Obv. **. IACOBVS . 6 . D . G . R . SCOTORVM .**, armoured bare headed bust right. Rev. **. NEMO . ME . IMPVNE . LACESSIT .** (date) **.** , thistle plant with two leaves and three flowering stems, crown above central flower (Stewart 1967, fig. 195).

	Weight g.	gr.	Die Axis	Date	
1197	6.14	94.7	150	1593	(B.939.1; S.5493). Bt Baldwin, 1994; ex Winstanley (HSAN 3572).
1198	5.98	92.3	30	1593	Obv. no stop after **SCOTORVM** (cf. B.939.1; S.5493). Bt Baldwin; ex Walters, lot 669 (part) (HSAN 3573).
1199	5.85	90.3	10	1594	(B.939.2; S.5493). Ex Walters, lot 669 (part) (HSAN 3574).
1200	5.35	82.6	275	1594	Rev. **9** over **6** in date (B.-; S.5493). Bt Baldwin, 1976 (HSAN 3575).
1201	6.08	95.8	180	1564 error	Rev. error date reading **1564** (B.-; S.5493). Ex Cochran-Patrick (1957), lot 149 (HSAN 3576).
1202	5.62	86.7	350	1594	(B.939.2; S.5493). Acq. *c.* 1950 (HSAN 3577).
1203	5.97	92.1	295	1564 error	Obv. **: IACOBVS .**. Rev. error date reading **1564** (cf. B.939.2; S.5493). Bt Spink, 1965; ex Marr (HSAN 3578).
1204	5.93	91.5	280	1595	Obv. no stop before **IACOBVS .**. Rev. **9** over **6** in date (cf. B.939.3; S.5493). Bt Spink, September 1967; ex Asherson. Inked number 3a (?) on reverse (HSAN 3579).
1205	6.11	94.3	210	1595	Rev. **MIE** for **ME** (cf. B.939.3; S.5493). Ex Walters, lot 669 (part) (HSAN 3580).
1206	5.97	92.1	180	1598	(B.939.4; S.5493). Bt Baldwin, 1976 (HSAN 3581).
1207	6.01	92.7	20	1598	Rev. small **9** in date (cf. B.939.4; S.5493). Bt Baldwin, 1976 (HSAN 3582).
1208	5.72	88.3	200	1598	(B.939.4; S.5493). Bt Spink, 1965; ex Marr (HSAN 3583).

PLATE 79

1197 1198 1199 1200

1201 1202 1203 1204

1205 1206 1207 1208

Before English Accession. SILVER *(cont.)*
Seventh coinage *(cont.) Ten shilling pieces (cont)*

	Weight g.	gr.	Die Axis	Date	
1209	6.09	94.0	240	1599	(B.939.6; S.5493). Ex Drabble II, lot 1204; ex Bearman; acq. Spink, 12 October 1908 (HSAN 3585).
1210	5.92	91.4	140	1599	Obv. . IACOB . (cf. B.939.6; S.5493). Bt Spink, September 1967; ex Asherson; ex Lockett II, lot 937 (part); ex Mackenzie, lot 332. Same obv. die as **1211** (HSAN 3586).
1211	5.81	89.7	340	1599	Obv. . IACOB . (cf. B.939.6; S.5493). Bt Baldwin; ex Walters, lot 669 (part). Same obv. die as **1210** (HSAN 3587).
1212	5.98	92.3	240	1600	(B.-, noted p. 379; S.5493). Ex R. C. Carlyon-Britton (HSAN 3588).
1213	6.01	92.7	195	1600	Obv. . IACOB .. Rev. . IMPVNIE . (B.-, noted p. 379; S.5493). Bt Spink, September 1967; ex Asherson; ex Lockett II, lot 937 (part) (HSAN 3589).
1214	6.04	93.2	20	1600	Obv. . IACOB . (B.-, noted p. 379; S.5493). Bt Spink, September 1967; ex Asherson; ex Lockett I, lot 385 (part) (HSAN 3590).
1215	5.98	92.3	170	1601	(B.-, noted p. 379; S.5493). Bt Spink, September 1967; ex Asherson; ex Lockett I, lot 385 (part) (HSAN 3591).

Five-shilling piece (1593–5, 1598–1601)

Theoretical weight 3.05 g, 47.1 gr: value 5 shillings Scots, revalued at 5 shillings and 4 pence in 1598.

As ten-shilling piece.

1216	2.96	45.7	210	1593	(B.-, noted p.380; S.5494). Bt Stanley Gibbons, 1975 (HSAN 3592).
1217	2.97	45.8	45	1594	(B.940.1; S.5494). Bt Spink, 14 January 1957. Same obverse die as **1219** (HSAN 3593).
1218	2.94	45.4	140	1594	(B.940.1). Bt Baldwin, 1976 (HSAN 3594).
1219	3.09	47.7	300	1594	(B.940.1). Bt Baldwin; ex Walters, lot 669 (part). Same obverse die as **1217** (HSAN 3595).
1220	2.95	45.5	40	1594	Rev. error in date corrected, **9** over **6** (cf. B.940.1; S.5494). Bt Spink, September 1967; ex Asherson; ex Lockett II, lot 937 (part) (HSAN 3596).
1221	2.97	45.8	350	1595	(B.940.2; S.5494). Bt Baldwin, 1976 (HSAN 3597).

1209 1210 1211 1212

1213 1214 1215 1216

1217 1218 1219 1220 1221

Before English Accession. SILVER *(cont.)*
Seventh coinage *(cont.)* *Five shilling pieces (cont.)*

	Weight g.	gr.	Die Axis	Date	
1222	2.89	44.6	320	1598	(B.-; noted p. 380; S.5494). Bt Spink, November 1994 (HSAN 3598).
1223	2.79	43.1	260	1598	Rev. error in date corrected, **8** over **6** (B.-, noted p. 380; S.5494). Bt Spink, November 1994 (HSAN 3599).
1224	2.80	43.2	140	1598	(B.-, noted p. 380; S.5494). Bt Seaby, October 1978; ex *SCMB*, item J123 (illus.) (HSAN 3600).
1225	2.95	45.5	275	1599	Obv. reads SCOTORVM .. (cf. B.940.3; S.5494). Bt Seaby, December 1972 (HSAN 3601).
1226	2.76	42.6	300	1599	(B.940.3; S.5494). Bt Baldwin, 1974 (HSAN 3602).
1227	2.81	43.4	305	1600	(B.-; S.5494). Bt Spink, 1965; ex Marr; ex R. Carlyon-Britton (HSAN 3603).
1228	2.69	41.5	170	1601	(B.-; S.5494). Acq. October 1988, from Mr. J. S. Cole of Coombe Bissett, Wiltshire, a field find (HSAN 3604).

Thirty-pence piece (1594–6, 1598–9, 1601)

Theoretical weight 1.53 g, 23.6 gr: value 30 pence Scots, revalued at 32 pence in 1598.

As ten-shilling piece.

1229	1.51	23.3	360	1594	(B.941.1; S.5495). Bt Spink, September 1967; ex Asherson; ex Murdoch, lot 1065 (part). Of fine work style (HSAN 3605).
1230	1.36	21.0	140	1594	(B.941.1; S.5495). Bt Baldwin, 1976 (HSAN 3606).
1231	1.31	20.2	210	1594	Obv. no i.m.. Rev. date reads **15944** (cf. 941.1). Bt Baldwin; ex Walters, lot 669 (part) (HSAN 3607).
1232	1.24	19.1	160	1595	(B.941.1; S.5495). Bt Spink, 10 December 1955 (HSAN 3608).
1233	1.31	20.2	50	1595	Obv. no stop after SCOTORVM (B.941.2; S.5495). Bt Baldwin, 28 June 1969 (HSAN 3609).
1234	1.46	22.5	270	1596	(B.-, noted p. 380; S.5495). Bt Spink, September 1967; ex Asherson (HSAN 3610).
1235	1.19	18.4	360	1598	Obv. no i.m.. Rev. date error correction with **8** over **6** (B.-, noted p. 380; S.5495). Bt Spink, September 1967; ex Asherson (HSAN 3611).
1236	1.46	22.5	250	1599	Obv. no i.m.. Rev. no stop after **1599** (B.941.3; S.5495). Bt Baldwin; ex F. Baldwin (HSAN 3612).

Twelve-pence piece (1593–6)

Theoretical weight 0.76g, 11.8 gr: value 12 pence Scots revalued at 10.75 pence in 1598.

As ten-shilling piece, obv. with pellet behind neck.

1237	0.62	9.6	200	1593	Obv. pellet behind neck omitted (B.-, noted p. 381; S.5496). Bt Spink, September 1967; ex Asherson (HSAN 3613).
1238	0.62	9.6	140	1593	(B.-, noted p. 381; S.5496). Acq. 8 December 1965; ex Thorburn; acq. Spink, April 1948 (HSAN 3614).
1239	0.57	8.8	45	Uncertain	Date uncertain, possibly 1593 or 1595 (B.942.2; S.5496). Bt Paramount, 12 February 1976; ex Revd. A. Mallinson (HSAN 3615).

1222 1223 1224 1225 1226

1227 1228 1229 1230 1231 1232

1233 1234 1235 1236 1237 1238 1239

Before English Accession. SILVER *(cont.)*
Seventh coinage *(cont.)* *Twelve pence pieces (cont.)*

	Weight g.	gr.	Die Axis	Date	
1240	0.64	9.9	170	Uncertain	Date unclear. Rev. LACACESSIT (cf. B.942; S.5496). Acq. 1976; ex Walters, lot 669 (part), where the date is given as 1594 (HSAN 3616).
1241	0.65	10.0	360	Uncertain	Date unclear (cf. B.942; S.5496). Bt Paramount, 13 February 1976; ex Revd. A. Mallinson (HSAN 3617).
1242	0.58	9.0	60	?1594	(B.-, noted p. 381). Bt Baldwin, 1976 (HSAN 3618).
1243	0.40	6.2	170	Uncertain	Date unclear (cf. B.942; S.5496). Bt Baldwin, 1976 (HSAN 3619).
1244	0.57	8.8	270	1595	(B.942.1; S.5496). Bt Baldwin, 1976; ex F. Baldwin. Same reverse die as **1245** (HSAN 3620).
1245	0.51	7.9	140	1595	(B.942.1; S.5496). Bt Baldwin, 1976. Same reverse die as **1244** (HSAN 3621).

Eighth Coinage, 1601–4

Thistle merk (1601–4)

Theoretical weight 6.79 g, 104.7 gr: value 13 shillings and 4 pence Scots, 11 deniers fine.

No i.m. on either side. Obv. crowned shield bearing lion rampant, IACOBVS . 6 . D . G . R . SCOTORVM. Rev. REGEM . IOVA . PROTEGIT . (date), crowned thistle flower with leaves (Stewart 1967, fig. 198).

1246	6.54	100.9	160	1601	(B.943.1; S.5497). Ex Walters, lot 669 (part) (HSAN 3622).
1247	6.39	98.6	180	1601	(B.943.1; S.5497). Ex Pye, lot 238 (part); ex Lingford II, lot 1180 (part) (HSAN 3640).
1248	6.37	98.3	210	1601	(B.943.1; S.5497). Acq. 1962; ex Dakers, lot 493 (part) (HSAN 3623).
1249	6.26	96.6	40	1601	(B.943.1; S.5497). Bt Baldwin, 1976 (HSAN 3624).
1250	6.56	101.2	240	1601	Rev. REGIM (cf. B.943.1; S.5497). Bt Spink, September 1967; ex Asherson; ex Lockett II, lot 938 (HSAN 3625).
1251	6.71	103.5	260	1601	(B.943.1; S.5497). Ex Cochran-Patrick (1936), lot 289 (HSAN 3626).
1252	6.31	97.4	160	1601	(B.943.1; S.5497). Bt Baldwin, 1976 (HSAN 3627).
1253	6.54	100.9	275	1601	Obv. reads SCOTORVI. Rev. date reads **161** (cf. B.943.1; S.5497). Ex Pye, lot 238 (part); ex Lingford II lot 1180 (part) (HSAN 3641).

1240 1241 1242 1243 1244 1245

1246 1247 1248 1249

1250 1251 1252 1253

Before English Accession. SILVER *(cont.)*
Eighth coinage *(cont.)* *Thistle merks (cont.)*

	Weight g.	gr.	Die Axis	Date	
1254	6.73	103.8	160	1601	(B.943.3; S.5497). Ex Cochran-Patrick (1936), lot 289 (part) (HSAN 3628).
1255	6.53	100.8	320	1602	Obv. RACOBVS (cf. B.943.3; S.5497). Bt Baldwin, 1976 (HSAN 3629).
1256	6.49	100.1	170	1603	(B.943.4; S.5497). Ex Pye, lot 238; ex Lingford II, lot 1180 (part) (HSAN 3642).
1257	6.30	97.2	210	1603	Obv. SCOTORVM **.** (B.943.4; S.5497). Bt Baldwin, 1976 (HSAN 3630).
1258	6.54	100.9	350	1603	(B.943.4; S.5497). Bt Baldwin, 1974 (HSAN 3631).
1259	6.76	104.4	180	1603	Obv. SCOTORVM **.**. Rev. stop after date (cf. B.943.5). Ex Cochran-Patrick (1936), lot 289 (HSAN 3632).
1260	6.42	99.1	45	1603	(B.943.4; S.5497). Bt Baldwin, 1976 (HSAN 3633).
1261	6.41	98.9	180	1603	Rev. stop after date (B.943.5; S.5497). Bt Baldwin, 1976 (HSAN 3634).

PLATE 83

1254 1255 1256 1257

1258 1259 1260 1261

Before English Accession. SILVER *(cont.)*
Eighth coinage *(cont.)* *Thistle merks (cont.)*

	Weight g.	gr.	Die Axis	Date	
1262	6.51	100.5	140	1603	Rev. stop after date (B.943.5; S.5497). Bt Baldwin, 1962; ex Dakers, lot 493 (part) (HSAN 3635).
1263	6.44	99.4	160	1604	Rev. stop after date (B.943.5; S.5497). Bt Baldwin, 23 March 1968 (HSAN 3636).
1264	5.75	88.7	300	1604	Rev. stop after date (B.943.6; S.5497). Bt Baldwin, 1976. Same reverse die as **1265** (HSAN 3637).
1265	6.33	97.7	340	1604	Obv. SCOTORVM .. Rev. stop after date (cf. B.943.6; S.5497). Bt Baldwin, 1976. Same reverse die as **1264** (HSAN 3638).
1266	5.92	91.4	210	1604	Rev. stop after date (B.943.6; S.5497). Bt Seaby, 10 August 1953. Found in Kent (HSAN 3639).

Half-thistle merk (1601–4)

Theoretical weight 3.40 g; 52.4 gr: value 6 shillings and 8 pence Scots.

As thistle merk.

1267	3.25	50.2	210	1601	(B.944.1; S.5498). Bt Baldwin, 1974 (HSAN 3643).
1268	3.35	51.7	140	1601	(B.944.1; S.5498). Ex Cochran-Patrick (1936), lot 289 (part) (HSAN 3644).
1269	3.22	49.7	130	1601	(B.944.1; S.5498). Bt Baldwin, 1976 (HSAN 3645).
1270	3.37	52.0	170	1602	(B.944.2; S.5498). Bt Baldwin (HSAN 3646).
1271	3.29	50.8	300	1602	(B.944.2; S.5498). Bt Baldwin; ex Walters, lot 669 (part) (HSAN 3647).
1272	3.16	48.8	340	1602	(B.944.2; S.5498). Ex Cochran-Patrick (1936), lot 289 (part) (HSAN 3648).
1273	3.15	48.6	360	1602	(B.944.2; S.5498). Bt Baldwin, 1976 (HSAN 3649).
1274	2.99	46.1	200	1603	Obv. SCOTORVM . (cf. B.944.3; S.5498). Bt Baldwin, 1974 (HSAN 3650).
1275	3.22	49.7	40	1603	Obv. O in IACO recut (cf. B. 944.3; S.5498). Ex Cochran-Patrick (1936), lot 289 (part). Same reverse die as **1276** (HSAN 3651).

PLATE 84

1262 1263 1264 1265

1266 1267 1268 1269 1270

1271 1272 1273 1274 1275

Before English Accession. SILVER *(cont.)*
Eighth coinage *(cont.)* *Half Thistle merks (cont.)*

	Weight g.	gr.	Die Axis	Date	
1276	3.31	51.1	190	1603	(B.944.3; S.5498). Ex Ryan II, lot 1369 (part). Same reverse die as **1275** (HSAN 3652).
1277	3.26	50.3	250	1604	Rev. stop after date (B.944.4; S.5498). Bt Baldwin, 1976 (HSAN 3653).

Quarter-thistle merk (1601–4)

Theoretical weight 1.70 g, 26.2 gr: value 3 shillings and 4 pence Scots.

As thistle merk.

1278	1.30	20.1	315	1601	(B.945.1; S.5499). Bt Seaby, *c.* 1948 (HSAN 3654).
1279	1.54	23.8	225	1601	(B.945.1; S.5499). Ex Walters, lot 669 (part). Same reverse die as **1280** (HSAN 3655).
1280	1.52	23.5	140	1601	(B.945.1; S.5499). Bt Baldwin, 1976. Same reverse die as **1279** (HSAN 3656).
1281	1.51	23.3	280	1602	Obv. IACOBS (cf. B.945.2; S.5499). Acq. *c.* 1951. Same obverse die as **1282** (HSAN 3657).
1282	1.59	24.5	140	1602	Obv. IACOBS. Rev. PROTEGIT, E over G and G over I (cf. B.945.2; S.5499). Bt Baldwin. Lord Stewartby noted this to be a plated forgery. Same obverse die as **1281**; same reverse die as **1283** (HSAN 3658).
1283	1.53	23.6	30	1602	Rev. PROTEGIT, E over G and G over I (cf. B.945.2; S.5499). Bt Baldwin, 1976. Same reverse die as **1282** (HSAN 3659).
1284	1.65	25.5	220	1602	(B.945.2; S.5499). Ex Ryan II, lot 1369 (part) (HSAN 3660).
1285	1.67	25.8	200	1602	(B.945.2; S.5499). Ex Cochran-Patrick (1936), lot 289 (part) (HSAN 3661).
1286	1.50	23.2	45	1602?	Date uncertain (?B.945.2; S.5499). Bt Spink, *c.* 1950 (HSAN 3662).
1287	1.60	24.7	125	1603	(B.-, noted p. 384; S.5499). Bt Seaby, 1975; ex *SCMB* June 1975, item SC3811; ex R. C. Carlyon-Britton (HSAN 3663).
1288	1.50	23.2	80	1604	(B.945.4; S.5499). Acq. 26 May 1992; ex Dolphin list 2, item 1544; ex J. K. R. Murray, lot 304 (part); ex R. C. Carlyon-Britton; ex Lockett I, lot 388 (part) (HSAN 3664).
1289	1.51	23.3	160	1604	(B.945.4; S.5499). Bt Spink, June 1989; ex Davidson (HSAN 3665).

Eighth-thistle merk (1601–3)

Theoretical weight 0.85 g, 13.1 gr: value 20 pence Scots.

As thistle merk.

1290	0.78	12.0	60	1601	(B.946.1; S.5500). Ex Cochran-Patrick (1936), lot 289 (part) (HSAN 3666).
1291	0.82	12.7	360	1601	(B.946.1; S.5500). Ex Walters, lot 669 (part) (HSAN 3667).
1292	0.78	12.0	130	1602	(B.946.2). Bt Baldwin, 1976 (HSAN 3668).
1293	0.77	11.9	40	1602	(B.946.2; S.5500). Bt Spink, September 1967; ex Asherson (HSAN 3669).
1294	0.84	13.0	170	1602	(B.946; S.5500). Bt Baldwin, 1976 (HSAN 3670).
1295	0.77	11.9	60	1602	Rev. PRTEGIT (cf. B.946.4; S.5500). Bt Baldwin, 1976 (HSAN 3671).
1296	0.72	11.1	40	1602	(B.946.2; S.5500). Bt Baldwin, 1976. Lord Stewartby noted the band of crown as broken (HSAN 3672).
1297	0.79	12.2	160	1603	(B.-, noted p.384; S.5500). Bt Baldwin, 1976 (HSAN 3673).
1298	0.74	11.4	190	1603	Obv. stop after SCOTORVM (B.-, noted p. 384; S.5500). Ex Cochran-Patrick (1936), lot 289 (part). Same dies as **1299** (HSAN 3674).
1299	0.76	11.7	360	1603	Obv. stop after SCOTORVM (B.-, noted p.384; S.5500). Bt Baldwin, 1974. Same dies as **1298** (HSAN 3675).

1276

1277

1278

1279

1280

1281

1282

1283

1284

1285

1286

1287

1288

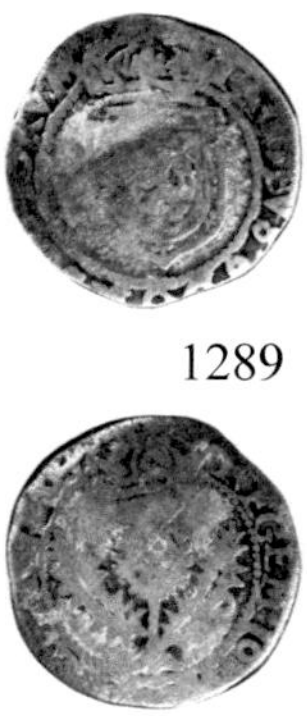
1289

1290

1291

1292

1293

1294

1295

1296

1297

1298

1299

Before English Accession. BILLON
Eightpenny groats or placks,

BILLON COINAGE

Eightpenny groat or plack, 1583–90 (undated)

Theoretical weight 1.81 g, 27.9 gr: value 8 pence Scots.

Obv. crowned shield bearing lion rampant. Rev. crowned thistle head with two leaves. 3 deniers fine.

Type 1

Obv. IACOBVS . 6 . D . G . R . SCOTOR'. without inner-circle. Rev. OPPIDVM . EDINBVRGI . without inner-circle (Stewart 1967, fig. 192; B.959.1–960.3; S.5511).

	Weight g.	gr.	Die Axis	
1300	2.00	30.9	10	Ex Ryan, lot 1369 (part) (HSAN 3739).
1301	1.80	27.8	260	Bt Baldwin, 1976; ex F. Baldwin (HSAN 3740).
1302	1.52	23.5	140	Bt Baldwin, 1976; ex F. Baldwin (HSAN 3741).
1303	2.08	32.1	20	Acq. 1976; ex Walters, lot 669 (part) (HSAN 3742).
1304	1.75	27.0	225	Ex Walters, lot 669 (part) (HSAN 3743).
1305	1.66	25.6	80	Bt Baldwin, 1976 (HSAN 3744).
1306	1.43	22.1	60	Bt Baldwin, 1976 (HSAN 3745).
1307	1.66	25.6	40	Obv. no stops. Bt Baldwin, 1976 (HSAN 3746).
1308	1.53	23.6	210	Bt Seaby, *c.* 1949 (HSAN 3747).
1309	1.42	21.9	250	Rev. as type 2, OPPID . EDINB. Ex Walters, lot 669 (part) (HSAN 3751).
1310	1.60	24.7	225	Rev. as type 2, OPPID . EDINB. Bt Baldwin, 1976; ex F. Baldwin (HSAN 3752).

Type 1 contemporary counterfeits.

1311	1.16	17.9	360	Contemporary counterfeit. IACOBVS . 6 . DG . R .. Rev. EDINBVRG. Bt Baldwin; ex F. Baldwin (HSAN 3765).
1312	2.13	32.9	360	IACOBVS . 6 . DG . R .. Rev. EDINBVRG. Ex Parsons, lot 766 (part) (HSAN 3766).

Type 2

Obv. IACOB' . 6 . D . G . R . SCO ., without inner circle. Rev. OPPID' . EDINB ., without inner-circle (B.960.4–961; S.5512).

1313	1.85	28.6	300	Rev. as type 1. Bt Baldwin, 1976; ex F. Baldwin (HSAN 3748).
1314	2.04	31.5	360	Rev. as type 1. Acq. 26 September 1954; ex Thorburn (HSAN 3749).
1315	1.56	24.1	180	Rev. as type 1. Bt Baldwin; ex F. Baldwin (HSAN 3750).
1316	1.84	28.4	140	Ex Parsons, lot 766 (part) (HSAN 3753).
1317	1.84	28.4	230	SCO;. Ex Walters, lot 669 (part) (HSAN 3754).

PLATE 86

1300 1301 1302 1303 1304 1305

1306 1307 1308 1309 1310 1311

1312 1313 1314 1315 1316 1317

Before English Accession. BILLON *(cont.)*
Eightpenny groats or placks (cont.) Type 2 *(cont.)*

	Weight g.	gr.	Die Axis	
1318	1.89	29.2	140	SCO;. Ex Walters, lot 669 (part) (HSAN 3755).
1319	1.79	27.6	200	SCO;. Bt Baldwin; ex F. Baldwin (HSAN 3756).
1320	1.88	29.0	260	SCO;. Bt Baldwin, 1976 (HSAN 3757).
1321	1.71	26.4	140	Bt Spink, 12 December 1956 (HSAN 3758).

Type 2, contemporary counterfeits.

1322	1.53	23.61	180	Cast contemporary counterfeit. Bt Baldwin; ex F. Baldwin (HSAN 3767).

Type 3

As type 2, with beaded inner-circles both sides. Rev. EDINB' . (B.962; S.5513).

1323	1.63	25.2	200	No stop after SCO. Bt Baldwin; ex Parsons, lot 766 (part) (HSAN 3759).
1324	1.81	27.9	170	Bt Baldwin; ex Walters, lot 669 (part) (HSAN 3760).
1325	1.38	21.3	315	Bt Baldwin; ex Walters, lot 669 (part) (HSAN 3761).
1326	2.08	32.1	20	Bt Baldwin; ex F. Baldwin (HSAN 3762).
1327	1.80	27.8	280	Bt Baldwin; ex F. Baldwin (HSAN 3763).
1328	1.17	18.1	150	Bt Baldwin; ex F. Baldwin (HSAN 3764).

Type 3, contemporary counterfeits

1329	1.19	18.4	150	Contemporary counterfeit of crude style. Rev. retrograde legend. Bt Baldwin; ex F. Baldwin (HSAN 3768).

Two-penny plack or half-plack, 1583–90 (undated)

Theoretical weight 0.91 g, 14.0 gr: value 4 pence Scots.

As eightpenny groat or plack but rev. thistle head with short stalk instead of leaves.

Type 1

As type 1 eightpenny groat or plack (B.-; S.5514).

1330	0.75	11.6	180	Ex Pye, lot 218; ex Lingford II, lot 1182 (part) (HSAN 3769).

Type 2
As type 2 eightpenny groat or plack (B.963–64.4; S.5515).

1331	0.81	12.0	220	Ex Parsons, lot 766 (part) (HSAN 3772).

Type 3

As type 3 eightpenny groat or plack (B.-; S.5516).

1332	0.60	9.3	220	No date stated. Bt Baldwin; ex F. Baldwin (HSAN 3770).
1333	0.74	11.4	280	Acq. 7 January 1954; ex Thorburn (HSAN 3771).

Hardhead or two-penny plack, 1588 (undated)

Theoretical weight 1.53 g, 23.6 gr: value 2 pence Scots.

First issue, August 1588

i.m. quatrefoil. Obv. only, crowned I R, . IACOB' . 6 . D . G . R . SCOTO'. Rev. . VINCIT . VERITAS ., crowned shield bearing lion rampant (Stewart 1967, fig. 199; B.965–66; S.5517).

1334	1.23	19.0	320	Ex R. C. Carlyon-Britton (HSAN 3773).
1335	1.73	26.9	345	Obv. SCO'. Rev. no stop before VINCIT. Unprovenanced (HSAN 3774).
1336	1.44	22.2	140	Obv. SCO'. Rev. no stop before VINCIT. Acq. 24 August 1955; ex Dakers, lot 506 (part) (HSAN 3775).
1337	1.20	18.5	280	Acq. September 1966; ex R. C. Carlyon-Britton (HSAN 3776).
1338	1.78	27.5	100	Rev. no stop before VINCIT. Bt Grover, 7 April 1954 (HSAN 3777).

1318 1319 1320 1321 1322 1323

1324 1325 1326 1327 1328 1329

1330 1331 1332 1333 1334 1335 1336

1337 1338 1339 1340 1341 1342 1343

Second issue, November 1588

i.m. quatrefoil both sides. Obv. as first issue. Rev. legend as first issue, crowned lion rampant left, two pellets behind (Stewart 1967, fig. 200; B.967.3–6; S.5518).

	Weight g.	gr.	Die Axis	
1339	1.72	26.5	170	Bt Baldwin, 1976 (HSAN 3778).
1340	1.67	25.8	170	Bt Baldwin; ex Winstanley (HSAN 3779).
1341	1.23	19.0	170	Bt Baldwin; ex Parsons, lot 766 (part) (HSAN 3780).
1342	1.22	18.8	20	Obv. SCO'.. Bt Baldwin, 1976 (HSAN 3781).
1343	1.60	24.7	110	Obv. SCO'.. Bt Baldwin, 1976 (HSAN 3782).

Before English Accession. BILLON *(cont.)*
Hardheads or twopenny placks (cont.) Second issue *(cont.)*

	Weight g.	gr.	Die Axis	
1344	1.46	22.5	180	Obv. SCO'.. Bt Baldwin, 1976 (HSAN 3783).
1345	1.49	23.0	160	Obv. SCO .. Bt Baldwin, 1976 (HSAN 3784).
1346	1.41	21.8	340	Bt Baldwin, 1976. Corroded, not illustrated (HSAN 3785).
1347	1.28	19.8	220	Obv. SCO'.. Unprovenanced (HSAN 3786).
1348	1.37	21.1	360	Obv. SCO .. Bt Baldwin, 1976 (HSAN 3787).
1349	1.33	20.5	220	Obv. SCO .. Bt Baldwin, 1976 (HSAN 3788).

Second issue, contemporary counterfeits

1350	1.36	21.0	360	Obv. SCO .. Bt Baldwin, 1976. Corroded, not illustrated (HSAN 3789).
1351	1.73	26.7	270	Bt Baldwin, 9 December 1968 (HSAN 3790).
1352	1.27	19.6	360	Bt Baldwin, 1976 (HSAN 3791).
1353	1.08	16.7	180	Bt Baldwin, 1976 (HSAN 3792).
1354	1.57	24.2	180	Bt Baldwin, 1976 (HSAN 3793).

Half-hardhead or penny-plack, 1588 (undated)

Theoretical weight 0.76 g, 11.8 gr: value 1 penny Scots.

i.m. quatrefoil both sides. Obv. crown above IR monogram, **. IACOB . 6 . D . G . R . SCO ..** Rev. **. VINCIT . VERITAS .**, crowned lion rampant left (Stewart 1967, fig. 201; B.968.1–2; S.5519).

1355	0.53	8.2	360	Acq. 26 September 1954; ex Thorburn (HSAN 3794).

Four-penny plack or 'Saltire' plack, 1594 (undated)

Theoretical weight, 23.6 gr, 1.53 g: value 4 pence Scots; 1 denier fine.

i.m. quatrefoil both sides. Obv. thistle plant with leaves over two crossed sceptres saltire, **. IACOB . 6 . D . G . R . SCO ..** Rev. **. OPPID . EDINB .**, a voided lozenge with a thistle head on each point (Stewart 1967, fig. 202; B.969.1; S.5520).

1356	1.46	22.5	360	Acq. 17 December 1965; ex Dakers, lot 506 (part) (HSAN 3795).
1357	0.86	13.3	360	Acq. 17 December 1965; ex Dakers, lot 506 (part) (HSAN 3796).

COPPER COINAGE

Twopence or 'turner', 1597 (undated)

Theoretical weight 3.82 g, 58.9 gr: value 2 pence Scots.

i.m. pellet both sides. Obv. bare headed armoured bust right, **IACOBVS . 6 . D . G . R . SCOTORVM**. Rev. **OPPIDVM . EDINBVRGI**, three thistle heads, two above one (Stewart 1967, fig. 203; B.970.1; S.5521).

1358	3.57	55.1	135	Ex Parsons, lot 766 (part) (HSAN 3797).
1359	3.51	54.2	30	Bt Spink, 1965; ex Marr (HSAN 3798).
1360	3.85	59.4	250	Obv. **OPPDVM**. Bt Baldwin, 1976 (HSAN 3799).
1361	3.35	51.7	135	Obv. **EDINBRGI**. Bt Baldwin, 1975 (HSAN 3800).

Penny, 1597 (undated)

Theoretical weight 1.80 g, 28.0 gr,: value 1 penny Scots.

As twopence or 'turner'. Obv. with single pellet in field behind head (B.970.2; S.5522).

1362	1.49	23.0	170	Bt Seaby, 10 August 1953 (HSAN 3801).

PLATE 88

1344 1345 1347 1348 1349 1351 1352

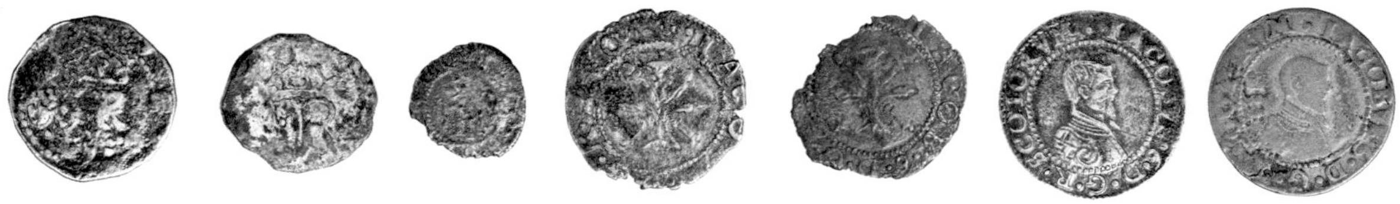

1353 1354 1355 1356 1357 1358 1359

1360 1361 1362 1363 1364

AFTER ACCESSION TO THE ENGLISH THRONE, 1603–25

GOLD COINAGE

Ninth Coinage, 1604–9

Unit or sceptre piece (undated)

Theoretical weight 154.83 gr, 10.0g: value 12 pounds Scots or £1 English, 22 cts fine.

i.m. thistle head/thistle head, Obv. king, crowned and armoured half-length, holding sceptre and orb, **. IACOBVS . D . G . MAG . BRIT . FRAN . & . HIB . REX.**. Rev. . (i.m.) **. FACIAM . EOS . IN . GENTEM . VNAM .**, crowned garnished shield, with arms of Scotland in second quarter only, dividing **I R**.

	Weight g.	gr.	Die Axis	
1363	9.68	149.4	100	Obv. **HIBR**, **BR** ligate (B.987.1; S.5463). Bt Seaby, 3 September 1981; ex *SCMB* September 1981, item EG 83, previously offered January 1981, item EG11 (HSAN 4840).

Double-crown (undated)

Theoretical weight 5.00 g, 77.40 gr: value 6 pounds Scots or 10 shillings English, 22 cts fine.

i.m. thistle head/thistle head. Obv. crowned bust right, **. IA . D . G . MAG . BRIT . FRAN . ET . HIB . REX .**. Rev. . (i.m.) **. HENRICVS . ROSAS . REGNA . IACOBVS .**, crowned shield, arms of Scotland in second quarter, dividing **I R**.

1364	4.95	76.4	180	(B. -, see page 431; S.5465). Ex J. K. R. Murray, lot 23; ex Hird, lot 120; ex Lingford II, lot 859 (HSAN 4841).

After English Accession. GOLD *(cont.)*
Ninth coinage *(cont.)*

Britain crown (undated)

Theoretical weight, 2.50 g, 38.60 gr: value 3 pounds Scots or 5 shillings English, 22 cts.

As double-crown.

	Weight g.	gr.	Die Axis	
1365	2.55	39.3	70	Rev. no stop before i.m. (B.-, see p. 431; S.5467). Ex Glendining, 14 December 1994, lot 169 (HSAN 4842).

Halfcrown (undated)

Theoretical weight 1.53 g, 23.66 gr: value 30 shillings Scots, 2 shillings and 6 pence English, 22 cts fine.

i.m. thistle head/thistle head. Obv. crowned bust right, **. I . D . G . ROSA . SINE . SPINA ..** Rev. **TVEATVR . VNITA . DEVS .**, crowned shield, arms of Scotland in second quarter (Stewart 1967, fig. 210).

1366	1.23	18.9	230	(B.-, see p. 433; S.5469). Bt Baldwin, 1980 (HSAN 4843).

Thistle crown (undated)

Theoretical weight 1.98 g, 30.50 gr: value 48 shillings Scots, 4 shillings English, 22 cts fine.

i.m. thistle head/thistle head. Acq. crowned rose, **IA . D . G . MAG . BR . F . & . H . REX..** Rev. **TVEATVR . VNITA . DEVS .**, crowned thistle (Stewart 1967, fig. 214).

1367	2.01	31.0	140	(B.988.2 – same dies; S.5471). Ex Pye, lot 184 (HSAN 4852).

Tenth Coinage, 1609–25

Unit (undated)

Theoretical weight 10.0 g, 154.83 gr: value 12 pounds Scots or £1 English, 22 cts fine.

i.m. thistle head/thistle head. Obv. half-length bust of king right, crowned and armoured, holding sceptre and orb, **IACOBVS . D . G . MAG . BRIT . FRAN . & . HIB . REX ..** Rev. **.** (i.m.) **. FACIAM . EOS . IN . GENTEM . VNAM .**, crowned garnished shield, with arms of Scotland in first and third quarters, dividing **I R** (Stewart 1967, fig. 204).

1368	9.70	149.7	330	(B.990.4; S.5464). Bt Spink, 10 August 1973. Holed at 7 o'clock (HSAN 4844).
1369	9.80	151.2	320	(B.990.4; S.5464). Bt Baldwin, 1982 (HSAN 4845).
1370	9.83	151.7	360	(B.990.4; S.5464). Acq. 31 July 1961; ex Lorimer (HSAN 4846).

Double-crown (undated)

Theoretical weight 5.0 g, 77.40 gr: value 6 pounds Scots or 10 shillings English, 22 cts fine.

i.m. thistle head/thistle head. Obv. crowned bust right, **. IA . D . G . MAG . BRIT . FRAN . ET . HIB . REX ..** Rev. **. HENRICVS . ROSAS . REGNA . IACOBVS .**, crowned shield, arms of Scotland in first and third quarters, dividing **I R**.

1371	4.84	74.7	350	Obv. **IACOBVS**, engraved letters R F in fields divided by bust (B.-, see p. 434; S.5466). Bt Baldwin, 9 August 1983 (HSAN 4847).
1372	4.91	75.7	210	(B.-, noted p. 434; S.5466). Bt Baldwin, 26 January 1996; ex Beresford-Jones, lot 508; ex Lingford II, lot 866; ex Cochran-Patrick (1936), lot 86; ex Roth II, lot 378; ex Murdoch part VIII, lot 1053 (HSAN 4848).

Britain crown (undated)

Theoretical weight 2.50 g, 38.60 gr: value 3 pounds Scots or 5 shillings English, 22 cts fine.

As double-crown (Stewart 1967, fig. 213).

1373	2.45	37.8	30	(B.991.5; S.5468). Acq. 1960; ex 'Rotterdam' (HSAN 4849).
1374	2.42	27.3	300	Rev. **IACOB .** (cf. B.991.5; S.5468). Ex Spink auction 107, 22 November 1994, lot 61 (HSAN 4850).

1365 1366 1367

1368 1369 1370

1371 1372 1373 1374 1375

Halfcrown (undated)

Theoretical weight 1.53 g, 23.66 gr: value 30 shillings Scots, 2 shillings and 6 pence English, 22 cts fine.

i.m. thistle head/thistle head. Obv. crowned bust right, **. I . D . G . ROSA . SINE SPINA .**. Rev. **TVEATVR . VNITA . DEVS .**, crowned shield, arms of Scotland in first and third quarters.

	Weight			
	g.	gr.	Die Axis	
1375	1.17	18.1	170	(B. 992.6; S.5469). bt Spink, 1972 (HSAN 4851).

After English Accession. SILVER
Ninth coinage.

SILVER COINAGE

Ninth Coinage, 1604–9

Sixty-shilling piece (undated)

Theoretical weight *c.* 29.9 g, *c.* 462 gr: value 60 shillings Scots, 5 shillings English.

i.m. thistle head both sides. Obv. king, crowned and holding sword riding right, rear caparison panel with a crowned thistle, **. IACOBVS . D ; G ; MAG ; BRIT ; FRAN ; & ; HIB ; REX.** . Rev. **. QVÆ . DEVS . CONIVNXIT . NEMO . SEPARET .**, garnished shield with Scottish arms in second quarter only.

	Weight g.	gr.	Die Axis	
1376	29.76	459.2	190	Obv. pellet stops, **. FRAN . Z . HIB .** (cf. B.972; S.5501). Acq. 1976; ex Walters, lot 670 (part) (HSAN 3676).
1377	29.85	460.6	250	(B.972; S.5501). Acq. 1976; ex Cochran-Patrick (1936), lot 290 (HSAN 3677).
1378	29.61	456.9	350	(B.972; S.5501). Rev. i.m. small thistle head. Bt Baldwin, 1976 (HSAN 3678).

Thirty-shilling piece (undated)

Theoretical weight *c.* 14.95 g, *c.* 230 gr: value 30 shillings Scots, 2 shillings and 6 pence English.

As sixty-shillings.

1379	14.68	226.5	180	(B.-, noted p. 418; S.5503). Ex DNW, 14 December 2004, lot 553 (HSAN 3679).
1380	14.62	225.6	350	(B.-, noted p. 418; S.5503). Ex DNW, 16 March 2005, lot 919 (HSAN 3680).
1381	14.89	229.8	310	(B.-, noted p. 418; S.5503). Ex Cochran-Patrick (1936), lot 291 (HSAN 3681).
1382	14.77	227.9	350	Obv. **; FRAN . & . HIB ;** (B.-, noted p. 418; S.5503). Bt Seaby, 13 April 1955 (HSAN 3682).

1376

1377

1378

1379

1380

1381

1382

After English Accession. SILVER
Ninth coinage *(cont.)* *Thirty shilling pieces (cont.)*

	Weight g.	gr.	Die Axis	
1383	14.43	222.7	260	Obv. pellet stops (B.-, noted p. 418; S.5503). Ex Walters, lot 670 (part) (HSAN 3683).
1384	14.97	231.0	240	(B.-, noted, p. 418; S.5503). Unprovenanced (HSAN 3684).

Twelve-shilling piece (undated)

Theoretical weight *c.* 5.60 g, *c.* 86 gr: value 12 shillings Scots, 1 shilling English.

i.m. thistle head both sides. Obv. armoured, crowned bust right, **. IACOBVS . D ; G ; MAG ; BRIT ; FRAN ; ET . HIB ; REX.**. Rev. **. QVÆ . DEVS . CONIVNXIT . NEMO . SEPARET .**, garnished shield with Scottish arms in second quarter only.

1385	5.76	88.88	230	Obv. **FRAN ; & . HIB ;** (cf. B.974; S.5505). Ex Walters, lot 670 (HSAN 3685).
1386	5.85	90.27	190	(B.974; S.5505). Ex Parsons, lot 766. Same obv. die as **1387** (HSAN 3686).
1387	5.87	90.57	45	(B.974; S.5505). Ex J. K. R. Murray lot 320 (part). Same obv. die as **1386** (HSAN 3687).

Six-shilling piece (1605–6, 1609, 9 cut over 7)

Theoretical weight *c.* 2.8 g, *c.* 43 gr: value 6 shillings Scots, 6 pence English.

As twelve-shillings, rev. with date above shield.

	Weight g.	gr.	Die Axis	Date	
1388	2.82	43.5	10	1605	Obv. no stops (B. 975; S.5507). Unprovenanced (HSAN 3688).
1389	2.70	41.7	320	1605	Obv. pellet stops, **FRAN . & . HIB .** (cf. B.975; S.5507). Bt Seaby, 1 October 1971 (HSAN 3689).
1390	1.99	30.7	110	1605	Obv. **: MAG . BRIT . FRAN . ET . HIB REX .** (B.975; S.5507). Acq. 19 August 1971; ex R. C. Carlyon-Britton (HSAN 3690).
1391	2.83	43.7	20	1606	Obv. no stops, **FRAN ET HIB** (cf. B. 975; S.5507). Acq. 28 May 1986; ex J. K. R. Murray; ex R. C. Carlyon-Britton (HSAN 3691).
1392	2.61	40.3	110	1606	Obv. **; FRAN . & . HIB ; REX .** (cf. B.975; S.5507). Bt Spink, May 2001; ex *NCirc.*, June 2001, item SC0003; ex Shuttlewood (HSAN 3692).

Two-shilling piece (undated)

Theoretical weight *c.* 0.90 g, *c.* 14.00 gr: value 2 shillings Scots, 2 pence English.

i.m. thistle head both sides. Obv. crowned rose, **.** (i.m.) **. I . D . G . ROSA . SINE . SPINA .**. Rev. **.** (i.m.) **. TVEATVR . VNITA . DEVS .**, crowned thistle head (Stewart 1967, fig. 211).

	Weight g.	gr.	Die Axis	
1393	0.93	14.4	200	Obv. **I ' D ; G ; ROSA.**. Rev. no stop before **TVEATVR** (cf. B.976.4; S.5509). Unprovenanced. Same obverse die as **1394** (HSAN 3693).
1394	0.85	13.1	315	Obv. **I ' D ; G ; ROSA**. Rev. (cf. B.976.4; S.5509). Unprovenanced. Same obverse die as **1393** (HSAN 3694).
1395	0.99	15.3	140	Obv. i.m. small thistle head, **I ' D ; G ; ROSA.** (cf. B.976.4; S.5509). Unprovenanced (HSAN 3695).
1396	0.98	15.1	60	(cf. B.976.4; S.5509). Unprovenanced (HSAN 3696).
1397	0.96	14.8	40	Obv. stop only after **SPINA**. Rev. no stop before i.m. (cf. B.976; S.5509). Unprovenanced (HSAN 3697).

1383 1384 1385 1386

1387 1388 1389 1390 1391

1392 1393 1394 1395 1396 1397

After English Accession. SILVER
Ninth coinage *(cont.) Two shilling pieces (cont.)*

	Weight g.	gr.	Die Axis	
1398	0.92	14.2	220	(cf. B.976.4; S.5509), ex R. C. Carlyon-Britton (HSAN 3698).
1399	0.93	14.4	130	Obv. ROS . A . (cf. B.976.4; S.5509). Unprovenanced (HSAN 3699).
1400	0.92	14.2	260	(cf. B.976.4; S.5509). Bt Baldwin (HSAN 3700).
1401	0.66	10.2	340	(cf. B.976.4; S.5509). Bt Baldwin, 1969 (HSAN 3701).
1402	0.81	12.5	260	(cf. B.976.4; S.5509). Bt Spink, 1965; ex Marr (HSAN 3702).
1403	0.78	12.0	340	(cf. B.976.4; S.5509). Bt Seaby, 1954; ex R. C. Carlyon-Britton (HSAN 3703).
1404	0.83	12.8	180	(cf. B.976.4; S.5509). Bt Baldwin (HSAN 3704).
1405	0.86	13.3	135	Obv. I ; D ; G ; (cf. B.976.4; S.5509). Ex Sotheby, 16 December 1977, lot 264 (part) (HSAN 3705).

One-shilling piece (undated)

Theoretical weight *c.* 0.45 g, *c.* 7 gr: value 1 shilling Scots, 1 penny English.

i.m. thistle head both sides. Obv. rose, . I . D . G . ROSA . SINE . SPINA .. Rev. . TVEATVR . VNITA . DEVS . thistle head.

1406	0.57	8.8	90	Obv. I : D : G :. Rev. stops uncertain (B.978; S.5510). Bt Spink, 1965; ex Marr (HSAN 3707).
1407	0.52	8.0	270	(B.978; S.5510). Acq. 24 December 1954; ex Thorburn (HSAN 3708).
1408	0.43	6.6	135	(B.978; S.5510). Bt Baldwin, 1969 (HSAN 3709).
1409	0.48	7.4	130	i.m. square pellet, I ; G ; ROSA ; SINE ; SPINA (cf. B.978; S.5510). Bt Spink, 1960 (HSAN 3710).

Tenth Coinage, 1609–25

Sixty-shilling piece (undated)

Theoretical weight *c.* 29.0 g, *c.* 447 gr: value 60 shillings Scots, 5 shillings English.

i.m. thistle head both sides. Obv. king, crowned and holding sword riding right, rear caparison panel with a crowned thistle, . IACOBVS . D ; G ; MAG ; BRIT ; FRAN ; & . HIB ; REX. . Rev. . QVÆ . DEVS . CONIVNXIT . NEMO . SEPARET ., garnished shield with Scottish arms in first and third quarters.

1410	29.90	461.4	190	(B.983.11; S.5502). Acq. 1960; ex Dakers, lot 499 (HSAN 3713).
1411	29.94	462.0	275	Rev. VAE in QVAE recut, V in CONIVNXIT recut (B.983.11; S.5502). Acq. 28 August 1956; ex Napier, lot 238 (part) (HSAN 3714).

Thirty-shilling piece (undated)

Theoretical weight *c.* 14.95 g, *c.* 230 gr: value 30 shillings Scots, 2 shillings and 6 pence English.

As sixty shillings (Stewart fig. 205).

1412	14.81	228.5	45	Obv. single pellet stops only (B.984.14; S.5504). Ex DNW 16 March 2005, lot 922 (HSAN 3715).

1398 1399 1400 1401 1402 1403

1404 1405 1406 1407 1408 1409

1410 1411 1412

After English Accession. SILVER
Tenth coinage *(cont.) Thirty shilling pieces (cont.)*

	Weight			
	g.	gr.	Die Axis	
1413	14.82	228.7	315	Obv. **: IACOBVS .**, remainder single pellet stops (cf. B.984.14; S.5504). Bt Baldwin, 1976 (HSAN 3716).
1414	13.84	213.6	360	(B.984.14; S.5504). Acq. 21 September 1954 (HSAN 3717).
1415	14.76	227.8	270	Obv. **D . G .**, **HIB .** (B.984.14; S.5504). Bt Baldwin, 15 October 1991 (HSAN 3718).
1416	14.63	225.7	360	Obv. single pellet stops only (B.984.14; S.5504). Bt Baldwin, 15 October 1991 (HSAN 3719).
1417	14.67	226.4	120	Obv. single pellet stops only (B.984.14; S.5504). Acq. 1960; ex Dakers. Same dies as **1419** (HSAN 3720).
1418	14.77	227.9	85	Obv. single pellet stops only (B.984.14; S.5504). Bt Baldwin, 1962 Same dies as **1418** (HSAN 3721).

1413

1414

1415

1416

1417

1418

After English Accession. SILVER
Tenth coinage *(cont.) Twelve shilling pieces* .

Twelve-shilling piece (undated)

Theoretical weight *c.* 5.60 g, *c.* 86 gr: value 12 shillings Scots, 1 shilling English.

i.m. thistle head both sides. Obv. armoured, crowned bust right, **. IACOBVS . D . G . MAG . BRIT . FRAN . & . HIB . REX .**. Rev. **. QVÆ . DEVS . CONIVNXIT . NEMO . SEPARET .**, garnished shield with Scottish arms in first and third quarters.

	Weight g.	gr.	Die Axis	
1419	5.80	89.5	10	Obv. no stop before **IACOBVS** (cf. B.985.15; S.5506). Bt Spink September 1967; ex Asherson; ex Lockett II, lot 939 (part); ex Bearman; acq. Spink 14 July 1905 (HSAN 3722).
1420	5.77	89.0	360	Rev. no stop after **SEPARET** (cf. B.985.15; S.5506). Bt Baldwin; ex Parsons, lot 766 (part) (HSAN 3723).
1421	5.78	89.2	150	Obv. small letters (B.985.15; S.5506). Bt Baldwin, 1976 (HSAN 3724).
1422	5.90	91.0	340	Small letters both sides (B.985.15; S.5506). Ex J. K. R. Murray, lot 325 (part) (HSAN 3725).
1423	5.64	87.0	170	Obv. small letters and numeral (B.985.15; S.5506). Ex J. K. R. Murray, lot 325 (part) (HSAN 3726).
1424	5.58	86.1	330	(B.985.15; S.5506). Ex J. K. R. Murray, lot 325 (part) (HSAN 3727).

Six-shilling piece (1610–19, 1622)

Theoretical weight *c.* 2.8 g, *c.* 43 gr: value 6 shillings Scots, 6 pence English.

As twelve-shillings, rev. with date above shield (Stewart 1967, fig. 215).

	Weight g.	gr.	Die Axis	Date	
1425	2.60	40.1	80	1610	(B.-; S.5507). Bt Spink, May 2001; ex *NCirc.*, June 2001, item SC0004; ex Shuttlewood (HSAN 3728).
1426	2.71	41.8	170	1611	(B.-; S.5507). Bt Spink, May 2001; ex *NCirc.*, June 2001, item SC0005; ex Shuttlewood. Holed (HSAN 3729).
1427	2.37	36.8	45	1612	(B. -, noted p. 427; S.5507). Bt Baldwin, 21 January 1987 (HSAN 3730).
1428	2.93	45.2	280	1615	(B.-; S.5507). Bt Spink, 17 May 1986 (HSAN 3731).
1429	2.73	42.1	140	1615	(B.-; S.5507). Bt Spink, May 2001; ex *NCirc.*, June 2001, item SC0007; ex Shuttlewood; ex Bute, lot 262 (HSAN 3732).
1430	2.77	42.7	220	1615	(B.-; S.5507). Bt Baldwin; ex Parsons, lot 766 (part) (HSAN 3733).
1431	2.69	41.5	220	1617	(B.-; S.5507). Ex Scaife, lot 1273 (HSAN 3734).
1432	2.54	39.2	250	1618	(B.-; S.5507). Ex DNW 16 March 1995, lot 933 (HSAN 3735).

1419 1420 1421 1422

1423 1424 1425 1426 1427

1428 1429 1430 1431 1432

After English Accession. SILVER.
Tenth coinage *(cont.) Six shilling pieces (cont.)*

	Weight g.	gr.	Die Axis	Date	
1433	2.88	44.4	260	1619	Obv. i.m. small thistle head (B.-; S.5507). Bt Seaby, 1 October 1971; ex R. C. Carlyon-Britton (HSAN 3736).
1434	2.35	36.3	80	1619	(B.-; S.5507). Bt Spink, May 2001; ex *NCirc.*, June 2001, item SC0008; ex Shuttlewood (HSAN 3737).
1435	2.88	44.4	330	1622	Obv. i.m. small thistle head (B.986; S.5507). Ex Pye, lot 251; ex Lingford II, lot 1191 (HSAN 3738).

COPPER COINAGE

On the provenances of the after-English accession copper coinage, see page 47.

Issue of 1614

Twopence or 'turner' (undated)

Theoretical weight, *c.* 2.50 g, *c.* 38.6 gr: value 2 pence Scots.

i.m. pellet both sides. Obv. thistle plant with two leaves and three flower heads, IACOBVS . DEI . GRA . MAG . BRIT. Rev. FRANCIE . ET . HIBERNIE . REX, lion rampant left, two pellets behind (Stewart 1967, fig. 216; B.993.1–2; S.5523).

	Weight g.	gr.	Die Axis	
1436	2.19	33.8	220	Bt Spink, 1965; ex Marr (HSAN 3802).
1437	2.12	32.7	170	Unprovenanced (HSAN 3803).
1438	2.59	40.0	180	Unprovenanced (HSAN 3804).
1439	2.10	32.4	180	Unprovenanced (HSAN 3805).
1440	2.13	32.9	30	Unprovenanced (HSAN 3806).
1441	2.33	36.0	170	Unprovenanced (HSAN 3807).

Penny (undated)

Theoretical weight, *c.* 1.25 g, *c.* 19.3 gr: value 1 penny Scots.

As twopence or 'turner'. Rev. with single pellet behind lion (Stewart 1967, fig. 207; B.994.3; S.5525).

1442	1.05	16.2	40	Bt Baldwin; ex Parsons (HSAN 3808).
1443	1.11	17.1	190	Bt Baldwin, 24 August 1955; ex Dakers, lot 506 (part) (HSAN 3809).

Issue of 1623

Twopence or 'turner,' (undated)

Theoretical weight, *c.* 2.00 g, *c.* 30.1 gr: value 2 pence Scots.

i.m. pellet both sides. Obv. thistle plant with two leaves and three flower heads, IACOBVS . D . G . MAG . BRIT. Rev. FRAN . & . HIB . REX, lion rampant left, two pellets behind (Stewart 1967, fig. 217; B.995.4; S.5524).

1444	2.25	34.7	90	Unprovenanced (HSAN 3810).
1445	1.37	21.1	20	Unprovenanced (HSAN 3811).
1446	1.92	29.6	45	Unprovenanced (HSAN 3812).
1447	1.88	29.0	280	Unprovenanced (HSAN 3813).
1448	2.19	33.8	145	Unprovenanced (HSAN 3814).
1449	1.94	29.9	280	Unprovenanced (HSAN 3815).
1450	1.72	26.5	220	Unprovenanced (HSAN 3816).
1451	2.12	32.7	140	Unprovenanced (HSAN 3817).
1452	1.64	25.3	130	Unprovenanced (HSAN 3818).
1453	2.04	31.5	220	Unprovenanced (HSAN 3819).
1454	1.98	30.6	330	Unprovenanced (HSAN 3820).
1455	1.43	22.1	180	Unprovenanced (HSAN 3821).
1456	0.83	12.8	160	Unprovenanced (HSAN 3822).

Penny, undated

Theoretical weight *c.* 1.00 g, *c.* 15.05 gr: value 1 penny Scots.

As twopence or 'turner'. Rev. with single pellet behind lion (B.-, noted p. 440–41; S.5526).

1457	0.98	15.1	300	Bt Baldwin, 24 August 1955; ex Dakers lot 506 (part) (HSAN 3823).

PLATE 95

1433 1434 1435 1436 1437

1438 1439 1440 1441 1442 1443

1444 1445 1446 1447 1448 1449 1450

1451 1452 1453 1454 1455 1456 1457

NON-CONTEMPORARY COPIES AND FORGERIES

Contemporary imitations have been listed alongside 'official' issues to enable ready comparison. The coins listed below are modern copies and forgeries fabricated sometime after the genuine coins were issued.

JAMES IV

	Weight g.	gr.	Die Axis	
1458	3.29	50.7	90	Lion or crown, i.m. crown. Rev. SA |LVVM . FAC . |PPLV |V TVVM . DNE* (B.-). Bt Baldwin, 26 January 1996. Bright metal. Lord Stewartby suggested that this was a 19th-century Jons forgery (HSAN 4797).

MARY

1459	6.86	105.8	220	First period, three-pounds or gold ryal, 1555, struck in lead, interior of crown not shaded. Possibly a lead copy or trial piece (Stewart 169; B.820). Acq. 11 August 1970; gift from P. Mitchell; ex Watters, lot 658 (HSAN 4823).
1460	7.61	117.4	360	First period, three-pounds or gold ryal, 1555, struck in base-metal, interior of crown shaded. Possibly a 19th-century electrotype. Unprovenanced (HSAN 4822).
1461	0.76	11.7	350	First period, penny, first issue, type Ia, i.m. lis, an 18th- or 19th-century forgery. Bt Baldwin, 1976 (HSAN 3368).
1462	5.74	88.6	300	Second period, ducat, 1558. A base yellow metal electrotype of the NMAS coin (*SCBI* 58, 984), possibly made in the 19th century (as B.888.1; Stewart 170). Bt Paramount, 1976; ex Revd. A. Mallinson (HSAN 4825).
1463	4.71	72.7	140	Second period, testoon, second issue, type B, 1560, Obv. i.m. . FRAN . ET . MA . D . G . R+R . ANCO . SOTOR Q. Rev. VICIT . LEO . DE . TRIB . IV DA . **1560**. Bt Baldwin, 1975. Cast white metal. Possibly a contemporary forgery (HSAN 2967).
1464	4.50	69.4	10	Second period, testoon, second issue, type B 1560. Obv. . SCOTOR . Q. Rev. no stop before VICIT., small crowns without cross, crowned thistle countermark over lis. Curious style, likely a modern cast copy. Bt Baldwin, 1975 (HSAN 2968).

JAMES VI

1465	15.80	243.8	360	Fourth coinage, thirty-shillings, 1585. Rev. . HONOR . , IVDITIVM., Xs in value with curule chair form, light and base, an 18th- or 19th-century forgery. Acq. 26 May 1992; ex Dolphin list 2, item 1510 (part) (HSAN 3545).
1466	4.31	66.5	100	Seventh coinage, ten-shillings, 1598. Bt Spink, September 1967; ex Asherson. Light weight and tooled both sides (HSAN 3584).

1458 1459 1460 1461 1462

1463 1464 1465 1466

SYLLOGE OF COINS OF THE BRITISH ISLES

1. FITZWILLIAM MUSEUM, CAMBRIDGE. Ancient British and Anglo-Saxon Coins. By P. GRIERSON. 32 plates, 1958.
2. HUNTERIAN MUSEUM, GLASGOW. Anglo-Saxon Coins. By A. S. ROBERTSON. 42 plates, 1961.
3. COINS OF THE CORITANI. By D. F. ALLEN. 8 plates, 1963.
4. ROYAL COLLECTION, COPENHAGEN. Part I. Ancient British and Anglo-Saxon Coins. By G. GALSTER. 30 plates, 1964.
5. GROSVENOR MUSEUM, CHESTER. Coins with the Chester Mint-Signature. By E. J. E. PIRIE. 16 plates, 1964.
6. NATIONAL MUSEUM OF ANTIQUITIES OF SCOTLAND, EDINBURGH. Anglo-Saxon Coins. By R. B. K. STEVENSON. 29 plates, 1966.
7. ROYAL COLLECTION, COPENHAGEN. Part II. Anglo-Saxon Coins: Æthelræd II. By G. GALSTER. (Publ. jointly with the Carlsberg Foundation.) 71 plates, 1966.
8. BRITISH MUSEUM. Hiberno-Norse Coins. By R. H. M. DOLLEY. 8 plates, 1966.
9. ASHMOLEAN MUSEUM, OXFORD. Part I. Anglo-Saxon Pennies. By J. D. A. THOMPSON. 42 plates, 1967.
10. ULSTER MUSEUM, BELFAST. Part I. Anglo-Irish Coins, John-Edward III. By M. DOLLEY AND W. SEABY. (Publ. jointly with the Trustees of the Ulster Museum.) 20 plates, 1968.
11. READING UNIVERSITY. Anglo-Saxon and Norman Coins; ROYAL COIN CABINET, STOCKHOLM. [Part VI.] Anglo-Norman Pennies. By C. E. BLUNT AND M. DOLLEY. (Publ. jointly with the Swedish Royal Academy.) 20 plates, 1969.
12. ASHMOLEAN MUSEUM, OXFORD. Part II. English Coins 1066–1279. By D. M. METCALF. 36 plates, 1969.

13–15. ROYAL COLLECTION, COPENHAGEN. Parts IIIA, B and C. Anglo-Saxon Coins: Cnut. By G. GALSTER. (Publ. jointly with the Carlsberg Foundation.) 158 plates, 1970. (3 vols.)

16. NORWEB COLLECTION. Ancient British and English Coins to 1180. By C. E. BLUNT, F. ELMORE JONES and R. P. MACK. 17 plates, 1971.
17. MIDLAND MUSEUMS, Ancient British, Anglo-Saxon, and Norman Coins. By A. J. H. GUNSTONE. 30 plates, 1971.
18. ROYAL COLLECTION, COPENHAGEN. Part IV. Anglo-Saxon Coins from Harold I and Anglo-Norman Coins. By G. GALSTER. (Publ. jointly with the Carlsberg Foundation.) 54 plates, 1972.
19. BRISTOL AND GLOUCESTER MUSEUMS. Ancient British Coins and Coins of the Bristol and Gloucestershire Mints. By L. V. GRINSELL, C. E. BLUNT and M. DOLLEY. 27 plates, 1972.
20. MACK COLLECTION. Ancient British, Anglo-Saxon, and Norman Coins. By R. P. MACK. 56 plates, 1973.
21. YORKSHIRE COLLECTIONS. Coins from Northumbrian Mints *c.* 895–1279; Ancient British and later coins from other mints to 1279. By E. J. E. PIRIE. 54 plates, 1975.
22. ROYAL COLLECTION, COPENHAGEN. Part V. Hiberno-Norse and Anglo-Irish Coins. By G. GALSTER with M. DOLLEY and J. STEEN JENSEN. 22 Plates, 1975.
23. ASHMOLEAN MUSEUM, OXFORD. Part III. Coins of Henry VII. By D. M. METCALF. 53 plates, 1976.
24. WEST COUNTRY MUSEUMS. Ancient British, Anglo-Saxon and Anglo-Norman Coins. By A. J. H. GUNSTONE. 35 plates, 1977.

25. NATIONAL MUSEUM, HELSINKI. Anglo-Saxon and Anglo-Norman Coins. By T. TALVIO. 41 plates, 1978.
26. MUSEUMS IN EAST ANGLIA. Morley St Peter Hoard *and* Anglo-Saxon, Norman, and Angevin Coins, and later coins of the Norwich Mint. By T. H. MCK. CLOUGH. 52 plates, 1980.
27. LINCOLNSHIRE COLLECTIONS. Coins from Lincolnshire Mints *and* Ancient British and later coins to 1272. By A. J. H. GUNSTONE. 68 plates, 1981.
28. CUMULATIVE INDEX OF VOLS. 1–20. By V. SMART. 1981.
29. MERSEYSIDE COUNTY MUSEUMS. Ancient British and later coins to 1279. By M. WARHURST. 39 plates, 1982.
30. AMERICAN COLLECTIONS. Ancient British, Anglo-Saxon and Norman Coins. By J. D. BRADY. 30 plates, 1982.
31. NORWEB COLLECTION. Tokens of the British Isles 1575–1750. Part I. Bedfordshire to Devon. By R. H. THOMPSON. 35 plates, 1984.
32. ULSTER MUSEUM, BELFAST. Part II. Hiberno-Norse Coins. By W. SEABY. (Publ. jointly with the Trustees of the Ulster Museum.) 16 plates, 1984.
33. BROOKER COLLECTION. Coins of Charles I. By J. J. NORTH and P. J. PRESTON-MORLEY. 130 plates, 1984.
34. BRITISH MUSEUM. Anglo-Saxon Coins. Part V. Athelstan to Edgar's Reform. By M. M. ARCHIBALD and C. E. BLUNT. 56 plates, 1986.
35. ASHMOLEAN AND HUNTERIAN MUSEUMS. Scottish Coins. By J. D. BATESON and N. J. MAYHEW, 116 plates, 1987.
36. STATE MUSEUM BERLIN. Anglo-Saxon, Anglo-Norman and Hiberno-Norse Coins. By B. KLUGE. (Publ. jointly with the State Museum Berlin.) 41 plates, 1987.
37. POLISH MUSEUMS. Anglo-Saxon and later medieval British coins. By A. MIKOŁAJCZYK. (Publ. jointly with the Archaeological and Ethnographical Museum in Łódź.) 20 plates, 1987.
38. NORWEB COLLECTION. Tokens of the British Isles 1575–1750. Part II. Dorset to Gloucestershire. By R. H. THOMPSON. 41 plates, 1988.
39. NORTH COLLECTION. Edwardian English Silver Coins, 1279–1351. By J. J. NORTH. 46 plates, 1989.
40. ROYAL COIN CABINET, STOCKHOLM. Part IV. Anglo-Saxon Coins: Harold I and Harthacnut. By T. TALVIO. 74 plates, 1991.
41. CUMULATIVE INDEX OF VOLS. 21–40. By V. J. SMART. 1992.
42. SOUTH-EASTERN MUSEUMS. Ancient British, Anglo-Saxon and later coins to 1279. By A. J. H. GUNSTONE with V. SMART and others. 78 plates, 1992.
43. NORWEB COLLECTION. Tokens of the British Isles 1575–1750. Part III. Hampshire to Lincolnshire. By R. H. THOMPSON and M. J. DICKINSON. 51 plates, 1992.
44. NORWEB COLLECTION. Tokens of the British Isles 1575–1750. Part IV. Norfolk to Somerset. By R. H. THOMPSON and M. J. DICKINSON. 50 plates, 1993.
45. LATVIAN COLLECTIONS. Anglo-Saxon and later British Coins. By T. BERGA. 12 plates, 1996.
46. NORWEB COLLECTION. Tokens of the British Isles 1575–1750. Part V. Staffordshire to Westmorland. By R. H. THOMPSON and M. J. DICKINSON. 51 plates, 1996.
47. SCHNEIDER COLLECTION. Part I. English Gold Coins and their Imitations, 1257–1603. By P. WOODHEAD. 83 plates, 1996.
48. NORTHERN MUSEUMS. Ancient British, Anglo-Saxon, Norman and Plantagenet Coins to 1279. By J. BOOTH. 64 plates, 1997.
49. NORWEB COLLECTION. Tokens of the British Isles 1575–1750. Part VI. Wiltshire to Yorkshire, Ireland to Wales. By R. H. THOMPSON and M. J. DICKINSON. 43 plates, 1999.

50. HERMITAGE MUSEUM, ST PETERSBURG. Part I. Anglo-Saxon Coins to 1016. By V. M. POTIN. 54 plates, 1999.
51. ESTONIAN COLLECTIONS. Anglo-Saxon, Anglo-Norman and later British Coins. By I. LEIMUS and A. MOLVÕGIN. 54 plates, 2001.
52. UPPSALA UNIVERSITY COIN CABINET. Anglo-Saxon and Anglo-Norman Coins. By E. LINDBERGER. (Publ. jointly with the University of Uppsala) 37 plates, 2006.
53. SCOTTISH MUSEUMS. English Coins, 1066–1279. By J. D. BATESON. 38 plates, 2001.
54. ROYAL COIN CABINET, STOCKHOLM. Part V. Anglo-Saxon Coins: Edward the Confessor and Harold II, 1042–1066. By F. COLMAN. Part VI supplement. Anglo-Norman Pennies. By M. BLACKBURN and K. JONSSON. 57 plates, 2007.
55. HERMITAGE MUSEUM, ST PETERSBURG. Part IV. English, Irish and Scottish Coins, 1066–1485. By M. MUCHA. 23 plates, 2005.
56. MASS COLLECTION. English Short Cross Coins, 1180–1247. By J. P. MASS. 82 plates, 2001.
57. SCHNEIDER COLLECTION. Part II. English Gold Coins, 1603 to the 20th Century. By P. WOODHEAD. 58 plates, 2001.
58. NATIONAL MUSEUMS OF SCOTLAND, EDINBURGH. Scottish Coins Part I. 1526–1603. By N. M. MCQ. HOLMES. 99 plates, 2006.
59. NORWEB COLLECTION. Tokens of the British Isles 1575–1750. Part VII. City of London. By R. H. THOMPSON and M. J. DICKINSON. 61 plates, 2007.
60. HERMITAGE MUSEUM, ST PETERSBURG. Part II. Anglo-Saxon Coins 1016–1066. By V. M. POTIN. 47 plates, 2011.
61. SCHNEIDER COLLECTION. Part III. Anglo-Gallic, Flemish and Brabantine Gold Coins 1330–1794. By P. WOODHEAD. 38 plates, 2010.
62. NORWEB COLLECTION. Tokens of the British Isles 1575–1750. Part VIII. Middlesex and uncertain pieces. By R. H. THOMPSON and M. J. DICKINSON. 68 plates, 2011.
63. BRITISH MUSEUM. Anglo-Saxon Coins I. Early Anglo-Saxon Gold and Anglo-Saxon and Continental Silver Coinage of the North Sea Area, *c.* 600–750. By A. GANNON. 37 plates, 2013.
64. GROSVENOR MUSEUM, CHESTER. Part II. Anglo-Saxon Coins and Post-Conquest Coins to 1180. By HUGH PAGAN. 34 plates, 2012.
65. NORWEGIAN COLLECTIONS. Part I. Anglo-Saxon Coins to 1016. By ELINA SCREEN. 76 plates, 2013.
66. NORWEGIAN COLLECTIONS. Part II. Anglo-Saxon and Later British Coins, 1016–1279. By ELINA SCREEN. 100 plates, 2015.
67. BRITISH MUSEUM. Anglo-Saxon Coins II. Southern English Coinage from Offa to Alfred *c.* 760–880. By R. NAISMITH, 2016.
68. THE LYON COLLECTION OF ANGLO-SAXON COINS. By S. LYON, 2016.
69. THE ABRAMSON COLLECTION. Coins of Early Anglo-Saxon England and the North Sea Area. By T. ABRAMSON, 2018.
70. NATIONAL MUSEUM OF SCOTLAND. Scottish Coins and Dies 1603–1709. By J. D. BATESON and N. HOLMES, 2017.
71. THE LORD STEWARTBY COLLECTION OF SCOTTISH COINS AT THE HUNTERIAN, AT THE UNIVERSITY OF GLASGOW. Part I. James IV to James VI 1488–1625. By WILLIAM A. MACKAY, 2021.

Published by the British Academy, except nos. 8, 34, 63 and 67 published by the Trustees of the British Museum/British Museum Press, and nos. 16, 31, 33, 38, 43–4, 46–7, 49, 57, 59, 61–2 and 69 published by Spink & Son Ltd.